INVISIBLE GENEALOGIES

Critical Studies
in the History
of Anthropology

VOLUME 1

Series Editors
Regna Darnell
Stephen O. Murray

REGNA DARNELL

INVISIBLE GENEALOGIES

A History of Americanist Anthropology

University of Nebraska Press

Lincoln & London

(∞)

Library of Congress Cataloging-in-Publication Data
Darnell, Regna.
  Invisible genealogies : a history of Americanist anthropology / Regna Darnell.
    p.   cm. — (Critical studies in the history of anthropology series)
  Includes bibliographical references and index.
  ISBN 0-8032-1710-2 (cloth : alk. paper) — ISBN 0-8032-6629-4 (pbk : alk. paper)
    1. Anthropology—North America—History. 2. Ethnology—Philosophy. 3. Indianists—
North America. I. Title. II. Series.
GN17.3.N7 D37 2001
301'.097—DC21   00-055956

Photo credits. Courtesy of the American Anthropological Association: Ruth Benedict, p. xxviii;
Franz Boas, p. 32; Alfred Louis Kroeber, p. 68; Edward Sapir, p. 104; A. Irving Hallowell,
p. 240; Claude Lévi-Strauss, p. 274; and Margaret Mead, p. 308. Courtesy of the American
Anthropological Association and the American Philosophical Society: Elsie Clews Parsons,
p. 206. Courtesy of Robert D. Farber University Archives, Brandeis University: Paul Radin,
p. 136. Courtesy of Robert G. Wheeler and John Benjamins Publishing Company: Benjamin
Lee Whorf, p. 172.

This is what anthropology looks like!
(with apologies to Gloria Steinem)

CONTENTS

ILLUSTRATIONS

This inaugural volume of Critical Studies in the History of Anthropology encapsulates the editors' conviction that there has been a longstanding gap in publication possibilities for history of anthropology as a critical theoretical enterprise engaging the very center of disciplinary practice. At least since the 1960s, when history of anthropology emerged as a specialization within the discipline, there has been a dialectic of praxis and reflexivity, a continuing "reinventing" of a discipline poised, sometimes uncomfortably, at the frontline of cultural contacts, clashes, and efforts to transcend virtually inevitable cross-cultural miscommunication. The future of something recognizable as anthropology depends crucially upon our responsiveness to rapidly changing conditions of global social order. That power relations are inevitable in culture contact, that communicative efforts are often abortive, that individuals transcend the constraints of their cultural upbringing, do not invalidate the effort. Much in our disciplinary past does not meet present-day standards of ethics, indeed, is ethnocentric at best. But while other social scientists continue to emphasize the gap between civilized and so-called primitive—a perspective deeply embedded in Western civilization—anthropologists have been listening to cultural others and trying to engage in dialogue. There are lessons in the failures as well as in the successes.

For the history of anthropology, the onset of the twenty-first century is both the best of times and the worst of times. On the one hand, the social sciences and humanities have been inundated by the ahistorical perspectives of so-called postmodernist philosophy and criticism. On the other hand, the work of interpretation has turned history as well as history of science into more critical, more clearly interpretivist, theoretical disciplines. New emphases on standpoint and the situatedness of all knowledge claims allow the historian of anthropology who is also a practitioner to talk about the past in its own terms, through the words and interactions of its participants, contextualized in their own times, followed by a reflexive turn to the contemporary relevance of earlier anthropological ideas.

Regna Darnell's *Invisible Genealogies: A History of Americanist Anthropology* treats the history of anthropology as an anthropological problem, approaching it through the characteristic disciplinary techniques of qualitative ethnography and participant-observation fieldwork. Subject position is taken as the central problematic of both ethnography and the history of science. Although other approaches can establish a critical discourse about disciplinary history aimed at producing practitioners and professionally socializing new generations of anthropologists who are aware of the past as it shapes the future, Darnell argues with considerable passion that continuity as well as revolution characterize the development of her field.

The invisibility of intellectual genealogies to latter-day practitioners, particularly in the case of the Americanist tradition associated with the work of Franz Boas and his first generation of students, suggests that professional attention in North America has been focused on other approaches; at the very least, American anthropologists since the Second World War no longer work exclusively or even primarily with Native Americans. Boasian ideas like cultural relativism, culture in the plural, and antiracism have become so commonplace in North American society, as well as in anthropology itself, that they are now perceived as natural components rather than as constructions emanating from the investigations of disciplinary predecessors.

The book explicates the core concepts of the Boasian paradigm, situating them in relation to social context, institutional framework, and professional network of participants. Each chapter focuses on a particular line of thought associated with one or more core Boasians and traces the congruities of these ideas with contemporary theoretical debates and preoccupations. Readers are invited to construct their own genealogies in continuity with a past that is subject to continuous reworking of productive ideas in new and ever-changing contexts.

The enterprise of critical history of anthropology is not restricted to anthropology, however broadly defined the discipline may be. Nor is it unmitigatedly critical. Critiques, positive as well as negative, come from myriad sources: from the people anthropologists used to study and with whom many of them now collaborate; from more positivistically inclined colleagues for whom the new cautiousness about grand generalization seems to invalidate the "scientific" status of anthropology; from literary critics who do not understand the constraints of commitment to something that can differentiate between a novel and an ethnography, that is, to something in the world outside the mind of the ethnographer; from general readers and fellow academics who continue to stereotype anthropologists as mere purveyors of the exotic; and from those in a variety of disciplines who fail to see the potential for generalization in ethnographic particularity.

The Americanist tradition explicated in *Invisible Genealogies* defines culture as a symbolic form that can be conveyed from one person to another, not only across generations but also across cultural boundaries. Anthropology has a long and often honorable history of negotiating this paradoxical tightrope between varying degrees of successful communication with ethnographic others and the exercise in translation that conveys something of that experience and understanding to an audience unfamiliar with the culture described. Just as contemporary ethnographers increasingly place themselves within the stories they tell about their relations with cultural others, historians of anthropology are telling stories about how they understand the disciplinary heritage of theories, methods, and ethnographic exemplars. In the Americanist tradition, these exercises produce parallel and mutually reinforcing results.

The position of the observer has been seminal to Americanist anthropology since Boas's legendary dissertation on the color of sea water. *Invisible Genealogies* lays to rest the idea that Boas was not a theoretician. Theory in our time again involves the effort to escape the constraints of a starting position by becoming aware of habitual patterns of language and thought. That Boas and many of his students were not systematic theoreticians does not mean that their theoretical commitments were not clear in the exemplars they presented to American public discourse about cultural difference. The "Native point of view" emerges from texts in an oral tradition whose performance in principle empowers the speakers to represent themselves to a larger world outside their own communities. The texts produced by anthropologists, presented in relation to their own disciplinary history, may fill a similar function in reminding anthropologists and explicating to others the possibility of thinking like an anthropologist.

—REGNA DARNELL AND STEPHEN O. MURRAY

When I first began to ponder how much of the fundamental character of North American anthropology derived from the Americanist tradition in the narrow ethnographic sense of specialization in the study of the American Indian, many of my colleagues, Americanist and non-Americanist alike, resisted my extension of the tradition to encompass the theoretical and methodological principles absorbed by American-trained anthropologists, regardless of where they did their fieldwork.

The invisibility of the Americanist tradition came home to me when I read a paper at the Canadian Anthropology Society several years ago on what I then called the Boasian text tradition (Darnell 1992). A distinguished Francophone colleague trained at an elite Anglophone North American university told me afterwards: "You almost make me want to be a Boasian." I responded, perhaps a bit flippantly: "But you already are." And indeed there were substantial overlaps between his position and the one I had outlined. Less flippantly, I resolved to revisit the sometimes perceived incommensurabilities of national traditions in anthropology, with a view to making explicit the continuities of Boasian theory, method, and practice in a range of contexts not usually interpreted as arising from this tradition.

The objective of this work is to deconstruct the "rhetoric of discontinuity" characteristic of contemporary anthropology in North America, with a view to illuminating theoretical, methodological, and ethnographic persistences from prior Americanist work. In the narrow sense, what I call the Americanist tradition developed around the wide-ranging study of the American Indian; it is associated with the historical particularism of Franz Boas and his students, which dominated the discipline in North America until after World War II. In a wider and more interesting sense, however, this tradition embodies a way of working that American-trained anthropologists exported around the globe with the postwar proliferation of anthropological field sites.

The Americanist tradition, in both of these senses, has been eclipsed in disciplinary memory, a process culminating in contemporary critiques of ethnographic authority loosely tied to the postmodernist turn across the social and human sciences. The very real continuity must now be rediscovered. Despite the invisibility of Americanist genealogies to many anthropologists who, I suggest, embody them, persistent links of ideas, personal contacts, and institutional arrangements continue to be crucial to defining disciplinary identity in North America.

Ironically, theoretical positions explored by early Boasians laid the groundwork for a number of contemporary developments that now deny their roots in the Americanist (or any other) past. What Clifford and Marcus (1986) hail as an "experimental moment" is neither reflexive nor momentary. To recover these invisible genealogies entails rethinking Boasian positions and testing their continuing relevance to the resolution of contemporary theoretical impasses. During the first half of the twentieth century, Franz Boas, Alfred Kroeber, Edward Sapir, Paul Radin, Robert Lowie, Ruth Benedict, Benjamin Whorf, Margaret Mead, Elsie Clews Parsons, and A. Irving Hallowell were among those who developed a collective Americanist paradigm around the cross-cultural study of meaning, based on participant-observation fieldwork and collection of linguistic and ethnographic texts. Contemporary feminist, postcolonial, and postmodern interests in narrative, dialogue, and standpoint are foreshadowed in the disciplinary texts reexamined here. Yet many contemporary proponents of these ideas stridently, even arrogantly, proclaim their autonomy from past, mistaken, contaminated versions of the discipline. Let us reclaim this suppressed past and reformulate its insights for our own times!

Because this book is about Americanist intellectual genealogies, it seems only fair to delineate the trajectory of the personal genealogy that has led me to this train of thought. There are no confessions here; much about my life and career is not part of this story. Nonetheless, the authorial stance is self-consciously personal, reflecting my own position within the Americanist tradition that I explore from the perspectives of a variety of its early participants.

I had one of the most old-fashioned anthropological educations possible in my generation; this experience has come in handy for doing history of anthropology. My first anthropology course was with Frederica de Laguna, one of Franz Boas's last doctoral students. The out-of-the-ivory-tower experiential flavor of her stories about Tlingit fishing villages quickly converted me (at least superficially) from English literature to anthropology. In retrospect, however, my double major linked the concerns and methods of the humanities and social sciences in ways of which I was not fully conscious at the time. I now have considerably more respect for what then struck me as the merely secondhand interpretive work of the literary critic.

In any case, the textbook for Anthropology 101 at Bryn Mawr College in 1961–62 was the 1948 edition of Alfred Kroeber's *Anthropology* (first published in 1923), its ethnographic exemplar Robert Lowie's *The Crow Indians* ([1935] 1956). My senior year I took history of anthropology from A. Irving (Pete) Hallowell (whose Ojibwe ethnography is still widely used in classes across Canada, including my own) and culture and personality with Freddy, who talked a lot about Hallowell's work. At that point I assumed anthropology itself was coterminous with the Americanist tradition and took for granted its overlap with the humanities.

I moved to the University of Pennsylvania for graduate work. Philadelphia in the late 1960s was a wonderful place to come of age intellectually and professionally, full of the heady conviction that ideas were important and that our politics could change the world. And indeed the world has not been the same since. At Bryn Mawr, an intellectually intense women's college where many students went on to become professional anthropologists (Karen Blu, Sherry Ortner, and Harriet Whitehead overlapped with me there), I acquired a confidence in my own standpoint that solidified into a reflexive feminist commitment shared by a number of strong women in my graduate student cohort, especially Judith Irvine, Elinor Ochs, and Susan Phillips. Theoretical work responding to challenges loosely encompassed under the label of poststructuralism or postmodernism only now reveals itself in the mature work of this generation.

At Penn I became further immersed in then-contemporary instantiations of Americanist scholarship. Dell Hymes, sometime protégé of Kroeber, Clyde Kluckhohn, Morris Swadesh, Harry Hoijer, and Carl Voegelin supervised my dissertation in history of anthropology. I took culture and personality and ethnohistory with Anthony F. C. Wallace, a student of Hallowell and Frank Speck. These are Boasian genealogies through and through (albeit even some of the names may be unknown to contemporary graduate students). The fad of the day, as culture and personality bit the dust, was ethnoscience or componential analysis, remembered today, if at all, as "emic" anthropology. Hymes, Wallace, and their Oceanist colleague Ward Goodenough were at the center of that movement across North America. Penn was inclined to the "God's truth" (Burling 1964) or "psychological reality" (Sapir 1933) version of theoretical adequacy, refusing to settle for "hocus pocus" or merely predictive formal modeling. For example, Wallace and Atkins (1960) explored multiple structurations of the "same" kinship system. Then, as now, anthropology was about figuring out what went on in people's heads when you couldn't get at it by projecting your own assumptions and experience. Cross-cultural ethnographic method stands squarely at the center of thinking anthropologically.

The addition to the Penn faculty of Erving Goffman in a cross-appointment between anthropology and sociology and of Bill Labov in linguistics, with Dan Ben-Amos and Kenneth Goldstein already in Folklore and Folklife and Sol Worth at the Annenberg School of Communication, heralded a new interdisciplinary synthesis. For me at least, this synthesis was grounded in anthropology and discussed endlessly in the University Museum coffee shop. The Center for Urban Ethnography coalesced just after I left Philadelphia, but its commitment to test theory against data from fieldwork was already central to Dell Hymes's ethnography of speaking/communication throughout the sixties. We began to construe construction of meaning by the individual in terms of (its accessibility through) the study of interaction. This, to my mind, is still the fun stuff. I came to appreciate how rare such matter-of-fact functioning of interdisciplinarity really is only in its absence, after I left Penn.

My articulation with the history of anthropology as a legitimate disciplinary specialization owes much to the serendipity of George Stocking's presence at Penn for a semester in 1967, precisely when my dissertation project was coming together. In some perhaps perverse form of resistance, I distinguished my own perspective from his by adopting (as did Dell Hymes and Pete Hallowell) the self-conscious stance of an anthropologist using anthropological (i.e., ethnographic) methods to study disciplinary history (Darnell ed. 1974, 1977b, 1982b). Reflexivity was not yet in fashion; Stocking (1968) emphasized the dichotomy between "historicism" and "presentism" and the methodological dangers inherent in positioning oneself within the latter. I was then, and remain, willing to risk those dangers. Further, both Stocking and I have written primarily for an audience of anthropologists; that audience is interested, sometimes in excruciating detail, in the anthropological work done by colleagues, past and present, as well as in the precedents and warrants for particular kinds of contemporary work. Anthropologists read history of anthropology as part of a professional socialization that consists in good part of constructing unique, individual genealogies for disciplinary practice. Like kinship relations, such genealogies are embodied, inalienably constructed relative to a particular ego.

The city of Philadelphia has long-standing attachments to the Americanist tradition in linguistics, ethnology, and ethnohistory, particularly through the American Philosophical Society (APS). I spent a lot of time at the APS during my Master's research on late nineteenth-century Philadelphia anthropologist Daniel Garrison Brinton (Darnell 1967, 1974a, 1988a) and my doctoral work on the transition from the Bureau of American Ethnology to Franz Boas (Darnell 1969, 1971, 1998a). I still sometimes think of myself as a Philadelphia anthropologist who happens to live elsewhere.

My fieldwork with the Plains Crees of northern Alberta began in 1969 when I went to the University of Alberta as a brand new assistant professor. I didn't get much training for meeting some of the Native Americans I had been studying secondhand over the better part of a decade. Pete Hallowell reported that it was cold up there and that he had learned to ride a horse in Edmonton in 1925. Dell Hymes told me he didn't think of me as a fieldworker, presumably because he thought I had become a pretty fair archival historian. But I was determined that my anthropology would be in the field as well as in the library, that I would be a "real" anthropologist. I found fieldwork transformative, my thinking fundamentally reoriented and my anthropology repositioned. My optimism for language maintenance and revitalization has been colored by the critical mass of traditional Plains Cree culture in northern Alberta. Such vitality can be taken for granted very few other places in Native North America today.

In 1969 the Vietnam War made it seem desirable to be American somewhere else. In retrospect I was remarkably naive; the contrast between east and west, Philadelphia and Edmonton, seemed more salient than the boundary between the United States and Canada. More than three decades later, now a dual citizen, I recognize that I emigrated with the mindset of a fieldworking anthropologist and that I have studied Canada as well as its First Nations (e.g., Darnell ed. 1971, 1973, 1977). My work on the history of Canadian anthropology (1975, 1976, 1997b, 1998c, 2000) has explored further the permeable boundary of Americanist research across the world's longest undefended border. I now speak in many professional contexts of "North America" rather than of "the United States" or simply "America;" Canada has functioned as a foil of "self" and "other" in my thinking about how Americanist anthropologists think. I have come to define myself in relation to two national cultures, each of which is in some sense "mine," although I am in another sense fully of neither.

I spent much of the 1980s researching and writing a biography of Edward Sapir (Darnell 1990a). Biography is a perplexing genre. The decisions an author makes in its writing are largely invisible, with the persona of the biographer appropriately embedded in the interstices of the text. Sapir initially intrigued me as a biographical subject because of the enormous range of his interests; I wanted to understand how the same mind could encompass several kinds of linguistics, ethnology and ethnographic semantics, folklore, the role of the individual in culture, poetics, music, and literary criticism. I chose to depict Sapir among his contemporaries, defined less by his own interiority (in any case, largely inaccessible to me) than by his position in a network of social relations. For the most part, I allowed the classic first-generation Boasians to speak for themselves about what they were up to, through their correspondence and public statements. This biography was, to my mind, an ethnographic project, implementing my own methodological commitment to the reality of events as perceived by participants. I learned to think about framing Sapir the person among other persons, human and otherwise, from friends and collaborators among the Crees of northern Alberta (especially Frances Thompson, Mary Rose Cardinal, and Roseanne Houle) as well as from colleagues and theories in Americanist anthropology.

There wasn't much of me in the biography of Sapir, at least on the surface. I was increasingly frustrated because I too had an opinion about subjects raised by Sapir and his contemporaries; yet the biographical genre, perhaps even the history of anthropology itself, had boxed me into being read merely as a commentator on the work of others. I noticed that many colleagues unreflexively relegated the Americanist tradition, in which I had been immersed intensely for so long, to the past. It was mere disciplinary history, closed, no more relevant than the classical evolutionism of E. B. Tylor and Sir James Frazer. I began to explore more open-ended genres of ethnographic representation and theoretical argumentation (Darnell 1985a, 1989b, 1991a), new forms that would allow established Americanist insights to resurface in contemporary, albeit often transformed, shapes. Adequate ethnography entailed representation in culturally appropriate structures of imagination.

For documenting and updating the Americanist genealogies sampled in this book, I settled on the genre of the discursive essay. This form is unabashedly idiosyncratic and persuasive, in rhetoric as well as in intent. I want to talk about the ongoing resonances of the Americanist tradition and the reasons we should respectfully remember, at the very least so as not to reinvent countless wheels. I am not proposing that we should stagnate within a mold cast in concrete by the early Boasians; to do so would be silly. Rather, I think we have thrown out too many babies with our bathwater, that there are continuities to our disciplinary past of which we have been only subliminally aware, and that the best of our contemporary work appropriately builds on Americanist persistences. An intellectually serious critique of contemporary anthropology, in my view, must engage theory and practice in the context of history. Tradition, my Cree friends say, is that which has continuity to the past.

Few academics are fortunate enough to reinvent themselves intellectually in midcareer. Renewed interdisciplinarity has been a particular blessing of my move to the University of Western Ontario in 1990. Doug Baer, Carole Farber, Alison Lee, Gaile McGregor, Calin Mihailescu, Ernest Redekop, Catherine Ross, Alison Wylie, and colleagues with/from QualMS (Qualitative Methods in the Social Sciences)—Pat Burman, David Flynn, Dennis Hudecki, Allan Jeffrey, Joe Lella, and Marshall Mangan—have reinforced my conviction that multidisciplines are best constituted as a by-product of intense conversations among friends.

This work at the intersection of theory and practice in Native North American ethnography and linguistics has been enriched by collaboration and friendship with Lisa Valentine and, more recently, Allan McDougall. Lisa was a student of Joel Sherzer, who was the linguist among my cohort at Penn; she and I shared a culture before we met. There is a continuity to the Americanist tradition that empowers both us and it. I thank the Social Sciences and Humanities Research Council of Canada for our three successive three-year grants to study discourse and identity in variants of English spoken by the First Nations of southwestern Ontario (Darnell and Valentine 1991, 1994; Darnell, Valentine, and McDougall 1997). Scholars rarely are enabled to speak to one another, their students, and their collaborators in research communities with such continuity. Thank you also to the team: Tim Bisha, Kathleen Buddle-Crowe, Lindy-Lou Flynn, Elizabeth Guerrier, Paul Hogan, Bruce Lawrence, Theresa McCarthy, Barry Milliken, Susanne Miskimmin, Molly Turnbull, Karen Pennesi, Craig Proulx, Marcia Simon, Dan and Mary Lou Smoke, Brenda Timmins, and Rob Wishart. This book reflects the theoretical side of the work that we have done together.

I honor the long-established focus of Western's Department of Anthropology in symbolic anthropology, inextricably enmeshed with linguistics; this is what brought me to London, Ontario. Judith Abwunza, Anne Brydon, Chet Creider, Carole Farber, Jim Freedman, John Gehman, David Maracle, Margaret Seguin-Anderson, Lisa Valentine, Rand Valentine, and Alison Wylie, although too few of them remain at Western, have made it mostly a joy.

Of recent years I have become much engaged with university politics, both in defense and in exercise of academic freedom and in presentation of the public face of the academy within a profoundly and increasingly anti-intellectual society. A university is, or ought to be, a place where people come together to think about things, to preserve and augment ongoing traditions of knowledge, to undertake a critique of society for the long-term benefit of society. Ideas have consequences, and our contemporary world desperately needs committed and articulate public intellectuals. Among such intellectuals, anthropologists have an especial role. I do not subscribe to the lamentably common view that contemporary critiques of anthropology from feminist, postcolonial, and various postmodernist standpoints constitute, or should constitute, the elegy for a moribund discipline. Instead I embrace the inherent vitality of an anthropology that is rapidly changing yet remains in continuous relation to its own internal critique, to strictures from the communities and individuals traditionally studied by anthropologists, and to challenges from interdisciplinary colleagues across the social and human sciences. Neither our past nor our present is static or closed off from revision and rethinking.

Chairing the Victor Turner Prize in Ethnographic Writing of the Society for Humanistic Anthropology in 1997 and 1998 led me to discover many fine books that, to my embarrassment, I probably would not have read without this inducement. This experience brought increasingly nuanced respect for the reflexivity of my fellow ethnographers and the foundational role of ethnography in our discipline, increasing both my humility as a writer and my certainty that Americanist themes indeed characterize broad segments of the anthropology practiced in North America today.

Another inestimable pleasure has been serving on Barbara and Dennis Tedlock's *American Anthropologist* editorial board. Despite the undeniable backlash, humanistic exploration, ethnographic experimentation, and interdisciplinary excursions have proved far from peripheral to anthropology, and it has been a heady sensation to feel for a time at the center, not persisting doggedly at a perceived margin.

The arguments presented in this book have emerged from invited talks, conference papers, and exploratory articles over the past decade (Darnell 1990c, 1992, 1995a, 1995b, 1997a). None has been published previously in present form. In addition to those singled out elsewhere, the following colleagues have responded to the emerging argument over its long gestation: Karen Adams, Michael Asch, Barbara Babcock, Lee Baker, Peter Bangarth, Stanley Barrett, Keith Basso, Jean Becker, Janice Boddy, Ivan Brady, William Bright, Robert Bringhurst, Jennifer Brown, Harold Conklin, John Cove, Julie Cruikshank, Raymond DeMallie, Peter Denny, Gary Dunham, the late Fred Eggan, William Fenton, Raymond Fogelson, Katherine and Don Fowler, Chris Frey, Frederic Gleach, Brian Given, Victor Golla, Eric Hamp, Richard Handler, Michael Harkin, Jane Hill, Dell and Virginia Hymes, Judith Irvine, John Joseph, Christine Jourdan, the late Roger Keesing, Michael Kenny, Douglas Kibbee, Konrad Koerner, Michael Kraus, Karl Kroeber, Paul Kroeber, the late Theodora Kroeber, Michael Lambek, Louise Lamphere, Stephen Leavitt, Penny Lee, Wendy Leeds-Hurwitz, James Lindahl, Andrew and Harriet Lyons, Michael Mackert, Pierre Maranda, Jonathan Marks, Marie Mauzé, David Maybury-Lewis, Bea Medicine, Barry Michrina, Bruce Miller, Antonia Mills, Bruce Nevin, James M. Nyce, Andie Palmer, Nancy Parezo, Douglas Parks, Jay Powell, Richard Preston, Robin Ridington, Blair Rudes, Allan Ryan, Mark Tyrell, Carl Urion, Elvi Whitaker, Wendy Wickwire, and H. C. Wolfart.

Stephen O. Murray has long been and remains the foremost trusted assessor and patient reader for all that I think and write on such matters. He remains also my sociological conscience—my personal Two Crows. His comments on the draft manuscript were invaluable, as were those of Fred Gleach and Gary Dunham. I remain, of course, fully responsible for the final argument.

I thank my family, the wellspring of life-enhancing chaos. My husband, György Ozoray, has undertaken to keep all big black dogs at bay. The Vanek gang keeps growing—stronger, wiser, and finer: Tracy, Kevin and Erika, Adam and Kim, Karin and Michael, and Rodney and Kristen (but, guys, I still get to be Hannibal Smith). And the usual motley assortment of descendants of the Great Lucy Mama-Cat, and György's very own garden.

Gary Dunham, an editor who is also an anthropologist, shares my own conviction that disciplinary history is sorely needed in anthropology, resulting in the Critical Studies in the History of Anthropology series edited by Steve Murray and myself. I honor the University of Nebraska Press's powerful assertion that history of anthropology, out-of-print Americanist classics, American Indian history and ethnohistory, and writing by contemporary Native Americans have much to do with one another.

The rhetorical strategies of this text are tailored to its interactive and pedagogical intentions; I have made these decisions deliberately. I have selected a few recurrent issues of presentist relevance to my own contemporary version of the Americanist tradition; in the process I have ignored issues that other commentators might choose to foreground. I quote heavily from works cited and from correspondence, lest the pungent flavor of the participants' disputations be lost. There is considerable internal diversity in the core Boasian engagements with a few key ideas (e.g., history vs. psychology, culture vs. the individual, science vs. the humanities, culture vs. history, language vs. culture); they did not always agree, but they shared a field of discourse. Ideas changed over time, although each core Boasian is associated with a small number of key positions; the treatment of each scholar is generally chronological on a given point. Footnotes are avoided in favor of parenthetical insertions because I want to encourage trains of thought in multiple directions and to capture the complexity of many generalizations. I have retained much of the colloquial rhythm of oral presentation, hoping for a less-than-passive reader response. I refer often to my own writing, not out of egocentrism but because this book draws together trains of thought long in progress. In-text references often cite sources that have influenced my thinking more generally than a specific passage (although specific references are given where warranted) and may provide the reader with a useful sense of intertextuality. References to contemporary work are necessarily rather arbitrary, and I am aware that others could have been chosen.

ABBREVIATIONS

APS   Franz Boas papers, American Philosophical Society, Philadelphia

BAE   National Anthropological Archives, Smithsonian Institution, Washington DC

NMM   Edward Sapir administrative files, National Museum of Man (now the Canadian Museum of Civilization) in Ottawa

UCB   Alfred Kroeber and Robert Lowie papers, University of California at Berkeley

UC   Anthropology department administrative files, University of Chicago

YU   Yale University Archives

YUDA   Yale University Department Archives

RUTH BENEDICT

Introduction

THE INVISIBILITY OF AMERICANIST GENEALOGIES

Resuscitating the Habits of Historicism

The contemporary variants of mature theory reveal a great deal about how well that theory functions as an explanatory model and about how useful it is as a theoretical framework or point of departure. But such explanatory usefulness is not the whole story. Such theory also invites historicism, the unpacking of underlying assumptions and evidence, at least in the first instance undistorted by presentist concerns (Stocking 1968). We must think historically while we are thinking theoretically. This simple methodological principle seems laughably obvious; after all, history as diachrony has returned to ethnographic descriptions with a vengeance in recent years. Yet as an anthropological historian with a deeply ingrained respect for the integrity of archival records and oral histories from the elders of our professional tribe, I am frequently nonplussed by the historical myopia of colleagues who ought to know better—who, if they stop to reflect, indeed do know where they come from and even take pride therein.

I want to reclaim the history of anthropology so that it can serve anthropologists as a means of constructing contemporary professional identities upon continuity with the past. Presentism in this reflexive sense, choosing issues for historical attention because they still matter today, is fully commensurable with historicism. It is only when we fail to distinguish the contexts of our own theoretical positions from those of the past that presentism becomes a methodological millstone.

This project arises in good part from the queries of my students, consistent over three decades, about where to find the theoretical insights of the early Boasians that I talk about with enthusiasm. It doesn't help when they read the works from which I learned to think about such Americanist issues as the idea of culture as symbolic form (Franz Boas), the concept of a continuum of cultures and civilization not restricted to our own (Alfred Kroeber), the locus of culture in the individual (Edward Sapir), the coevalness of ethnographic subject and anthropologist (Paul Radin), the relation of language and culture to thought and reality (Benjamin Whorf, Ruth Benedict), the genres of ethnographic representation (Elsie Clews Parsons), the humanistic heritage of anthropology and its ethnographic writing (A. Irving Hallowell), the interpretivist options in contemporary anthropology (Claude Lévi-Strauss, Clifford Geertz, George Marcus), and the politics and epistemology of anthropological knowledge (Dell Hymes, James Clifford, Edward Said). The contemporary reader requires historicist framing for these ideas; they are dated in style of presentation, embedded in the times and contexts of their writing, nonetheless germinal, worth retrieving.

Frustration with anthropology's habitual unreflexive presentism has goaded me into tracing the groundedness of our present "experimental moment" (Clifford and Marcus 1986) in terms of continuity or persistence rather than of disjuncture and innovation. *And Along Came Boas: Continuity and Revolution in Americanist Anthropology* (Darnell 1998a) documents the institutional and theoretical roots of Boasian innovations in a preexisting Americanist tradition centered around the Bureau of American Ethnology. The contributors to *Theorizing the Americanist Tradition* (Valentine and Darnell 1999) explore the resonances of this tradition in contemporary praxis across the Americas. Finally, in the present volume, "invisible genealogies" are made explicit through my readings of historicist continuities and contemporary adaptations of Americanist ideas.

The received history of our discipline is rarely interrogated theoretically. Its unilinear succession of dominant paradigms is so lacking in subtlety that the methods of historical reasoning developed in our conventional ethnographic encounters should immediately raise suspicions of superficiality.

First, according to the seamless narrative, came the classical evolutionism of Edward Burnet Tylor, Lewis Henry Morgan, and Sir James Frazer. Franz Boas's critique of this evolutionary paradigm, construed in retrospect to have been formulated largely in negative terms, then produced the historical particularism usually assumed to be tantamount to North American anthropology and deemed to have ended with the Second World War. Modern anthropology began, according to this traditional cautionary tale, with the participant-observation fieldwork and functionalist theory of Bronislaw Malinowski, with the mystique of the anthropological rite of passage in encounter with the un-sullied "primitive." This was powerful rhetoric, much of it emanating from Malinowski himself; he was a lyrical writer and a charismatic showman. In second stage functionalism, the story continues, A. R. Radcliffe-Brown soon cleaned up Malinowski's act with a turn from symbolic to social structure. Classical British social anthropology moved even further toward structuralism in response to the work of Claude Lévi-Strauss, albeit removing much of his ra-tionalist, universalist logic in a characteristic adaptation to Anglophone em-piricism and behaviorism. The resulting functional-structural hybrid passes, if anything does, for conservative consensus as anthropology enters the new mil-lennium. To be sure, there have been various challenges to orthodoxy loosely labeled as poststructuralist or postmodernist. But the verdict on these new and hardly unified dispensations is still out; supporters and detractors are equally passionate.

That changes are in order, however, can no longer be doubted. I contend that these changes, and their reception, are best understood in relation to what anthropologists already know about themselves and their work. Since the pub-lication of Thomas Kuhn's *The Structure of Scientific Revolutions* in 1962 (with the 1970 revision including a postscript about misreadings of the original argu-ment), academic disciplines have construed their histories in terms of non-cumulative theoretical paradigms of "normal science," followed in due course by accumulation of "anomalies" leading to "scientific revolutions" ensconcing new normal sciences. Kuhn's original formulation included speculation that the social sciences, and certainly the humanities, would prove to be "pre-para-digmatic." To have a paradigm, therefore, became critical in the eyes of many social scientists, reinforcing their claims to do "real" science (that being un-derstood as a good thing).

Kuhn correctly captured the social construction of scientific change and the consequent incommensurability of successive theoretical paradigms, empha-sizing networks of practitioners whose peer judgment provided consensus for establishing and elaborating scientific theories. At the same time, however, he glossed over the process, the social organization underlying the gradual emer-gence of a meaningful paradigm shift. Nor was it clear how long a paradigm ought to last; Kuhn's examples, such as the Copernican Revolution, were more cosmology than specific theory and were measured in centuries, not in the decades in which contemporary scientific changes succeed one another.

Joseph Rouse imagines a "radical Kuhn" whose implied critique of representation sees "communities of believers" replacing "communities of practitioners" (Rouse 1987:32). In the absence of value-neutral standards for judgment, competing theories can only be evaluated by comparison to one another. The illusion of scientific progress, then, reflects the writing of history by the winners. Rouse thus contends that science is better understood as a field of practices than as a retrospective textbook codification of uncontested results. Kuhn might well have disagreed, producing a more conservative reading of his own position. It is the difference between what Bruno Latour (1987:4) characterizes as "ready-made science," already reified for textbook consumption, and "science in the making," the doing of the work in the first place, a process never predictable or controllable in advance.

For the disciplinary historian writing within the continuous flow of paradigmatic contentions and contestations, process is the intriguing part. How does one paradigm come to succeed another? How do successive or simultaneous paradigms coexist? How and why do individuals switch allegiances? How do students decide which basket will contain how many of their eggs— and how do they hedge their bets? How many scientific paradigms does a social science practitioner live through in the course of a career spanning perhaps four decades (see Hill 1980)? Such questions require us to attend to continuities and overlaps as well as to changes.

Anthropologists already have some paradigmatic models for studying the history of their discipline. We apply the same methods to the history of anthropology that we do to the study of ethnographic communities. Way back in 1965, in the first issue of the *Journal of the History of the Behavioral Sciences*, A. Irving (Pete) Hallowell noted the familiarity, at least among American anthropologists, of this adaptation of ethnography to ethnohistory and by extension to the history of anthropology, resulting in instrumental acquisition of the sleuthing and interpreting skills of the archive historian. His own documentary contextualization of the northern Ojibwes provided a decisive methodological exemplar. Although he never explicitly said that historians were inclined to be myopic, I suspect that Pete thought it would be more difficult to teach anthropological interpretation to historians than to teach archival skills to anthropologists.

Hallowell's methodological emphasis also altered the professional marginalization of the history of anthropology, history previously understood as the memories of the oldest member of a department. However crucial the respectful recording of the experiences and insights of our professional elders, history of anthropology also includes the analyst's view, whether from within the discipline or from outside it. Hallowell himself produced both detailed archival investigations in history of anthropology (e.g., Hallowell 1960) and reminiscences of early Philadelphia anthropology based on his own participation (e.g., Hallowell 1964, 1967).

Dell Hymes employed a parallel rhetoric of continuity, urgency, and humanistic significance in talking about the Americanist philological/textual tradition and about the histories of linguistics and anthropology. In each case, practitioners have failed to take seriously the diversity and complexity of the patterns and events characterized. In 1962 at the Social Science Research Council conference, which stands as a convenient moment of origin for history of anthropology as a self-conscious anthropological specialization, Hymes whimsically explored the question of who should write the history of anthropology. He mused that anthropologists who shared their tribal knowledge were less than enchanted when historians did not take their words literally and went away to listen at other campfires—despite the irony that anthropologists have long been in the business of doing the same thing to others. "Informants" have a legitimate stake in being believed, in having their words taken literally. This conundrum is clearer when we ourselves are on the other side of the encounter.

This exemplary tale is replicated in contemporary reports. To take a single example, Andrew Shryock (1997) describes the resistance met by his efforts to weave together narrative accounts of the competing genealogies of Bedouin lineages into a unified account of Jordanian national identity. Standpoint epistemology was unacceptable to narrators who sought his allegiance, because each was convinced that his or her version was uncontestable truth, ontology rather than mere epistemology.

Dennis Tedlock (1995), on both ethical and theoretical grounds, interrogates the history of anthropology in the performative dialogic form he has long advocated for ethnographic reportage, arguing persuasively that our inherited methodologies suppress the dialogue of field notes into a format where only one person can speak at a time. The honorable exceptions he cites are almost all linked to the Americanist tradition, for example, the work of Paul Radin, Gladys Reichard, Victor Turner (an Americanist grafting on British stock), Clifford Geertz, but also the French anthropologist Marcel Griaule. Even Malinowski (though not Radcliffe-Brown) has moments of sounding like an Americanist.

Just as we are observers affecting the observed in our fieldwork, so is our professional practice intertwined with our historical practice. It should not surprise us, therefore, that a specialization in history of anthropology has developed more strongly in American than in British anthropology. National tradition is a powerful influence on, if not determinant of, paradigmatic commitments. Such traditions, however, are normative rather than absolute. Greater internal variability doubtless also accompanied the vastly greater scale of American anthropology relative to British. Evans-Pritchard's historical apostasies to the contrary, classical British social anthropologists have tended to privilege synchronic rather than diachronic study of ethnographic communities. Contemporary inheritors of this tradition (e.g., Jean Comaroff 1985; John and Jean Comaroff 1992), despite institutional affiliation with the hybrid Americanist and British tradition of the University of Chicago, do not cite Americanist grapplings with history when they exhort social anthropologists to relegitimize a history shorn of its prior evolutionary baggage.

Perhaps, however, I overstate the case. If so, it is in part a result of personal exposure. My initial encounter with British social anthropology was in the rather formidable person of Meyer Fortes, at a Wenner-Gren conference on national traditions in 1968. I particularly recall his vehement self-satisfaction in reporting that he had forbidden historian John Burrow to sit in on his anthropology lectures because it was not *his* discipline's task to wonder about the social structure of some African tribe. I felt very American(ist) as I silently mused that Burrow's (1966) very fine book on Victorian evolution would have been even finer had its author been more conversant with issues in contemporary British anthropology as a context and source of continuity for his treatment of the preceding classical evolution.

I am not alone. Dennis Tedlock, in lyrical defense of the necessity for dialogical anthropology, calls for a return to things anthropologists knew long ago and seemingly have forgotten:

> There was a time when the same anthropologists who worked on producing ethnographies also worked on text collections, but that came to an end when American cultural anthropology was diverted from its course by British social anthropology, which tended to treat the utterances of natives as falsehoods and illusions concealing truths that could be revealed only by anthropologists. The collection of texts fell to other field-workers whose concerns were narrowly lin-

guistic and who increasingly pursued their careers in academic departments separate from anthropology. (Tedlock 1995:5)

The "turn away from language" and "the older Boasian philology" were correlated with "a change in the center of gravity of North American anthropology from the Americanist tradition of recovering the Native American past to a more globally conceived imperial anthropology, concentrated especially in the newly emerging spheres of U.S. economic interest in the Pacific and Latin America" (Tedlock 1995:5).

The mutual unintelligibility of the British and Americanist sensibilities was further reinforced for me by Adam Kuper's comment (personal communication 1990) that he had never really understood the emphasis on language in American anthropology. Not that there is no precedent in British social anthropology for studying language: John Firth, the teacher of Michael Halliday, was a student of Malinowski, whose *Coral Gardens and Their Magic* (1935) and appendix to Ogden and Richards's *The Meaning of Meaning* (1923) set out a methodology for ethnographic semantics. But as in the case of history, these matters are not in the forefront of the British tradition and seem to have required rediscovery.

History of anthropology, virtually from its emergence as a specialization, has taken a backseat to other modes of theoretical reflexivity. These days most of us take for granted the inseparability of investigator and investigated, the inextricability of professional practice and personal standpoint. The greater difficulty is that history and theory often are not clearly distinguished. Theory is more sophisticated when it acknowledges the context in which ideas were and are propounded in the world. Chronology matters; ideas do not emerge in a vacuum. It is easy enough to criticize earlier work by applying contemporary standards, but at the price of eclipsing the context and continuity of ideas; this price is too high.

Contemporary enthusiasm for reading "against the grain" potentially distorts the intentions and relevance of previous contributions. Americanists have learned that it is respectful to listen to the words of the people studied, people who are not dupes but experts, analysts, even theoreticians. Analogously, we can and ought to attend to the words of our professional predecessors: We can disagree in ways that acknowledge prior argument and evidence in their own terms as well as in those of the contemporary critic.

I am far from suggesting that the cultural critic should not take issue with previous work. Rather, there is an enabling double hermeneutic in our theoretical and historicist methodology, just as there is when we do ethnographic fieldwork and return to write up the results. In the first stage of this hermeneutic, we suspend disbelief in order to understand in local terms, keeping in mind that "the Native" is also an ideologist. In the second stage, we establish meaning in translation, aiming to remove the exotic from the world of the "other," for the edification of a reading audience that has not been there. Both the understandings we (re-)present and our own theorizings are situated knowledges (Haraway 1988). Our theorizing remains forever sloppy if we do not acknowledge these multiple and shifting contexts, particularly as we move between and across the poles of our double hermeneutic.

Recovering the Complexity of Our History

Like most seamless narratives, the received history parodied above perpetuates, if only by the superficial romp-through, a series of inaccuracies that mask the complexity of the actual interactions of anthropological paradigms during the twentieth century. My own strategy is to rehabilitate parts of the Americanist tradition associated with Franz Boas and his early students as the baseline for a contemporary theory of cultural knowledge and social interaction focused on language, symbol, and meaning. In order to establish historical and epistemological continuity to contemporary anthropology, I will draw upon some postmodernist impulses that both attract and repel me; many of these are foreshadowed in Boasian work. I hope to recover some of the complexity of the historical development of Americanist anthropology, to free it from what all too often seems a static canonical form frozen in the time of the last buffalo hunts on the Great Plains and peopled with the equally frozen Amerindians who were its privileged subjects. Rigor mortis is incompatible with critical theory, then as now.

To be sure, there has been an intimate relationship between anthropology in North America and the study of the American Indian. Hallowell (1960) argued persuasively that urgent practical problems of coexistence with and administration of the Indians created the broad scope of the discipline, encompassing ethnology or cultural anthropology, linguistics (of unwritten languages), (prehistoric) archaeology, and physical or biological anthropology.

Historians and ethnohistorians, conversely, have emphasized the crucial role of the Indians in the emergence of an American identity. A number of early amateur anthropologists were statesmen and administrators of the nascent nation, for example, Albert Gallatin, Thomas Jefferson, John Pickering, Peter Stephen Duponceau, Lewis Cass, and Henry Rowe Schoolcraft (Berkhofer 1978; Bieder 1986; Deloria 1998; Smith 1950; Wallace 1999). Their studies looked to Europe for theoretical inspiration; they were homegrown scholars-on-the-spot who could contribute American data on language and customs to the increasingly systematic comparative ethnology of eighteenth-century universalist Enlightenment rationalism. Although most had some direct contact with Native Americans, these Americanist ethnologists were primarily armchair scholars, their theories based on data from men of affairs (traders, missionaries, and military officers). Although not professional scientists, they formed the core of practitioners necessary to articulate a paradigm around the study of the American Indian. Because they wanted to place the Indian relative to the global diversity of cultures and languages, these scholars tended to homogenize the diversity of New World aborigines, assuming, for example, that all Amerindian languages were "polysynthetic," in contrast to the "analytic" European languages. Interpretation of the typology was unproblematically evolutionary.

Oral tradition to the contrary, Americanist anthropology did not emerge full-blown from the mind and institutional machinations of Franz Boas, although it certainly attained its particular twentieth-century form in relation to his herculean efforts at professionalizing and giving academic status to the discipline. In a paradigm shift of Kuhnian proportions, at least in retrospect, anthropology moved from the work of the amateur rationalist savants toward professionalization with the founding of the Bureau of American Ethnology by Major John Wesley Powell in 1879 (Darnell 1998a).

Professionalization inevitably modified the conditions of anthropological work, producing salaried positions, participation in a network of peers sharing some degree of consensus about work to be done, evaluation of its quality, funding for research, access to publication, and professional training. These innovations, consolidated gradually during the late nineteenth century, dramatically enlarged the contexts in which anthropological research could be pursued. Institutional changes interacted with new theoretical perspectives and emerging social networks to produce a clear paradigm shift.

Disciplinary affiliation became increasingly significant. Major Powell himself was an army officer and geologist, mostly self-trained, who turned to ethnology after an early career as explorer, geographer, and politician. Powell's (1878) modeling of the arid lands of the American Southwest as a complex interaction of environment, technology, and culture (land use) was anathema to land speculators and politicians. His strategic retreat to ethnology, drawing on his fieldwork with the Utes and Shoshones in the Southwest, was an astute political retreat rather than a shift in discipline (Stegner 1954); his research already spanned several conventional disciplines. The early bureau staff were also, of necessity, trained in other disciplines or careers; there were as yet no academic programs in which they could have obtained doctoral credentials in anthropology.

Powell and his staff (optimistically funded by the United States Congress because of the practical need for accurate information about the Indians) devoted themselves assiduously to mapping the cultural and linguistic diversity of the continent. Under bureau auspices, participant-observation fieldwork was carried out, long before Malinowski, by Frank Hamilton Cushing, James Mooney, James Owen Dorsey, and Francis LaFlesche.

The synthesizing collaborative projects of the bureau culminated in a linguistic classification published under Powell's name in 1891. On this increasingly professionalized institutional baseline, Franz Boas began to consolidate what in retrospect would become the dominant paradigm of twentieth-century American anthropology. As the bureau's honorary philologist, Boas edited the *Handbook of American Indian Languages* (1911a, 1922), which provided exemplary grammars of American Indian languages with illustrative texts. Languages were selected to represent the range of psychological variation across the continent, a direct challenge to the single American Indian pattern taken for granted by the eighteenth-century evolutionist savants.

I have argued elsewhere (Darnell 1998a) that neither professionalization nor Boasian hegemony over the discipline were unassailably in place until some years after the end of the First World War. In the interim Boas gradually honed his theoretical critique of evolution, assembled institutional resources in universities (initially in collaboration with museums), and trained personnel with university credentials in anthropology as he defined it. By the time the *Handbook* appeared, Boas controlled the manpower (*sic:* the early Ph.D.s were mostly men, despite the feminist haven Boas created at Columbia, beginning around 1920 with Ruth Benedict, Margaret Mead, Elsie Clews Parsons, Ruth Bunzel, Gladys Reichard, Esther Goldfrank, Ruth Landes, Rhoda Métraux, and others) to enforce his vision of Americanist anthropology.

Boas was the victor who wrote the history of anthropology, giving no quarter to his intellectual or institutional competitors. In the first decade of the twentieth century, he was wont to target the recently deceased Daniel Brinton's evolutionary theory without naming him (e.g., Boas 1904); by implication, however, the critique also applied to Powell. For ensuing generations of academically trained Boasians, oral history has eclipsed the process of emergence of the Americanist tradition we know today.

Boas and Powell had much in common, sharing a commitment to mentalist anthropology, to ethnology and linguistics rather than to archaeology, material culture, and museums (Darnell 1998a). Language was key to Powell's classification of tribes and their framing within an evolutionary model of culture drawn from Lewis Henry Morgan's *Ancient Society* (1877). Although Boas rejected the bureau's party-line evolutionary interpretation, he built his own historical particularist theory directly on the philological data accumulated under Powell's auspices. Moreover, Powell, like Boas, was convinced that the words of informants recorded in texts constituted crucial ethnological and linguistic data for anthropological interpretation. Powell and Boas further agreed on the uniquely North American four-square definition of anthropology (although Powell never ventured into physical anthropology).

In the context of these continuities, let us turn to the version of the Americanist tradition constructed around the intellectual and institutional leadership of Boas and transmitted to and by his students and their students. A superficial reading suggests that the center of gravity of North American anthropology moved overseas after World War II. In contrast, I argue that careful attention to what the early Boasians were up to reveals significant continuities to contemporary practice in our late modernist, or for those who prefer, postmodernist times.

Distinctive Features of the Americanist Tradition

My proposed catalog of the distinctive features of the Americanist tradition is neither finite nor closed. Nor are these features fully separable, except in a heuristic sense. The list is normative rather than exhaustive; to discover another feature would not invalidate those identified here. I have selected themes that interest me; these lie largely at the intersection of cultural anthropology and linguistics, in the realm of meaning-making. Despite the ostensible inclusiveness of the Americanist four-field net, not everyone, even in

North America, is an Americanist. For example, almost everyone cited by Lawrence Kuznar (1997) as a "scientific anthropologist" would be difficult to include under the term.

Sharing some or all of the preoccupations of the Americanist tradition does not confine a given anthropologist to a box that no other influence can possibly penetrate. Unlike Schrödinger's cat, moreover, the models of anthropologists can be interrogated, both reflexively and ethnographically, as to their viability and intertextuality. The boundaries of national traditions and subdisciplinary specializations prove in practice highly permeable, at least insofar as they are embodied in individual practitioners.

Although it seems to me that these distinctive features form an interrelated package, this is not a finite system model. It is inductive—historical or cosmological rather than scientific in the narrow sense (see Boas 1887 on the distinction between history and science). Here, then, is my list, with some indications of continuity to contemporary praxis:

1 / Culture is a set of symbols in people's heads, not (or at least not merely) the behavior that arises from them. Observation of behavior is certainly legitimate, but the meaning of a behavior observed by an outsider depends on the words that explicate it. Boas's Northwest Coast diaries make clear his delight in collecting a mask for the American Museum of Natural History and enhancing its scientific value by also collecting its story (Rohner and Rohner 1969:38). There is a long-established tradition in many North American museums of appointing curators of linguistics: Boas held such a position in New York, Kroeber in California, Sapir in Ottawa (alongside his position as Director of the Anthropological Division of the Geological Survey of Canada). Dell Hymes was a curator of linguistic anthropology (a term that would be anachronistic for the first-generation Boasians) at the University [of Pennsylvania] Museum when I was a graduate student, and my fellow graduate student Michael Foster was a linguistic curator at the National Museum of Man (now the Canadian Museum of Civilization) in Ottawa. What, then, does a linguist curate? The interpretation of cultural objects, including words. Where does she or he get the words to curate? From texts. Where do the texts come from? From the collaboration of linguists and anthropologists with Native persons, past or present.

Claude Lévi-Strauss in La Voie des Masques (The Way of the Masks 1982) adopts, for theoretical as well as ethnographic purposes, Boas's insistence that objects are intelligible only in terms of their accompanying cultural texts. In fact, the domain plasticity of Lévi-Strauss's concept of structure allows him to move freely between visual and verbal representations. Similarly, Edward Sapir (in Irvine 1995) noted that observing a Nootka ceremony did him little good until someone told him in words what it all meant. I suspect that he liked the words—which could only come from a member of the culture—better. Boas, equally at sea in the midst of his fieldwork, noted disingenuously in his diaries: "George Hunt was not here, and so I did not know what was going on" (Rohner and Rohner eds 1969:188).

Without *both* the behaviors and their explications in words, we have what I have always thought of as "man from Mars" ethnography; it is commonplace in the anthropological literature. Non-Americanist anthropologists have been wont to ridicule the Americanist tradition for reconstructing cultures that no longer function—on the basis of "mere" words. I would argue, in contrast, that words are universal devices for the construction of meaning, both within and across cultures. What may have begun as a disadvantage to be overcome has become a strength. But then I am unabashedly an Americanist.

The anthropologist or linguist inevitably appears obtuse when forced to invent meanings on the basis of observation alone. Moreover, to consult a member of the culture being studied is not an entirely artificial construction of meaning. People habitually speak among themselves about the meanings of things, events, and actions. Children in every culture must learn to be human, in particular local ways, in the course of a socialization that in turn provides models to teach outsiders, including anthropologists. The primary difference is that background context can be more fully taken for granted by a child raised within the framework of his or her traditional language and culture. Our job as anthropologists is to assimilate and make explicit the framework that such a child takes for granted.

2 / Language, thought, and reality are mutually entailed in ways that are accessible to investigation. Americanists have habitually approached culture as a symbolic form articulated in words. The study of Native American languages, therefore, has been understood as the ideal entrée into Native thought and worldview. Grammatical categories, which divide the world in terms unique (at least as an assemblage) to each language, seem to predispose members of different speech communities to interact differently with the world and with one another. "Language, thought, and reality" is the three-pronged formulation that psycholinguist John B. Carroll (1956) used to title his selection of the writings of Benjamin Lee Whorf, student of Sapir and principal architect of the so-called (Sapir-)Whorf hypothesis of linguistic relativity. The relationship of language and culture is too complex to be determinative and too intuitively attractive to be ignored.

Attention to the significance of language as symbolic form characterizes Americanist cultural anthropologists as well as linguists. Boas was particularly adamant about the urgent need of linguistic description for the scholarly record as well as for use in the communities where languages were spoken. The Boasian program committed the student, at least in principle, to produce a grammar, a dictionary, and texts for each language and culture studied. In 1903, Boas clarified his expectations for students:

> I have instructed my students to collect certain things, and to collect with everything they get information in the native language and to obtain grammatical information that is necessary to explain their texts. Consequently, the results of their journeys are the following: they get specimens; they get explanations of the specimens; they get connected texts that partly refer to the specimens and partly simply to abstract things concerning the people; and they get grammatical information. (quoted in Berman 1996:270)

Though few of these students were primarily linguists, a surprising number of them tried to follow Boas's dictate. Exemplary dissertations presented between 1892 and 1926 include Alexander Francis Chamberlain on Missasauga language (1892), Roland Burridge Dixon on Maidu language (1900), John Reed Swanton on Chinook morphology (1900), Pliny Earle Goddard on Hupa language (1904), William Jones on Algonquian word formation (1904), Edward Sapir on Takelma language (1909), Leo Frachtenberg on Northwest Coast languages (1910), and Gladys Reichard on Wiyot grammar and texts (1926).

3 / Texts from Native speakers of Native languages are the appropriate database for both ethnology and linguistics. Collecting texts requires the anthropologist to work closely with one or a small number of speakers. I have argued elsewhere (Darnell 1990c) that this method focuses anthropological and linguistic attention on how cultural knowledge is uniquely structured in the mind of each of its members. That anthropologists and linguists have sometimes overgeneralized from such unique constructions of worldview to whole culture patterns does not invalidate the sophistication and complexity of the intuitions of what Paul Radin called the "philosophers" from the cultures studied by anthropologists. All ethnographers seek out individuals who are personally and intellectually compatible and who can collude with them to construct cocreated texts and translate across cultural and linguistic boundaries. There is a shared faith, however qualified, that texts will reveal structure.

Ideally, the *same* set of texts provides grammars, ethnographies, and cross-cultural psychologies. The grammars are based on more or less spontaneous consecutive narrative as a methodological defense against the imposition of Indo-European grammatical categories. The ethnographies are collaborative texts inscribing voices from oral traditions. They are not "our" words but "theirs." "We" record what "they" know that "we" do not. It makes sense, at least some of the time, to skip the intermediary "we," that is, for "them" to record what "they" know. The dichotomy remains discriminatory, even though it aspires to privilege the traditionally silenced.

Linguistic and ethnological texts also form a database for psychological studies of the individual and the impact of culture upon him or her. It is no accident that culture and personality developed out of the Boasian/Americanist text tradition, with a grafting from psychoanalytic life history. Texts are created by individuals, regardless of the degree to which they reflect whole cultures. The personal characteristics and preoccupations of those individuals are implicit in the linguistic and ethnological information encoded in the texts.

Americanist texts have always resulted from consultation and collaboration. Contemporary anthropologists are continuously refining the coevalness of such collaborations (Fabian 1983). Texts must not be obtained surreptitiously from persons unauthorized to speak of collective knowledge and must be contextualized, in publication as well as in the field, in the relationships between particular anthropologists and particular Native persons. We stand in a long historical tradition, albeit one yet to attain its potential for full collaboration. By becoming aware of emergent forms of collaboration over our shared history, scholars and Native persons alike can build on both previous and ongoing efforts.

4 / There is considerable urgency to record the knowledge encoded in oral traditions as part of the permanent record of human achievement. By the end of the nineteenth century, Native American languages and cultures were disappearing rapidly, with dramatic declines both in population and number of speakers of traditional languages. By 1995, only 209 languages were still spoken, less than half the number at European contact. Moreover, only 46 were still spoken by children; that is, only 1 language out of 5 still has generational continuity of speakers (Goddard 1996:3).

Edward Sapir ostensibly abandoned Germanic philology on the grounds that the Boasian challenge to record aboriginal languages before they were utterly lost was more important than ongoing scholarship on established Indo-European texts. This was undoubtedly not his only reason for switching professional allegiance, but it instantiates the rhetoric of urgency that unmistakably pervades early-twentieth-century North American anthropological literature and personal correspondence. To this day, concern with the futures of endangered languages remains an Americanist preoccupation.

We know now that many purportedly dying languages have proved remarkably resilient, both in terms of linguistic revitalization and demographic growth, despite the dire prognostications of many anthropologists and linguists (Chafe 1962). Nonetheless, the loss becomes less reversible in each generation virtually everywhere.

5 / "Traditional" culture is a moving target, always changing and adapting to new circumstances. It is located in the contemporary practices of communities whose interests and concerns direct the work of anthropologists. The label "traditional" is used with considerable rhetorical force in contemporary Native American communities and in their interactions with non-Native institutions and individuals. "Tradition" does not imply returning to some idealized pure culture that existed before Columbus spearheaded the invasion of the "new" world. Native Americans recognize that their societies, like those of white people, whether in Europe or America, have changed in five hundred years; all peoples have a history in which living traditions are continuously invented and reinvented.

This discourse is, of course, very different from the non-Americanist one about "invented traditions" that somehow lack authenticity because they are continually constructed by contemporary communities, often without attention to the scientific authority of the anthropologist to define their culture. In my view, anthropologists, in the field and in their writing alike, must respect both the cultural heritage and the contemporary practice of the peoples with whom they work. "Tradition," in such a discourse, refers to that which is continuous with the past, in line with the practices and values of a moral community. Native people themselves can and should define what is traditional within their own communities. They do so in terms of innovations that serve to maintain the identity of the community and its members in relation to their collective histories and personal agencies. "Tradition," in Native American terms, holds much of the meaning that "culture" embodies for anthropologists. If it is invented, we must celebrate its creativity and adaptability under conditions of change. That anthropologists sometimes produce alternative interpretations for other purposes is, of course, another matter.

6 / Native people are subjects and collaborators, not objects for study. The urgency of linguistic and cultural revitalization projects in particular communities has facilitated collaboration, with an implicit division of labor between the anthropologist as recorder, translator, annotator, and procurer of publication outlet and the native language speaker with knowledge to be passed on and motivation to transmit her or his knowledge under conditions of rapid culture change, even through unfamiliar forms like writing or multimedia technology. The resulting commodification of texts, an objectification or reification of knowledge removed from its traditional context of oral transmission and public performance, has produced mixed results: conflict, both external and internal, but also grounds for further collaboration.

Working closely with a native speaker on texts in a language previously unknown to the investigator, and often previously unwritten, forces the investigator to attend to how an individual speaker constructs the meaningfulness of her or his culture. Sapir, Boas, and their contemporaries were convinced that texts provided evidence of the Native point of view that would not be falsified by the standpoint of the observer. The resulting texts could be analyzed and reanalyzed, or they could simply be valued for their own sake—as distilled records in the words of particular individuals of the knowledge systems of their cultures. Not every native speaker of a Native language, however, was a potential contributor to such an exercise. Anthropologists sought out articulate members of these cultures who were willing to talk to them, often conflating this role with the status of experts, so deemed by their own communities. In practice, many of those willing to talk were marginal, of mixed blood, or removed from their communities to residential schools at an early age.

Boasians, and some of their BAE predecessors, habitually taught native speakers to write their own languages and record texts in the absence of the anthropologist. Boas's own long-term collaboration with George Hunt on the Kwakiutls (now known as the Kwakwaka'wakw) exemplifies the method:

Jeanne Cannizzo (1983), Judith Berman (1996), and Darnell (2000) argue persuasively that Hunt's unique version of Kwakiutl culture constituted it for anthropology in something other than its own terms. Certainly, Boas accepted the authenticity of Hunt's texts with greater alacrity than did his successors.

Undeniably, writing down these texts was the non-Native's way of preserving knowledge from an oral tradition (despite the inherent artificiality of phonetic representation based on dictation) (Murray 1983). Nonetheless, the intent of the textual methodology was to ensure replication of "the Native point of view." Implicitly, occasionally explicitly, the Americanist texts stood alongside what Matthew Arnold valorized as the best that had been known, thought, and expressed in human civilization (Stocking 1968). Our own generation is certainly more skeptical than Boas's about the possibility of capturing "the Native point of view." Humanistic optimism has frayed around the edges. Contemporary sensibilities also cringe at the implied arrogance of the Boasian textual privileging of written information, but this arrogance often coexisted with respect for the spoken words and underlying knowledge systems of the speakers who produced the texts. Reliance on texts guarantees an ineluctable quiddity that constrains imposed interpretation.

Americanist anthropology enriches contemporary theory through the evolving ethics of fieldwork. Research with human subjects is particularly problematic in vulnerable communities. Despite the ambiguities of informed consent, anthropologists are accustomed to our subjects reading what we write; we work together or we do not work at all. Dennis Tedlock's chapter title "Reading the Popul Vuh over the Shoulder of a [Mayan] Diviner and Finding out What's so Funny" (1983) provides an ironic reversal. We should not be surprised that Mayan diviners have preserved in oral tradition both the form and the humor of traditional knowledge forced underground by colonial repressions. Moreover, we are more accustomed to worrying about the reactions of the Native people who read what we write and impose their ethical and political agendas on us than are colleagues who work in distant areas.

We have not always had cause to congratulate ourselves. For example, the political economy of the Boasian tradition enjoined that texts appear under the name of the linguist or anthropologist who recorded them and controlled their form, rather than under the name(s) of the persons whose words came, through the texts, to represent their cultures and languages for generations of anthropologists and linguists. Agendas of evolutionary typology, structural modeling, language classification, and disciplinary theorizing have too often overwhelmed the Native point of view, overshadowing more proximate concerns with cultural and linguistic genocide, political and economic development, and a host of local issues.

On the question of authorship, I think with pleasure of John Fredson's texts spoken in Kutchin, an Athabascan language of the Northwest Territories and Alaska, and recorded at Camp Red Cloud, Pennsylvania, by Edward Sapir in 1923. Sapir's choice of Kutchin was integral to his larger study of the Athabascan language family, particularly the role of tone in historical inference about Athabascan and its possible connections to Asia (Krauss 1986). Sapir never did fieldwork in a Kutchin community and never published the Fredson texts (although they will appear in the Sapir collected works series now being issued by Mouton de Gruyter of Berlin). In 1982 these texts were published by the Alaska Native Languages Center in Fairbanks. The orthography and translation were arrived at in consultation with the contemporary Kutchin community. The texts appeared under the authorship of Fredson (with an easily missed notation that Edward Sapir wrote them down). The linguistic value of these texts, many Americanists would argue, is enhanced immeasurably today by the powerful political message of the transfer of ownership of the words back to the language community of the original speakers. Appropriation of knowledge expressed in words is just as significant, in local terms, as appropriation of material objects or skeletal remains.

The claim to local ownership of spoken words as intellectual property is a contemporary Native American political position requiring that presently practicing anthropologists become comfortable with the roles of facilitator and translator rather than that of author. It is unnecessary, however, to denigrate the textual work done throughout the twentieth century simply because its sensitivities to aboriginal-white relations are not those of our own time. A historicist stance requires us to look seriously at the conditions of collaboration at the time of text production as well as to acknowledge the importance of these texts for contemporary Native peoples, anthropologists, and linguists alike. John Fredson would not have recorded his texts without Sapir's initiative and resources. For contemporary Kutchin communities, this record has become an irreplaceable resource, which they now collaborate, among themselves and with outsider linguists, to preserve and expand in a dynamic political agenda.

The relationship between scholars and Native people must be reconstituted in every generation. Many Americanists welcome such realignments, acknowledging that our purposes often have not been congruent with those of communities or consultants and that we are aware of the depth of meaningful interpretation possible to a member of the culture but inaccessible to the anthropologist who arrives as a tourist and ultimately goes home to another place. Practitioners of the Americanist tradition negotiate every day the terms on which we live alongside Native communities and individuals. This contemporary Americanist scholarship is unmitigatedly political and remains ethically ambivalent. That individuals among us are liked or even loved by the people we study and work with does not resolve the internal colonial or postcolonial asymmetry of our structural relationships of power to them.

7 / **Fieldwork takes a long time.** Few of us "do" a culture and hurry on to the next. I've been at it for over three decades now, as have many of my most respected Americanist colleagues. Fieldwork in North America lends itself to ongoing commitment, in ways that are impossible in much of the Third World. Repression of Fourth World peoples often excludes researchers with access to international public opinion. Whether it be a result of logistic ease of access to a "field" located among ourselves or a response to Native North American pedagogical principles, understanding is expected to come slowly, in a spiral, in sustained interaction with the same people over the course of one's own life cycle. Rapport and trust emerge gradually over a period of years. People who have known one another for a long time do not have to start their stories at the beginning. They share an interpretive code born of experience, despite different backgrounds and many experiences that are not shared. Moreover, Native North American societies tend to be age graded, to understand knowledge as emerging over a lifetime in relation to experience. Anthropologists, like Native Americans, are expected to learn things that matter in due course and in appropriate contexts. Observation is far preferable to interrogation.

Many Native people have told me over the years that they hate telling stories to white people because the stories have to be so long. That is, what is obvious to any civilized Native person has to be stated explicitly for outsiders. To do so is boring and unaesthetic for the Native person. The differences in criteria for effective storytelling involve interactional styles as well as shared knowledge. Despite these barriers, a surprising number of non-Native Americanists have been invited to receive the patient teachings of elders about their traditional languages and cultures.

Why These Genealogies Are Invisible

One begins to wonder if all these factors are obvious. In fact, they are not. I am increasingly convinced that there is a deep and long-established gulf across national traditions. American, British, and French anthropologists, for example, far too often talk past one another without realizing they do so. Cross-cultural miscommunication applies to professional debates as well as to more traditionally ethnographic encounters.

Let me illustrate in terms of one of my favorite pieces of archival documentation, a confrontation preserved in anthropology departmental records at the University of Chicago. Edward Sapir was hired in 1925 as the superstar expected to revitalize Chicago anthropology within an interdisciplinary social science synthesis funded by the Rockefeller Foundation and closely tied to the Chicago school of sociology (Darnell 1986a, 1990a; Murray 1986). Sapir resigned in 1931 to accept a call to Yale University and its Institute of Human Relations. He left behind a lavishly funded (for the time) research program and field school with the Navajo, which depended heavily on his own collaboration with Father Berard Haile and Navajo "informant" (the accepted term at the time) Albert "Chic" Sandoval.

Sapir's replacement as the central theoretician of Chicago anthropology was A. R. Radcliffe-Brown, who was emphatically not an Americanist (despite his extensive use of American Indian data during his Chicago sojourn). Chicago at the time was the only academic program in pre–World War II North American anthropology to maintain theoretical and institutional independence from Boas (see Darnell 1998a for details). Sapir, however, retained considerable loyalty to the fundamental tenets of the Boasian paradigm, among them the crucial importance of Native language texts. He knew that publication of texts was difficult to arrange. Publishers objected to the typographic complexities of American Indian orthographies and to the small, specialized readership of the resulting volumes. Nonetheless, Sapir assumed that Chicago department chair Fay-Cooper Cole (also a former Boas student) would see to such mundane matters on his behalf, if not on Haile's.

Radcliffe-Brown, however, professed not to understand why anyone would value texts such as those collected by Father Haile. He wrote to Cole: "What are such texts as these for? I wish Sapir had enlightened me on this. I read his letter over without finding out just what one does with such texts. . . . Authoritative it will certainly be. But just what will be done by scholars with these texts? . . . I am clear on this: that if they are to be treasured merely because they are disappearing, and because they are accurately transcribed . . . their publication would then be supported by mere antiquarian sentiment" (Radcliffe-Brown to Cole, May 1932, UC). Sapir recoiled at this challenge to the very premises of the Americanist method and the almost sacred integrity of the texts, responding to Cole that Haile's texts must be understood as "a priceless linguistic document" (Sapir to Cole, 22 May 1932, UC). He found it inconceivable to "see a beautiful piece of work made hash of because of the hostility of a supercilious gentleman." It is difficult to imagine any British anthropologist of this period relying on the word "beautiful" to cement the legitimacy of a method of research. ("Supercilious" was a word used rather frequently by Boasians in reference to Radcliffe-Brown.)

Cole, eager to avoid public confrontation between successive prima donnas of the department, mediated by focusing on how to edit Haile's material rather than on the legitimacy of the text method itself. Cole assured Sapir (25 May 1932, UC) that he had exaggerated Radcliffe-Brown's position (which Cole must have realized was not the case). Sapir (2 June 1932, UC) interpreted this to mean that Cole shared his own position. Partially mollified, he agreed to a compromise of additional ethnographic notes to make the texts more accessible to nonspecialist readers. But he continued to insist that "Brown" (the foreshortened form of his name being a characteristic Boasian strategy for deflating the perceived affectation of Radcliffe-Brown's personal style) must not be permitted to transform the Haile texts into a mere general overview of Navajo ritual. The texts themselves were the ideal entrée into the Native point of view, "what the ritual means to the Navaho."

Sapir returned to the subject of his nemesis:

> You see, from my standpoint that meant not only was the priceless linguistic material as such to be disregarded . . . but that all my own Navaho fieldwork was, by implication, judged a waste of time, that I might, so far as he was concerned, never have trained Father Berard . . . , that nobody cared for elaborate accounts of specific Navaho rituals anyway, and that we in America had better get busy and learn something from functionalism as to how a truly readable volume should be prepared. . . . It was all as if some Smart Aleck were to put the proffered texts of the Homeric poems aside with a supercilious remark. (Sapir to Cole, 2 June 1932, US)

Haile and Sapir speculated that Cole hoped to evade his obligation to publish the masses of collected texts. Their seeming paranoia was not unrealistic: The texts languished in limbo for years, eventually inspiring Sapir's most lyrical defense of the textual basis of Americanist ethnography. Less than a year before his death, he wrote to Cole:

> I'm not particularly interested in "smoothed-over" versions of native culture. I like the stuff in the raw, as felt and dictated by the natives . . . , the genuine, difficult, confusing, primary sources. These must be presented, whatever else is done. . . . There are too many glib monographs, most of which time will show to be highly subjective performances. We need to develop in cultural anthropology that anxious respect for documentary evidence that is so familiar to the historian, the classical scholar, the Orientalist. We'll *have* to do this, willy nilly, if we are to keep the respect of our colleagues. . . . If we're not careful, thoughtful and essentially not unfriendly colleagues will be getting more and more restive and saying, "Yes, this is all most interesting and I admire the beautiful synthesis that you have made, but where is the raw evidence? I can't tell whether a given statement is common native knowledge or is merely your interpretation of one man's say-so. (Sapir to Cole, 25 April 1938, UC)

Sapir's Boasian commitment to allowing members of studied cultures to speak in their own words and their own language is unmistakable here, though his target in 1938 may have shifted from Radcliffe-Brown to Margaret Mead and Ruth Benedict, neither of whom was comfortable with the linguistic thrust of the early Boasian program. Sapir's impassioned defense of the textual method, in any case, reflected his unwavering conviction that texts were the only reliable source of authentic cultural understanding. (Today we might object that there is no such thing as raw data, but there are certainly degrees of distance from actual words and events.)

There is a "fundamental dichotomy" between anthropologists who want to be scientists and those who are indifferent to the label for what they do. The distinction is highly correlated with the divide separating the British and the Americanist traditions, epitomized by the confrontation of Radcliffe-Brown and Sapir over the significance of American Indian texts. I am "often faintly startled to realize how many colleagues do not share even the basic assumption that what anthropologists (ought to) study is the construction of meaning across cultures and languages" (Darnell 1996:35). The basic premises of the Americanist tradition are, for me, not negotiable. This conclusion was something of a surprise, given how deeply I have always professed, and continue to profess, the value of eclecticism of both discipline and method.

Do I have an axe to grind? Yes, of course. I am intrigued by what Lowie called the Boasian "super-intelligentsia"—Sapir, Paul Radin, Ruth Benedict, and Alexander Goldenweiser (Lowie 1959:133)—and by the intersection of language, symbol, and interaction across cultural communities. I want to trace and celebrate my own genealogy, in the context of a responsible, documented historicism.

Every practicing anthropologist has a unique genealogy, understood as a way of tracing her or his relationship to the ideas, institutions, and social networks of the profession. These are more complex than practitioners usually consciously realize. Whether or not they have attended an elite university, most American anthropologists have been taught by people who can tell personal stories about both disciplinary founders and major contemporary figures (Murray 1994). The shallow time depth of the professional discipline produces a rapid approach to founding ancestors who are personalized for their students by contemporary elders. Durkheim, Marx, and Weber, in contrast, are more distant and left no direct students (comparable to those of Boas); further, I suspect that anthropologists are, by the tools of their trade, more inclined than sociologists to personalize their genealogies.

When my professional life had fewer tendrils across disciplines and my mentors were anthropologists whose names were familiar to my students, I used to draw for them meandering charts of the personal network that kept me in touch with the far reaches of our discipline. My last history of anthropology class at Alberta was enchanted when I retrieved from memory the name of Sapir's secretary (Elaine Blakeney) who married his Ottawa colleague Diamond Jenness. History became real, humanly accessible.

I argued that an active professional network could connect you with someone who was expert in almost any given subject, with one or at the most two intervening links. Beyond the small size of the field of anthropology, this method is particularly well suited to characteristic anthropological claims to holistic scope, potentially including everything knowable about humankind and its environment, both social and natural. Many practitioners, myself included, take pride in the claim that anything can be anthropology, if thought about anthropologically. An anthropologist can, and often does, change his or her area of interest several times during a career. Although some colleagues may be bored or irritated by the new focus, few will deny that it is anthropology.

In another sense, genealogy is an individual's unique articulation, through teachers and close colleagues, to areas of theoretical, methodological, or ethnographic specialization. Such genealogies initially emerge from professional socialization. Linked genealogies constitute both a diachronic lineage through the history of the discipline and the synchronic structure of relations of a network of colleagues. Each anthropologist has a story to tell, a story whose complexity expands over the trajectory of a career. Collectively as well as individually, these stories make sense out of what we find colleagues doing and thinking about—and with whom. Genealogies are shared; they produce consistent products, characterized by family resemblances rather than by isomorphisms. Individual idiosyncrasies coexist with cultural patterns. We all enhance the memories of our most famous ancestors, claiming the elite of the discipline as our own wherever possible.

Why, then, do genealogies disappear from professional awareness? Although their disappearance seems remarkable, even counterintuitive, I suggest several reasons for the phenomenon.

1 / The specialization and expansion of North American anthropology brought on by the Second World War eroded most practitioners' sense of the discipline as a single intellectual community and social network. Documenting the final throes of colonialism gained momentum in the 1960s, more theoretically since about 1980. Coupled with existential guilt over the complicity of anthropology with empire, documentation of this process seemed to many more urgent and engaging than reconstruction of memory cultures in North America. It became fashionable to denigrate the search for pristine, precontact culture and to so characterize all Americanist work. Yet the illusion embodied in the concept of the ethnographic present, as still deployed in British social anthropology, is as problematic as the stereotyping of all Americanist work in this vein.

It is as if our British colleagues thought that Americanists would not be reduced to eliciting narratives if the rituals and practices were still in use. Not too long ago, I heard a lecturer who works in one of the more isolated areas of our contemporary global society respond to a question, as if it did not much matter: "Oh, they haven't actually carried out these ceremonies for a generation at least." So this contemporary ethnography differed from the stereotypical Boasian reconstruction of memory culture largely in that its illusionary ethnographic present purported to be based on behavioral observation rather than on retrospective explication by members of the culture. Ironically, however, the behavior was precisely what was missing, and the methodology had not changed in response.

Even after years of hanging out with the Plains Crees of Alberta, I still bought into the idea that traditional culture somehow must be closer to the surface in isolated former colonial locales than in the obviously complex and rapidly changing strategic symbolic adaptations I saw around me in northern Canada. When I lived in Africa for three summers in the mid-1980s, however, I quickly discovered that cultural vitality is not measured by intensity of contact or contemporary political autonomy. There, as in Canada, extensive mixtures of traditional and modern were largely unproblematic for the people we talked to, and they did not worry about identity or community (though both were changing rapidly). In fact, historical contingencies may make people more reflexive, more determined to exercise personal agency in constructing meaningful cultural identity.

2 / Genealogies become submerged because their insights are so taken for granted that one need not justify or even bring to conscious awareness their basic standpoints. In a somewhat different context, E. Valentine Daniel noted: "There are those theories which, by virtue of their long-standing naturalism in the social sciences as well as their partial integration into common sense (e.g., Marxism, psychoanalysis, functionalism, and most pervasively, Cartesianism), can be mistaken for descriptivism. . . . Because of the easy sense they make, their distinctiveness as theory—providing a way of *seeing* the world—becomes blurred and fades into appearing to be one with what is discovered in reality" (Daniel 1996:5).

The very success of an idea can eclipse its revolutionary character, especially in retrospect. Sociologist Robert Merton called this "obliteration by incorporation" (Stephen Murray, personal communication). The most obvious anthropological example is the incorporation of cultural relativism into the North American worldview, at a critical juncture when American isolationism was being shattered by world events and had to be reconstituted rapidly during and after the Second World War. The culture-at-a-distance project of Margaret Mead and Rhoda Métraux (eds. 1953) was foundational to this national reorientation toward cultural difference; Ruth Benedict's aesthetic distillation of Japanese culture in *The Chrysanthemum and the Sword* (1946) epitomizes the best of this tradition. Another case is the singular poignancy of the critique of scientific racism by Franz Boas (1938) and Ruth Benedict (1940) in response to the rise of Nazism. Finally, the anthropological concept of culture in the plural, as a necessary feature and emergent creation of all human groups, exemplifies democratization of the existence of culture or civilization (which I am inclined to equate, as did E. B. Tylor) understood as a civil standard of order and value.

Anthropologists trained in North America since the Second World War, which includes most of our living elders, have absorbed the basic tenets of the Americanist tradition almost subliminally, without necessarily thinking of themselves as Americanists. The exciting stuff has seemed to be the rest, the paradigms over which there was professional debate and dissensus. So the substratum of unquestioned Americanist assumptions became more and more deeply masked from conscious awareness. It became background rather than figure, out of the focus of conscious attention.

3 / The third factor, which I understand less clearly, is that the Americanists who continued to work with aboriginal North Americans did not dispute this paradigmatic territory, did not claim centrality to virtually all sociocultural anthropology on this continent. They weren't a contentious lot, for the most part, at least in relation to outsiders, and they stuck to cultivating their own disciplinary gardens. Many Native American groups withdraw rather than confront whenever possible; "their" anthropologists have apparently learned this lesson well.

Perhaps the deaths of Edward Sapir in 1939, Franz Boas in 1942, Benjamin Whorf in 1944, and Ruth Benedict in 1948, around the time of the Second World War, created a sense of vulnerability that also mitigated against confrontation. Another group of founding elders died around 1960 (Robert Lowie in 1957, Paul Radin in 1959, Clyde Kluckhohn and Alfred Kroeber in 1960, Leslie Spier in 1961). The discipline was poised for expansion and differentiation just as it was becoming less Americanist.

4 / Boas himself would probably have explained the eclipse of Americanist genealogies by what he called "secondary rationalization." His model of culture was not a rationalist one, like those his evolutionary predecessors had proposed. Rather, he hypothesized deep loyalties remaining below consciousness for most people most of the time. Trained anthropologists were not immune to human nature, which inclines toward rational justification for beliefs

and actions actually based on emotion. Boas worried that the "shackles of tradition" could only be broken by self-consciousness, which was difficult to attain (cf. Hatch 1973:55–57); it required an external observer/analyst. Intellectual heirs have evaded the perceived romanticism of the Boasian model.

5 / Anthropologists may have failed to apply insights acquired from their ethnographic work to the written traditions within which they report it. Native American oral traditions acknowledge the sources of their knowledge, lines of transmission through story and experience. There is something distancing about the mere fact of writing, which depersonalizes knowledge and standpoint, making each author's formulation appear to arise de novo. By our own professional standards, however, we should know that all knowledge, not only that transmitted through oral tradition, is situated in the standpoints of its originators and transmitters. Perhaps there is still some knee-jerk mistrust of oral tradition.

Whatever the full set of reasons (which I assume to be unknowable in any straightforward or complete sense), there has been a public eclipse of the Americanist tradition, not in its centrality as much as in the acknowledgement thereof (see Murray 1999 for quantitative demonstration of this persistence).

Why the Americanist Tradition Persists

In a permutation of the rhetoric of discontinuity employed by critics of Americanist traditions, I am often told, by Americanist and non-Americanist colleagues alike, that it's a shame there is no work on "Indians" at the meetings of the American Anthropological Association or the Canadian Anthropology Society these days. Well, yes, it would be a shame—if it were true. When I count the sessions on Americanist topics and the Americanist papers in other sessions, however, they number far more than those for any other single ethnographic area. I have done this reckoning systematically for the Canadian meetings (Darnell 1997b) and found the results consistent with the self-reported fields of specialization of university-employed Canadian anthropologists. In 1995–96 every Canadian department had at least one Americanist in at least one subdiscipline. Indeed, the majority of faculty in several departments had Americanist specializations (though not necessarily exclusively). The correlation was even higher in the case of linguistic anthropologists, confirming that this linkage still embodies a solid Americanist continuity.

I attribute this continuing focus on Americanist topics to various causes. The theoretical training of the present generation of North American–trained academic anthropologists made it virtually impossible, I suspect, to become a practicing professional without knowing quite a lot about the Native peoples of North America. Even the University of British Columbia, where there has been until recent retirements a clustering of British-trained anthropologists, maintains a pervasive commitment to the First Nations of the province. If the demographics of the Canadian profession are changing, then it is crucial to identify and preserve what is of value from both British and American traditions. On the other hand, Native peoples themselves now demand that expertise be placed at their disposal—so perhaps would-be Americanists, regardless of training, have very little choice after all. And perhaps that is a good thing.

Another factor in the persistence of specifically Americanist specializations is that anthropologists are people who get involved in things. They have a tendency to work where they live, even if they also work somewhere else. The pragmatics are necessarily attractive, but the consequences for the work are nonetheless substantial. If I am correct in my contention that the relationship of Native American communities and anthropological communities is a reciprocal one, at least in a sufficient number of cases to make the ideal plausible, then it may follow that for a long time Native Americans have been teaching anthropologists how to behave in a civilized fashion and respond to local communities' needs and concerns. Vine Deloria Jr. (1969, 1997) has been consistently explicit about this strategy. It is to the good if we also think of ourselves this way. Ray Fogelson recently argued (in Valentine and Darnell 1999) that we must become wards of the communities in which we work if we are to continue to work. That sounds more reasonable than it did even a generation ago, which, I believe, is one of the still emergent legacies of Americanist genealogies, invisible or not.

Those accustomed to working in what have until recently been isolated areas of the world, moreover, will be forced to follow suit, willingly or otherwise (Asad 1973; Hong 1994). This likelihood is enhanced by anthropology's increasing return home for field sites. George Marcus (1998:3–29) suggests a pattern of initial fieldwork in exotic and essentialized traditional cultures, with later fieldwork more or less at home and reflecting contemporary global and diasporic realities. Micaela di Leonardo (1998) reverses the argument, rendering the diversity of contemporary North American culture more exotic through a process of defamiliarization.

The Plan of the Work

In the remainder of this book, I explore some of the key conceptual sites of the Boasian version of the Americanist tradition, hoping for an endpoint relation of cogent promise for the future of anthropology, albeit without the (unattainable) coherence of a master narrative or a finished story. The past and the present are interrelated, such that the vitality of anthropology arises most productively from acknowledgment of continuity in the construction of professional identity.

The core ideas of the Boasian paradigm are interrelated; I have drawn exemplars from a range of works by several authors that pick up these thematic preoccupations in diverse ways. Boas was rarely a systematic theoretician; nonetheless, the pieces of his program have a certain theoretical coherence, which elucidates his often contemporary-sounding rejection of premature grand theory. In our own time, the Enlightenment tradition, which is the source of our culture as well as of anthropology itself, has come under serious question; traditional bases of Western science now seem increasingly ethnocentric, prejudging the validity and richness of alternative thought-worlds. Our social science—although perhaps the indictment applies less to anthropology than to others—has closed off prematurely the chance to learn from reciprocal conversations across cultural boundaries.

Where does this story end? It doesn't. These continuities are becoming our future because it is still worthwhile to engage Americanist ideas. They are part of our own genealogies whether we work on American Indian reservations or in urban centers around the globe; in small communities we now know are not bounded, in diasporic communities, or in those whose identity is grounded in ties to particular land; in multiple field sites or in a single community where all persons are known to one another. The way we do our work has deep roots in the fertile soil of the Americanist tradition. Nevertheless, the story is ongoing. We do not yet know whether we will call the forthcoming branches and their offshoots "Americanist" or, indeed, "anthropology" (see Hymes 1969; Said 1978). We do know that we stand at an embarkation point for an emergent standpoint with a past as well as a future.

FRANZ BOAS

CHAPTER 1

History and Psychology as Anthropological Problems

Boas and the Boasians in the History of American Anthropology

The central historiographic question in twentieth-century North American anthropology has been the impact of the formidable presence of Franz Boas at center stage. Boas and his students controlled the intellectual direction and social organization of North American anthropology at least until the end of the Second World War. Commentators on the history of anthropology, both internal and external, have concurred that, whatever the final evaluation of his intellectual leadership, Boas excelled as an institutional leader (see Murray 1994 for the distinction between these two types of leadership). During the first two decades of the twentieth century, Boas's machinations established an institutional framework in universities for the professional training of anthropologists, with museum collaboration sponsoring and often publishing their fieldwork (Darnell 1998a).

Theoretical assessment of Boas's role in the development of the discipline, however, has oscillated between extremes of adulation and vitriolic critique. It has become fashionable to dismiss "the five-foot shelf" of Kwakiutl ethnography as the metaphorical antithesis of interpretive or postmodernist anthropology. The claim that Boas was not a theoretician has long cried out for nuanced reexamination from sufficient distance to lower the short-term stakes. Despite the continuities foregrounded in this work, it is no longer necessary to distinguish oneself from Boas in order to function as an anthropologist in North America.

Leslie White (1963, 1966) presents a particularly virulent permutation of the argument that Boas's deeply ingrained disquiet over the possibility of grand theory halted disciplinary progress. White acknowledged that Boas's critique of the excesses of armchair theorizing by classical evolutionists was salutary in its time. But that time, in his view, had long passed, whereas Boas continued to exert his considerable institutional power to prevent others from going beyond his outdated research program. White wrote with more than a modicum of self-interest; marginalizing Boas was tantamount to asserting the legitimacy of his own revitalized evolutionary theory. If White's model failed to take anthropology by storm, blame could be laid on obstacles set in place by Boas.

In a more modulated response to neo-evolutionary advances on historical particularism, Marvin Harris (1968) continued to read the history of anthropology through a single plot-line, culminating in his own brand of "techno-environmental determinism." Like White, he acknowledged the significance of Boas's late nineteenth-century critique of evolution and the need at that time to establish an adequate ethnographic database for a return to nomothetic theory. This scientific revolution having been completed, Boas (despite the normal science established by working out the details of the antievolutionary program) could be relegated to the past.

Boas's former students rallied around to meet the challenges to his retrospective reputation as a theoretician. Most saw their own work as continuous with "historical particularism," the theory that replaced evolution for the Boasians. This paradigm involved commitment to reconstruct the past of each culture in its own terms on the basis of evidence specific to it. Melville Herskovits wrote a somewhat eulogistic biography of Boas in 1953. Official memoirs of the American Anthropological Association edited by Ralph Linton in 1943 and Walter Goldschmidt in 1958 relied on topical essays by colleagues whose disciplinary specializations derived from some aspect of Boas's work. No single contributor could match their mentor's scope across the subdisciplines (although in archaeology and physical anthropology, Boas had largely concentrated on problems of utility to cultural anthropology) or even across the increasingly disparate specializations in cultural anthropology. The year after Boas's death, Leslie Spier wrote: "Boas had to concern himself with the whole field of anthropology in a way that may never be forced on another man. . . . Where some of the later students seem to be more systematic because they stayed with one topic, one cannot but feel that this was the result of rather narrow interests, of too limited a conception of anthropology" (Spier 1943:11). The overall scope of North American anthropology, by implication, was represented solely by Boas, both as exemplar and as publicist. Nevertheless, Spier depicted this broad scope as cumulative rather than as theoretically integrated. In a sense, therefore, the variegated apologia for historical particularism by its latter-day practitioners accepted, or at least failed to counter, the neo-evolutionist charge that Boas's theoretical alternative to evolution had been mere descriptivism.

The paradigm developed by the early Boasians was not shared in all its details by any particular individual, or, indeed, integrated or formally articulated by Boas himself. His own work changed over time and shifted topics without revision of prior positions, without synthesis. Nevertheless, postwar proliferation of anthropological specializations was foreshadowed in the range of earlier work intended to elaborate and fill in the details of the Boasian program. Seen from within, there was considerable diversity among the Boasians; for an observer standing outside their shared disciplinary culture, however, common assumptions and methods loomed larger. This observer effect was exacerbated for those who felt unjustly excluded from the Boasian core group (i.e., George Dorsey, Leslie White, Clyde Kluckhohn).

The early Boasians shared a heady sense of solidarity, viewing themselves as rewriting the history of anthropology, creating a professionally respectable and scientifically rigorous discipline whose practitioners were loyal to a common enterprise. In a simplified biological metaphor ignoring the Boasians' own emphasis on the psychological integrity of social groups, Stocking compared Boasian anthropology to a Victorian family:

> Thus, Boas's basic anthropological viewpoint may be seen as a kind of intellectual gene-pool, containing a limited number of traits, some dominant, some recessive, whose manifestation in his descendants was affected by the genetics of their affinal relationships and the environments in which their phenotypes developed. The outcome might be a considerable divergence within the patriline but this divergence was limited by the original genetic make-up of the intellectual father and by his continuing presence in the disciplinary environment, as well as by a certain tendency to intellectual endogamy. (Stocking 1976:19)

Some of this gene pool came, of course, from outside anthropology, especially as insights from European psychology were incorporated after Freud's first visit to America in 1909.

Life in the Boasian family did not always run smoothly. Paul Radin, for example, attributed theoretical tensions to Boas's personality; he was "personally a powerful figure who did not tolerate theoretical or ideological differences in his students." Boas deployed a "mechanism of intense personal involvement and loyalty" to "make a generation of students an extension of himself and his ideas," setting a rigidly controlled program for successive generations (Stocking 1976:19). "The work of Boas's former students tended to reflect the particular phase of Boas's thinking with which they come into contact while they were his students. . . . Insofar as Boas's students dominated the field, American anthropology became an elaboration of different phases of Boas's career, each phase being represented by a different age and sex grouping of his students" (Radin 1933:xxv–xxvi). Ironically, however, Radin exempted himself from the determinism of such cohort fixation, insisting that his own patrimony consisted of the "example of intellectual independence" (Radin 1933:xxviii).

The intimacy of the early core group enabled intense mutual fertilization of ideas, established a productive normal science with a sense of shared mission, and frustrated individual attempts to develop ideas beyond the pale of the shared Boasian standpoint. Stocking distinguishes "strict" Boasians (Robert Lowie, Leslie Spier, and Melville Herskovits), "evolved" Boasians (Margaret Mead and Ruth Benedict), and "rebellious Boasians" (Alfred Kroeber, Edward Sapir, and Paul Radin) (Stocking 1974 ed.:17); the nature of the rebellion, however, remained within the larger fold, each protégé taking "one aspect of the Boasian assumption" and carrying it "farther than Boas himself would accept." Radin was a self-conscious rebel throughout his career, Sapir tangled with Boas when his linguistic specialization led him to reformulate crucial tenets of the paradigm, and Kroeber labored to maintain the autonomy of his California research program; their careers remained, however, in an orbit with Boas at the center.

Specialization within Boasian cultural anthropology increased rapidly after about 1920 as each former student carved out his or her own theoretical niche, dividing up the holistic range of Boas's own work. This paradigmatic diversification confirmed and solidified the position of cultural anthropology at the center of the North American discipline. Archaeology and physical anthropology held somewhat subsidiary roles, their theoretical questions arising from cultural anthropology (at least from the standpoint of Boasian theoreticians of culture). Linguistics held an anomalous role because, during the period of incipient specialization, it was both a subdiscipline of anthropology and an increasingly autonomous discipline in its own right. Sapir partially bridged the gap in that he was simultaneously a core Boasian ethnologist, a founder of the culture and personality approach, which emerged in the interwar years, and a major player (along with Leonard Bloomfield) in the professionalization of linguistics. Sapir's influence on the Boasian cultural paradigm, moreover, failed to draw his fellow ethnologists closer to linguistics. Figure 1 delineates this diversification in terms of some of its core participants.

The writings of the former students, and students of Boas's former students, conveyed respect and often affection for the man himself. Margaret Mead (1959, 1974) was the most eloquent advocate of Boas's benign dictatorship over the distinctive North American anthropological tradition. Although the intensity of her rhetoric suggests defensiveness about her own divergence from the ostensibly shared paradigm, she remained adamant about the centrality of Boas to the core of her own professional identity. Other former students doubtlessly shared her sense of common commitment within the culture of Americanist anthropology.

Nonetheless, Mead's interpretations of Boasian tradition were highly selective. She appropriated a spokesperson role in the reorientation of the paradigm from history to psychology and made a blanket assertion that Boas supported the innovations she and Ruth Benedict introduced. This turn to new questions was by no means as discontinuous as Mead would have it. Nor were she and Benedict the sole contributors to the revised synthesis. The changes were grounded in the oscillation between problems of history and psychology that Boas, virtually from the beginning of his career, explicitly defined as the theoretical center of his anthropology.

Boas as theoretician worried a small number of ideas throughout his career, evincing the tenacity of a dog with a particularly juicy bone. The analytic discreteness of race, language, and culture, codified in his introduction to the *Handbook of American Indian Languages* in 1911, preoccupied him throughout his career. In 1940, two years before his death, Boas used this same conceptual triad to title a volume of his selected works. His other great idea was the relativism and historical contingency of cultural categories, explored in *The Mind of Primitive Man,* also in 1911. These two ideas have been so thoroughly incorporated into North American anthropological praxis that they now appear trivial and unproblematic. But in 1911 they were theoretically innovative. Boas proposed to flesh out these conceptual packages through fieldwork directed both toward "the Native point of view" and the reconstruction of culture history from the present distribution of traits assumed to have diffused among neighboring groups. He was so successful that the theoretical nature of his original motivations is now largely invisible.

Boas never produced a synthetic ethnography or life history among the Kwakiutls (Kwakwaka'wakw). But then he never promised to do so; in fact, it

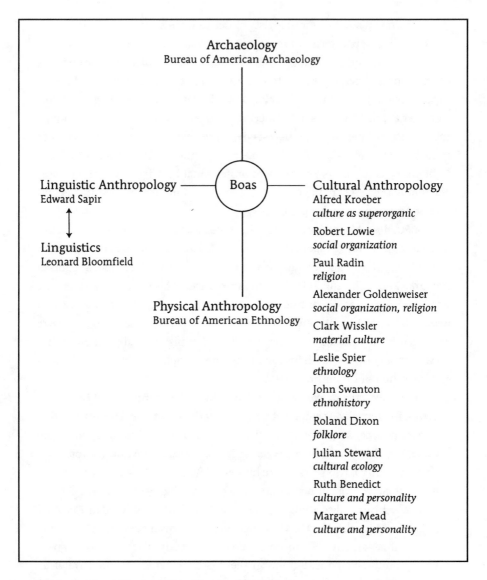

Archaeology
Bureau of American Archaeology

Linguistic Anthropology — Boas — Cultural Anthropology
Edward Sapir
Alfred Kroeber
culture as superorganic

Robert Lowie
social organization

Linguistics
Leonard Bloomfield
Paul Radin
religion

Alexander Goldenweiser
social organization, religion

Physical Anthropology
Bureau of American Ethnology
Clark Wissler
material culture

Leslie Spier
ethnology

John Swanton
ethnohistory

Roland Dixon
folklore

Julian Steward
cultural ecology

Ruth Benedict
culture and personality

Margaret Mead
culture and personality

Figure 1. Diversification of the Boasian Paradigm

is unclear whether he thought such a thing was possible. He preferred to let the materials, primarily textual, speak for themselves, attributing to them an unassailable objectivity. (In hindsight, however, it does not follow from the fact that texts are objects that they speak for themselves. On the one hand, much of the background interpretive knowledge underlying traditional texts has been lost within contemporary communities; on the other hand, successive generations of Americanists have provided the context that Boas apparently assumed to be self-evident.)

Boas expected texts to be used in the construction of grammars, ethnographies, life histories, and public understandings of other cultures (i.e., in linguistics, ethnology, psychology, and public discourse). He appears to have assumed his anthropological audience sufficiently sophisticated to recognize the implicit theory without being hit over the head with it; his technical reports were not intended for a general audience. On the one hand, Boas as theoretical commentator preferred the minimalist aesthetic characteristic of an Indian narrative, avoiding the risk of distorting his data by saying too much. Certainly his pedagogical style, about which some of his students expressed major reservations, was of the sink-or-swim school. On the other hand, he presented the largest possible amount of as close to raw descriptive data as he could get.

Subsequent generations, however, have preferred their theory explicit and labeled as such. Boas's penchant for embedding theory in his ethnography has buried his generalizations deeply in professional (un)consciousness. How many of us, after all, spend a great deal of time reading canonical ethnographies or ethnographic texts (exclusive of those directly relevant to our own fieldwork sites)? If we do, those we read are for the most part by British social anthropologists who have not hesitated to tell us why we should read their monographs. Americanist work has been eclipsed by the willingness of successors to dismiss the ethnographic theory and practice underlying the Boasian texts.

The emphasis on history meant that, even while reconstructing memory cultures, the Boasians acknowledged the effects of culture change, refusing to enshrine the ethnographic present so beloved of the British tradition. Culture change was interpreted, however, as a detriment to reconstructing traditional cultures rather than as a subject of interest in its own right. Acculturation became a focus only in the 1930s (e.g., Redfield, Linton, and Herskovits 1936).

Boas first addressed the question of psychological patterning in language in "On Alternating Sounds" (1889), a significant precursor of Sapir's definition of the concept of the phoneme in terms of its "psychological reality" for native speakers of a given language (Sapir 1925, 1933). For Sapir the issue was the unique pattern of sound contrast internal to each language. Boas, however, concentrated on how nonnative speakers misheard and consequently mispronounced unfamiliar sounds according to the habits of their first languages. He intended to counter stereotypic dismissal of complex Native American sound systems as random because they were heard variably from the standpoint of contrasts familiar to Europeans. In fact, Boas applied his cultural relativism to his own culture as well as to those he studied "in the field." Tolerance for customs elsewhere became an ethnographically edged sword pledged in service to social critique at home.

Methodologically, Boas was eager to pin down the phonetic detail of each language, features of sound not previously known to Indo-European speakers. He carried over this logic of unique patterning of habitual thought to his work on grammar. After a brief spate of survey mapping in historical linguistics on the Northwest Coast under the combined aegis of the Bureau of American Ethnology and the British Association for the Advancement of Science in the 1880s, he turned to the "psychological" question of grammatical categories. Sound systems and vocabulary were less likely than grammar to produce psychological insights.

As in the sound-systems argument, Boas wanted to establish that familiar Greek and Roman grammatical categories could not adequately represent particular patterns of languages with diverse histories and pattern integrations. Radin praised Boas for "treating aboriginal cultures as unknowns" (Radin 1933:8), that is, for not letting preset categories interfere with the task of ethnology. Ignoring the linguistic focus of Boas's argument, Radin disputed the assumption that the cultural facts would speak for themselves. The objectivity of a natural science model was impossible in reconstructing culture history because it had "too many imponderabilia" (Radin 1933:12).

History and Psychology as the Poles of Boasian Theory

Boas used the terms history and psychology in ways that now seem awkward, inextricable from the context of their original formulation. For him these poles of culture theory were sides of the same coin, their definitions mutually entailing. What now seems an absence of substance and exemplar was less a question of ideological posturing than of the axiomatic character of Boas's theoretical move away from the unilinear certitudes of an outmoded evolutionary paradigm. He needed a method, a conceptual apparatus, that was simultaneously qualitative and rigorous, a way to control the observer effect and draw "people without history" (Wolf 1982) into the purview of anthropological science. History and psychology were the hooks on which Boas wanted to hang the descriptive data amassed by ethnologists in the field.

In "The Study of Geography" (1887), Boas already made clear that science and the amalgam he referred to alternatively as history, geography, or cosmography posed separate kinds of questions and therefore required different methods. Both were legitimate parts of an anthropology that encompassed the natural and the social sciences. The same phenomena could be studied either from a nomothetic or an idiographic standpoint, moving between the methods of cosmographer and physicist. In "The Aims of Ethnology" in 1888, Boas already distinguished "the critical analysis of the characteristics of each people" from "the laws governing the life of peoples," from *Kulturgeschichte* (culture history) to *Völkerpsychologie* (folk psychology) (Boas 1940:629, 634).

Although Boas's temperament led him to prefer the methods of science, he shifted repeatedly throughout his career between the two strategies. Sapir, during his period of enthusiastically analyzing his colleagues according to Jung's personality types, characterized Boas as fundamentally ambivalent, a feeling introvert whose scientific training led him to privilege thinking over feeling, in a futile attempt to exclude human subjectivity from his anthropology (Sapir to Lowie, 20 May 1925, UCB). Sapir's own predilections ran rather more to the humanistic pole.

For Boas psychology was a domain of scientific laws; his doctoral work was grounded in the purported objectivity of Machian psychophysics. His career turn to ethnology, however, shifted the order of questions; he decided that the database on which the ultimately psychological questions of anthropology could be answered was historical. Moreover, there was a poignant urgency to ethnographic salvage work, whereas theory could be postponed in favor of recording rapidly disappearing traditional knowledge. Perhaps conditioned by his training in geography, Boas's detailed study of particular cultures emphasized spatial distributions of culture elements as clues to reconstruct the successive temporal contacts of peoples without written history. Geography became a substitute for history under cultural conditions precluding its conventional application.

Psychology, in this formulation, referred primarily to how particular culture traits were nonrandomly combined as a result of borrowing and culture contact. Elements were selected for elaboration and integrated into new cultures. Boas was uninterested in random sampling, apparently assuming that whatever the anthropologist discovered was somehow representative by virtue of its integration into the culture. Thus grammars could be constructed on the basis of texts from a single speaker, and knowledge of a culture was assumed not to vary substantially among its members. (He did not, however, explicitly elaborate the underlying assumption that culture is [fully] shared.)

Boas was inclined to discuss element distributions in quantitative terms, hoping thereby to transcend the observer bias to which his initial training in physics made him acutely sensitive and which jeopardized the very possibility of objectivity in the social sciences. His research program rested on the ostensibly objective properties of some kinds of ethnological objects, particularly texts and artifacts. Texts acquired materiality by being written down. Boas sought to understand the uses of such objects and how they were understood by their creators: "I have spared no trouble to collect descriptions of customs and beliefs in the language of the Indian, because in these the points that seem important to him are emphasized, and the almost unavoidable distortion contained in the descriptions given by the casual visitor and student is eliminated" (Boas 1909:309). Such an approach would make the social and ritual practices of a given group intelligible to an outside observer: "All of these [collectible objects] are used in the daily life of the people, and almost all of them receive their significance only through the thoughts that cluster around them. For example, a pipe of the North American Indians is not only a curious implement out of which the Indian smokes, but it has a great number of uses and meanings, which can be understood only when viewed from the standpoint of the social and religious life of the people" (Boas 1907:928). History and psychology were ethnology's twin avenues to mental process, both past and present: "Thus it happens that any array of objects is always only an exceedingly fragmentary presentation of the true life of a people. . . . The *psychological* as well as the *historical* relations of cultures, which are the only objects of anthropological inquiry, cannot be expressed by any arrangement based on so small a portion of the manifestation of ethnic life as is presented by specimens" (Boas 1907:928; emphasis mine). Boas's most explicit statement of the value of texts came a few years later in *Tsimshian Mythology*: "Material of this kind does not represent a systematic description of the ethnology of the people, but has the merit of bringing out those points which are of interest to the people themselves. They represent the autobiography of the tribe" (Boas 1916b:393). By the following decade, Mead, Benedict, and others would begin to elaborate the integration of such quasi-objective elements, employing a qualitative and humanistic methodology that was far from alien to Boas's own speculations.

Early in his career, perhaps as a carry-over from his scientific training in physics and geography, Boas emphasized the possibility, albeit at some unspecified future time, of arriving at "laws governing the growth of culture" (Boas 1898:2). He envisioned an ordered series, in which historical interpretation necessarily preceded psychological. When laws analogous to those of the natural sciences failed to emerge, Boas retreated to a deconstructionist rhetoric of what he considered premature generalizations distorting the increasing body of ethnographic data against which potential "laws" could be tested: "As we have penetrated more deeply into these problems we have observed that the general laws for which we have been searching prove elusive, that the forms of primitive culture are infinitely more complex than had been supposed, that a clear understanding of the individual problem can not be reached without taking into consideration its historical and geographical relations" (Boas 1906:642).

"Complex" is a key word in this discourse; recognition of complexity might even render generalization impossible. Particular ethnographic studies demonstrated that culture change did not proceed everywhere in a unilinear sequence, as predicted (or perhaps merely taken for granted from the outset) by the evolutionary model. Moreover, the parts of a culture changed at different rates. Patterning was located in individual cultures rather than in a rigidly determinative (evolutionary) progression. Indeed, Boas's priority in the critique of premature generalization and oversimplification in cultural evolution foreshadows the attention to complexity of more recent syntheses in biological evolution. Diffusion seems a better model than unilinear historical diversification for the plenitude of forms in the Burgess shales as interpreted by Stephen Jay Gould (1989). The social sciences have pioneered in providing models for complexity and interdeterminacy that have in turn proved useful in the so-called hard sciences.

Boas's impulse to theoretical adequacy is clear here, although the method is deconstructive, possibly even destructive, rather than reconstructive. What it is not is atheoretical. The need to examine the observer bias of the anthropologist as fieldworker and cultural analyst has not passed, as evidenced in much contemporary theorizing across the social and human disciples. Boas might well have enjoyed Jacques Derrida's efforts to disentangle what is implicit and unquestioned in the culture of the West and whether we are ever justified in identifying patterns as already existing in social and natural worlds beyond the observer. Despite his failure to present an integrated replacement theory, no one seriously suggests that Derrida is not a theoretician.

I have argued elsewhere (Darnell 1977a) that the turn to cultural and psychological patterning in Boasian anthropology arose without substantial discontinuity from the trait distribution studies of the 1920s. Alexander Goldenweiser's deconstruction of totemism in 1910, Leslie Spier on the Plains sun dance in 1921, and A. Irving Hallowell on circumpolar bear ceremonialism in 1926 set parameters for a normal science genre. The model adapted easily to archaeology where artifacts could be interpreted only in the broader context of an assemblage and its areal distribution.

Ruth Benedict's comparative study of elements of the Plains vision quest (1923), what she called "the concept of the guardian spirit," appeared a decade before her best-selling *Patterns of Culture* (1934b). On the surface, the thrust of these two works is quite different. For Benedict, however, there was nothing anomalous in the quintessentially Boasian movement from historical inference based on trait distribution to psychological interpretation of the integration within a single culture. They were sides of the same coin, her successive models continuous rather than disjunctive.

Radin, following Boas's encompassing theoretical dichotomy, considered these exemplars "complex historically and psychologically, as well as variable" (Radin 1933:138). The number of common traits was less significant than "the observer's evaluation of them" (Radin 1933:143). Boas's students were all "somewhat perturbed by the apparent denial of tribal individuality" in the quantitative trait element method (Radin 1933:145). Rather, whole complexes took their character from a particular cultural setting. Sapir referred to these trait element studies as "the body of historical critiques that anthropology owes to Boas" (Sapir to Benedict, 25 June 1922, in Mead 1959). Accepted Boasian wisdom was that trait elements added up to history, insofar as it was accessible in societies without written records.

Lowie, even less inclined to theoretical generalization than Boas himself, willingly settled for "fruitful correlations" rather than scientific laws (Lowie 1963:13). Simultaneously, he captured the processual model inherent in Boas's move from evolution to culture history with his famous, though often mis-interpreted, comment: "But no such [evolutionary] necessity or design ap-pears from the study of culture history. Cultures develop mainly through the borrowings due to chance contact. Our own civilization is even more largely than the rest a complex of borrowed traits. . . . To that planless hodgepodge, that thing of shreds and patches called civilization, its historian can no longer yield superstitious reverence" (Lowie 1920:440–41). I am inclined to read "cul-tures" in the plural and "our civilization" as the ends of a continuum rather than as essentialist disjuncture; that the insights of studying so-called primi-tive cultures can be brought to the understanding of contemporary North America implies that the two are fundamentally similar in their engendering processes.

This passage has often been attested as evidence that the Boasians gave up on generalization. Lowie's point, however, was not that patterns were absent but that their locus was contemporary, in the integration of cultural elements of diverse historical origin. Classical evolutionists were mistaken to seek invar-iant laws of cultural process: Origins were not recoverable by methods avail-able to the ethnologist, and cultures accumulated elements from all available sources and wove them into a new fabric, a synchronically integrated *social* fabric.

Lowie's theoretical claim was doubly prophetic. First, he argued that only when viewed at a given moment in time could patterns be expected to emerge from the unique history of any given culture. This is functionalism without the label, little different from the functionalisms of Malinowski and Radcliffe-Brown. Lowie took it for granted in 1920, although Malinowski's *Argonauts of the Western Pacific* appeared only in 1922. This reading confirms the frequent Boasian assertion that functionalism was nothing new; the British disciples of Malinowski and Radcliffe-Brown seemed to the Boasians to make much ado about very little. Second, a few years later, Mead and Benedict would make ex-plicit a reading in terms of the psychological integration of individual cultures. Or, as Sapir formulated the turn to psychology, the locus of culture is in the in-dividual, and each individual acts creatively in the context of a cultural pattern.

Lowie's apparently contentious claim, therefore, differed from those of his contemporaries working within a diffusionist model more in rhetorical vir-tuosity than in content. Spier, for example, saw the sun dance as producing a variety of patterned expressions, each coherent in its own terms:

Tribal individuality has been expressed principally in pattern concepts of organization and motivation. Since there is no difference in the character of borrowed or invented traits which are incorporated in the sun dance and those
which are rejected, it follows that the determinants must be sought in the conditions under which incorporation proceeds. . . . The character of the individual contributions to the ceremonial complex and the diversity in receptiveness
and interests explain in part the elaboration and individualization of the several sun dances. (Spier 1921:453)

Calling them all "sun dances" was a generalization of some magnitude. The
plural reasserted the particularism of local forms.

Hallowell cataloged "man's relation to the animals of his environment,"
especially the bear, in its "socio-psychological" rather than in its utilitarian aspects (Hallowell 1926:3-5). Historical processes had to be shown in detail in order to finally lay the evolutionary ghost to rest. In isolation, available data on
bear ceremonialism were superficial. "Collectively, however," the partial and
uninterpretable descriptions acquired a cumulative character, demonstrating
"a more or less unique . . . attitude . . . toward the bear" (Hallowell 1926:22).
Like Boas, Hallowell moved from history to the psychology that would be the
focus of his subsequent career. Only after the analyst had disentangled such
historical contacts and intersections based on trait distributions would it be
possible to turn to pattern integration, focusing on psychological reality for
members of a culture: "Each culture exhibits its own peculiar combination of
features which cannot be deduced from any general principles of association.
[Studies are needed of] specific cultures in terms of their own range of values
and concrete expressions. . . . Only in this setting do qualitative terms . . . have
any real force as descriptions of subjective attitudes" (Hallowell 1926:18). Both
the historical and the psychological were systems of interpretation.

The method remained historico-geographical. Only diffusion could explain
why particular traits were found over wide areas, albeit in different combinations. Until the turn to psychology, trait distributions were mapped and
counted, with limited attention to variability within specific cultures. In light
of such quantitative assumptions, Hallowell felt justified in postulating a "bear
ceremonialism complex" with diverse psychological manifestations built on
common historical roots; each culture integrated borrowed materials. Traits
whose combination could not reasonably be accidental, however, were not
necessarily psychological. The controlling spirit notion was the exception; iso-

lated cultural practices might remain uninterpretable, despite being attested across wide areas as a result of historical continuities.

The Boasian Model of Culture Change: Diffusion

At the time of Boas's initial Northwest Coast fieldwork, the priority of his sponsors was mapping the languages and cultures of the area. Therefore, he duly attempted historical generalizations within a single culture area on the basis of linguistic relationship, accepting the common wisdom that language was the best candidate for a single classificatory variable. As early as 1888, he suggested that Tlingit and Haida were related languages, as were Nootka and Kwakiutl (Darnell 1998a). His last major statement on the genetic relationship of languages was presented to the World's Fair Congress in Chicago; he recognized only four linguistic stocks on the Northwest Coast that could "be explained only by the assumption of a common origin" (Boas 1894:342).

By 1890 the period of survey mapping of basic cultural and linguistic units was over. The general framework having been established, Boas could turn to more detailed problems. In 1901 he proposed a handbook of American Indian languages to the Bureau of American Ethnology; he had now trained "a sufficient number of young men" to make such a project feasible (Boas to Zelia Nuttall 16 April 1901, APS). As honorary philologist of the Bureau, Boas organized the fieldwork and designed the "analytical" format, exercising rigid control over the personnel of a project intended to provide models for future scholars writing American Indian grammars. The *Handbook* is perhaps the single project where his control could not be challenged, and some of his former students rallied round to do their part in the collective project. Those who participated were the marginally linguistic ethnographers, not including Sapir, Boas's chosen successor in linguistics. Sapir's sketch of Takelma was postponed until the second volume because it did not fit the overall format; it was too long and the textual illustration was excessive for the format. (It was also too elegantly done to serve as an exemplar for scholars without Sapir's training or talent.) Missionaries and amateur anthropologists, including most of the staff of the Bureau of American Ethnology, were also excluded.

By the time the first volume appeared in 1911, Boas's general skepticism about "permanent classification" (the provisional character of all classification was part of his methodological critique of evolution) had caused him to reconsider his previous genetic hypotheses for Northwest Coast languages. He rejected his own prior linking of Haida, Tlingit, and Athabaskan, with a conservatism that would become even more pronounced in response to Sapir's increasingly bold genetic hypotheses.

The *Handbook of American Indian Languages* emphasized "analytic descriptions of particular languages"; in practice, they provided synchronic structural grammars that minimized historical problems (Stocking 1974:475). Comparison was psychological. Psychological pattern inhered in grammatical categories, understood without evolutionary implications. Language revealed psychology because it was less conscious than the rest of culture. Between the initial conception of the *Handbook* and the appearance of its first volume, then, Boas's focus shifted from ethnographic survey to detailed reconstruction of particular culture histories (for example, inferring migrations and culture contacts from the distribution of particular folklore motifs among contiguous tribes).

Boas had minimal training in linguistics, having taught himself techniques of language description while doing fieldwork in the Arctic (Müller-Wille 1998)—perhaps one reason he developed a psychological (i.e., synchronic and descriptive) rather than a historical approach to grouping American Indian languages: "One of the remarkable features of American anthropology is the multiplicity of small linguistic families the origin of which is entirely obscure to us. The investigations made during the last ten years suggest that there may be larger entities in existence based on similarity of the psychological foundations of language rather than on phonetic similarity. This hypothesis is based on the observation that in several regions [i.e., the Northwest Coast] neighboring languages, although quite diverse in vocabulary, are similar in structure" (Boas to Woodward, 13 January 1905, APS). Lack of training in Indo-European comparative method forced Boas to approach linguistics as a discovery procedure, a tool for ethnological interpretation; he had little vested interest in the validity of phonetic similarity as a criterion of long-term genetic relationship. In fact, the more he emphasized diffusion in his model of cultural process, the less he was interested in genetic classification as an index to the past.

Boas's diffusion model worked well for the distribution of folklore elements on the Northwest Coast, providing a reasonable interpretation of the history of the area in terms of the interaction of diverse groups over time. The causes of attested cultural similarity were complex, and Boas invoked both history and psychology to explain observed variance. He wrote to John Wesley Powell at the Bureau of American Ethnology: "The longer I studied, the more convinced I became that customs, traditions and migrations are far too complex in their origin to enable us to study their *psychological* causes without a thorough knowledge of their *history*. [Moreover] the fate of an individual does not influence himself alone, but also all succeeding generations, . . . no event in the life of a people passes without leaving its effect upon later generations" (Boas to Powell, June 1887, BAE; emphasis mine). This statement suggests methodological caution, but Boas clearly questioned whether the methods at hand could ever produce adequate histories, not to mention psychological profiles.

Boas stressed that the same surface phenomenon could develop "in a multitude of ways" (Boas 1896a:275). The role of any given cultural element could be understood independently of its origin, synchronically and functionally; its origin was likely to be unknowable. This viewpoint followed from the critique of evolution, with its insidious imposition of uniform laws of historical development. Diffusion and migration reflected particular historical events that were sources of culture change (Boas 1920:181–82).

Diffusion, the primary mechanism of history, was the alternative theoretical concept enabling Boas to attack the premises of evolutionary method, particularly the assumption of independent invention based on the psychic unity of mankind. Diffusion provided a methodological focus for fruitful research, both Boas's own and that of his students. Generalizations about evolutionary process—if they turned out to be feasible—would have to await detailed studies of particular historical cases. Sounds of a language, folktale motifs, baskets, and beliefs were diverse elements that Boas assumed behaved similarly in their susceptibility to borrowing and reintegration; the advantage of language as largely independent of "secondary rationalization," that is, as unconscious (Boas 1911a), was rarely mentioned in the diffusionist historical projects. Psychology, insofar as it entered at all, reflected the German Romantic view of the "genius" or spirit of a people, a somewhat mystical and superorganic concept, unsatisfying to Boas.

Boas probably was not thinking about linguistics when he elaborated his diffusion model. Yet his later critiques of linguistic method were based on the assumption that diffusion was the dominant process of culture change. Culture history was fundamentally spatial or geographical, hardly a surprising conclusion for a former geographer (though it was far from the environmental determinism Boas had hoped to test in his early fieldwork among the Eskimos of Baffin Island).

Boas's explanation of his methods for reconstructing past history on the basis of present distribution of folklore elements was remarkably consistent over his various treatments. As early as 1891, he argued that "the only method open to us [in the absence of written records] is that of comparison" (Boas 1891:437). His program consisted of three stages: study of component parts, analysis of their mode of distribution, and psychological understanding of the processes of dissemination and amalgamation (Boas 1891:445). "Psychological" meant subconscious secondary rationalization rather than "the Native point of view."

For Boas (1895:429) borrowing was the primary process whereby folklore elements attained their present form: "Mythologies as we find them now are not organic growths, but have gradually developed and obtained their present form by accretion of foreign material. Much of this material must have been adopted ready-made, and has been adapted and changed in form according to the genius of the people who borrowed it." The "genius of the people who borrowed" various elements of myth was the core of the psychological in Boas's mature thought.

In line with his consistent analytical distinction of race, language, and culture as explanatory variables, element distribution did not coincide with "linguistic divisions" (Boas 1896:427). Generalization could not proceed from linguistic evidence to cultural process. Diffusion and linguistic relationship were incommensurate methods of approaching history.

By 1914 Boas's claims were even stronger: "There is no tribe in North America whose tales can be considered as purely local products uninfluenced by foreign elements" (Boas 1914:479). The original form of an element could not be retrieved by any known method, and elements were constantly being modified. Simple plots were widely distributed, but each culture integrated the elements differently: "The imagination of the natives has played with a few plots, which were expanded by means of a number of motives that have a wide distribution, and . . . there is comparatively little material that seems to belong to any one region exclusively, so that it might be considered as of autochthonous origin" (Boas 1916a:403). Boas thus gave up on the question of "archaic residue" in culture (folklore); the nature of culture contacts on the Northwest Coast, with its extremes of cultural and linguistic diversity, did not encourage use of historical linguistic methodology.

While Boas was consolidating his own model, his students also began to use diffusion as an integrative culture process. Lowie's much maligned "shreds and patches" statement did not reject the possibility of historical inference so much as it qualified the methods of adequate reconstruction. Diffusion constituted an integral part of the Boasian paradigm, which represented progress for ethnology although not necessarily for linguistics. The other side of the Boasian diffusional coin was the genetic model of culture change. Although it was implicit in his own logic, Boas failed to develop the implications of this model, and language rather than culture became his exemplar.

The Sapir Model of Culture Change: Genetic Relationship

Although history was certainly a critical pole in Boas's model of culture, his definition of history led to conflict with former students for whom geography was less relevant and time depth more so. Opposition crystallized around what would be meant by "history" in the study of the American Indian.

Primary among the proponents of divergent models was Sapir, whose initial training in Indo-European linguistics distinguished him sharply from other Boas students who produced American Indian grammars. Although Sapir's early work was predictably Boasian, he increasingly applied the methods and insights of Indo-European philology to anthropological (i.e., cultural) problems, often to the consternation of his anthropological mentor, Boas. The result was an alternative model of cultural process (see Chapter 3), to which Boas's "temperamental-methodological inhibitions" (Stocking 1976:68) rendered him increasingly antagonistic.

The so-called Boas-Sapir controversy is well known in the folk history of anthropology. The issues were both temperamental and intellectual. Lowie, who knew both protagonists well, explained their moments of "mutual irritation and estrangement" in terms of a "tenuous . . . parental-filial bond." "A hostile critic once described Boas as a Prussian drill-sergeant, and a friendly commentator called Sapir something of a prima donna. Neither of these casual utterances is acceptable, yet it is significant that they could be made at all; no one would ever refer to Boas as a prima donna or to Sapir as a martinet" (Lowie 1965:7).

Morris Swadesh (1951) noted that, although each man recognized both genetic and areal influences on the development of particular cultures, Boas stressed "diffusional cumulation" over time, whereas Sapir stressed "archaic residue" from a common historical past. These were sides of the same historical coin. Sapir, on linguistic analogy, simply inverted the conventional Boasian historical logic. In retrospect, of course, the poles are not mutually exclusive.

The consequences of this perceived polarization for the subsequent development of American anthropology were considerable. First, Boas's position changed in midcareer. His early work on the Northwest Coast had used linguistic classification extensively to group tribes; he now turned instead to the diffusion of cultural elements. Having arrived at this model, moreover, his position became increasingly rigid. Second, Sapir's divergent model of culture history, which distinguished between the effects of "diffusional cumulation" and "archaic residue" on internal linguistic grounds, meant that language could classify the data of the ethnologist.

Sapir shared many of Boas's basic assumptions about the scope and methods of describing unwritten languages. Boas insisted on the urgency of recording dying languages and of using language as a tool to reconstruct North American culture history. He was considerably less sanguine than Sapir about the latter possibility. Sapir argued that language, because of its peculiar internal structure, provided a uniquely rigorous method for historical reconstruction. Nonetheless, to see Boas as interested only in diffusion and Sapir only in genetic relationship is an unwarranted oversimplification; in practice, both men dealt with both subjects. The argument between them, however, encouraged both to make extremist theoretical statements, in a kind of "complementary schizmogenesis" (Bateson [1936] 1958).

In his descriptions of particular languages, Sapir was careful to assess evidence for borrowing and psychological integration of borrowed traits as well as evidence for genetic relationship. *Time Perspective in Aboriginal American Culture: A Study in Method* (1916), his most extensive contribution to the theory of culture history in the Boasian mode, summarized and rendered explicit the Boasian program of historical reconstruction based on diffusion. Simultaneously, Sapir went beyond Boas in stressing the special potentials of linguistic structures for such reconstruction. Language had formal properties absent from other parts of culture.

Time Perspective was written at the behest of Kroeber, who explicitly sought Sapir's linguistically conditioned attention to genetic relationship. Ever the peacemaker, Kroeber doubtlessly preferred not to challenge the limitations of the diffusion model directly on Boas's ethnological home ground. Because Boas was only secondarily a linguist, Kroeber hoped that he could get away with a critique that would open up wider ranges of historical method. The responses of Kroeber, Lowie, and Radin to the paper suggest a tacit conspiracy if not a full-scale rebellion.

Sapir's linguistic methods could circumvent the limitations of the diffusion model (without falling into the unilinear logic of the classical evolution that Boas had critiqued in the late nineteenth century) by grappling with "the accumulating but unorganized evidence on the time element in the history of the American race and civilization," which lacked "historical records and more or less trustworthy traditions running back some distance" as were found in Asia or Oceania (Kroeber to Sapir, 7 December 1914, NMM). American anthropology had "reached a pretty thorough understanding of the several local types of culture and their interrelations," making further survey ethnography unnecessary. Generalizations now seemed possible about "the length of time involved in these local developments, as well as in such general cultural traits as may be specifically American." American anthropologists, including archaeologists, were "particularly remiss and unimaginative" about historical inference, showing "the most scrupulous reference to geography" alongside "an almost punctilious avoidance of the factor of time." Linguistic inference held the key to further progress.

Kroeber, because of his interest in ethnological uses of historical inference, was eager to undermine the methodological one-sidedness of the Boasian program according to its founder, seeking generalizations from the increasing body of ethnographic evidence. At Zuni in 1916 Kroeber pioneered in experiments with seriation; his later Peruvian archaeological work also focused on the need for time perspective in ethnology. To inject time perspective into ethnology required linguistics in the absence of archaeological stratigraphy. Although Kroeber and Sapir foresaw no contradiction to the diffusion model, Boas, with escalating vehemence, polarized the methods and their underlying assumptions.

Initially demurring that he was not the best person for the task, Sapir eventually took up Kroeber's challenge to confirm the place of history in American ethnology, formulating the problem in theoretically conventional Boasian terms as a contrast between "descriptive or psychological" and "strictly historical" comparative frameworks (Sapir to Kroeber, 14 December 1914, NMM). Sapir agreed about "our timidity in grappling with the time elements in the history of culture" because "so many of our men are trained rather in descriptive or psychological comparison than in strictly historical comparative work," which, to him, meant linguistic work. Linguists knew how to eliminate "extraordinarily complex" ethnological and linguistic features of recent or "quite secondary origin." Features "demonstrably of secondary origin" were useless "from the point of view of historical reconstruction."

Like Kroeber, Sapir saw the issue as one of ethnological method. Characteristically, he focused on the "timidity" of historical reconstructions. His own reliance on linguistic inference produced frustration with "descriptive and psychological" explanations of cultural facts. The whole problem of secondary origin came from the emphasis of the diffusion model on unusual features of the present system. The linguistic model, in contrast, sought remnants of patterns from earlier historical periods, patterns that were often peripheral to the present structure of a language.

The perspective that opened up was like "a long-exposure star-chart, in which the immensities of space are indeed reduced to a flat, but in which the extent and direction of movement of the nearer bodies, the planets, are betrayed by short lines" (Sapir 1916:8). The ten-thousand-year time depth for human occupation in the Americas was "hopelessly inadequate" (Sapir 1916:78). Sapir was far more optimistic than Boas, both in method and by temperament.

Sapir thought Kroeber was overly concerned with absolute time depth in North America, which, in any case, would usually prove inaccessible. He intended to stress method rather than facts because of the limited amount of reliable data. He cited examples from more than sixty American tribes; few were elaborated beyond a sentence or two. But infusion of historical perspective, however preliminary and tentative, was essential (Sapir to Kroeber, 14 December 1914, NMM); despite "supposed contrast to many English ethnologists" and Boasian "pride" in the American "historical sense," the present culture areas retained a "purely descriptive rather than historical bent." That is, the contrast between North American and British anthropology was epitomized, for Sapir, by disagreement about the meaning of history.

As Kroeber had hoped he would, Sapir enjoined fellow Americanists to maximize the explanatory power of their historical method. He formalized what his fellow Boasians had been doing for a long time. The age-area hypothesis assumed that culture traits clustered at their point of origin. A wide distribution implied great time depth; recent diffusion was found at the peripheries of a distribution. For example, the Nootka totem pole with one figure could be assumed to be older than the Haida and Tsimshian versions with several superimposed figures (Sapir 1916:13). To cite another example, the dependence of Plains culture on the buffalo "has given a dramatic tone to all of Plains culture." But its value "as a historical criterion" dissolved if it proved to be "ethnologically secondary." It remained interesting "from a purely descriptive or psychological standpoint . . . to differentiate Plains culture more markedly than anything else from neighboring cultures." This "type of reasoning is, of course, perfectly familiar to us in linguistic work" and it was "always of course easier to do this in linguistics than in culture anyway" (Sapir to Kroeber, 14 December 1914, NMM).

That is, Sapir self-consciously used language in analogy to culture to establish relative if not absolute time depth in ethnology. He did not so much reject the uncodified postulates of Boasian diffusional studies as he supplemented and extended them based on his own training in comparative linguistics. Inference based on geography was merely "descriptive"; a genuinely historical science must use not only diffusion but also time depth arrived at through comparative linguistic reconstruction. Language, though part of culture, was not interchangeable with it—a methodological boon to the historical analyst. Language, indeed, had a superorganic quality of great heuristic or methodological significance.

In 1916 little could be said about historical documents, Native testimony, or archaeological stratigraphy, forcing all of the Boasians to focus on ethnological (largely diffusional or geographic) or linguistic evidence. Sapir stressed that cultural anthropology was increasingly becoming "a strictly historical science" (Sapir 1916:391). Interestingly, from his point of view anthropologists had turned to psychological explanations largely because information about time sequence was not available to them, that is, by default. Sapir acceded to Boas's certainty that history was the ultimate anthropological problem and psychology the ultimate way to approach it. Regardless of the conclusions of folk psychology, anthropology needed histories of specific cultures, even if details could not be retrieved from available data. Sapir hoped to provide a dual-pronged methodology to "inject a chronology into this confusing mass of descriptive fact" (Sapir 1916:392)—a methodology focusing on generalized events that were amenable to reconstruction.

Historical reconstruction lacked a single criterion. Cultural elements had to be interpreted in their social context, weighing the relative validity of particular elements anew in each case. The elements and complexes "that go to make up the whole of a culture are never isolated phenomena but . . . they enter into all sorts of relations" (Sapir 1916:402). This is a straightforward statement, firmly grounded in Boasian praxis, about the functional integration of present-day cultures, however divergent the sources of their particular elements. Lowie's "shreds and patches" were re-formed in the course of borrowing and adaptation.

Sapir stressed the artificiality of the dichotomy between diffusion and common heritage, with the really intriguing question being the relative age of the two processes. This was, of course, precisely the argument of his linguistic work. Sapir differed from Boas in believing that language was quite different from culture, a "more compact and inherently unified conceptual and formal complex" (Sapir 1916:51). Changes in language proceeded more slowly and evenly than those in culture, tending to be consistent in direction. (Crucially, foreign influences could be detected by the application of phonetic laws.) Secondary rationalizations that distorted historical explanations produced by cultural members were relatively rare in cases of linguistic change.

Because Boas found the emphasis on phonetic laws exasperating, overstated, and methodologically suspect, Sapir and Boas talked past each other despite extensive overlap in their theories in every aspect but emphasis. In Sapir's view of North American linguistic history, only multiple migrations of peoples with already differentiated languages could account for the present diversity of American language families. Borrowing as a result of extensive contact operated concurrently with genetic diversification, even at considerable time depth.

Figure 2 abstracts the alternative models. Boas's diffusion model stressed that the origins of traits were diverse, arbitrary, and unrecoverable. What was amenable to scientific explanation was their psychological integration in a single culture at a given moment in time. Sapir's genetic model assumed that an original language developed gradually into various new forms that continued to reflect their common origin. The features of such a protolanguage could be reconstructed based on surviving contemporary languages; this historical continuity explained present cultural diversity. Language was the key to culture history. Sapir could use either model, depending on the problem at hand; Boas, however, was unwilling to think from Sapir's premises or to allow theory to move far from data. The full Boasian position, therefore, cannot be found in Boas alone but must be extrapolated from the uses his students made of the variety of historical, linguistic, and psychological models available to them.

Although it was to stand as the synthesis for the potentials of Boasian historical method, the reaction of other Boasians to *Time Perspective* was mixed. Kroeber, who started the whole argument, begged off reviewing it, suggesting

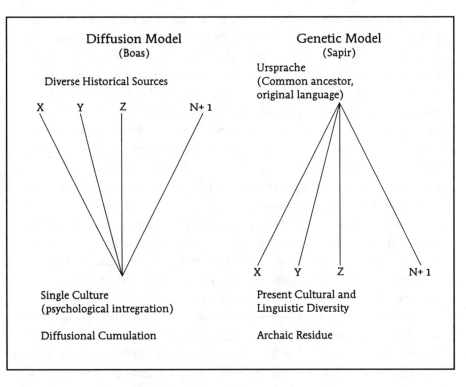

Figure 2. Contrasting Models of Historical Process

Radin, who was well known for his historical fervor (Kroeber to Sapir, 21 August 1917, NMM). The review was eventually produced by Lowie, who found the ethnological inferences unduly involuted but praised the linguistic section (implicitly as a useful expansion of the Boasian approach as practiced by Boas): "I think your views on culture areas are thoroughly sound and the insistence on their non-equivalence and on their *historical* evaluation, while carrying immediate conviction, has not been made before in definite form, so far as I remember. Further, all you say on the ethnological inferences from linguistic data, while perhaps only an adaptation of Indo-Germanic methods to the American field, is most suggestive and ought to have a direct influence on working anthropologists" (Lowie to Sapir, 14 January 1916, NMM).

Lowie's review praised Sapir for applying the linguistic material which he knew best; "he expounds methods that have proved significant in Old World investigations, but have hitherto remained strangely unfamiliar to the majority of American ethnologists" (Lowie 1919:75). Lowie also approved Sapir's questioning of the validity of culture area classifications: "He is certainly warranted in insisting that the culture areas established descriptively as classificatory devices are not chronologically equivalent and require sequential evaluation" (Lowie 1919:76). The Boasian critique of evolution underscored the claim that each culture area had a unique history such that the units in a culture area classification were not comparable.

Interestingly, Lowie was the most conservative of the Boasians about certain kinds of historical inferences, especially those deriving from oral tradition. He accepted such evidence only if confirmed from external sources. Whereas Sapir (1916:396) inferred both direction and source of migration from historical narrative, Lowie argued that each tribe would have a contradictory claim about invention and origin of culture traits: "The fact that one of them must be correct does not establish the methodological validity of accepting native traditions as history" (quoted by Payne and Murray 1983:337). Goldenweiser countered that the Indians themselves distinguished between myth and history. Taking the argument to absurdity, he noted: "Who would doubt the word of a woman who tells of having witnessed a child being run over by a street car, solely on the ground of his knowledge that the woman believes in ghosts" (Payne and Murray 1983:336–37).

In retrospect, Lowie thought that *Time Perspective* contributed more to the logic of ethnology than to its content: "Precisely because Sapir is so eminently sane, he is obliged to qualify every principle of procedure beyond the point of practical utility" (Lowie 1965:11). Radin (1933:55) emphasized that only a phi-lologist could set criteria for arriving at time perspective in aboriginal North America. The degree of necessary qualification to any generalization dem-onstrated to Radin the futility of the exercise. "That a clear-headed man like Sapir will go to such lengths simply indicates anew how compulsive is the need we feel for giving aboriginal cultures historical depth" (Radin 1933:59). The compulsion was Boas's, although Sapir worked out the details.

In fact, Sapir's essay was both the classic theoretical statement and the be-ginning of decline for the centrality of the culture element model (except in California where Kroeber employed it into the 1930s). Increasingly, the Boasi-ans differed among themselves in problems and methods. A more configura-tional approach to ethnology evolved within the ensuing decade. Moreover, the seeds of Sapir's bold revision of the linguistic map of North America were already present in *Time Perspective*. His six-unit classification of American In-dian languages shed a different kind of light on "how these languages grew out of their origins and what the causes of the changes have been" (Kroeber to Sa-pir, 27 December 1920, UCB). Sapir's fellow ethnologists preferred tentative conclusions to awaiting detailed philological results, while Kroeber tried to make the new results sound conservative: "Boas' purely analytical and descrip-tive work has of course been badly needed, and is still; but it is also time that we proved we were not always evading the historical problems. I do not believe we need fear any excessive swing of the pendulum toward speculation. Boas' in-fluence in the direction of a soundly critical attitude will remain with us per-manently" (Kroeber to Sapir, 27 December 1920, UCB). The point was not to jettison the diffusion model, which he believed Boas applied in exaggerated form, but to supplement it.

Sapir's disillusion with Boas's (lack of) historical thinking was already of long standing. Radin, sympathizing with his frustrations, wrote to Sapir about Boas's inconsistencies between ethnology and linguistics. In ethnology his interests were historical, but in linguistics he insisted on descriptive or "psy-chological" work. "To my mind this is a fundamental error in method of ap-proach, though I fully recognize that both historical and psychological inter-ests have their place" (Radin to Sapir, 3 March 1913, NMM).

Radin formulated the problem in fully Boasian terms, as a shifting pendu-lum between history and psychology. Boas was reluctant to accept proofs ob-

vious to "any trained philologist" and assumed "an original condition of society—characterized by an unlimited number of linguistic stocks" (Radin to
Sapir, 1 June 1913, NMM). Sapir recognized the fundamentally methodological
character of his disagreement with Boas, who "allows his judgment to be influenced by a preconceived like or dislike" (Sapir to Radin, 10 June 1913, NMM).
Sapir assumed "a time when the members of a linguistic group have diverged
so much that their genetic relationship is difficult to detect." Many languages
"are genetically related where we shall never be able to establish such relationship" (Sapir to Radin, 10 June 1913, NMM). There were limits to the conservatism of language (as reflected in sound correspondences). For Sapir, however,
the residual, unmarked category remained prior genetic relationship.

Linguistics had to move beyond the views of Boas and adopt the methods of
Indo-European philology in order to interpret the ethnological record adequately. Sapir attributed Boas's intransigence to his lack of "personal experience in historic grammar or comparative linguistics"; "personal training and
interest influence one's scientific point of view" to "an alarming extent" (Sapir
to Leo Frachtenberg, 8 January 1915, NMM). ("Purely historic" meant "comparative" in the Indo-European sense.)

As Sapir's linguistic method increasingly diverged from that of Boas, he
wrote to nonlinguist colleagues about the revisionist ethnological implications
of his emerging radical linguistic classification (Sapir 1921a). Degrees of genealogical relationship would reveal "fascinating perspectives" for ethnology
(Sapir to Frank Speck, 1 August 1920, APS). Linguistic method could produce a
classification of "great interest to ethnologists as providing a definite historical
background. . . . One can almost see movements of population" (Sapir to
Lowie, 9 September 1920, UCB). Sapir sought an audience within Boasian cultural anthropology.

He was still thinking about historical inference within the ethnological
framework of *Time Perspective*. The six units of the 1921 classification were "presumably genetic," leaving open the possibility that some similarities might
have complex or multiple causes. The avoidance of premature generalization is
vintage Boasian. Even in his better known 1929 formulation of the six units,
Sapir acknowledged the difficulties of distinguishing in particular cases between genetic relationship and diffusion. He remained convinced, however,
that linguistic method could distinguish them in principle, even though the
particular classification remained "probably only a first approximation to the
historic truth" (Sapir 1929:139).

Sapir considered it unreasonable to restrict attention to the history of particular groups in isolation. "It would be easy to relieve oneself of the burden of constructive thinking and to take the standpoint that each language has its unique history and therefore its unique structure" (Sapir 1921b:20). But he refused to follow this easy path.

Boas's Reaction to the Sapir Classification

Boas reacted with growing alarm to Sapir's historical work, virtually interpreting the six-unit classification as a personal attack. His unwillingness to push the limits of the comparative method in the study of unwritten languages was fully consistent with the logic underlying his critique of evolution. History had a different meaning for Boas than for Sapir or Kroeber. As a result of their challenge to his method, Boas was forced to articulate his position in theoretical terms.

Boas chided his former student for generalizing in the absence of adequate "corroborative evidence":

> There are, of course, several ways possible in which similarities may have originated. There may be a diffusion of mannerisms of speech that are diffused without reference to linguistic groups, or it may be that we have a differentiation from a common stock. While I do not think for a moment that new grammatical forms may not originate, I should want very sound proof before accepting such a change in form as that which occurs between Tsimshian and Chinook. The psychological shift that is involved in this matter is so fundamental [compared to borrowing] that it is difficult to understand how it can be brought about. I should rather suppose for the two cases an exceedingly long history of independent development. To my mind . . . habits of speech that transgress linguistic boundaries [i.e., areal features of language] must be taken into account. (Boas to Sapir, 22 July 1918, NMM)

As far as Boas could see, Sapir was interested in no explanation other than common origin.

Sapir, however, willingly accepted the complexity of evidence in particular cases. He disagreed with Boas primarily about what would count as "corroborative evidence." Boas accepted that the psychological character of a language was stable over time but not that genetic diversification could be traced reliably through its conservation of sound changes from different stages in the past.

Nor would Sapir have denied that "habits of speech" crossed the boundaries of linguistic families. Such diffusional processes were not, in his view, incompatible with a genetic explanation for other kinds of linguistic similarities.

Boas cautioned Sapir against applying the Indo-European method to classifying unwritten American Indian languages: "Far-reaching similarities, particularly between neighboring languages must be due to historical causes" (Boas to Sapir, 18 September 1920, NMM). Not enough was known "to decide definitely whether we are dealing with a gradual development of divergence" or whether language should be treated like any other part of culture. That is, he refused to acknowledge special properties of language for historical reconstruction or the legitimacy of probable relationship between languages or language families. Only diffusion could be a decisive answer, with the burden of proof resting on historical connection. "In the same way as the cultural life of a people originated by the confluence of the most diverse courses which are integrated and developed by the people themselves, so in the same way languages may owe much more than is ordinarily assumed to foreign sources and . . . this material is gradually integrated into the new forms" (Boas to Sapir, 18 September 1920, NMM). Boas preferred quantitative trait survey to linguistic inference.

Even before Sapir published his radical classification, Boas felt his own theoretical position sufficiently threatened to merit public disclaimer. He stated in the *American Anthropologist* that a number of his former students, "largely through the influence of Dr. Edward Sapir," had begun to "compare, on the basis of vocabularies [although actually much of the evidence was morphological], languages which apparently are very distinct" with an effort to "prove far-reaching relationships" (Boas 1920:211); Boas deplored this trend, which countered his own conviction that American linguistic comparisons "should proceed from the study of fairly closely related dialects towards the study of more diverse forms." Therefore, Boas found it "desirable to state briefly the *theoretical* [emphasis mine] points of view upon which my own attitude has been and still is based." He recanted his 1894 interpretation of morphological similarities among Northwest Coast languages as genetic, feeling that a definite answer was unattainable: "I do not mean to imply by this that all the languages must have developed entirely independently, but rather that, if there was an ancient common source of several modern languages, they have become so much differentiated that without historical knowledge of their growth, the attempts to prove their interrelation cannot succeed" (Boas 1920:212).

Boas believed that independent evidence was needed from written documents, comparable to those available for Indo-European languages, before inferences about distant genetic relationship could be taken as demonstrated (precisely counter to the arguments Sapir and Leonard Bloomfield would soon put forward on the applicability of Indo-European methods to the study of unwritten languages, a keystone of the autonomous profession of linguistics that arose in the mid-1920s.) Despite his respect for Indo-European philology, Boas worried about the lack of independent historical evidence of comparable quality for unwritten American languages. His solution was to collect texts that could be subjected to multiple analyses over time:

> A control of our results and deeper studies based on material collected by us will be all but impossible. Besides this we must furnish in this way the indispensable material for future linguistic studies. What would Indo-European philology be, if we had only grammars made by one or two students and not the live material from which these grammars have been built up, which is, at the same time, the material on which philosophic study of the language must be based. . . . As we require a new point of view now, so future times will require new points of view and for these the texts, and ample texts, must be made available. (Boas to Holmes, 24 July 1905, APS)

Theory, in this case historical reconstruction, could be put off indefinitely. The problems of historical inference remained methodological. Only the diffusion model could not be disproved; Boas explicitly disclaimed the reliability of the *Ursprache* or original-language model for North America:

> If these observations regarding the influence of acculturation upon language should be correct, then the whole history of American languages must not be treated on the assumption that all languages which show similarities must be considered as branches of the same linguistic family. We should rather find a phenomenon which is parallel to the features characteristic of other ethnological phenomena—namely, a development from diverse sources which are gradually worked into a single cultural unit. We should have to reckon with the tendency of languages to absorb so many foreign traits that we can no longer speak of single origin, and that it would be arbitrary [i.e., undemonstrable] whether we associate a language with one or another of the contributing stocks. In other words, the whole theory of an "Ursprache" for every group of modern languages must be held in abeyance until we can prove that these languages go

back to a single stock and that they have not originated, to a large extent, by the process of acculturation. (Boas 1920:217)

"Acculturation" here refers not just to processes of culture change observable in the present but also to change that has occurred from times immemorial in all cultures, with or without writing. For Boas the capacity of cultures to "absorb" (i.e., integrate) elements acquired by accretion from chance contacts with other cultures made origins inaccessible. Psychological dimensions of cultural integration functioned to mask historical ones.

Boas's argument was not new. In 1917, in his introduction to the first volume of the *International Journal of American Linguistics,* as in the *Handbook of American Indian Languages* (Boas 1911a, 1922), classifications based on different criteria could not be expected to overlap and many linguistic families had "complex" origins. The caution remained methodological rather than substantive: "It is not safe to disregard the possibility of a complex origin of linguistic groups, which would limit the applicability of the term 'linguistic family' in the sense in which we are accustomed to use it. . . . The proof of genetic relationship, however, can be considered as given, only when the number of unexplained distinct elements is not over-large, and when the contradictory classifications, to which reference has been made before, have been satisfactorily accounted for" (Boas 1917:204). Historical linguistic inferences were based on identifying remnants of past linguistic stages, a virtual inversion of Boas's diffusion model in which evidentiary weight was placed on exceptions as counterexamples that negated theoretical generalization.

Having failed to convince Sapir privately before publication of his classification, Boas apparently did not consult him further before making his public disclaimer. Sapir expressed his consternation about whether to reply as well as his personal ambivalence toward Boas to Lowie:

It is becoming increasingly clear to me that his whole approach is so different from mine and from that of the vast majority of linguistic students that the attempt to argue about the theoretical basis can only result in mutual irritation. He bandies far too many semi-philosophical categories to suit me. . . . His wholesale use of the idea of diffusion must also strike anyone that has real experience with the brass tacks of linguistic history as rather absurd. . . . Historical inference is not easily possible for Boas, certainly not in languages. As soon as he tries it, he loses his ground, gets involved in cloudy principles, and all tied up in fruitless inhibitions. I never saw a man who was so overawed by a feeling of the impossibility of certain things. Intuitionally, he is almost a child; he has a perfect genius for hitting upon unplausible or unfortunate hypotheses. And have you noticed this? He will never take a preliminary theory of some magnitude and see where it will lead him, test it out pragmatically. He prefers to prance on one spot. But I've said enough. I would not for the world run afoul of him. A family quarrel would not be edifying and would help no one. And I like him too well personally. (Sapir to Lowie, 15 February 1921, UCB)

Sapir considered himself part of the Boasian "family," but he was frustrated by Boas's failure to accept historical reconstruction based on linguistic evidence. Sapir did not see his classificatory work, or the informed linguistic intuition on which it was based, as radical; in linguistic work, he was as concerned with method as was Boas. He expected most of his colleagues to side with his oscillation between complementary historical approaches.

As late as 1929 Boas began his presidential address to the Linguistic Society of America by reiterating his arguments against use of the genetic model pioneered by Sapir. Boas explicitly postulated hybrid languages whose particular histories would remain forever inaccessible. American Indian languages could not be grouped "rigidly" with each linguistic family "shown to have developed to modern forms" because "many of the languages have multiple roots" (Boas 1929:225). It was left for future scholars to develop more explicit methods for areal linguistics, based on the logic of Boasian diffusionism (Bright 1976; Haas 1978; Sherzer 1976).

Disciplinary Consequences

The conflict between Boas and Sapir, then, was far more divisive than a simple disagreement about what constituted sufficient evidence for genetic relationship in particular cases. At least from Boas's point of view, Sapir's approach attacked the core of anthropological method and theory. Although many of Boas's students diverged from his positions in particular analytical cases, Sapir, more than any of the others, succeeded in questioning the very premises on which Boas's own anthropology rested—and thereby potentially expanding them for his fellow Boasians.

This irresolvable divergence from Boas in models for cultural process was undoubtedly one reason Sapir increasingly identified himself as a linguist in the second half of his career. Boas's intransigence made Sapir's position increasingly awkward. Moreover, the founding of the Linguistic Society of America in 1925, with its journal, *Language,* provided an easy alternative professional identification. In the same year, Sapir left Ottawa to become a professor of anthropology and linguistics at the University of Chicago. At Yale from 1931 until his death in 1939, he also held a joint appointment in his two disciplines. The increasing autonomy of linguistics as a discipline tended to decrease the role of linguistics within anthropology and consequently the authority of Boas. Boas had an honorary rather than a constitutive role in the LSA, while Sapir and Leonard Bloomfield were recognized as the leading American linguists of the 1930s. In this new framework, Sapir found ample support for his contention that the methods of Indo-European philology were applicable to the study of unwritten languages. Feedback from nonanthropological colleagues in linguistics encouraged him to speak to an audience to whom he need not justify his basic assumptions.

Although the later history of linguistics has tended to oppose Sapir and Bloomfield, particularly over the issue of Sapir's "mentalism," the two men shared a common program to a large extent. Increasingly, anthropologists who did linguistics were specialists who did not concern themselves with the full body of anthropological theory. Sapir's students in the 1930s tended to be either in linguistics or in culture and personality. Few even attempted to combine the two specializations of their teacher. Moreover, much of the research was on English, for example, the work by Morris Swadesh and Stanley Newman on semantics. Sapir's definition of the concept of the phoneme in 1925 led to the morphophonemics of the 1930s. "The circle around Sapir" (Hymes and Fought 1975:1023) increasingly separated itself from anthropology. Stocking (ed. 1976:71) argues that, although more linguistic dissertations continued to be written at Columbia under Boas, Sapir's students were more influential because they were trained specifically in linguistic methods: "The development of the sophisticated structuralist methods of linguistic analysis had left more broadly-trained anthropologists of the 1930's somewhat behind the development of the field; and those few who had participated in the process were, ironically, isolated from anthropology by their preoccupation with American Indian work in a period when anthropology was turning overseas" (Stocking 1976:73).

Although the dispute over appropriate models of historical reconstruction is, of course, not the only factor in the increasing separation between linguistics and anthropology, it suggests an underlying rationale in the increasing specialization of anthropology after the Second World War, as represented in

Figure 1. Cultural anthropology began its internal diversification in the 1920s, when none of Boas's first generation of students cast their anthropological nets as widely as did their teacher. Boas's perceived insistence on orthodoxy, with himself as arbiter, further polarized the specializations. Despite forays into other areas, each former student had one or more specializations. Alongside the new discipline of linguistics, language came to be seen less as a part of culture than as a separate system requiring study in its own terms. Moreover, the ethnological issues of time perspective that concerned Sapir were increasingly dealt with by archaeology and physical anthropology as more extensive data and more sophisticated methods developed. Linguistics attained its own direction; by default, therefore, the critical mass of Americanist anthropology remained firmly within cultural anthropology.

Although the Boasian historical program as such has receded into the past, linguists continue to work historically. Interestingly, however, the canons of evidence for genetic relationship of languages are now much more conservative than in Sapir's day. These stringent standards, however, derive more from linguistics per se than from its anthropological adjuncts. The psychological prong of the Boasian program worked its way through culture and personality to ethnoscience, still seeking access to the Native point of view; it lives on in text collection, life histories, sociolinguistics, and other meaning-oriented domains of contemporary sociocultural anthropology. These positions were developed by Boas's students in various directions, all of which took for granted the baseline of oscillation between history and psychology in the study of culture.

ALFRED LOUIS KROEBER

CHAPTER 2

Culture as Superorganic

Alfred Louis Kroeber, Boas's first Ph.D. in anthropology from Columbia, began to build an anthropological base at the University of California, Berkeley, in 1901 and contributed to the establishment of a distinguished Boasian lineage that would dominate the discipline in North America for more than half a century and continue to influence its national tradition into the present and beyond. When Boas died in 1942 at the age of eighty-four, Kroeber succeeded him as the grand old man of Americanist anthropology, a position he held until his own death in 1960, also at the age of eighty-four. Both were organizational and institutional as well as intellectual leaders, carving out a niche for anthropology as a preponderantly academic discipline and for their shared version of what was increasingly called in North America "cultural anthropology" as opposed to ethnology. Kroeber himself was a key player in this redefinition around the concept of culture. The prior distinction of descriptive ethnography based on fieldwork and theoretical ethnology from the evolutionists' armchair became outmoded through the successful critique of evolution. This national tradition differed considerably in emphasis from what the British called "social anthropology."

The unity of standpoint in Americanist anthropology to which both Kroeber and Boas aspired held fairly firm during Kroeber's lifetime. But he had no successor as guru and spokesperson for the North American discipline as a whole. Fragmentation and specialization gained momentum during the 1960s as the postwar breakdown of American isolationism opened up fieldwork opportunities around the globe, while at home university expansion facilitated growth and intensified institutionalization. In the same broadly interdisciplinary context that had led Boas to his characteristic North American emphasis on four-square anthropology, academic departments sought faculty for new specializations—particularly in culture change, culture and personality, cultural ecology (even a revamped evolutionism), and various anthropologies of meaning (ethnoscience, componential analysis, symbolic anthropology, ethnography of communication, interpretative anthropology) (Ortner 1984; Murray 1994).

Entire departments no longer expected to share the assumptions and methods of the Boasian paradigm. Nonetheless, the new dispensations drew on Boasian roots. Persistences were masked by a rhetoric of discontinuity, albeit not as strident as the one with which Boas himself had attacked the fundaments of the classical evolutionary paradigm. Kroeber's position on culture, in contrast to Boas's avoidance of theoretical manifesto, provided a visible and thereby vulnerable target for declarations of independence from the domination of the Boasian paradigm (e.g., White 1963, 1966; Harris 1968); in practice apostasies were institutional and personal as well as theoretical and substantive. As in the course of any scientific revolution, nuances among predecessors were elided.

Kroeber, far more than his mentor, systematized, theorized, and popularized the scientific position implicit in the Boasian program. Like Boas, Kroeber foregrounded culture rather than society as the core of thinking anthropologically. Culture in its anthropological sense referred to the ways of life of the range of known human groups and constituted anthropology's claim to discrete status among the social sciences; in Kroeber's view, the culture concept transcended the ambiguity of the discipline's multiple roots in the natural sciences and humanities (Kroeber 1950a, 1950b, 1952). For all its importance in unifying the early twentieth-century discipline, however, Kroeber's anthropology has not weathered well. His insistence on culture as "superorganic" rightly strikes contemporary anthropologists as static and reified. Kroeber's insistence on defining history more in spatial than in temporal terms, despite its honorable roots in Boasian studies of diffusion (e.g., Wissler 1917, 1923), vies, to its detriment, with the combinations of historical documentation and oral history that now bring the pasts of what Eric Wolf (1982) called "the people without history" fully into the modern world. Something very like Kroeber's concept of culture is at stake when contemporary anthropologists reject the centrality of this concept to what anthropologists (ought to) do.

Whereas the sciences "decompose" or deconstruct phenomena, Kroeber insisted that "the distinctive feature of the historical approach" was "descriptive integration," in which "the phenomena are preserved intact" (Kroeber 1952 [1935]:63; throughout this chapter, dates in brackets refer to the essay's original publication date). This integration was the job of the historian and the primary role of the anthropologist. Cultural or superorganic phenomena were more "complex" (Kroeber's quotation marks) than the inorganic, "epiphenomena—from the standpoint of analytic processual science." Defining time sequence as a mere secondary attribute of history circumvented the Boasian sociological and functionalist impasse in which history was a valid enterprise but historical reconstruction was not (1952 [1935]:64). Time relations were precisely the phenomena to be reconstructed. Kroeber went so far as to suggest that "all historical procedure is in the manner of a reconstruction" and could never be "objectively verifiable" (1952 [1935]:64). Historians were less often aware of the social construction of their interpretations than anthropologists.

Kroeber was adamant that anthropologists could provide reliable "time history for the poor dateless primitive," albeit with "more approximative results" because of the absence of "even one document written before our day" (1952 [1935]:65). The great divide between history and historical reconstruction, he argued, was artificial and glossed over the reconstruction implicit in any historical interpretation. Kroeber's position is fully consistent with more recent critiques of the subjectivities of conventional history (e.g., Collingwood 1936; White 1973). Contemporary ethnohistorians find ample evidence of Native point of view implicit in conventional documents and habitually turn to oral history to supplement written records (e.g., Brown and Vibert 1996). Because he dealt with historic civilizations as well as with so-called primitive societies, Kroeber was well situated to theorize the relation between history and culture in terms of creative combination of disciplinary sources and methods. In "So-called Social Science" in 1936, Kroeber criticized history for clinging to "narrative," to events rather than their patterns, viewing "any larger culture history askance" (Kroeber 1952 [1936]:74). Anthropologists were fortunate in the constraints of their subject matter: "The rarity of recorded events in primitive life has helped to force anthropologists into recognition of the forms or patterns of culture, and from this into the clear recognition of culture as such. In short, perhaps more than any other group, they discovered culture. . . . Anthropologists became explicit and culture-conscious" (Kroeber 1952 [1936]: 75). Kroeber's rationalization of the subdisciplinary structure of Boasian anthropology relegated time to background; specializations included "the dateless primitives" (ethnology), "the dateless prehistoric" (archaeology), "the unwritten languages" (linguistics), and "the racial history of man" (physical anthropology) (Kroeber 1952 [1936]:75). Fieldworking Boasians found that all cultures were complex, none easily mastered, and took these factors as further grist for the critique of evolution.

Kroeber acknowledged the scale of the primitive as crucial to the anthropological "discovery" of culture: The "very remoteness" of "these small, apparently insignificant, easily mastered cultures" made them "much more readily treatable objectively," producing the impersonal dispassion essential to science (Kroeber 1952 [1936]:76). Anthropology had to move beyond its origins; results would remain "unimpressive as long as anthropological concern remain [ed] timidly attached to primitives alone" (1952 [1936]:77). In 1936 Kroeber was responding to an incipient trend, exemplified by the Lynds' study of Middletown (1929), to work at home in North America, rather than breaking new ethnographic ground. But it fit well with his own long-standing interest in complex societies through history.

There could be "no testing of historical data or interpretations by experiment"; the historian only "infers" the "probabilities of fact, of relation, of significance" (Kroeber 1952 [1938]:79). Kroeber characterized the historian's task as "complex." Preserving the complexity and variability of individual events played against imposing "a certain coherence of meaning."

Kroeber's insistence that history as understood by the anthropologist must link the study of isolated small-scale societies with that of the great civilizations known to conventional history, in principle a far from trivial ambition, in practice grasped at typology of culture area and growth cycle rather than at process. Grand synthesis eluded Kroeber.

Read in terms of the stated aspirations of his methodologically austere theory of culture and history, Kroeber's oeuvre reflects a coherent train of thought linking early Boasian thinking about the interpretation of human diversity and similarity through time and space to more promising contemporary reformulations. His attempted syntheses were largely abortive, but his will to explain, or at least to classify, "configurations of culture growth" (the title of his 1944 compendium) continue to challenge his successors.

Culture as Anthropology's Autonomous Level of Explanation

Kroeber's assemblage of his theoretical essays in 1952 unabashedly clung to the explanatory domain of culture as his first principle, closely followed by history, given "the nature of culture to be heavily conditioned by its own cumulative past" (Kroeber 1952:4). Like Boas he defined history not primarily as narrative but as increasingly broad contextualization "of quality and of organizing pattern" integrating culture traits (Kroeber 1952:5).

Kroeber presented himself more as descriptor than as theoretician of culture, having produced "contributions to factual knowledge or . . . organization of knowledge or . . . first-level generalization from it" (Kroeber 1952:vii). But he wanted to be remembered as a theoretician. Because few readers care about "all this factualism," Kroeber abstracted passages on culture from his substantive works to impose "a kind of unity" centering around "a theory about the kind of thing culture is: about its properties and typical manifestations, its relation to other kinds of things, and how it is most fruitfully viewed and investigated" (Kroeber 1952:vii). His "culture" was definitely a thing, one with the potential to unite Americanist anthropology (see Kroeber and Kluckhohn 1952).

Kroeber conceded that phenomena in the real world did not automatically separate culture from the "mixture of behavior, events, institutions, individuals, and psychic and somatic reactions which constitute the primary and raw material of the historical and social sciences" (Kroeber 1952:vii). Kroeber maintained the line between personal and scientific at some psychic cost; he never entirely got over the challenge to his objectivity with the death of his friend Ishi, the last survivor of the Yahi tribe, in 1915. The anthropologist was supposed to isolate the level of the cultural. Insisting that his own temperament leaned toward the typologizing trends of the sciences, Kroeber attempted to maintain the impersonal distance characteristic of the scientific method narrowly conceived. Like Boas, he foregrounded the historical.

Kroeber's version of natural history was akin to the particularism of Boas's critique of evolution. He sought "widening generalization and understanding, not hypotheses which are then tested" in a laboratory (Kroeber 1952:vii). Kroeber denied any "absolute difference in method of inquiry" while acknowledging that "conceptual hypotheses" tended "to remain implicit longer" in the study of culture than in more experimental inquiries. Through direct observation, theories "emerge gradually and pile up as we rearrange and reinterpret our facts by trial and error; they are mostly an end-product" (Kroeber 1952: vii). Without apology, he observed: "I am not a formal theoretician. My natural and first interest always has been in phenomena and their ordering: it is akin to an aesthetic proclivity, presumably congenital" (Kroeber 1952:vii). Several years after his retirement in 1946, Kroeber reflected: "The theory was just sweated out piecemeal and slowly over fifty years" (Kroeber 1952:3). The length of his career and the consistency of his culturological position led Kroeber himself to telescope the development of his thought by revisiting earlier formulations without revision.

"The Superorganic," published in the *American Anthropologist* in 1917, still stands as Kroeber's most characteristic theoretical statement about culture, despite his frequent declaimers over four succeeding decades that he had merely claimed the so-called superorganic as one of several autonomous levels of structure among natural phenomena, clearly distinguishable from both the inorganic and the organic. Kroeber claimed little originality: The term "superorganic" was adopted (without its evolutionary connotations) from Herbert Spencer; Boas already had "estimated very justly many of its properties and influences." Kroeber considered Boas, Lowie, and Spier as his allies in "laying bare the skeletal structures of cultures" (Kroeber 1959:402). The plural "cultures" is telling, although Kroeber did not emphasize the contrast of ethnographic and theoretical. In any case, he and Leslie White were left to defend "the thesis of a distinctive cultural level" (Kroeber 1952:4). In 1952 Kroeber agreed with his (unnamed) latter-day critics that his argument might sometimes have "lapsed" into "mysticism." But he insisted that recognition of distinct levels of phenomena need not carry such limitations.

Kroeber admitted that Benedict's characterization of cultural wholes in terms of temperament or ethos had considerable "affinity" with his own understanding of pattern, configuration, or gestalt. Nonetheless, her psychological level of analysis "returned largely to a subcultural level" (Kroeber 1952:5), to which he did not subscribe (at least as the business of anthropology). For Kroeber, Benedict's use of cultural evidence to arrive at psychological generalizations typified the anthropological misuse of such pervasive unities. He was unsure, however, whether "this psychological result" derived from "a bent in the ethnologists" or resided "in the nature of things." He even speculated that the cultural level of analysis might be incapable of transcending description. Moreover, psychological orientations proposed by ethnologists were "still largely in cultural terms" from the psychologist's point of view (Kroeber 1957:73), serving well neither cultural nor psychological approaches (a critique that can now be taken for granted).

Benedict's "psychological orientations" influenced the "slant" of a particular culture, much as did the personality orientation of individuals. The patterns of interest to Kroeber, in contrast, "are nexuses of culture traits which have assumed a definite and coherent structure, which function successfully, and which acquire major historic weight and persistence" (Kroeber 1952 [1943]: 92–93). This integration did not come ready-made; a culture was "highly composite in the origin of its constituent materials" (1952 [1943]: 93). This point was made by Lowie (Kroeber 1957:87), whose famous dictum made only "passive allusion" to the original sources constituting a culture; "shreds and patches" did not refer to the "ultimate structuring" of "constituent materials" in contemporary terms, through which he agreed with Kroeber that integration emerged (Lowie 1920:440–41). Lowie envisioned a continuum between culture and civilization rather than a stark dichotomy of classification or method. Even Boas, "with his critical negativism toward all anthropological schemes about culture" (Kroeber 1957:87), never implied that culture traits drifted about randomly. The early Boasians, in short, believed it was possible to know things about the history of peoples without written history.

Kroeber emphasized the affinity between his own position and Lowie's, seeming almost puzzled because "nobody would accuse Lowie of mysticism or of lack of clarity" (1952 [1948]:112), as he himself was accused repeatedly. Although Lowie did not use the term "superorganic," he certainly spoke of culture as a "distinct domain," "a thing *sui generis*," and "a closed system." Kroeber assumed in retrospect that his own "autonomous *forces*" (his emphasis) of culture must have earned him the charge of mysticism.

Kroeber correctly recognized the danger of arbitrariness in isolating the boundaries of cultures and their contacts in order to compare them. "Anthropologists have acquired considerable skill in presenting culture-wholes of tribal size as discrete units" and in documenting how things pass from one culture to another at this scale of civilization (Kroeber 1952:6). He was virtually unique among his Boasian contemporaries, however, in testing the validity of the culture concept on "the outward segregation and inner consistency . . . of large civilizations" (Kroeber 1952:6). Throughout his career, Kroeber was fascinated by issues of scale and the degree to which simple and complex societies would prove similar in kind.

The value of the superorganic concept was primarily heuristic, "more effective if directed at an isolable set of factors than at several interacting ones" (Kroeber 1952:7). Analysis proceeded one level at a time. As an anthropologist, Kroeber had "personally chosen or become addicted to" the cultural level as "the most consistent with an integrative-contextual or 'historical' approach" (Kroeber 1952:7). Factors of the individual in culture were held constant in order to explore the explanatory potential of the cultural level.

In the first flush of Americanist enthusiasm for European psychology, perhaps best dated from Freud's American visit in 1909 (when he shared a platform at Clark University with Franz Boas), several prominent Boasians tried to integrate their anthropology with the study of the individual and personality. Although Kroeber himself underwent psychoanalysis as part of his psychoanalytic training and became a practicing analyst for several years after the death of his first wife in 1913, he always kept the two levels of understanding separate. Changing professions was a serious option at one point, but crossing from the superorganic to the psychological within anthropology failed to tempt him (T. Kroeber 1970; Darnell 1990a).

Individuals were largely unconscious of the operation of the cultural, for example, in the timing of inventions. "It is only from the point of view of the several individuals involved that simultaneity and co-occurrence exist" (Kroeber 1952:8). Culture, manifested as the expression of genius, allowed the anthropologist to move from individual description to cultural analysis. "Genius," for Kroeber, was "a function of cultural growth" rather than a property of individual minds, evidenced by the "clustering of great minds," the "style-like pattern [which] evokes or releases the required innate individual talents" (Kroeber 1952:8). From such a standpoint, individuals entered "only as a cog in the mechanism of intercultural transfer, stimulus and creativity"; Kroeber "carried out this methodological suppression without qualms" (Kroeber 1952:8), ruthlessly. The cultural view, as opposed to the "raw" phenomena treated by the historian, was "not only collective" but "also almost inevitably long-range." Only distance could capture "the dynamism or flow or growth" (Kroeber 1952:8). Archaeology appealed to Kroeber because it already filtered out extraneous individualisms. Language, impersonal in its basic structures, came a close second for aesthetic satisfaction.

This aesthetic is very different from the one Sapir derived from the study of linguistic form. Language was a part of culture with characteristic properties that lent it to formal manipulation and discovery of regularity, but Kroeber still considered language relatively unimportant in the overall inventory of human achievements. His analogy of grammar to culture emphasized that, although grammars were unconscious, their overall patterning "can be discovered by analysis and can be formulated." The formal properties of culture were similar, although "larger, more varied and complicated . . . as well as more substantive and less autonomous" (Kroeber 1957:106).

Kroeber carefully stipulated that the apparent determinism of the superorganic level "contains a concealed factor of striving and will" embodied in individuals (Kroeber 1952:9). It simply wasn't the task of the anthropologist to deal with this analytic structural level. An analogy clarified his point: To a geologist, a coral reef was an accumulation of secretions, while to a zoologist it was a growing organism composed of individual living polyps with a modicum of free will. Each science had its own expertise and its own level. And Kroeber appointed himself to speak for anthropology in circumscribing its domain.

In retrospect, Kroeber identified 1917 as the height of his superorganic phase: "I thought I stood at the threshold of glimpsing vague, great forces of predestination" like those of Spengler soon to come. Three decades later, he was less sanguine about the grand generalizations, acknowledging that the causation he sought then was based in a "naive," "old-fashioned [i.e., Newtonian] mechanics" (Kroeber 1952:9). The implications of cultural relativism, analogizing from a metaphorical adaptation of Einsteinian physics that suggested new processual models for the social sciences, were only beginning to open up; chaos and complexity theories were still far in the future. Kroeber would have found these changing science metaphors fascinating.

Retrospectively, Kroeber read "The Superorganic" as "a sort of raid into enemy territory," a deconstruction of "the false reading into the biological process of a distinctly sociocultural mechanism," unambiguously depicting anthropology as more than a poor country cousin in its "relations with biology" (Kroeber 1952:20).

Introducing the 1917 essay in 1952, Kroeber suggested that it had attracted more attention from related social science disciplines than from his own disciplinary colleagues, "presumably because its contentions have largely passed into their common body of assumptions" (Kroeber 1952:22). The (then-)contemporary reading of "an antireductionist proclamation of independence from the dominance of the biological explanation of sociocultural phenomena" no longer fit his own recollections of the period when the paper was written. He recalled no sociobiological "oppression or threatened annexation," rather "a diffused public opinion, a body of unaware assumptions, that left precarious the autonomous recognition of society, and still more that of culture" (Kroeber 1952:22). Confusion about the explanatory potentials of "race" and "civilization" posed far greater challenges to the Boasian synthesis.

Kroeber amended his earlier usage of "culture," "civilization," and "history" as having failed to accurately separate out the level of society from that of culture; he now preferred the more inclusive term "sociocultural" (Kroeber

1952:22). He also "retracts" the "unwarranted reification" of culture for which he had been criticized in the interim. Disclaimers aside, his apologia for the superorganic accurately reflected his continuing commitment to an anthropological concept of culture that remained remarkably consistent over his career of nearly six decades.

Kroeber insisted that binary discriminations, "a way of thought characteristic of our western civilization" (Kroeber 1952 [1917]:23) were invaluable in the progress of science. For him, the classifying bent of the civilization that produced modern science was a good thing, not one to be suspected as arbitrary logocentrism. The binary distinction between organic and cultural was pivotal to defining the scope and method of anthropology. Because evolution worked at the organic level, it was misapplied to cultural phenomena; such reasoning by analogy broke down as soon as anything was known about culture at its own level of analysis. Civilization evolved by accumulation rather than by replacement and was not inherited biologically. Men and birds did not fly in the same way; polar bears and Eskimos adapted differently to the harshness of the same environment. Speech was unique to humans. The cultural level reflected "something deep" in human evolution (Kroeber 1952 [1917]:28). Kroeber's reworking reflected cultural infusion into the neo-evolutionary synthesis of the 1950s that arose around the centennial of Darwin's *The Origin of Species.*

In line with the earlier Boasian critique of evolution, Kroeber insisted that the difference between human and animal was "only in small measure a question of high and low" (Kroeber 1952 [1917]:30–31). Indeed, human history consisted of changes in culture that would be impossible within organic evolution. Human "tradition is something super-added to the organisms that bear it, imposed upon them, external to them" (Kroeber 1952 [1917]:32). Man[kind], therefore, was both organic and superorganic or cultural; the challenge for the anthropologist was not to confuse the two levels.

Kroeber argued that the "shifting of mental and emotional point of view" to the cultural interpretation of racial and ethnic differences constituted "as absolute a turning upside down of attitude . . . as when Copernican doctrine challenged the prior conviction of the world" (Kroeber 1952 [1917]:34). Ironically, given that anthropology's cultural revolution has yet to be universally acknowledged, the Copernican "revolution" was Thomas Kuhn's paramount exemplar for "the structure of scientific revolutions" (Kuhn 1962). (Such critiques persist, even within anthropology, as in the ongoing vendetta of Derek Freeman against the memory of Margaret Mead, which is, beneath the rhetoric, a sociobiological attack on the Boasian culture concept [Côté 1994; Freeman 1983, 1999].)

Kroeber countered the argument that had not yet been made: Heredity and civilization could be substituted for one another only as a "crass" "act of illiberality" (Kroeber 1952 [1917]:35); that is, his point was located at the very core of the Boasian paradigm. The "acquired heredity" of Gustav LeBon, Lester Ward, and Herbert Spencer fell into place once it was assigned to the realm of the superorganic (Kroeber 1952 [1917]:35). Eugenics was a particularly virulent confusion between cultural and organic levels.

Civilization, in Kroeber's view, could exist only in the mind. Minds, of course, were grounded in the organic, in biology. But culture was not an individual phenomenon; mental ideas were transmitted in society, not organically but superorganically. Confounding heredity and environment in observable everyday behavior prevented proper understanding of civilization as "a body or stream of products of mental exercise" (Kroeber 1952 [1917]:40), its essence nonindividual. Heredity, for Kroeber, operated solely at the individual level, already banished from his anthropology.

The concept of genius was Kroeber's hook on the analytic autonomy of culture and the individual. He hypothesized that the incidence of inherited genius (understood to have different varieties of unusual ability) was invariant across space and time. But history recorded only the actions of geniuses fortunate enough to live in a time and place prepared for their potential genius. The "germ" (Kroeber 1952 [1917]:43) of an invention might come long before its cultural recognition, as with Gregor Mendel and modern genetics; or inventions might be effectively simultaneous when the cultural groundwork was already in place.

Kroeber's enthusiasm was reserved for the superorganic, for these "pulsing events" that "reveal a glimpse of a great and inspiring inevitability which rises as far above the accidents of personality as the march of the heavens transcends the wavering contacts of random footprints on clouds of earth" (Kroeber 1952 [1917]:44). As soon as "interest shifts from individually biographic elements" to civilizational ones, "the presence of majestic forces or sequences pervading civilization will be irresistibly evident" (Kroeber 1952 [1917]:45). Consequently, differences among individuals were different in kind from those among cultures. Individuals varied similarly everywhere, but the weight of accumulated civilization created dramatically diverse outcomes.

History epitomized the social sciences in refusing to focus on the individual as such. But "the current view of history" held the "obviously illogical assumption" that civilization was merely "a sum total of the psychic operations of a mass of individuals" (Kroeber 1952 [1917]:49). Lamentably for Kroeber, the great man theory of history was (and still is) deeply entrenched in the individualism and anthropocentrism of Western civilization.

The move from organic to cultural evolution was qualitative, "a leap to another plane" analogous to the origin of life itself (Kroeber 1952 [1917]:49). The discontinuity was so dramatic that the rate of organic evolution had actually declined. Indeed, "not only the content of civilization but the complexity of its organization" had increased (Kroeber 1952 [1917]:51). Because we have misapplied the methods of the natural sciences to phenomena properly located in the domain of the cultural, the "processes of civilizational activity are almost unknown to us" (Kroeber 1952 [1917]:51). Kroeber's classic paper ended with an implicit plea to develop methods of purely civilizational analysis. He was, in 1917, wildly optimistic that this would be possible, that laws analogous to those of the organic realm would emerge from the appropriately specific (i.e., ethnographic) study of the superorganic. In retrospect, he concluded: "What I was dreaming of, as a distant possibility, was a true processual science causally explaining the pageant of the history of culture" (Kroeber 1952:52). The merely social, the interaction of organic individuals, like the merely biological, could not explain cultural process. The 1917 argument effectively set the stage for Kroeber's mature testing of the culture concept among the world's great civilizations and presaged his meticulous application of Boasian historical method to qualify premature generalizations of an over-enthusiastic latter-day evolutionism, in history as in anthropology.

The Dream of Synthesis and the Failure of Nerve

Kroeber was among those whom Isaiah Berlin labeled the hedgehogs of intellectual life. At least in the theory of culture, Kroeber worried a few ideas throughout his career; even his Peruvian and southwestern archaeology fell under this overarching umbrella. His work on civilizations, both past and present, carried over the assumptions of method and interpretation from his firsthand fieldwork in small isolated American Indian communities. Each provided a new arena for testing theory against empirical data to produce a cross-cultural science of anthropology. Kroeber expected evidence from multiple sources to converge, both across the scale of cultures studied and in the mutually confirming subdisciplines of anthropology. His paradigmatic textbook, titled simply *Anthropology* (1923), exemplified the scope and rigor of the Boasian Americanist position. Kroeber wanted to be a scientist, or perhaps better, he longed for (meta)history to be a science.

Process in cultures was closer to natural history than to social science; in his own view, Kroeber was "not by temperament a social scientist." "Historical Reconstruction of Culture Growths and Organic Evolution" in 1931 marked a turning point, a parting company with "my guru Boas," who "disapproved of my tendency to historical reconstruction" although this difference of opinion "never interfered with our personal friendship" (Kroeber 1952:57). The disclaimer reflected longstanding ambivalence in Kroeber's relationship to Boas. After many years of resisting his mentor's efforts to draw him back from California into the Columbia-centered fold, during which Kroeber carefully avoided direct conflict, all the while stubbornly preserving his institutional and intellectual autonomy, he finally declared personal and professional independence from Boas over the issue of the superorganic.

The divergence was not, however, absolute. Kroeber's emphasis on the age and area principle, similar in biology and cultural anthropology, and his interest in the distribution of cultural phenomena were vintage Boasian. Simultaneously, however, he moved from complexes of cultural traits (not necessarily connected to one another) to "configuration" (an integrated pattern of multiple elements) and "the totality of structure" in a particular case as determining variation and historical trajectory (Kroeber 1952 [1931]:59). His "cautious optimism" that origins might be accessible to cultural analysis (Kroeber 1952 [1931]:60), however, was thoroughly un-Boasian in its implicit retrieval of evolutionary aspirations at a time when the very mention of origins was anathema in conventional Boasian circles.

Kroeber acknowledged the practical difficulties of cultural analysis, attributing them to the relative youth of anthropology, with its "smaller and less intensively organized and classified body of accurate fact" resulting in "less exact" "critical standards" than those of the natural sciences (Kroeber 1952 [1931]:61). Anthropology had only recently "consciously discovered process in culture" (see Kroeber 1952 [1917]; Sapir 1916); it was now poised to move beyond "a descriptive prolegomena" (Kroeber 1952 [1931]:62) to codification and synthesis.

Kroeber asserted that "the idea of basic pattern has not been wanting in anthropology." Sapir's was the clearest articulation because language, in "its precision of form facilitates analysis" (Kroeber 1952 [1943]:86). Although Kroeber acknowledged nonlinguistic cultural patterns as "relatively short-lived," he believed some were "more basic or primary and on the whole older," while others were "more superficial, secondary, and transitory" (Kroeber 1952 [1943]:86). He distinguished historical, which (at least among preliterate peoples) lacked control over "time perspective," from physiological or functionalist approaches to culture, the latter moving "from the contemporary directly into generalization, perhaps into universals" (Kroeber 1952 [1943]:87).

Modern anthropologists were better at analysis of cases than at comparison. Comparative studies were based on traits or items rather than "whole cultures or systems" (Kroeber 1952 [1943]:89). Kroeber was relatively uninterested in the natural world, being preoccupied instead with the domain of the superorganic. Omer Stewart recalls that in 1954 he glossed over human modifications of the environment because anthropology was "too busy on the whole to pay much attention to extra-cultural relations" (Stewart 1998:161).

Kroeber first attacked the question of culture growth in *Cultural and Natural Areas of Native North America* in 1939, asserting that culture was "relatively uniform" within each of eighty-four discrete areas. Because content and "richness" of ecological and cultural systems were highly correlated, he envisioned "approximately objective" measures of cultural identity" (Kroeber 1952 [1939]: 337). Each major culture area of North America demonstrated at least one "climax or focus of cultural intensity." Although his treatment of major world civilizations was still embryonic, Kroeber remained an optimist: "Both in art and in degree of systematization the more outstanding American cultures seem to conform to a general pattern of culture growth, the outlines of which gleam through the known historic civilizations. Further, the very concept of climax, or, if one will, culture center, involves not only the focus of an area but also a culmination in time" (Kroeber 1952 [1939]:343). In retrospect, this attempted grand synthesis reified the very process it aspired to illuminate. Time and space somehow mythically coalesced. The idea of regionally specific forms of culture growth "now seems to be hopelessly compromised, not the least by the way it reproduces essentialist notions of culture" and "fences off communities" so that the complexity of their histories is erased (Vibert 1997:25).

Despite its difficulties by contemporary standards, this train of thought led Kroeber to apply Boasian historical method to known civilizations, a project culminating in his monumental *Configurations of Culture Growth* (1944).

Kroeber was not the first culture historian to identify recurrent phases of development across civilizations. Each contributor had his own vision: "Spengler sees immanent predestination, Toynbee normal free will, Sorokin a pendulum beat between sensate and ideational proclivities" (Kroeber 1952 [1949]:135). Kroeber most fully characterized these various efforts, all in his view highly unsatisfactory, in his Messenger Lectures on the Evolution of Civilization at Cornell University in 1956 (published as Kroeber 1957).

Arnold Toynbee's *A Study of History* (1972) hypothesized "parallel processes" causing regularities in the origin, growth, breakdown, and disintegration of civilizations; content could be traced from one civilization to its successors. But Kroeber rejected the "quasi-psychological" character of these growth processes (Kroeber 1952 [1943]:373). Toynbee wanted to compare "the life histories of societies" and "the psychological and moral factors that determine the courses of these histories" (Kroeber 1957:127). Despite the purported essentialism and conditioned by Boasian attention to diffusion, Kroeber worried that "few societies or civilizations are wholly unrelated; the majority have some external relation" (Kroeber 1952 [1943]:374). Among nonliterate societies, Toynbee dealt with only the Eskimo, the Polynesian, and the Andean. A civilization was the minimal "unit of historical intelligibility," with a "fundamental ideology," a "master plan" (Kroeber 1963 [1948]:20, 21).

Oswald Spengler, though oblivious to quantitative assessment, recognized the significance of "fundamental patterns of culture" (i.e., Kroeber's superorganic) extracted from influence of individual biography (Kroeber 1944:825). Spengler's organic analogy, however, led him to overestimate the discreteness of cultures as wholes; "the question at issue in all such cases is to learn how far the analogy extends and where it ends" (Kroeber 1944:827). "Fixed parallel stages," the single controlling key pattern, and inevitable death were unproven and likely to be disconfirmed by particular evidence (Kroeber 1944:828), again a Boasian methodological asceticism. Kroeber conceded that "the limits of cultures can be drawn differently from the limits which I have observed" (Kroeber 1944:830), as indeed they were by others who tackled similar comparative projects. But he continued to think imposition of such boundaries was both possible and desirable.

Kroeber judged Spengler close to an anthropologist, "a complete cultural relativist." He first realized "that science shares at least a degree of the relativity that is characteristic of all human culture" (Kroeber 1957:65). Spengler's method alternated detail with contrastive pattern (Kroeber 1957:83). But he short-circuited historical interpretation by dealing only with the coherence of "each of his great cultures in their active phase" (Kroeber 1957:85). The validity of Spengler's generalizations rested on "one's presuppositions" about whether the products of a single civilization really were significantly similar over time (Kroeber 1957:95). Unintelligibility to members of other cultures was one index of such similarity (Kroeber 1957:97). Civilizations were incommensurable.

Kroeber stressed that Spengler's thinking was fundamentally nonbiological. He was, furthermore, too impatient to exclude "commonplace universals" before building an edifice of style (Kroeber 1957:102). In contrast, Kroeber presciently understood the coherence of culture styles to be "partial," "variable," and gradually emergent (Kroeber 1957:103). The elements of a coherent culture took time to coalesce and assimilate in a new context.

Whole-culture styles, for Kroeber, could only result from "secondary spread and assimilation within the culture;" they were not primary phenomena as Spengler thought (Kroeber 1957:152). A "total civilization" might be "recognized on a broader base, allowing an ultimately wider range of patterns and styles" (Kroeber 1957:157), as in Western society since about 1900. To truly understand these matters, however, required an ethnographer's eye: "The study of civilizations must progress beyond preoccupation with a small number of highly contrastive great cultures and must include minor, derivative, and even humble cultures, of course with emphasis according to importance. . . . [We] should aim at still greater inclusiveness and less haphazardness of selection" (Kroeber 1957:158–59).

Despite his critique of Spengler, Kroeber insisted in other arenas that his own usage of the organic analogy was not, or at least not exclusively, metaphorical. Human life was biological as well as cultural (Kroeber 1957:74). Cultural products were more plastic and individual because they were unconstrained by heredity; cultural phenomena "vary in larger arcs" (Kroeber 1957:76). (With Kroeber's characteristic penchant for qualifying any generalization, the neo-evolutionary synthesis demonstrated forms of organic life that arrived at their own kind of coherence [Kroeber 1957:77]).

Kroeber thought his own work added methodological focus to process manifest in history. Historians, in his view, habitually refused to "face the problem of the qualitative separateness of cultures" (Kroeber 1952:330), of their boundedness. He agreed with Lowie that any culture was "in some degree an artificial unit segregated off for expediency" (Kroeber 1952 [1946]:379). Kroeber was fully aware of his shift from the range of human cultures to the "range of man's most developed cultures," the Oikoumene or inhabited world known to the Greeks (Kroeber 1952 [1946]:379). The Oikoumene was "a great web of culture growth," rich in style, content, and values, moving "almost like a wave or pulsation" (Kroeber 1952 [1946]:392). While many of his contemporaries (e.g., Goldenweiser 1922) tried to apply the term "civilization" to the so-called primitive societies that were the mainstay of anthropological fieldwork, Kroeber chose to focus on the uniqueness of civilization itself.

In introducing a posthumous collection of his later papers on culture and history, Kroeber's widow, Theodora, emphasized that only an anthropologist could have written *Configurations of Culture Growth* (Kroeber 1963:xvii). Kroeber wanted to "delimit" the boundaries of cultures so that they could be compared as wholes (Kroeber 1963 [1953]:3); criteria included discontinuity in space or time, language, religion, political and military development, economy and technology, and style. With the exception of the last, these criteria are commonplaces of Boasian anthropology. "Style," for Kroeber, involved the creative, qualitative and transient in culture (Kroeber 1963 [1953]:14), "a self-consistent way of behaving or of doing things" (Kroeber 1963 [1958]:40). Its unidirectional growth allowed him to "speak of a style as if it were a life history" (Kroeber 1963 [1958]:43).

Nonetheless, Kroeber continued to exclude the individual or the psychological from cultural analysis. *Configurations of Culture Growth* differed from the national character studies of Mead and Benedict in being "diachronic and transcultural . . . and strictly inductive . . . concerned with the non-holistic activities of culture, such as painting or philosophy" (Kroeber 1963 [1958]:74). Kroeber insisted that "culture history" must free itself from "the entanglements of individuals" (Kroeber 1944:25). His theory of genius was little changed from 1917; indeed, he noted (Kroeber 1944:12) his own priority in theorizing simultaneous inventions as evidence of cultural rather than of psychological forces.

When I first read *Configurations of Culture Growth* in Frederica de Laguna's senior seminar on culture and personality some three and a half decades ago, I was incensed at its soporific compilation of more than I ever wanted to know about the typologies of civilizations (including the ancient Near East, the ancient Mediterranean, Japanese, Chinese, Arabic, Sanskrit, Greek, Latin, Persian, European [sometimes broken down into separate nations], Egyptian, and Islamic) and their areas of expressive or material achievement through time (with compendious chapters on philosophy, science, philology, sculpture, painting, drama, literature, music). When I complained to Freddy that I was excruciatingly bored, she agreed that Kroeber's generalizations had not come forth; she smiled conspiratorially: "It was such a magnificent failure!"

Kroeber began with the methodological assumption that "inductive comparison" was impossible without "orderly arrangement" of phenomena. He concentrated on explanations in terms of cultural pattern, arguing that these necessarily preceded "the underlying psychology" (Kroeber 1944:vii). The project involved "one of the forms which culture takes," that is, "the frequent habit of societies to develop their cultures to their highest levels spasmodically, especially in their intellectual and aesthetic aspects" (Kroeber 1944:5). Kroeber wondered if such "clusterings" or "spurts" might be in the mind of the beholder. He was willing to settle for documenting a "tendency toward order" (Kroeber 1944:6). The "configurations" of his title occurred in time, space, and "degree of achievement" (Kroeber 1944:6). He sought to document rather than to explain the behavior of cultures. Cultural florescences came in pattern waves, an image possibly derived from his reading of physics.

The cultures Kroeber could find comparative facts about included some "native American." Despite their "presumably complete historical disparateness," however, clear data were seldom available, especially for culture sequences (Kroeber 1944:24). European culture had no greater principled importance than did any other culture. The constraints on selection of cases were purely pragmatic.

At least half a dozen major cases were apparently independent in origin and development, allowing at least descriptive generalization. The disadvantage of the method was that it forced Kroeber to extract data from their cultural context and assume oversimplified equivalences of activities and patterns. Kroeber noted somewhat sheepishly that he had "allowed" a chapter on philology because "though it is the least important of the activities dealt with, its configurations are neat" (Kroeber 1944:25).

Kroeber's foray into the philosophy of science led him to assume that natural science, as furthest from the "subjective core in the life history of each of us and in the history of early human knowledge," was easy for humans to study (Kroeber 1957:80). Culture was easier to understand than psychology because "the greater co-ordinations and configurations are more easily recognized" (Kroeber 1957:81). The naturalistic intent of Kroeber's project precluded religion because he could not estimate growths and declines, given its dependence on "emotional intensity" (Kroeber 1944:799). Intellectual and aesthetic (i.e., cognitive and affective) activities were different in kind, facilitating the distance necessary for science.

Kroeber acknowledged his dependence on "certain recurring metaphors" of "growth, patterns, saturation, realization, pulse, dissolution." "More precisely denotive terms" were unavailable (Kroeber 1944:26). He avoided "cycle" because its connotations of precise recurrence were yet undemonstrated (Kroeber 1944:27). The argument remained historical "in the sense of being variably individuated, rather than shaped by fixed principles" (Kroeber 1944:788). Over seven hundred pages later, Kroeber found "no evidence of any true law, nothing cyclical, regularly repetitive, or necessary" (Kroeber 1944: 761). Ruefully, he reiterated the lessons of failure: "If there are to be explicit comparative findings, comparison must be undertaken as such; and if the chief conclusion proves to be the difficulty of comparing precisely and reliably, that will be at least a wholesome if disappointing result. I confess to some lowering of expectations in the course of my work" (Kroeber 1944:762). The method was descriptive or narrational; culture configurations stood out "as stripped skeletons rather than softened, mixed, and blurred" by the addition of individual or cultural agency (Kroeber 1944:761). Kroeber derived this predilection from his ethnological work "with primitive cultures" (Kroeber 1944: 761). The effort at sociological comparison had precluded historical context (Kroeber 1944:762). Duration and rate did not seem to increase over time or to show clear patterns of recurrence. The age and area principle measured these civilizations in space (Kroeber 1944:813), but failed to provide the temporal or stylistic regularities Kroeber had hoped for.

Particular cultures could and did die, both by population extinction and by absorption or displacement. "Primitive cultures are dying in this way every year before the 'impact of civilization'" (Kroeber 1944:819). Nonetheless, it was impossible for a society to become "cultureless" (Kroeber 1944:818). Nor was cultural death necessitated by the organic analogy (Kroeber 1944:821). Kroeber worried whether culture growth occurred in a symmetrical normal curve. This phenomenon was difficult to measure (Kroeber 1944:773). Further, "there may be no single normal type" (Kroeber 1944:777). Fractal patterning, its form repeated across scales, was not yet a possible explanation.

Kroeber was eager to avoid value judgment, settling for the view that "cultures do not necessarily either age or progress, but that they do undergo variations in vigor, originality, and values produced" (Kroeber 1944:822). Despite his massive compilation, we still know very little about these matters. Nonetheless, Kroeber ended on a note of some dignity: "My own feeling is that the growth-configuration approach results rather in a multiplicity of specific historic findings. These are occasionally new, more frequently a shifted emphasis or realigned interpretation. And the endless events of history are lifted out of their level of near-uniformity into organized relief, by an attitude which consciously recognizes pattern-growth configurations in their space-time relations as well as in their value relations" (Kroeber 1944:846).

The completion of his compendious failure did not dispel Kroeber's obsession with a taxonomy of civilizations. He left an unfinished manuscript published in 1962 under the title *A Roster of Civilizations and Culture: An Essay on the Natural History of the World's Cultures, Living and Extinct.* As for Lowie in 1920, culture and civilization were synonymous, although "larger and richer cultures" were more likely to be called civilizations (Kroeber 1962:9). Cultures, both past and present, seemed to "grade into one another in space and time in a vast continuum" (Kroeber 1962:10) rather than in a simple dichotomy. Cultures and the histories that created them were interdependent. Anthropologists and historians alike were "relativists," with no absolute or final ideas of cultural value (Kroeber 1962:11). Anthropologists, faced with unrecorded time depth and limited access to individual creations of culture, usually had fewer data than historians.

Anthropology rejected its heritage in organic evolution for a more "modest and sober undertaking" (Kroeber 1962:14). The larger cultural traditions called civilizations could not be studied exhaustively by a single investigator. "But societies of the size of tribes, and possessing cultures of limited scope, did seem to warrant hope that they could be known with reasonable accuracy and characterized holistically" (Kroeber 1962:15). Kroeber explicitly avoided generalizing about culture growth cycles, restating his 1944 thesis in terms of empirical questions for ongoing research: "Culminations of cultural activity, with their rises and declines, do tend to suggest that cultures as well as organisms may have a normal life course or trajectory. Certainly many styles of creativity appear to run such a course, and the idea may be extensible to whole cultures. But this is something to be investigated, not assumed as a premise and then proved by the selected cases that fit the assumption" (Kroeber 1962:17).

The civilizations of Native North America were characterized as "minor." Despite the extensiveness of his firsthand fieldwork among them, Kroeber's language was evolutionist in its patronizing overview of local diversities: The hundreds of "petty nations" were usually called "tribes"; they were of "fairly uniformly lower level of culture as compared with our own, or even with that of the native peoples of the relatively advanced 'Nuclear' area" (Kroeber 1962:55). Moreover, the number of such tribes led Kroeber to conclude that their cultural differences "could not have been very great nor important as compared with our own civilization." Indeed, "slight" but "regular" differentiation was virtually predictable (Kroeber 1962:55). Kroeber proposed to measure such diversity quantitatively, by "isolable or definable items of culture," as he had done in his California trait surveys in the 1930s (Kroeber 1962:56). By inference, culture change in North America was gradual but steady, resulting in dramatic disruption and conflict only with the coming of Europeans (Kroeber 1962:57). Items of cultural content recurred widely but were "selected" in each particular context with "some distinctiveness of organization . . . into a coherent pattern or functioning plan" (Kroeber 1962:59). Cultures began to cohere on a small scale, through a cumulative effect of area and population increase. Archaeology documented the "natural order of events" entailed by the "birth of civilizations" (Kroeber 1962:60). Despite the absence of a dichotomous gulf between cultures and civilizations, the nonliterate cultures of North America were "incipient but only partly achieve higher civilization" (Kroeber 1962:60).

Citing Boas, Kroeber noted that Old and New World civilizations differed in distribution of basic traits such as the wheel, the plow, stringed instruments, riddles and proverbs, and iron manufacture; all such absences were in the New World. From "this set of negative distributions," Boas inferred not that the Old World was superior but that extreme caution was needed about explaining invention in terms of the psychic unity of mankind (Kroeber 1962:74). Old and New Worlds were necessarily understood as developing independently. The great inventions of the Oikoumene did not move beyond the classical world of their birth (Kroeber 1962:76).

Complexity and the Reformulation of the Culture Concept

Kroeber's questions about the relationship of culture to civilization and consistency in the development of particular civilizations have proved more interesting than his answers. Our own generation's approach to these questions cuts through some of the impasses that led to his failed synthesis. His unsuccessful grapplings with the nature of complex order are now amenable to generalization through recent amalgams of mathematics, physics, and computer graphics modeling capacities generally glossed as chaos or complexity (Gleick 1987; Prigogine and Stengers 1984).

The property of "self-organization" allows "spontaneous crystallization of order out of complex systems" (Lewin 1992:25). For Roger Lewin, as for Kroeber, "configurations of culture growth" seem to cry out for elusive generalization: "I asked speculatively whether the rise and fall of complex societies might also be described by the science of Complexity. Wild idea, I said, but I'd been reading studies of the inexorable rise and fall of civilizations through history, and the repeated pattern seemed to this naive spectator to have the right 'smell' about it" (Lewin 1992:29) Lewin, a science journalist, posed this question to Stuart Kauffman, who had moved from medicine to biochemistry to plectics, the science of complexity, with its assumption that order crosses the boundaries of conventional disciplines and must be studied wherever it is found. Lewin's initial reaction, as a student of neural networks, was that civilizations were a different order of phenomena (as indeed Kroeber argued in his distinction of organic and superorganic). But Kauffman changed his mind, concluding that cultural and biological worlds shared structures of complexity.

Lewin's introduction to complexity for lay readers, subtitled "life at the edge of chaos," is both a description of the point where nonlinear, nonrecursive patterns arise and a metaphor for the rapidly changing face of contemporary science. Chaos opens up new visions of order accessible to human understanding. Lewin begins and ends with a single powerful cultural example, the population and depopulation of Chaco Canyon in the American Southwest; "The View from Chaco Canyon" leads to the metaphorical "View from the Edge." Order in a global system is an emergent property, impossible to pin down in detail but possible to model as a process. The "edge of chaos" entails modeling of intermittency.

A millennium before our own time, Chaco Canyon was the center of Anasazi culture, "a web of economic, political, and religious influence that encompassed more than a hundred thousand square miles" (Lewin 1992:2). The "exuberance" of the culture was reflected in its architecture, its irrigation for farming under marginal conditions, and its symbolic system (Lewin 1992:5). A road thirty feet wide and straight regardless of land contour transcended mere function, despite its role linking 150 to 200 outlying settlements spread over a hundred-mile span yet sharing "a unified social system of some kind" (Lewin 1992:6). Stone, pottery, seashells, and turquoise were imported from distant locations, probably for seasonal ritual occasions; yet the central Great Houses of Chaco Canyon were not densely populated.

Lewin began to think about these matters at a conference called "Organization and Evolution of Southwestern Prehistoric Societies" at the Santa Fe Institute, established in 1984 to study "general phenomena," including those of culture, from interdisciplinary perspectives. Questions about "the larger pattern of Southwest prehistory" included the failure of maize agriculture to modify dramatically the scale of social organization over three millennia, with a "burst of new forms of social organization" after about A.D. 200, a regional center in Chaco Canyon between 900 and A.D. 1150, and a permanent (so far) collapse thereafter (Lewin 1992:9). These phenomena are precisely the kinds that Kroeber discussed as florescences and declines for the world's historically attested civilizations. Archaeology as well as complexity theory have progressed considerably since Kroeber's day.

Anthropologists and biologists, however, usually lack the mathematical modeling skills to describe complexity at Chaco Canyon. Only computers can model the mathematical deep order of complex nonlinear systems: "We're looking for the fundamental rules that underlie all these systems, not just the details of any one of them" (Chris Langdon in Lewin 1992:1). Murray Gell-Mann suggests that human societies are "in effect, kinds of cultural DNA," with "institutions, customs, traditions, and myths" as their schemata. As Kroeber dimly realized: "Complex adaptive systems are pattern seekers" (Lewin 1992:15); the units are not individual biological organisms.

Far beyond Newtonian mechanics, predictability eludes grasp in nonlinear chaotic systems. Yet surface complexity is "generated by a relatively simple set of subprocesses," although their particular interaction cannot be specified precisely (Lewin 1992:12). A biological ecosystem, the modern capitalist economy, and the archaeology of Chaco Canyon, perhaps even human consciousness, clarify and exemplify similar forms of order (Lewin 1992:13–14). Kroeber, although lacking the tools to formulate systematically the order in complexity, grappled with a similar insight.

Meanwhile, back at Chaco Canyon in about A.D. 200, a rapid "phase transition" from foraging bands to a more specialized social organization produced more intense pottery utilization, irrigation, and increasing sedentarism tending toward state formation (Lewin 1992:17). The cultural expansion at Chaco Canyon paralleled the process in the Cambrian explosion of faunal forms recorded in the fossils of the Burgess shales and exemplifying Stephen Jay

Gould's punctuated equilibrium theory of natural selection. In both cases, a "vacant ecology" produced a "coincidence" of biological and cultural patterns, an "increase in variety of social conventions" (Lewin 1992:18). By A.D. 1100, Chaco Canyon had reached maximum exploitation of this cultural/ecological niche. Both social and biological evolution involved "an initial scatter of new forms, and then it gets harder and harder to improve on them" (Kauffman in Lewin 1992:19).

Anthropologists have attempted classifications of band, tribe, chiefdom, and state—in which Kroeber (e.g., 1939) was much interested; but local variations and unilinear classificatory schema have plagued such neo-evolutionary models. Chaco Canyon, for example, lacks the "monumental architecture and elaborate burials" usually associated with a chiefdom (Lewin 1992:20). More interesting than the categories of a static typology is the virtual equivalence of the archaeologists' "hinge points," evolutionary biologists' "punctuations," and physicists' "phase transitions" (Lewin 1992:20). The patterns Kroeber identified intuitively were the "attractors, states to which the system eventually settled, depending on the properties of the system" (Lewin 1992:20). The pattern around an attractor, produced by population interaction, was more stable than the sequence or content/form. With implicit caution for the traditional neo-evolutionary models of social structure, Langdon notes that each evolutionary system is unique, "so you can't compare them directly with anything" (Langdon in Lewin 1992:22).

Complexity emerges spontaneously and appears to increase over time. Nonetheless, order comes with a price, particularly in the vulnerability of the system to breakdown. To equate complexity with progress, therefore, is a dangerous conflation deeply embedded in Western cultural practices. Stated in extreme form by Gould: "Progress is a noxious, culturally embedded, untestable, nonoperational idea that must be replaced if we wish to understand the patterns of history" (Gould in Lewin 1992:139). Belief in progress is wish fulfillment, to which anthropologists are much prone. Fascination with consciousness is another "punctuation in the history of life" (Lewin 1992:146) with which humans may be overly preoccupied.

Causes of the collapse at Chaco Canyon, including drought, are unique to this system, whether or not human land use was a contributing factor. But the very fact of collapse confirms the overall cyclic pattern predicted by complexity theory (Lewin 1992:194). The focus shifted briefly to Mesa Verde, previously on the periphery of the cultural climax, before a further collapse. Once the balance supporting the network of communities destabilized, decline proceeded apace.

Complexity theory has been applied to a wide variety of systems in nature and culture, including the origin of life, the dynamics of evolution, the complexity of human societies, and the earth itself as a global system. Richard Nemesvari even applies the concept of strange attractors to interpretation of successive generations of passion and destruction in *Wuthering Heights,* a novel that seems to break with the controlled order of most English fiction of its time. The apparent opposition of nonlinear dynamical systems is resolved into interdependence of the characters with the aperiodic recurrence characteristic of a chaotic system. Households framed on the moors create a "representative microcosmic system" (Nemesvari 1997:16). Expectations that class will determine social relationships dissolve before the chaotic interactive system created among the characters; the results are patterned across a variety of scales but are not predictable. Interpretation from outside the chaotic system leaves gaps in explanation—the failures of interpretation that so plagued Kroeber's civilizational investigations.

Human ecodynamics is an emerging field of particular interest to archaeologists. Complexity theory reaches beyond functionalist ecology to coevolutionary process focusing on human-modified environments. Despite its counter-intuitive feel and the absence of simple cycles for nonlinear dynamic systems, chaos theory explains why humans cannot be neutral observers of interdependent socionatural systems. The reciprocity within any such system defies conventional predictability, producing irreversible self-organization, encompassing random variation, and entraining recursive patterns at "higher scalar levels" (McGlade 1995:117, after Prigogine and Stengers 1984). Agricultural communities are less stable "than their natural counterparts" because of weeds, insects, and disease; the ecosystem, much simpler than any natural one, thereby becomes more vulnerable to destabilization. Population increase then makes perturbation-dependent systems "brittle" and dependent on "a chain of managed causalities" in a resilient "metastable" relationship of "multiple domains of attraction" evaluated by their ability to absorb and utilize change (McGlade 1995:124–25). Coevolutionary arguments reconstitute the traditional life sciences, with environment and ecosystem no longer existing independently of human social systems. Such emergent organization requires no external intervention. Generalization, then, must rest on issues of scale of observation and boundedness of socionatural systems. Human agency, in a way that would have intrigued Kroeber, is minimized in such a nonfunctionalist model.

Issues of scale are crucial to anthropological adaptations of complexity theory. "What is required is a recognition of the value of perspective, without the assumption that the universe is a totally knowable, integrated totality" (Gare 1995:107). At simpler levels of more detailed observation, patterns are easier to identify; the exemplar is the fractal coastline, self-similar but not quite replicated at multiple scales. Anthropologists are constrained by the scale of human observation, resulting in a characteristic method wherein the "relativizing effect of knowing other perspectives exist gives the observer a constant sense that any one approach is only ever partial" (Strathern 1991:xiv). This approach challenges anthropologists' traditional "stereotyped defensiveness about the small-scale nature of their own forays into complex societies" (Strathern 1991:25); the discipline has *chosen* a scale of observation, not merely accepted it as entailed by the study of isolated small-scale societies. Anthropology, as an interest group within the social sciences, has a "point of view from which the world is evaluated" (Strathern 1991:31), which retains "the participant's right to passionate criticism" (Strathern 1991:32).

Thus any standpoint, for example, the feminist one, will be partial because gender is not the whole person. Pluralism thus "creates a discourse encompassable by no single participant" (Strathern 1991:34). Totality recedes before a series of partisan positions. Consequently, anthropologists' generalizations based on Native points of view may be reread as "enlargements" framing the activation of social relationships at a wider scale (Strathern 1991:104); potential loss of information is not necessarily failure to conform to the same nonlinear pattern. In Strathern's view, anthropological comparison balances sets of complexity "suspended" in "relativity" (Strathern 1991:108). Further, the "exchange of perspectives" requires the ethnographer to take a standpoint independent from that of his or her consultants; to share viewpoints is to forego complexity.

The indissolubility of an interactive system from within mirrors the observer effect so crucial to the humanistic or historicist pole of the Boasian paradigm. The "recursive epistemology" of Gregory Bateson can be read as an oscillation between observer standpoint at the methodological center and distance from which observation is possible at the margins (Harries-Jones 1995:9). Anticipating chaos theory, Bateson de-emphasized human agency, seeking patterns in which human consciousness and the self-organization of

organic systems were virtually indistinguishable. Progress in learning or thinking, then, involved awareness of the self moving into new systems of relations
(Harries-Jones 1995:43). For Bateson, reflexivity was the key to coevolution;
"the pattern which connects" was not restricted to the human domain (Harries-Jones 1995:178). Recursive systems create gaps that are the space for imagination; only humility in application of the human moral order to the natural
world can produce an interconnected sustainable development (Harries-Jones
1995:223). Interestingly, it is the anthropologist dealing with complexity who
breaks through the failure of Kroeber's superorganic concept of culture to deal
with the creativity and freedom to act of the individual in culture, a potential
dehumanization of the human and natural worlds shared by much work
within the emerging chaos/complexity paradigm.

Style, Women's Fashion, and Cultural Wholes

After the failure of his grand synthesis in *Configurations of Culture Growth*,
Kroeber revisited the impulse to model patterns after the relationship between
style and civilization. He still wanted to know how civilizations happen. They
were, he claimed, among the most "complex" and "subtle" phenomena
known to us (Kroeber 1957:1). Kroeber assumed their causes must be equally
complex, although that now seemed less clear than in 1944.

On a scale considerably smaller than that of the cultural whole, Kroeber
worried another topic through successive instantiations. He first tried to write
about fluctuations in women's fashions and their correlation with political
and social unrest in 1919, returned to the question in more statistical terms in
1940, and revisited the implications in 1957 in *Style and Civilization*. The volume title suggests that, for Kroeber, the question was closely related to that of
Configurations of Culture Growth. This work was his most successful application of the argument about the autonomy of the impersonal superorganic level
of culture.

Even while speaking about "style," seemingly individual in locus, Kroeber
insisted upon "the superpersonal flow of form," arguing that dress fashions
"arise obscurely, are due to undetermined causes, and are almost wholly
shaped and executed, as well as accepted and used anonymously, by the great
nameless throng" (Kroeber 1952 [1949]:127). Kroeber was fascinated by what
Clyde Kluckhohn called the "covertness" of value patterns, with lack of awareness underscoring their impersonal quality. Indeed, "much of the collective in

culture" was a product of irrationality at the level of the individual (Kroeber 1952 [1949]:130).

Dress fashion intrigued Kroeber because it was "so fluidly capricious" yet was susceptible to quantitative and objective characterization. In 1919 he spoke "blithely of law or at least of order and regularity in civilization" (Kroeber 1952 [1919]:334). The language of Kroeber's pattern statements included "rhythm," "beat," and "underlying pulsation" (Kroeber 1952 [1919]:334). The march of fashion followed a cycle longer than the normal human life, underscoring that its consistencies could not be attributed to the actions of individuals.

This early optimism reflected delight in finding culture patterns at all. But Kroeber acknowledged that he was not then "seeking to establish recurrent uniformities between different cultures" (Kroeber 1952:329). The iterative cycles of culture growth, for him, resuscitated the comparative project of evolutionary anthropology with more reliable methodology.

Statistical analysis moved from impasse to "short-term and individual fluctuations of fashion," without ever leaving "the cultural level" (Kroeber 1952: 329). With Jane Richardson, Kroeber summarized three hundred years of dress fashion. The resulting correlation was not about the internal relationships determining changes in fashion but "more a matter of adjustive relations between basic patterns of different segments of culture" (Kroeber 1952:358). Kroeber identified consistent "oscillations," with a full cycle taking about a century; he then attributed the correspondence of this duration with the length of the average business cycle to "coincidence" (Kroeber with Richardson 1940; Kroeber 1952:359). He speculated that dress patterns might, like language, respond to "unconscious patterning," Sapir's term for speakers' knowledge of the grammar of their own languages. Alternatively, extremes of proportion could succeed one another through internal momentum. "Nonstylistic" or psychological factors were acknowledged but deemed irrelevant to cultural analysis (Kroeber 1952 [1940]:368).

"Both style and civilizations are sociocultural phenomena" (Kroeber 1957: 149). A style was necessarily selective, assuming selection among alternatives (Kroeber 1957:150). "Style" had predictive value because it reflected historical connections (Kroeber 1957:2). Dress styles "can be stated more precisely" and "supported by more objective evidence" than art styles. Utility, erotic allure, social effect, and novelty interacted creatively to produce a "rate of change which tends to be constant" albeit "frivolous" (Kroeber 1957:8). Dress styles moved in a pendulum, while art styles exhausted themselves (Kroeber 1957:10). The com-

plexity of a whole-culture "configuration" did not yield to overall characterization as easily as a "style" in a limited domain of a single culture.

Richardson and Kroeber identified a calm period between 1835 and 1905,
preceded by "at least 45 agitated and fluctuating years" and followed by at least
30 years of "instability" (Kroeber 1957:11). Kroeber was still intrigued by the
mechanism of the correlation between women's clothing styles and "decades
of social and political unrest" (Kroeber 1957:12). If he were to "guess" about
the intervening two decades, the "restlessness" would probably have subsided
(Kroeber 1957:15). Both domains were unsettled (form), but the particular directions of dress pattern change (content) were not predetermined (Kroeber
1957:17). The ideal shapes of women's dress in a variety of cultures were "expressions of something long enduring in the civilization" (Kroeber 1957:21).
That is, fashion changes proceeded from or around a baseline. Thus "fashion
style works *against* its basic pattern" in times of war and revolution (Kroeber
1957:21). Perhaps the correlation was not so arbitrary after all!

Kroeber went on to suggest that there might be "analogues of certain qualities of styles . . . in the forms of life itself," speculating "on how the immediacy
of our knowledge affects the course of science" and the distinctions between
civilizations and individuals (Kroeber 1957:58). Great men and their social
contexts became almost sides of the same coin, or at least there was "no conflict" between them (Kroeber 1957:58). *Configurations of Culture Growth* convinced Kroeber that artists frequently appeared "standing outside a constella-
tion, randomly alone" (Kroeber 1957:59).

"Any whole-culture style that may be discoverable must be regarded as composite in origin, secondary, and derivative." But Boasian diffusion took borrowed elements and created "a construct built up from particulars" (Kroeber
1957:71). Any anthropologist was aware that "small societies" were not highly
differentiated internally; "the mass of the culture is modest, compared with
that of a great civilization." Kroeber concluded that it behooved his colleagues
"to transfer their approach from their little cultures to the great ones" with "a
strong faith that they also possess a pervasive unity and a strong internal coordination that can be formulated" (Kroeber 1957:72).

Setting the Stage for a New Concept of Culture

Robert Redfield, most notably among Kroeber's younger contemporaries, attempted to draw the societies traditionally studied by anthropologists into the

larger context of civilization. Accepting the Chicago School of Sociology axiom that cohesive local societies changed with the advent of "the atomized, heterogeneous, disorganized city," he contrasted the "moral order of the folk" and the "technological order of civilization" (Wolf 1982:11); Wolf's critique rests on Redfield's failure to see the interconnections of center and periphery, how the "people without history" are in fact part of the larger history of European expansion and conquest.

For Redfield, the moral order attained new degrees of order in civilization, "marked by self-consciousness, . . . sense of deprivation, and . . . conscious creativeness" (Redfield 1953:50). Internal growth and meeting of peoples (i.e., diffusion) combined to create particular cultural developments. Redfield suggested that "style of life" captured "what is most fundamental and enduring about the ways of a group persisting in history" (Redfield 1953:51). Civilization was an outgrowth or "transformation" of "the primitive world" (the title image of Redfield's Cornell lectures on the philosophy of history). Redfield was intrigued by the possibility, against the expectations of the cultural evolutionists, that "people with very different specific contents of culture may have very similar views of the good life" (Redfield 1953:52). Both "culture" and "style of life" "imply some harmony of parts and some continuity through time" (Redfield 1953:52), although Redfield professed himself unable to describe "the specific styles of life which civilization creates" (Redfield 1953:53). Like Kroeber, he retreated from the complexity of civilizations to their parts understood as styles.

Redfield directly addressed Kroeber's understanding of progress in culture or civilization, praising him because he "found more than Boas had found" (Redfield 1953:160). Despite his austere methodology, Kroeber attempted to pin down the cumulative character of technology and science, acknowledged a "transformation in judgment" with lessened reliance on magic and superstition, and noted declining obsession with "the outstanding physiological events of human life" (Redfield 1953:160–61). According to Redfield, ignoring the failures of generalization in *Configurations of Culture Growth*, Kroeber decided that, overall, the human race was moving through history toward civilization. More interestingly for Redfield, Kroeber "identified here a change in human valuing" or ethical judgment (Redfield 1953:161). Redfield concluded that the relativism of anthropology could be exaggerated: "I think we do in fact appraise the conduct of primitive people by standards different from those by which we judge civilized people and yet also . . . according to the historic trend which has tended to make the totality of human conduct more decent and more human." (Redfield 1953:163) Local customs were all very well but universal standards were eventually applied, whether reflexively or otherwise. Redfield was clear that this "double standard of ethical judgment toward primitive peoples is a part of my version of cultural relativity" (Redfield 1953:163). He held his values as a product of his own civilization.

Alexander Goldenweiser took a position more akin to Kroeber's when he argued that "the differentia of individual civilizations" had no predictable determinants in biology, environment, psychology, history, or sociology. Rather, culture operated autonomously "in the specific historical fates of each local culture in its particular geographical and historical setting" (Goldenweiser 1922:401). Any attempt to arrange civilizations in "ascending series" caused them "to break up into their constituent elements, each of which has undergone a distinctive development . . . in degree and in kind" (Goldenweiser 1922:126). Goldenweiser was adamant that "no parallelism except of a most general sort" existed "between the different aspects of each civilization" (Goldenweiser 1922:127).

Indeed, his textbook on *Early Civilization* treated each of his five text cases (the Eskimos, the Tlingits and Haidas, the Iroquois, the people of Uganda, and the people of Central Australia) from three different standpoints: economic and industrial development; art, religion and magic; and social structure. Goldenweiser refused to admit any difference in kind. His five tribes "insofar as they are *primitive*" (his emphasis) remain "first and foremost human civilizations, displaying the static and dynamic characteristics which are encountered in every organized human society" (Goldenweiser 1922:117). Not only was the psychological make-up of "the mind of primitive man" similar across cultures and civilizations, but civilization itself reflected "common humanity" (Goldenweiser 1922:115). What we call civilization arose from "creativeness of the individual," "psychological and sociological inertia," and "historic relations between human groups" (Goldenweiser 1922:300–301). Imported elements were always present; thus diffusion had much to offer, especially relative to evolution.

Eric Wolf draws on Kroeber's comparative understanding of "the dimensions and limits of human nature" through "the most extreme expressions" of culture (Wolf 1999:16–17). To Kroeber's example of ancient Mexican human sacrifice, Wolf added National Socialist Germany (the moral dilemma of his own coming of age) and Boas's Kwakiutls with their "unusual intensity of cultural activity" (Kroeber 1962:61) in potlatch giveaways. The very flamboyance and the "high drama" of these cases, as Kroeber suggested, shed light on the range of human nature, the links between power and ideas through history (Wolf 1999:16–17). Wolf explicitly attributes his ethnographic method of "descriptive integration" to Kroeber and Redfield (Wolf 1999:18).

Nonetheless, *Envisioning Power* takes the heirs of Kroeber to task for failing to go beyond culture "as a self-generating and self-propelling mental apparatus of norms and rules for behavior" (Wolf 1999:19). Stresses leading to "ecological, social, political, or psychological crises" (Wolf 1999:274) in these three cases lead Wolf to compare Kwakiutl, Aztec, and Nazi extremisms as similar in their historical relations to power despite differences in surface form and degrees of cultural elaboration.

The opposition of civilization and culture is false. If the concept of culture is to retain its utility, "we must transform it" (Wolf 1999:287), a worthy challenge because we still don't understand "how the human mind can produce such great socially patterned variability" (Wolf 1999:288). The culture concept, in fact, still enables anthropologists to link ethnographic particularism to theoretical insight: "The concept of culture remains serviceable as we move from thinking about what is generically human to the specific practices and understandings that people devise and deploy to deal with their circumstances. It is precisely the shapeless, all-encompassing quality of the concept that allows us to draw together—synoptically and synthetically—material relations to the world, societal organization, and configurations of ideas. Using 'culture,' therefore, we bring together what might otherwise be kept separate" (Wolf 1999:288). Kroeber is right in this analysis, that anthropology's uniqueness resides in its capacity to revamp the culture concept from superorganic rigidity to a more open-ended, flexible future.

Johannes Fabian, among the most vocal critics of the culture concept that has dominated North American anthropology throughout the Boasian century, envisions culture as a complex entity existing "outside individual minds" (Fabian 1998:x), essentially Kroeber's position. Fabian is eager not to throw out the baby with the bathwater, even though cultural difference, culture in the plural, has suffered from overemphasizing intellectualism. He juxtaposes the "deconstructive, nonontological, nonpersonal" strand of contemporary culture theory (embodied in Foucault as well as in Kroeber) from the "constructive notion of culture as praxis," speaking of popular culture rather than of "culture 'tout court,'" entity rather than process (Fabian 1998:xi, 1). Indeed, for Fabian, global systems theory reenacts Kroeberian reification of culture.

"Popular culture" allows Fabian to emphasize process and discursive strate-gies producing knowledge of it. Arguably, Kroeber used "style" and "fashion" to similar ends. This framing discourse maintains the ethnographer in the foreground and acknowledges ongoing and negotiated relations of power, "moments of freedom" from constraint or determinism; ethnography remains a powerful form of knowing because such freedoms, like culture, exist only in the plural (Fabian 1998:21). Contradiction necessarily remains at the center of the popular culture discourse. Fabian aspires to break down anthropology's historical obsession with the "other" as "doomed" "disappearing objects" (Fa-bian 1998:24). Like anthropology, popular culture at its best challenges author-ity: "Could it be that anthropology, at least for moments, actually parodies, subverts, and resists imperialism—not so much by intentions or correct politi-cal attitudes as by its practices and creations, the way popular culture chal-lenges the powers that be?" (Fabian 1998:31).

Fabian, failing to acknowledge Kroeber's use of time sequence when avail-able, is highly critical of Kroeber's penchant for privileging space over time at the core of his history: "In older versions, practices counted as (parts of) cul-ture only if they could be assigned to distinctive geographic areas . . . A meth-odological corollary of such a theory was that culture—never mind how much its inner, organic, or ideal unity was celebrated—was thought of as a combina-tion of parts. A static record, the spatial distribution of elements, called culture traits, could then be translated into history; spatially bounded culture areas could be understood as traditions" (Fabian 1998:71).

In Fabian's view, Kroeber's spatial approach to diachrony was static because it assumed that culture traits and patterns would hold still for the analyst to study them. The individual, both as observer and as creator of culture, failed to emerge. Contemporary studies of ethnicity and globalization have similar Kroeberian limitations because they foreground space rather than time. The actual relationship between ethnicity, identity, and local conditions is consid-erably more complex (Fabian 1998:74–75). Examples, including "fashions of dress," musical and dance styles, visual art, and religious movements, are con-sumed around the world, encouraging a fusion of time and space that elides the detail of actual cultural circumstances, moving betwixt the global and the local specifics (Fabian 1998:81).

The debate over reenvisioning culture continues—and we will return to it in Chapter 8. What remains intriguing about Kroeber's position, however, is that it has invited caricature, an easy target for those who want to emphasize the individual in relation to culture or to historicize the discipline in more processual ways than Kroeber was able to devise; at the same time, culture as superorganic has stimulated ongoing debate, both within anthropology and in the wider history of the sciences and social sciences in mainstream Western culture. Kroeber's concept of the superorganic has proved inadequate but refuses to go away; it is the nearly inevitable starting point for revisionist theorizings.

EDWARD SAPIR

CHAPTER 3

Culture Internalized

Kroeber's paper on the superorganic in 1917 sparked a flurry of minor rebellion among the core Boasians. The early students had divided up their mentor's anthropological program, each pursuing a focus somewhat narrower than Boas's own (see Figure 1, Chapter 1). It was as if the six blind men of Hindustan had poked about at an elephant named culture and reached very different understandings of its essential attributes. Kroeber in particular retained a touching faith that the diverse investigations of his fellow Boasians would delineate a unified beast whose overall configuration would assure disciplinary autonomy and scientific prestige to anthropology. Kroeber's ambitions were institutional as well as intellectual, including loyalty to anthropology. During the First World War, about which Boas and many of his former students were lukewarm, German and/or Jewish intellectuals with radical political leanings were, at the very least, suspect to an American scientific elite focused on patriotism and the utility of scientific results (Stocking 1968:274). In this context, Kroeber's position seemed to him so self-evident that he was taken aback by the backlash to the "superorganic" from at least some of his own comrades in arms.

Polarization of his former students' positions reflected tensions inherent in Boas's foundational position—scientific vs. historical method, historical reconstruction vs. the psychological world implicit in the Native point of view, and determinative constraint vs. the creative capacity of culture itself. The Boasians divided this terrain according to their personal inclinations, with Kroeber, Lowie, and Spier generally following a culturological path, while Goldenweiser, Radin, Sapir, and Benedict chose a more psychological line of reasoning than Lowie's relatively "pedestrian" version of the collective research program (Lowie 1959:133). Goldenweiser retrospectively characterized Lowie as the "Gibraltar of scientific orthodoxy in American anthropology"

(Goldenweiser 1941:159); this was not entirely a compliment. Kroeber, despite a "many-sidedness" equaled only by Boas, misguidedly insisted on superorganic culture, boxing history into culture trait distributions; Goldenweiser blamed Kroeber's psychological defensiveness on a "rich personality" trying to be "safe" rather than innovative (Goldenweiser 1941:158).

Both Lowie and Kroeber implicitly worried that Sapir, Radin, and Goldenweiser somehow were cheating, that their version of the Boasian dispensation glossed over the essential features of the core concept of culture, that what the mavericks focused on was peripheral to the real business of anthropology. Goldenweiser waxed ecstatic over Sapir's "genius" in analyzing linguistic form and praised his later work, using similar models for linguistics and culture, as "cultural studies": Sapir "turned to culture, both primitive and modern," with a characteristic psychiatric approach. "In his preoccupation with the individual he became a leader among the 'moderns'" (Goldenweiser 1941:159). Kroeber presumably remained among the "ancients."

Lowie was the sole core Boasian seemingly unthreatened by the divergence of views among his contemporaries. Boas's students "have often differed from their teacher and from each other," while Kroeber as well as Sapir and Radin, "have repeatedly expressed their dissent from cardinal 'Boasian' views, and even I have uttered misgivings on certain points" (Lowie 1963:412). Indeed, Lowie, also retrospectively, saw the differences as more significant than the similarities, at least in contexts within the in-group. Healthy debate would lead to scientific progress; he contributed to it by combating heresies within Boasian ranks.

Internal revolt was spearheaded by Sapir, the most literary and humanistic of the initial cohort. In 1917, Sapir was oblivious to undertones of conflict among his Boasians, enraptured by his own exploration of psychoanalysis and belles lettres, the seeds of a nascent synthesis around the locus of culture in the individual, the creative capacity of culture itself (from the standpoint of the individual), and the potential variability of a culture across its members. His position, first articulated in response to Kroeber's manifesto on the superorganic, anticipates much of the contemporary critique of the anthropological concept of culture. Although Sapir did not fully develop the implications of his own position, in part because of his premature death in 1939 at the age of fifty-five, his revisions of the received Boasian tradition constitute a genuinely alternative culture theory. The initial formulation challenged Kroeber's reification of culture and marginalization of individual agency. The turn to psychology during the interwar years established the legitimacy of this alternative within American anthropology that was pursued by many among Sapir's successors, largely under the rubric of culture and personality. Sapir himself preferred to frame the question as "the impact of culture on personality." During the 1930s at Yale's Institute of Human Relations, he was forced into a new defense of symbolic and qualitative concepts of culture against encroaching behaviorism.

Significant features of the Sapirian alternative include: the relation of group and individual, the effect of the creative individual in a given cultural context, the impact of culture (through socialization) on individual creativity, variability and management of conflict in social organization as well as in normative cultural principle, the relation of life history and individual self-fulfillment to the viability of cultures as wholes, the symbolic consensual character of culture itself, and the lack of essential disjuncture between "primitive" and "modern" at the level of individual personalities. These questions remain intelligible, even pressing, half a century after Sapir's death.

The significance of the Sapirian alternative was elided for intervening generations by the omission of "Do We Need a Superorganic?" from the canonical edition of Sapir's papers in 1949. David Mandelbaum clarified this editorial decision to his collaborators: "The later personality papers make the same points and more incisively without the kind of personal reference that this reply necessarily has" (Mandelbaum to Murray Emeneau, Harry Hoijer, and Verne Ray, 21 July 1947, Sapir family documents). Rather than acknowledging these rifts as necessary parts of a vital normal science, Mandelbaum attempted to showcase Boasian unity (and perhaps placate Kroeber, given the California publication venue) by sweeping internal dissent under the rug. Whatever the short-term merits of this decision, the consequence was to bury fundamental differences in perspective among the Boasians and mask continuities to the revisionist social science of our own day.

Anthropology without the Superorganic

"Do We Need a Superorganic?" was the opening salvo in Sapir's articulation of a theory of culture firmly grounded in the Boasian paradigm even while moving beyond it. The rhetorical flourish of Sapir's title in responding to Kroeber's 1917 paper exemplifies his self-conscious opposition to cultural determinism, his awareness that culture and the individual were merely sides of the same coin within the domain of human behavior carved out by the fledgling discipline of anthropology. Sapir's opposition to culture as superorganic was not yet tied directly to interdisciplinary excursions into psychology and psychiatry; he was just beginning to read seriously about psychiatry and psychoanalysis (Darnell 1986b; Darnell, Irvine, and Handler 1999: section 3). In his critique of Kroeber's position, Sapir attempted to redefine the historical pole of Boasian anthropology to focus on individual action and motivation in addition to the impersonal forces of culture, even in the case of unwritten traditions where individual biography remained methodologically inaccessible in the past beyond the reach of oral history.

When Kroeber's piece appeared, Sapir assessed his likelihood of successfully challenging the status of the superorganic as Boasian orthodoxy. He tested the waters to Lowie (10 July 1917, UCB), characterizing Kroeber's argument as "dogmatism and shaky metaphysics." Kroeber's "excessive undervaluation" of the role of the individual in history was mere "abstractionist fetishism"; Sapir indulged in the very psychologizing that Kroeber deplored. Were he to reply in the *American Anthropologist,* as he was considering, Sapir hoped fellow Boasians would also protest.

Only Goldenweiser took him up on it. His approach was to treat Kroeber's superorganic as "peculiarly his own" rather than as speaking for Boasian anthropology as a whole (Goldenweiser 1917:448). Its implicit cultural determinism would prove inadequate in particular cases because it was merely quantitative and ignored the accidents of history and the actions of individuals on their cultures. Indeed, the sui generis quality of Kroeber's superorganic was better located in the "biographical individual" as constituting a "historic complex." Each individual uniquely combined "biological, psychological, and civilizational factors," with history as the outcome (Goldenweiser 1917:448). No superorganic was needed.

Kroeber responded to Sapir's public attack (24 July 1917, UCB) with a further disclaimer: He saw himself as merely codifying Boasian practice (implicitly thereby staking out a territory for North American anthropology with himself as its spokesperson). Somewhat patronizingly, he attempted to persuade Sapir that there was no fundamental disagreement: "I've left absolutely everything to the individual that anyone can claim who will admit to the social at all . . . What misleads you is merely that you fall back on the social at such occasional times as you're through with the individual; whereas I insist on an unqualified place, an actuality, for the social at all times" (Kroeber to Sapir, 24 July 1917, UCB. Sapir's response (29 October 1917, UCB) acknowledged a "common tendency" to avoid "conceptual science" in favor of history. Psychology should remain "in its place as much as possible." The magnitude and character of that place remained tactfully unstated in the interest of surface consensus.

Kroeber was less than mollified, charging that Sapir failed to meet his duty to encourage the growth of the Boasian discipline: "I don't give a red cent whether cultural phenomena have a reality of their own, as long as we treat them as if they had. You do, most of us do largely . . . If we're doing anything right, it deserves a place in the world. Let's take it, instead of being put in a corner. That's not metaphysics; it's blowing your own horn" (Kroeber to Sapir, n.d. November 1917, UCB) Kroeber's position was conventional in the social sciences. Sociologist William Fielding Ogburn chided Sapir (31 December 1917, NMM) that Kroeber's superorganic model was much more useful; it led to pragmatic, explanatory analyses. Sociologists, of course, were even less inclined by professional socialization than anthropologists to focus upon the role of the individual in culture and history. Sapir clarified to Ogburn his "rather heterodox" views of the individual in history: history "in terms of book formulae that take no account of the individual is, to my mind, but a passing phase of our hunger for conventional scientific capsules into which to store our concepts" (Sapir to Ogburn, 14 January 1918, NMM).

Sapir never changed his mind, writing to Kroeber only months before his death:

> Of course, I'm interested in culture patterns, linguistic included. All I claim is that their consistencies and spatial and temporal persistences can be, and ultimately should be, explained in terms of humble psychological formulations with particular emphasis on interpersonal relations. I have no consciousness whatsoever of being revolutionary or of losing an interest in what is generally phrased in an impersonal way. Quite the contrary, I feel rather like a physicist who believes that immensities of the atom are not unrelated to the immensities of intersteller space. In spite of all you say to the contrary, your philosophy is pervaded by fear of the individual and his reality. (Sapir to Kroeber, 25 August 1938, UCB)

The study of the individual still seemed to him more interesting than that of culture, superorganically conceived. Explaining the latter in terms of the former was not reductionism but acknowledgement of levels of structure in the same phenomena.

At about the same time, Sapir (25 October 1938, published in Stocking

1980:8–10) wrote to Philip Selznick, then a student reflecting on culture and personality. Implicitly Sapir critiqued the work of Margaret Mead and Ruth Benedict, which then seemed to have carried the day, for its failure to distinguish properly between culture and the individual. Sapir separated himself from the "radical wing of anthropology," suggesting that only serious study of personality development and organization could clarify the complex interdependency between culture and the individual; Sapir was increasingly impressed by Freudian developmental models. Indeed, the insights of anthropology narrowly conceived "such ideas as cultural relativity and psychological reinterpretation of cultural forms," reached an impasse rapidly, going little beyond common sense. "Exotic" cultures could elucidate cultural history but not "the meaning of personality organization in cultural terms." Clinical experience, inaccessible to normal anthropological method, was the most productive approach. Benedict and Mead, in contrast, mistook mere analogies for "psychological realities." Such "'as if' psychological pictures" were far too "glib"; rigorous methodology was essential, scientific rather than "aesthetic or poetic." Sapir was a poet, but he knew the difference between poetry and science. He further cautioned the young Selznick that universals or normalities across cultures should not be dismissed out of hand; the psychiatric mandate to generalize about individuals everywhere had its merits.

Sapir's initial formulation, however, was internal to the Boasian paradigm. His published critique in 1917 was superficially tactful, although brutally frank in challenging Kroeber's personal objectivity (the "emotional impetus" of his argument) in presenting a position predicated on scientific objectivity. Sapir reformulated the stakes—shifting from the relation of organic and superorganic to the discrete methods of the natural and social sciences (cf. Boas 1887). The rejoinder began aggressively: "Nothing irritates a student of culture more than to have methods of the exact sciences flaunted in his face as a salutary antidote to his own supposedly slipshod methods" (Sapir 1999 [1917]:33; throughout this chapter, dates in brackets refer to the essay's original publication date). The anthropologist "deals with an entirely different order of phenomena" (Sapir 1999 [1917]:33); that order encompassed both the cultural and the individual.

Effort to soften the critique was qualified. Sapir granted that a "rigidly historical and anti-biological interpretation of culture" had some merits (though "rigidity" was hardly a positive attribute for him); further, the organic vs. social distinction held only "in the main," with considerable "doubts . . . on special points." Kroeber committed the "common fallacy of confounding the cultural advancement of a group with the potential or inherent intellectual power of its individual members" (Sapir 1999 [1917]:34).

Like Goldenweiser, Sapir relegated Kroeber's position to one of personal "standpoint" rather than of disciplinary foundation. Kroeber was "the victim of a too rigidly classificatory or abstractionist tendency" that "overshoots" the domain of the cultural relative to that of the individual (Sapir 1999 [1917]:34). Framing the argument in the language of standpoint both detracted from Kroeber's credibility in the particular debate and exemplified the more general Boasian position that standpoint resided at the epistemological core of social or historical science methodology.

"Standpoint" and the Individual in Culture

"Standpoint" functioned as something of a technical term in Boasian discourse of the interwar years (although "point of view" and other circumlocutions sometimes served as functional synonyms). Standpoint was particularly crucial to Sapir because of his focus on the creative capacity of the individual, both as member and as analyst of culture. But it was salient also in the work of some of his contemporaries and used in a way congruent with present-day feminist standpoint epistemology. In contemporary terms, Sapir's position would be characterized as epistemological realism; history and culture are constructed on the basis of real events, although no particular witness or authority can ever expect to arrive at an objective or final interpretation. Emphasis on standpoint in this self-conscious way establishes a substantive continuity from the qualitative side of the Boasian paradigm to contemporary theoretical perspectives (which, indeed, we might label as "standpoints"). Thus it is crucial to exemplify the pervasiveness and range of Boasian usage.

For Boas the position of the observer was the fundamental fact of science, which for him included anthropology. This is why he placed so much emphasis on "the Native point of view" and distinguished it analytically from his own anthropological standpoint as external observer. Boas's fundamental paper on the distinction between the social or human and the natural sciences in 1887 revolved around the crucial role of standpoint in determining the appropriate method to study fundamentally different kinds of phenomena: "From the standpoint we occupy," the two kinds of science must be taken on their own terms because inevitably any "judgment will be founded on the mental disposition [i.e., preconception] of the judge" as to the relative value of the aesthetic (the natural sciences) or the affective (the human sciences) (Boas 1940:140). History and geography, what Boas called "cosmography" in the manner of Alexander von Humboldt, fell with the arts because their study included "the way in which the mind is affected by the phenomena" being studied (Boas 1940:140).

Boas also used the term "standpoint" to gloss "the Native point of view." In "Some Principles of Museum Administration", Boas insisted on the multiple functions and meanings of an Indian pipe "which can be understood only when viewed from the standpoint of the social and religious life of the people" (Boas 1907:928). The observer must deliberately manipulate standpoint, the angle of vision, to transcend his or her own biases.

Standpoint was also closely linked to cultural relativism. In his introduction to Ruth Benedict's *Patterns of Culture*, Boas suggested that not every culture would have a dominant theme as did those Benedict selected for her analysis but that the motivations of the individual were the key to making intelligible the "relativity of what is considered social or asocial, normal or abnormal;" indeed, patterns of unfamiliar cultures necessarily appeared abnormal, even pathological, "when viewed from the standpoint of our civilization" (Boas in Benedict 1934b:xv). The task of the anthropologist, of course, was to invert the standpoint and translate the oddity of other cultures into a comprehensible normalcy.

Sapir understood standpoint as the positioning of the individual observer, whether within a culture studied by the anthropologist or of the individual anthropologist choosing a point of view appropriate to a particular problem. In "Culture, Genuine and Spurious in 1924," he asserted that the anthropological use of culture as something belonging to every human group, regardless of complexity, was a question of disciplinary standpoint (Sapir 1999 [1924]:48); analytic attention to the significance of particular culture traits in a given culture or civilization, for example, the French, also constituted a standpoint (Sapir 1999 [1924]:51).

Perhaps most crucially, given the theoretical importance he placed upon individual creativity, Sapir insisted that his focus was a standpoint, not an exclusion of the interest of culture as an alternative analytic standpoint (Sapir 1999 [1924]:62). His argument with Kroeber over the superorganic was unnecessary because the standpoints of the individual and culture were valid for different kinds of problems. Almost anything could be understood from multiple standpoints: "Even the Alphabet from this [psychiatric] standpoint becomes a datum of personality research. As a matter of fact, the alphabet does mean different things to different people" (Sapir 1999 [1938]:360).

An individual might illustrate religious behavior in his society from the standpoint of the social scientist without feeling the emotions usually entailed in that behavior within his society (Sapir 1999 [1926]:83); it was crucial not to confuse these standpoints. Of the two, analysis from the standpoint of "personal expression" posed the greater difficulty (Sapir 1999 [1927]:120). From the standpoint of a parent, for example, theories about personality conditioning failed to capture the "stubbornly nuclear" character of each child (Sapir 1999 [1930]:223). There were some things that the standpoint of "scientific theories" could do and others that it could not; the symbolism of "personal behaviour," for example, largely eluded the grasp of science (Sapir 1999 [1934]: 323).

Even linguistic structure, which many of Sapir's contemporaries took to be fixed and employed passively by speakers of a given language, boiled down to standpoint. Sapir was the American discoverer of the concept of the phoneme (Sapir 1925, 1933) which he understood as "unconscious behavior," "standpoint," and "psychological reality." In each case, he sought analytic language to discuss patterning that left room for individual creativity.

Cultural relativism, a kingpin of Boasian theory (see Chapter 5) was a generalization from standpoint. For Sapir, for example, the psychiatric concept of "adjustment" made no sense because it took for granted judgment "from the standpoint of the requirements, real or supposed, of a particular society" (Sapir 1999 [1932a]:289). Theoretical models that failed to acknowledge the positionality, but not necessarily the arbitrariness, of standpoint were inadequate models from the start. Anthropology offered its fellow social sciences a view from outside standpoints that otherwise were likely to persist without awareness of ethnocentrism. Objectivity did not disappear in Sapir's concept; rather, it was correlated with distance of the observer from the standpoint of self-interest that might jeopardize clear analysis: "The suggested classification is based on an analysis of groups from an objective standpoint; that is, from the standpoint of an observing non-participant or the standpoint of humanity or the nation or any other large aggregate in which the significance of the individual as such tends to be lost" (Sapir 1999 [1932a]:297). Standpoint transcended the position of the individual as actor.

The logic of standpoint also applied to the boundaries between scientific

disciplines: The same behavior could be social from the standpoint of the social scientist and individual from that of the psychologist (Sapir 1999 [1926]:
76). Both standpoints were legitimate, and neither need be condemned because they were not the same. Sapir's fondness for such a position was crucial
to his mediating role in the interdisciplinary social science synthesis of the
1920s and 1930s (see Darnell 1986a, 1990a for details); consensus was attainable if distinguished representatives of the various disciplines, predominantly
sociology, psychology, and anthropology, agreed to retain their particular approaches and evaluate other approaches as distinct in standpoint from their
own and, therefore, nonthreatening.

The usage closest to Sapir's among his contemporaries was that of Alexander Goldenweiser, his coconspirator in challenging Kroeber's superorganic
argument. On the one hand, Goldenweiser's 1922 textbook used standpoint to
argue that Northwest Coast art was "a many-sided cultural symbol, most intimately associated with almost every aspect of the life of the people" (Goldenweiser 1922:69); on the other hand, "a logical standpoint" external to the cultures studied might reveal contradictions, even to the point of establishing
something like the "primitive mentality" proposed by Lucien Lévy-Bruhl
(Goldenweiser 1922:386). The book was organized around three standpoints
from which "early civilization" could be viewed: the economic, the mythologi-
cal, and the sociopolitical (Goldenweiser 1922:127). Goldenweiser further employed standpoint with reference to theoretical options for the anthropologist,
for example, to refer to the choice of evolutionary theory or the absence of cultural traits an outside observer might expect (Goldenweiser 1922:125); theories
were ways of looking at things rather than statements of context-free truth.

Some Boasians used "standpoint" in more pragmatic ways, less as a source
of verifying different observations of the same reality than to critique points of
view other than their own. For example, Kroeber, for whom religion and
science were incommensurable, noted: "From the standpoint of strict reality
alone, the findings of religion are pure figments, whatever their claims"
(Kroeber 1952:159). The Native point of view was invalidated by the more authoritative "standpoint" of the scientist.

In Sapir's favorite metaphor, consistent with his reliance on "standpoint"
as a technical term, culture and the individual were two sides of the same coin.
The individual would always attempt to modify the "never-ending flux" of "the
form and content of social activity." From the standpoint of the culture, however, "the content of an individual's mind is so overwhelmingly moulded by

the social traditions to which he is heir that the purely individual contribution of even markedly original minds is apt to seem swamped in the whole of culture" (Sapir 1999 [1917]:34).

Sapir was interested primarily in the standpoint (my usage of the term, not his) of the individual: "It is always the individual that really thinks and acts and dreams and revolts" (Sapir 1999 [1917]:34). Such individual actions became "social data" when they "somehow contribute in sensible degree to the modification or retention of the mass of typical reactions called culture" (Sapir 1999 [1917]:34). This distinction, however, could only be applied from the analyst's point of view. The behaviors themselves, "psychologically considered," embodied no such dichotomy. The distinction was imposed and "essentially arbitrary, resting, as it does, entirely on a principle of selection." Moreover, this selection "depends on the adoption of a scale of values." It was not objective, but a matter of standpoint. Therefore: "Needless to say, the threshold of the social (or historical) *versus* the individual shifts according to the philosophy of the evaluator or interpreter. I find it utterly inconceivable to draw a sharp and eternally valid dividing line between them" (Sapir 1999 [1917]:34–35). Individual reactions thus "constantly spill over into and lend color to" social reactions. *This* was the kind of culture concept for which Sapir could muster enthusiasm.

Returning to Kroeber's version of culture, Sapir charged that it involved "a social determinism amounting to a religion to deny to individuals all directive power, all culture-moulding influence" (Sapir 1999:35). He argued that no mysterious "social force" was necessary to explain the cultural factor in inventions and scientific theories; rather, the apparent lack of individual control could be attributed to "the fixity, conceptually speaking, of the objective world" (Sapir 1999 [1917]:35). Therefore, the real issue was the historical vs. nonhistorical sciences, not the organic vs. superorganic realms of phenomena. "The social was but a name for those reactions or types of reaction" depending on "a cumulative technique of transference, that known as social inheritance"; this, at our present state of knowledge, "merely implies a heightening of psychic factors" (Sapir 1999 [1917]:37). It followed that the social sciences derived their peculiar character from "a modulus of values" rather than from "an accession of irresolvably distinct subject matter." The "unbridgeable chasm" between organic and psychic lay in "immediacy of experience" (Sapir 1999 [1917]:37).

Sapir declined to explore further the "philosophy of the nature of mind" that divided his position from Kroeber's, but it was there with a vengeance: "The break lies entirely in the principle of selection that respectively animates the two groups of sciences" (Sapir 1999 [1917]:37). The social sciences were different from psychology because of this selection rather than because of some mysterious superorganic force. Kroeber was further mistaken in attempting to deal with an experiential distinction of standpoint in terms of merely conceptual distinctions. What Sapir called "experiential irresolvability" was illustrated by geology, which was conceptually divisible into chemistry and physics but also dealt with the historical particulars of the "world of directly experienced phenomena from the ideal world of conceptual science" (Sapir 1999 [1917]:37). Sapir subtly reoriented Kroeber's example; experience had a human object and individuality that the collective behavior of polyps did not. Sapir professed himself bored by the conceptual (i.e., theoretical) sciences, preferring to learn or be surprised by the historical, experiential phenomena that encompassed the study of the individual rather than of the merely social or conceptual. History, then, became something very different for Sapir than for Kroeber: It involved the "'historical,' not conceptual, treatment of certain selected aspects of the psychic world of man" (Sapir 1999 [1917]:37).

(Interestingly, Sapir did not draw linguistic analogies in his culturological critique. His approach to linguistic patterning was indisputably superorganic; individual unconsciousness of grammatical categories and sound correspondences were the keys to historical inference on linguistic grounds [see Figure 2, Chapter 1]. The use of language in culture was what facilitated human creative capacities, which were not superorganic.)

Sapir then turned to the nature of generalization in the historical and non-historical sciences. A sociological law would retain its validity if 99 percent of known cases were consistent, despite failure to explain the lone (or rare) exception. A Newtonian physical law, in contrast, would be utterly discredited by a single counterexample: "There is something deeper involved here than relative accuracy. The social 'law' is an abbreviation or formula for a finite number of evaluated phenomena, and rarely more than an approximately accurate formula at that; the natural 'law' is a universally valid formulation of a regular sequence observable in an indefinitely large number of phenomena selected at random" (Sapir 1999:39). (The laws of quantum mechanisms, in contrast, are statistical, suggesting that the single counterexample critical method may be self-defeating, even in the natural sciences.)

In definitional matters Sapir believed he and Kroeber were in agreement. He differed, however, in finding it "perfectly possible to hold this view of history without invoking the aid of the 'superorganic'" (Sapir 1999:40). If Kroeber had focused more directly on "the uniqueness of historical phenomena," he would have had little reason to eliminate the individual as understood by Sapir. Nor would he have sought the wrong kind of historical generalizations. Despite its surface civility, the critique was devastating to Kroeber's case, indeed incommensurable with it.

The Anthropologist's Quest for "Genuine" Culture

Throughout his career, Sapir was determined that anthropology must offer North American society a critique of its own excesses, a return to values and scales of human contact less alienating to self-realization. *Bildung,* to become a cultured person, is the goal of education for the individual in the German-Jewish culture from which most of the early Boasians came (see Liss 1996). Sapir, after all, was a poet, who attributed to so-called primitives his own capacity for creative self-expression and reflexive cultural critique. Many of his colleagues failed to understand the humanistic and critical thrust of "Culture, Genuine and Spurious"; it was Sapir's declaration of individual and cultural relativism, a paean to quality in the Aristotelian sense. The ambiguity of method and vocabulary was reflected in its successive audiences. Its first section, Sapir's exegesis of the concept of culture, in and out of anthropology, appeared in *The Dial* in 1919 and, with a sequel, in *The Dalhousie Review* in 1922; both periodicals reached an educated general public. Only in 1924 did Sapir present a version targeted to his social science colleagues. It appeared in the *American Journal of Sociology,* the house organ of Chicago sociology, just as Sapir was moving to Chicago's joint sociology and anthropology department as a theoretician of culture. This was the piece he chose to introduce himself.

Sapir employed the terms "genuine" and "spurious" in two different senses. First, he wanted to counter the spurious popular idea that only high civilizations or the elite within them truly had culture. Genuineness was not dependent on level of civilization or societal complexity. Second, the paper's title dichotomy characterized the way in which every social system functioned to satisfy individual needs, including emotional and aesthetic as well as rational and intellectual. It followed that only the individual within a given culture had the capacity to assess its genuineness.

Contemporary responses to the paper ranged from appalled to nonplussed.

Ogburn warned Sapir (31 August 1922, NMM) that more obviously sociological vocabularies would produce more interesting results, showing the "varying parts of culture, correlation, original nature, and adaptation." It was "unscientific" not to separate science and art. "You seem to be struggling to articulate something that you feel emotionally rather than coldly and scientifically." Sapir's aesthetic intention to dissolve the art/science dichotomy was meaningless to Ogburn. In terms of the contemporary interdisciplinary critique of culture, however, his argument reads quite smoothly.

Sapir's discussion of three incommensurable definitions of culture attended least to the anthropological one (which he theorized against the grain of the Boasian mainstream). The emphasis of the anthropological construct on cultural contents decentered the "unifying feeling-tone" (Sapir 1999 [1924]:47), which linked genuine cultures across degrees of societal complexity. Whereas Kroeber was quite certain he knew what a culture was, at least in terms of an inventory of its elements, Sapir worried about what kind of a good thing culture was. He was careful to note, however, that the anthropological standpoint involved resistance to value judgment, that is, cultural relativism. One definition of a "genuine" intellectual was someone who could talk to what Radin called a "primitive philosopher."

Sapir also rejected the idea of an elite culture based on individual refinement, although he maintained its emphasis on the need for ideal types. Sapir's own class hang-ups emerged in his disdain for the snobbery and artificiality of what he saw as spurious culture in his own society. Ironically, the dispassionate aloofness of the elite intellectual linked him or her to the past rather than to the genuineness of the present. Sapir wanted to claim (Western) history in his heritage as a genuine intellectual.

The third sense of culture characterized the "spiritual possessions of the group rather than the individual" (Sapir 1999 [1924]:49). It was not a quantitative measure of content but an evaluation from within, of "how what is done and believed functions in the whole life of that people, on what significance it has for them" (Sapir 1999 [1924]:50). This version of the culture concept was tied to romanticism and emerging nationalism in Europe, the "genius" of a people. Sapir was adamant that "genius" was not biologically based or useful in service of national chauvinism, but "the resultant of purely historical causes" (Sapir 1999 [1924]:50); he inverted Kroeber's attribution of genius to individuals, as biological capacity.

The qualitative approach to the integration of culture raised issues of subjectivism of judgment not fully resolved by Sapir's contrast of French and Russian styles, if only because "strict parallels between the spirit" of these two European nations "force[d] an emphasis on contrasts" (Sapir 1999 [1924]:53) rather than on continua and individual variability.

Genuine culture, the title construct, was, then, scarcely anthropological at all. It was not the ideal form of a specific culture but a potential quality of every culture, "inherently harmonious, balanced, self-satisfactory, . . . the expression of a richly varied and yet somehow unified and consistent attitude toward life" (Sapir 1999 [1924]:54). The significance of one element came only relative to others. Within such a culture, "nothing is spiritually meaningless" (Sapir 1999 [1924]:54). Efficiency, highly valued in the America of the 1920s, was the antithesis of genuineness. The opposite of this "sterile externality" was the salmon fisherman of the Northwest Coast (Sapir 1999 [1924]:55). Sapir's quintessential example of spurious contemporary industrial culture was the telephone operator (whom he refers to as a "girl"), whose "technical routine" lacked expressive or integrative value in her life (Sapir 1999 [1924]:55). She was far less fulfilled than the Indian salmon fisherman who felt no comparable sense of frustration. The genuine culture was internal; it applied at the level of individual rather than of group. (There may be some unresolved gender conflict in Sapir's assignment of genuine culture among so-called primitives to male roles and its spurious counterpart to females in his own society.)

So-called progress involved superficial "sophistication," "a merely quantitative concept that defined the external conditions for the growth or decay of a culture" and had little to do with genuineness (Sapir 1999:56). Even though we moved toward "a cleaner and healthier, and, to a large extent, a more humanitarian existence," we must distinguish these very real advances from their price in individual alienation from culture (Sapir 1999 [1924]:56).

The "sensitive ethnologist" was privileged to see at first hand "the frequent vitality of culture in less sophisticated levels" (Sapir 1999 [1924]:57). The "well-rounded life of the average participant in the civilization of a typical American Indian tribe" was all the more poignant because white contact had produced a "bewildered vacuity . . . an uneasy sense of the loss of some vague and great good" (Sapir 1999 [1924]:57). Sapir, at least in this rhetorical frame, regretted the "fading away of genuine cultures" far more than the physical and material genocide he had also witnessed firsthand. (By contemporary standards, there was a certain callousness inherent in the characteristic Boasian distance of the observer from the observed [see Buckley 1996 on Kroeber's disregard for the genocide underlying the plight of Ishi; the last survivor of the genocide against small tribes of California Indians was romanticized as an individual saved by white benefactors, in this case anthropologists who took no responsibility for the plight itself].)

The "grimmest joke" of American culture was that so few arose to claim their "cultural patrimony": "Part of the time we are dray horses; the rest of the time we are listless consumers of goods which have received no least impress of our personality. In other words, our spiritual selves go hungry, for the most part, pretty much all of the time" (Sapir 1999 [1924]:60). As in the superorganic debate with Kroeber, Sapir concluded that culture and the culture of the individual were interdependent rather than opposed (Sapir 1999 [1924]: 60). An individual needed a culture, but every culture came with the capacity to reframe it to individual ends.

Sapir disputed the self-congratulatory stereotype that America was a genuine culture because it was new among nations. Rather, he suggested that "signs of a genuine blossoming of culture" reflected "America coming of age" (Sapir 1999 [1924]:61). His preference for the richness and maturity of European culture was palpable.

To attain self-realization in Sapir's own world required, in his view, considerable alienation from the cultural mainstream. Many contemporaries shared his doubts about the "spiritual maladjustments" of then-contemporary North American society. Nonetheless, a reasonably satisfying position could be arrived at through poetry, music, and art, that is, the "spiritual heightening" of the functions remaining to the individual in an economically and politically specialized civilization (Sapir 1999 [1924]:54).

Modern sophisticated cultures withdrew mastery of everyday environment from individuals and posed a severe challenge to the "truly cultured" individual (Sapir 1999 [1924]:62). Direct creativity was the most obvious path, though one could also be linked more passively to the richness of one's own tradition. "The place of the individual in our theory of culture" involved, in sum, self-mastery and spiritual freedom. Art was the particular province of genuine culture because "the impress of the self is most direct, least hampered by outward necessity" (Sapir 1999 [1924]:67).

To be cultured was to be tied to one's social milieu, not to be a hermit. Sapir feared that a "renaissance" was unlikely to thrive "in the critical atmosphere of today" (Sapir 1999 [1924]:65). Detachment and cynicism preserved individuality but did not automatically create genuine culture. Nonetheless, Sapir saw himself as one who could keep up with the turbulent spiritual currents of this troubled time (Sapir 1999 [1924]:66). He seemed to expect that he would remain a prophet in the wilderness, perhaps a legacy of his perceived bitter isolation in the late Ottawa years (Murray 1981). The academic version of "Culture, Genuine and Spurious" appeared in the year of his first wife's death.

Sapir concluded with some prescient remarks on what he called the "geography of culture." Genuine culture was a restricted local phenomenon, involving "something like direct intensive spiritual contact" with "the common cultural heritage" (Sapir 1999 [1924]:67). In Boasian historicism, therefore, diffusion diluted the genuineness of culture. Sapir did not explore this observation but turned to the utopian hope of internationalism and the lingering ties of nationalism (and localisms more generally): "Internationalism, nationalism and localism are forms that can be given various contents . . . [We must] know what it is that we are to be internationalistic about" (Sapir 1999 [1924]:68). Since "a generalized international culture is hardly thinkable," the remarkably contemporary challenge was to link internationalism with social and political units "not too large to incorporate the individuality that is to culture as the very breath of life" (Sapir 1999 [1924]:68). Sapir lamented the shallowness and homogenization of cultures in New York, Chicago, and San Francisco and called for a revitalization, a resistance that might yet produce "better yet, a series of linked autonomous cultures" that were truly genuine (Sapir 1999 [1924]:71).

The Need for Interdisciplinary Triangulation

Sapir's university career, beginning only in 1925, reinforced his uneasy distance from the Boasian mainstream. During the preceding fifteen years, he had directed the anthropological program of the Canadian government. The Division of Anthropology mandated a rather rigid focus on the Canadian Indian. Sapir willingly complied as long as funding for fieldwork and publication made up for the annoyances of bureaucratic administration. But the First World War dramatically disrupted this idyllic research enterprise, and Sapir became increasingly restive in Ottawa.

The Sapir of received anthropological tradition contributed seriously to several disciplines, including linguistics, anthropology (which he defined in increasingly interdisciplinary terms), and psychology/psychiatry. This is a significant switch from his early work, which tended to be very specialized in linguistics. Sapir does not appear to have realized how little interest the average anthropologist, even allies firmly committed to the place of linguistics in anthropology, had in linguistics as such. For example, when he worked on Yana for Kroeber in California in 1907–8, he expected to concentrate on the ideal output of a definitive dictionary, grammar, and texts. He never fully appreciated the pressures on Kroeber to classify the languages and cultures of the state for more practical purposes. Given this essential conflict of aims, especially under financial pressures of declining support for anthropology, Kroeber could hardly have retained Sapir permanently. Around the same time, Sapir's perfectionist streak also clashed with Boas's editing of his Takelma grammatical sketch for the *Handbook of American Indian Languages*. Sapir refused to follow the format, and his brilliant grammar was relegated by Boas to the second volume. Sapir's assumption that everyone shared his devotion to detailed linguistic work inclined him to unrealistic career management strategies. He lost out on positions at the Chicago Field Museum, the Bureau of American Ethnology, and the Universities of California and Pennsylvania. Naiveté undaunted, he adopted his linguistic mapping priorities as the key to historical reconstruction of American Indian languages in Ottawa, where he would, for the first time, organize a research program around his own priorities.

After the initial euphoria wore off, however, Sapir yearned for wider recognition of the importance of his work. Ethnology per se had always bored him. Kroeber thought he wasted his time by not building up a school of American linguistics (difficult, given that he had no students in Ottawa) and by avoiding grand generalizations of potential classificatory utility to ethnologists until all evidence was in. Sapir took this advice seriously and sought to ensure the relevance of linguistics, developing the insights of his application of linguistic method for ethnological inference, also at the behest of Kroeber, into his revisionist classification of American Indian languages five years later (Sapir 1916).

Between 1917 and his departure from Ottawa in 1925, Sapir published some two hundred poems, mostly in small literary magazines, and a volume of his own poetry. Poems served him well as a distancing mechanism for his own emotions; he was further gratified by his participation in the Ottawa literary elite. He had far more in common with Indian Affairs Commissioner Duncan Campbell Scott in the realms of poetry and music than of Indian assimilation policy. Moreover, his poems and literary reviews renewed and solidified his ties to the New York intelligentsia in which various Boasians, especially Benedict and Lowie, were active participants.

In his early psychoanalytic explorations, Sapir did not typically distinguish between personal motives and intellectual outreachings. Personal catharsis led him to psychoanalysis, but he approached its insights with a distanced and analytic eye (Darnell 1986b). He was skeptical in his correspondence with Boas's friend Lyman Wells about psychologists' use of cross-cultural data, but the long-term result was a major shift in his professional persona, from reasonably party-line Boasian to innovative cultural theoretician. This trajectory led him to the University of Chicago in 1925 and to Yale in 1931.

Sapir began to revise his Boasian culture theory without direct stimulus from colleagues in psychology or psychiatry. The superorganic debate focused his developing argument that culture had its locus in the individual, consequently that there were as many cultures as individuals. Sapir moved from his own creative and aesthetic impulses to the creativity of the individual in culture.

The call to the University of Chicago accelerated his progress toward an interdisciplinary rather than an exclusively anthropological theory and audience. Chicago was the only North American university offering a serious program in anthropology that was not directly under Boasian control in the 1920s. The department was chaired by Fay-Cooper Cole, a former Boas student whose own work leaned toward archaeology; formal autonomy from the much larger and more prestigious Chicago sociology department came only in 1929 (and deployed Sapir's prestige for implementation). The symbolic interactionism of the Chicago school reoriented surveys of social problems in the city of Chicago toward ethnography by applying anthropological fieldwork methods. Cross-fertilization proceeded through intellectual and interactional crossovers, particularly Robert Redfield, a Chicago-trained anthropologist married to the daughter of sociologist Robert Park and sometime protégé of Sapir (Darnell 1986b, 1990a; Murray 1986). Only a few years before he introduced Redfield to the "pedants and potentates" at the Rockefeller Foundation's annual Hanover Conference, Sapir himself had to be introduced to these same wheelers and dealers of the emerging interdisciplinary social science. The Chicago sociologists were secure at Hanover because their fieldwork in the city of Chicago was the only database then available for testing hypotheses about the role of personality in culture.

Sapir never converted his fellow social scientists to the genuine culture argument. It had arisen from his ambivalence toward the negative effects of World War I on the pursuit of science, in ways apparently unshared by Boasian colleagues. Yet ironically, it had made him marketable. Cole invited him to Chicago in 1925 because he could collaborate with the Chicago sociologists, attract funding from major foundations (especially the Laura Spellman Rockefeller Memorial Fund), and was eager to cross disciplinary boundaries. Although Sapir thought he was being hired as a linguist and an Americanist, that is, in recognition of his past work, support for his appointment came from outside Boasian anthropology, which was itself just settling into widely acknowledged paradigmatic status. Sapir's openness to theoretical innovation and willingness to analyze his own as well as "primitive" society made him a palatable Boasian spokesman in the eyes of the Chicago sociologists.

Sapir took to his new role like a duck to water. Indeed, he spent the last fifteen years of his life in the academic jet set of his day, bankrolled by Rockefeller Foundation munificence and energized by conversations with psychiatrists, psychologists, and Chicago sociologists; he was the catalyst (Darnell 1986a, 1990a). Sapir believed that the ideas of anthropology crossed the boundaries of conventional disciplines, that anthropology must not allow itself to be conceptually (i.e., theoretically) restricted by its conventional focus upon the so-called primitive and exotic.

Ironically, given the thrust of his mature thought, Sapir is remembered today primarily as the premier linguist among his contemporaries, within a four-field scope that required every ethnologist to incorporate language within the purview of culture. Indeed, Sapir's ethnography focused on linguistic labels for cultural facts as his colleagues did not (Darnell and Irvine 1994:19–21). He wrote to Wilson Wallis: "What we are after in studying primitive peoples is, to a large extent, to get their scheme of classification. This scheme must be more or less reflected in their own language . . . I think that one can do a great deal with linguistic material even if one is not out for a special linguistic study as such" (Sapir to Wallis, 10 June 1913, NMM).

Sapir was forced to take his position as culture theoretician outside the Boasian paradigm because the majority of his fellow Boasians were closer to Kroeber's notion of culture as superorganic than to Sapir's alternative. His fellow iconoclasts, Goldenweiser and Radin, were in no position to appropriate the role of mainstream spokesman. Sapir's challenge to Boasian orthodoxy, however, drew on the reputation for "genius" established by his linguistic work. Even Boas admitted Sapir's primacy in this field.

Perhaps the best index of Sapir's peripherality in the core ethnological areas of Boasian anthropology is the coherent program sketched out in his contributions to the prestigious *Encyclopedia of Social Sciences* between 1931 and 1934. Sapir did not receive the juiciest assignments. Lowie, Kroeber, and Clark Wissler served on the editorial team on behalf of American anthropology; Boas was on the Board of Directors. Sapir's crucial entry on language reflected his acknowledged specialization. But in culture he was assigned tangential entries: fashion, custom, group, personality, and symbolism. Nonetheless, Sapir himself took these essays seriously, even assigning them to his Yale seminar on "the impact of culture on personality." "Taken together . . . [they] present a succinct view of Sapir's maturing theory of culture, society and the individual as presented for an interdisciplinary social science informed by, but not exclusive to, anthropology" (Darnell, Irvine, and Handler 1999:255).

The contrasting and cross-referenced arguments on fashion and custom updated the superorganic debate so seminal to Sapir's theory of culture. Fashion fascinated Sapir because it served, depending on one's standpoint, as exemplar of custom maintained by departure from it or as expression of individual personality. The contrast to Kroeber's insistence on fashion as cultural pattern rather than individual action was dramatic. Sapir insisted that fashion could be taken seriously to explore the relation of individual and culture. Its "psychological complexity" (Sapir 1999 [1931b]:267), although rarely considered by social actors, was accessible to analytic purview.

Moreover, fashion was "a historical concept . . . A specific fashion is utterly unintelligible if lifted out of its place in a sequence of forms" (Sapir 1999 [1931b]:268). Like a phoneme, an individual element of fashion formed a point in a pattern, meaningless outside its system of contrasts. Whereas Kroeber had discussed women's hemlines in terms of changing political contexts, Sapir was more intrigued by possible individual motivations. Like Benedict he worried about the vulnerability of those who were out of step with their culture. His distempers about American society, including his own unresolved issues of gender and class, emerged clearly from the examples he chose.

For an anthropologist, Sapir, like Kroeber, was oddly unconcerned with cross-cultural examples. The unwritten histories of most so-called primitive societies presumably precluded finding evidence for comparable speculation. Sapir acknowledged that the "individual in society is only rarely significantly expressive in his own right" (Sapir 1999 [1931b]:273), but his tone was more cynical about his own society than that of Kroeber's virtual cultural determinism. Sapir cited Kroeber and Lowie in the appended bibliography but did not explore their culturological arguments.

"Custom," predictably, interested Sapir primarily because individuals attached feelings to such patterns. Again, he avoided cross-cultural examples, defining custom in opposition to "the more refined and technical anthropological concept of culture" (Sapir 1999 [1931a]:256). Anthropologists were particularly denotative and objective in their usage; custom had a more affective tone and thus applied well "to geographically remote, to primitive or to bygone societies" (Sapir 1999 [1931a]:256). Sapir was trying to be scientific.

Sapir compared customs to fashions, suggesting that what began as "isolated behavior patterns of a customary nature" rapidly "group themselves into larger configurations which have a formal cohesion" and were "rationalized as functional units" by members of the group in question "whether they are such historically or not" (Sapir 1999 [1931a]:258). This alternative patterning of diffusion and integration was as close as Sapir came to Kroeber's "configurations of culture growth." He emphasized the integration of cultures. It was "only by slow processes of transfer of use and progressive integration of all these socialized modes of behavior" that "a complex system of unified meaning arises" (Sapir 1999 [1931a]:259). This process, moreover, was dynamic; new values were likely to set up disharmonies needing further integration. The "life of language" provided particularly cogent examples (Sapir 1999 [1931a]:259).

Custom was "stronger and more persistent in primitive than in modern societies" because conformity was "psychologically necessary" (Sapir 1999 [1931a]:260). Only writing created "an impersonal arbiter" for custom that removed it from the realm of the sacred. Limited division of labor further mitigated against experimentation with custom. Even within the modern world, there were degrees of adherence to custom, with rural areas being far more conservative. Modern cities exemplified the "complex community" (Sapir 1999 [1931a]:261). A single individual was likely to participate in society through a variety of social roles that enabled strategic manipulation of custom for personal ends. Modern society placed more value on individuality. Despite its constraining quality, custom allowed the individual to learn and express group solidarity efficiently. References were mostly to anthropologists; custom was an anthropological province, as fashion was not.

Sapir began his discussion of "group" by emphasizing that the relation of individual and group within the social sciences depended on disciplinary standpoint. The cohesion of groups required "some interest" holding them together (Sapir 1999 [1932b]:294). Sociology tried to classify kinds of groups, but Sapir was more interested in the symbolisms illustrated by various kinds of groups. His own classifications applied more easily to "the modern civilized world" than to the folk or primitive ones. Sapir believed that his taxonomy was based on "an objective standpoint" that might focus on the nature and intensity of individual participation (Sapir 1999 [1932b]:297). Subjective and objective views could not be discrete because most subjective identification was unconscious. Group participation ranged from physical to symbolic on a continuum. Group emotion was more important than the distinction between primary face-to-face relationships and larger scale groups. A complex modern society had "more groups of more or less psychological significance than it possesses individuals who participate in these groups"(Sapir 1999 [1932b]: 298). The references for the discussion of group were sociological; anthropologists had their concept of culture instead.

The interdisciplinary contingent remembered Sapir's charisma and verbal fluency, his "mellifluous" words and his "ineffable gift of tongues" (Darnell 1986a). Nonetheless, he was not the only silver-tongued orator of his generation. Sapir's perspective expanded dramatically as a result of his collaboration, perhaps first motivated by personal adjustment to the guilt and despair surrounding the death of his first wife (Perry 1983), with interactional psychiatrist Harry Stack Sullivan. The interdisciplinary triumvirate of Sapir, Sullivan, and political scientist Harold D. Lasswell persuaded others to participate in the construction of a yet unnamed multidiscipline emerging around the study of the individual in culture, the very problem that had worried Sapir as theoretician of culture at least since 1917.

Sapir simultaneously redefined the Boasian, and by extension the anthropological, point of view for these new interdisciplinary colleagues, partly and perhaps ironically on the basis of what he was learning from them. Sapir adamantly refused the role of expert witness on the trivia of the exotic. The man who told his Yale seminar that nothing was trivial (Bingham Dai, personal communication) insisted that culture and personality must be conceived the same way in modern industrial society as in the presumably simpler cultures traditionally studied by anthropologists. Sapir carefully chose examples from the familiar everyday world that he shared with his students (smoking cigarettes, playing the piano, earning a living).

Disciplinary boundaries aside, Sapir increasingly functioned as a sociologist in the broad sense. His chapter on the relations between sociology and anthropology in a volume edited by Ogburn and Goldenweiser, his recalcitrant Boasian colleague, avoided altogether the traditional anthropological focus on the primitive (in Darnell, Irvine, and Handler 1999 [1927]). The social science envisioned by Sapir interposed society as a mediating term between culture and the individual, all three taken as symbolic constructs of the analyst, not found prefabricated in the world.

Sapir was eager to make up time lost during his perceived isolation in Ottawa and quickly learned to translate his notions of the individual into the psychologists' field of discourse—personality. He sought a "dynamic" social science corresponding to the "dynamic psychology" highly touted in the period. Along with Sullivan, he came to see mental illness as culturally conditioned in ways accessible through studying the interaction of the individual with the environment, both social and natural. Anthropology had led Sapir to expect individual creativity within cultural tradition. The life history technique of the clinical psychiatrist opened new vistas for interdisciplinary collaboration. Sapir did not, however, formulate a concrete plan to proceed from theory to practice.

Renegade Chicago sociologist William I. Thomas provided a useful foil. Thomas wanted to follow his monumental life history–based study of the Polish peasant (Thomas and Znaniecki 1927) with a similar study of Scandinavian culture—close enough to his own to allow member intuition but different enough to pose contrast. Thomas's theoretical interests arose directly from empirical projects designed to test them, and he interacted pragmatically with the psychiatrists at the interdisciplinary conferences. He wanted access to clinical observations, usually impossible for a nonpsychiatrist on ethical grounds as well as on those of credentialization. Perhaps because he had another kind of data to trade, Thomas got his access.

At Hanover, Sapir rapidly became a core participant, ensuring anthropological influence disproportionate to his discipline's size. Usually the sole Boasian in these hallowed halls, Sapir did not threaten those with disciplinary homes in psychology or sociology. He was not pushing a specific disciplinary or personal agenda; he presented himself as a naive amateur asking questions and mediating among methods and professional vocabularies. Sapir stood outside the particular projects and translated, evoking implications and interconnections. He rarely criticized anyone's work, simply reframing it in terms of larger issues so as to incorporate everyone into the collaborative network. His sharply negative comments were reserved for what he considered the spuriously scientific facade of statistical analysis without adequate theoretical underpinnings.

Sapir blossomed under these conditions. His enthusiasm for new ideas was contagious, and at last he felt appreciated.

Sapir and Sullivan organized two symposia of the American Psychiatric Association in the late twenties. Sullivan, however, was too peripheral to the emerging professionalism of psychiatry to effectively push his case for interactional studies of mental patients. Sapir, cautious in face of the new emphasis on training analysis as the credential sine qua non for clinical practice, presented himself in an uncharacteristically low-key manner, quietly asserting his conviction that psychiatry and anthropology/sociology could balance each other's strengths and weaknesses if only psychiatrists would become sensitive to the social domain and to research rather than simply to the ad hoc clinical treatment of patients. Both Sapir and Sullivan were convinced that psychiatric training was too rigid to move beyond its professional blinders to study culturally conditioned personality.

By the second American Psychiatric Association conference, however, Sapir had gained confidence. He discussed his own research in quasi-experimental studies of voice quality and phonetic symbolism (actually carried out largely by Stanley Newman). Sapir attempted to impress upon the medically trained participants in this conference that he was "scientific" in their terms—a reasonable prelude to effective dialogue.

Much of the transcript (Darnell, Irvine, and Handler 1999: section 1) involved brief, enthusiastic exchanges between Sapir and Sullivan. The participants must have been convinced. When it came time to sum up, they turned to Sapir to propose a follow-up program, ignored his characteristic diffidence as a rhetorical device, and assumed he had a concrete research program to propose. Apparently off the top of his head, Sapir outlined a three-pronged attack with each group of participants contributing at a different level: The psychiatrists would study mental patients through detailed life histories; the sociologists would study normal individuals in American society; and the anthropologists would study the exotica. Sapir did not associate himself with any of these positions. There is no evidence that he had any specific idea about how to do cross-cultural fieldwork on the organization of personality. Sapir's own fieldwork was with linguistic materials, which were usually not emotionally sensitive; even his ethnology was largely a by-product of collecting linguistic texts. His last major linguistic fieldwork was in 1929. Moreover, he was an intensely private man in the expression of his own deeper emotions. He was unable to envision the relationship one would need with an informant to record a life history and uncertain of his own objectivity in interpreting such materials even if he could obtain them. Theoretically, it was easy to see what had to be done; practically, however, Sapir envisioned training students, preferably from anthropology, to do the actual work. These students would undergo psychiatric training analysis before attempting to study personality cross-culturally in participant-observation fieldwork. Sapir himself, however, always carefully avoided undergoing analysis, declining to reexamine what he considered the traumas of his personal life.

Ironically, Sapir's interest in psychology had deep roots in the linguistic fieldwork that required him to work closely with a small number of conservative elderly speakers of disappearing languages (Darnell 1990b). He came to see the world through the eyes of these speakers as individuals. He also responded enthusiastically to bilingual "informants" who were inclined to analyze their native languages: Tony Tillohash for Southern Paiute, Alex Thomas for Nootka, and Chic Sandoval for Navajo. Their insights were fundamental to his theoretical formulation of the psychological reality of the phoneme. His literary-ethnographic experiments identified strongly with Nootka individuals (see Chapter 6). And yet there was a point beyond which he would not go.

Meanwhile back at Hanover, Sapir responded greedily to the Rockefeller Foundation plan for an interdisciplinary seminar for foreign students who would provide a database for cross-cultural study of personality by analyzing their own cultural backgrounds. The "informants" would be both social scientists and members of the cultures to be analyzed. The crucial test case could not have been more clearly posed. Sapir was the only person with the charisma and interdisciplinary prestige to lead the proposed seminar. The problem was location, not personnel. The Rockefeller Foundation was interested in integrated research projects, and the Chicago social scientists pursued their research projects largely independently. An institutional alternative emerged at Yale, where psychologist Mark May, also a core Hanover participant, was building the Institute of Human Relations into an administrative umbrella for interdisciplinary collaboration independent of particular university departments. Sapir, given his favored role as synthesizer and theoretician, quickly volunteered to lead the seminar on a Chicago sabbatical in 1931–32.

Sapir's move to Yale in 1931 had almost nothing to do with anthropology. Indeed, in the same year he turned down an offer to return to Columbia as Boas's successor, along with Kroeber (who also declined). Sapir enjoyed his authority as interpreter of the Boasian tradition to an interdisciplinary audience and declined to retreat to the more restrained confines of the Boasian discipline.

Yale president James R. Angell was determined to acquire the prestigious project and resolved to entice Sapir to Yale permanently. Angell, a newcomer to Yale, did not even notify the sociologists under whose domain anthropology had hitherto fallen when he hired Sapir as head of the newly formed department. Sapir was soon to learn, to his dismay, that the evolutionary sociology of Albert Keller, disciple of William Graham Sumner, was diametrically opposed to virtually every tenet of Boasian anthropology. Further, the proponents of Yale sociology were integral to the old boy network around which the university was organized. From the beginning, Sapir's position was more precarious than he realized.

For Sapir, Yale was the logical culmination of his increasing involvement with interdisciplinary social science during his Chicago years. Recalling childhood poverty and continuously plagued by impinging financial disaster, Sapir foresaw the first financial security of his career. The social elitism of Yale seemed far from the immigrant world of New York's Lower East Side. He was both attracted and repelled by Yale. The possibility of anti-Semitism apparently did not occur to him, despite the warnings of Chicago colleagues. Sapir was a nonpracticing Jew who advocated assimilation. It took Yale's anti-Semitism plus the rise of Hitler to return him to sympathy with the tradition of his childhood.

Sapir failed to appreciate the intensity of May's commitment to integrated research programs. Although neither May nor Angell cared about American Indian languages, Sapir consistently used his Institute of Human Relations research allotment to sponsor his students' linguistic fieldwork. His personal route to interdisciplinarity was marginal to anything else at the institute. Adding insult to injury, Sapir also pursued his interests in personality independently of the institute, with Sullivan and other nonlocal cronies from the conference circuit. His prestige made his carping about the situation at Yale particularly detrimental to the institute's plans for integration.

Unsurprisingly, Sapir's version of personality studies failed to prevail at the institute. Integration of the social sciences coalesced around Clark Hull's behavioristic psychology, which differed dramatically from Sapir's qualitative and symbolic approach. Many of those who rallied round came from the Sumner-Keller, pre-Boasian sociological tradition, which was anathema to Sapir. It is unlikely that he thought anyone could take this work seriously, and in any case Sapir was not a team player. The gap widened rapidly.

The dichotomy between the qualitative/symbolic thrust of Sapir's vision and the more scientifically oriented side of interdisciplinary science was contested in particularly vitriolic form at Yale in the late 1930s (Darnell 1998b). That these issues still rattle cages was demonstrated at the 1986 meeting of the American Anthropological Association in a session commemorating Sapir's departmental nemesis George Peter Murdock. John Whiting, a student in the Murdock camp, which restructured Sapir's program rapidly after his death in 1939, responded to a question about Sapir's role at Yale: "Sapir, you see, was not a scientist, he was a poet." Clearly there were those who responded to the charisma of Sapir and those who resented it, who felt that his personal magnetism was inappropriate, that "science" should be more objective. Personal style was at least as important as intellectual content in sustaining bitterness and hostility over competing approaches to human behavior.

Meanwhile, the Impact of Culture on Personality Seminar was postponed until 1932–33 on practical grounds. Sapir invited John Dollard to move from Chicago to Yale with him, apparently envisioning an amicable division of labor in which he would present the "culture" and Dollard the psychoanalysis and personality. Dollard, however, allied himself with May and the integrative social science of the Institute of Human Relations.

No one in the final contingent of thirteen scholars representing eleven countries and several disciplines (with sociology predominant) was already familiar with the interdisciplinary discourse that had become second nature to Sapir. To his chagrin, basic groundwork would have to precede the testing of personality theory by these fellows. For all his parleying this interdisciplinary synthesis into research opportunities for young anthropologists, to the end of his life Sapir envisioned the cross-cultural study of personality in Boasian terms. His lectures in the psychology of culture, reconstituted by Judith Irvine (1994), remain thoroughly conventional in their Boasian, even Kroeberian, cultural vista. In practice, Sapir turned to the individual only after thoroughly analyzing culture. For someone who had been thinking in interdisciplinary terms for some time, Sapir's seminar program was remarkably conservative. The fellows read in advance three Boasian classics (Boas's 1911 *The Mind of Primitive Man,* Wissler's 1923 *Man and Culture,* and Kroeber's 1923 *Anthropology*), Thomas Dewey's pragmatic philosophy, and Robert and Helen Lynd's sociological study of Middletown (1929). They were supposed to study North American society before returning to their own countries. Although Sapir asked each fellow to send an advance psychological autobiography, the seminar worked its way quite leisurely toward the study of personality.

In practice, Sapir lectured on anthropology and Dollard on psychology. Sapir acted as master of ceremonies for a parade of visiting lecturers whose individual points of view were not integrated for the fellows by Sapir or anyone else. He seems to have played to the audience of visitors rather than to the students, who spent more time with Dollard, further accentuating the fragmentation inherent in the seminar organization.

After the school year, the students dispersed for summer research, mostly in North America. The project had not produced rapid empirical verification of personality theory and the Rockefeller Foundation declined to support an additional year. Of the fellows, only Bingham Dai remained in North American academia. The great synthetic effort, then, had no lasting results.

Sapir and Sullivan made one last effort at interdisciplinary collaboration, but this too was stymied by lack of funding. As chairman of the Division of Psychology and Anthropology of the National Research Council, Sapir convened an optimistic ad hoc committee on training fellowships for the cross-cultural study of personality. The dynamic duo envisioned Stanley Newman as the first fellow (Darnell 1989a). Ruth Benedict sat on the committee but remained aloof from the largely non-Boasian enthusiasms of Sapir and Sullivan. Both organizers, however, were deferential, needing to show common Boasian cause to impress the psychiatric audience. Tensions remained over the relationship between the abnormal in North American society and the normal in other societies (Benedict 1934a). Sapir and Sullivan, although neither wanted to appropriate the terms of abnormal psychology directly, glossed over this issue. From the psychiatric point of view, the issue was another version of the Boasian commitment to studying socialization, that is, culture rather than biology as the primary determinant of individual motivation and behavior.

Sapir was particularly eager to secure the participation of Adolf Meyer, who agreed to commute to New York to supervise training analyses to be carried out by neo-Freudian psychiatrists Karen Horney and Erich Fromm. Meyer, whose dynamic psychology was much in fashion at the time, thought the research fellows would be able to carve out an employment niche for themselves. He worried about "how to get from the anecdotal stage, which now is used for mutual animation among philanthropists [hardly an endorsement of interdisciplinary social science!], to a basis that would be almost respectable" (Darnell 1990a:324). Meyer was also determined not to tie the program to any particular brand of psychiatry. Discussions of credentials centered on training analysis for the new breed of researchers, unblinded by the preconceptions of any discipline, especially psychology.

By 1935 the heyday of foundation support for the social sciences was over. The vision was ever receding in personal terms as well: Sapir had his first heart attack in 1937, and Sullivan never obtained money for an interdisciplinary research institute.

Sapir's pioneering work continues to be cited in programmatic terms but was never supported by a program of validating research results. The Kardiner-Linton seminars of the 1940s established the collaborative reality of which Sapir and Sullivan only dreamed. Within anthropology the Benedict-Mead intuitive equation of whole cultures with personality types increasingly held sway after Sapir's death. He dismissed this work as superficial, with little of the individual in its "psychological" focus. The methods of the time were inadequate to pursue questions of intracultural variability (see Wallace 1952, 1961). Mead outlived the others and was outspoken in her assessment of their contributions, thus further eliding the distinctiveness of Sapir's position.

In retrospect the abortiveness of particular projects detracts from recognition of the holistic vision that Sapir drew from anthropology and elaborated in the brief, shining moment of interwar interdisciplinary funding. The strong, possibly excessive, quest for scientific objectivity that dominated the social sciences in North America over the ensuing two decades has now given way to methods more congenial to Sapir's anticipatory visions. He maintained the respectability of such an alternative to behaviorism until it could be taken up by a new generation.

Despite the conservatism of entrenched disciplines, genuine interdisciplinarity has blossomed today around the so-called postmodernist turn in the social sciences and humanities. Sapir claimed a critical place for anthropology in that discourse: to counter otherwise ethnocentric theories and purported exemplars. Sapir did not concede anthropology's claim to realism, the possibility of representation, or the symbolic character of human expression. He insisted on the well-tried anthropological method of microanalysis geared to elucidating the Native point of view. Individuals were endowed with agency in culture change, and cross-cultural data were applied to the critique of North American society. At the boundaries of the social sciences and humanities, Sapir's vision guides us away from the nihilism and rhetorical shortsightedness for which the self-styled postmodernists in anthropology have been extensively chastised, both within the discipline and outside it.

PAUL RADIN

CHAPTER 4

Philosophizing with the "Other"

Paul Radin provides a link between two lines of argument within a larger reassessment of the Boasian paradigm.

First, the Boasian text tradition entails a symbolic and ideational definition of culture as knowledge encoded in the words of native speakers of languages or members of a culture. This tradition provides a context for contemporary ruminations on ethnographic rhetoric that betide intense and productive collaborations with expert members of other cultures, drawing from and feeding into Western academic traditions across the humanities and social sciences. For the first time since the 1930s, we may have the makings of a truly interdisciplinary social science.

Second, the "coevalness" called for by Johannes Fabian (1983) extends the capacity to philosophize, to theorize, from "us," the so-called "civilized," to "them," the so-called "primitive." Texts provide both Radin's evidence and his comparative method, the attitudinal grounds on which cross-cultural conversations become possible and the role of the individual in history emerges despite the absence of conventional written records. Radin's position is neither the analyst's comparative perspective of Boas nor the superorganic internal necessity envisioned by Kroeber. Rather, it embodies a fierce individualism more consonant with the genuine, situated culture of Sapir's alternative.

Radin was the maverick among the first generation Boasians, a Trickster-shape shifter in the figure used by his Native American interlocutors. He was oblivious to institutional forms that seemed to him to constrain creativity and individuality; he moved blithely from one job to another, sorely challenging the ability of his colleagues to find ways of supporting him. Anthropology was more "a way of life" than a career or "specialized discipline" (Diamond 1981: 73). He was, in fact, highly suspicious of intellectuals in his own society because they were "dependent upon the establishment" (Diamond 1981:75). Radin was a man of words, the "inner unity" of his work having a poetic quality (Diamond 1981:69) that brought alive the inner world of the Winnebagos and other tribes. "Above all," he "never merely analyzed the lives of people called primitives; by some alchemy of insight he transmuted himself, time and again, into their spokesman" (Diamond 1981:77), attempting to see the world from "the Native point of view" rather than merely reporting how the Natives said they saw their worlds. Radin emphasized the positive features of aboriginal civilizations and sought a concept of human nature through which civilizations could meet on equal terms. He was an outspoken critic of the Boasian anthropology that he paradoxically embodied.

Primitive Man as Philosopher

Primitive Man as Philosopher was first published in 1927 and reissued in paperback thirty years later with "no changes whatsoever in the older text" (Radin [1927] 1957:vii). Radin added a new introductory chapter on "methods of approach in the study of aboriginal philosophy," which subtly altered the framework for the volume as a whole, and an appendix on "new religious-philosophical formulations attempted by the American Indian" (Radin [1927] 1957:vii), adopting the life history genre, which had proliferated in the interim, in no small part due to his own efforts, as a means of integrating cultural description and individual experience.

The most significant revision was the loss of the now-pejorative epithet "primitive" and its replacement by the more neutral and politically correct (even more so today than in 1957) "aboriginal" to describe philosophers from traditions other than our own. Surprisingly, however, Radin did not comment on this change in terminology, and it was not extended consistently through the new edition. He implicitly defended the relevance of the original formulation rather than reworking it in more contemporary terms; publisher's costs and the complexities of resetting type may, however, have played the decisive role.

Radin's analytic language also differs from contemporary practice in referring to primitive "man" as philosopher. He did not dismiss the possibility that some women might also be philosophers, although he did not discuss it either. For Radin, inclusive language was a nonissue: The Winnebago philosophers he knew were men, and, in the case of an honorable exception, the masculine pronoun would be generic. In any case, retention of the terms "primitive" and "man" has precluded proper continuous appreciation for a minor masterpiece of the Americanist tradition that spans anthropology and linguistics.

Interestingly, philosophers today more often read Radin than do anthropologists, perhaps because they are less conditioned by professional socialization, if indeed they are so conditioned at all, to speak respectfully of the range of human cultures and the intellectual capacities of their members. On the one hand, Radin's deceptively straightforward ethnography of so-called primitive thought poses a still-unmet challenge to mainstream analytic philosophy. On the other hand, however, we must attend to the potential incommensurabilities of how philosophers of non-Western cultures think and how anthropologists think about how those philosophers think (see Bloch 1998).

Philosophers are inclined to "worry" about the coherence of philosophical systems through a methodology euphemistically labeled as "thought experiment." From the point of view of an anthropologist with experience of cross-cultural diversity or of a linguist with exposure to unfamiliar systems of grammatical categories, introspection cannot possibly produce alternative forms of life or ways of thought as complex as those already existing in the world and accessible to philosophers who choose to explore them, regardless of their discipline. These thought-worlds are multiple because of the finite but unspecifiable number of alternatives to our own philosophical tradition and the many ways of being "other," long attested by the ethnographic record.

The same objection applies to the insistence by linguists of the transformational dispensation that only native speakers can produce grammatically decisive intuitions about their languages. A linguistic competence that begins with the principled exclusion of communicative competence becomes downright mystical. The further claim that data from native speaker intuition can produce an inventory of linguistic universals gainsays the sophistication and complexity of what native speakers of all languages, not just those in which linguists are habitually trained, know by virtue of their socialization in a particular culture. The currently fashionable search for universals is problematic insofar as it alienates individual agency and cultural diversity or precludes recognition of linguistic and cultural change.

The challenge for linguistic theory, as for analytic philosophy, is to get at genuine alternatives in languages, cultures, and worldviews. Cross-cultural researchers quickly discover that alternative epistemologies cannot be derived from the culture or language of the external observer. Insofar as there turn out to be universals, they should be arrived at empirically from the overlap among attested alternatives. The crucial methodological caveat is that the categories of the researcher must hold no special privilege.

Radin intended *Primitive Man as Philosopher* to teach a popular audience the characteristic Boasian standpoint of cultural relativism. He worried, although perhaps in a different way than philosophers do, about the facile assumption of a North American mainstream educated audience that so-called primitive peoples were conceptually as well as technologically inferior to them. His preface mounted an explicit defense of "people whom we have been accustomed to call uncivilized" (Radin [1927] 1957:ix). Popular judgment was unreflexive, based almost entirely on the absence of writing. Radin emphasized that the European idea of the primitive was almost immediately romanticized, with all non-Western peoples "lumped" in a monolithic contrast with so-called civilization despite attested differences among their cultures (Radin [1927] 1957:x).

Radin's argument, in opposition to the social evolutionism of the early anthropology of E. B. Tylor and his intellectual descendants, was a self-conscious "rebellion . . .[derived] in large measure from the American ethnologists" trained by Franz Boas (Radin [1927] 1957:xi). Radin liked to think of himself as a rebel and he was certainly acknowledged as such among the Boasians (e.g., Lowie 1959:133). He defended the core premise of cultural relativism or linguistic relativity with a fervor reminiscent of the contemporary convert to postmodernism. Nonetheless, his opposition to covert forms of racism, scientific or otherwise (still deeply embedded in Western consciousness from Arthur Jensen to Philippe Rushton), remained thoroughly Boasian.

The need to "examine anew the older assumptions" that "threaten to become fixed traditions among psychologists, sociologists and historians" required the anthropologist (which, for Radin, included the linguist) to convey to the North American public the rarely acknowledged high "level of intelligence among primitive peoples" (Radin [1927] 1957:xii). He set out to counter the unproblematic assumption that the individual in a so-called primitive society was "completely swamped by and submerged in the group" and that "thinkers and philosophers as such do not exist—in short, that there was nothing even remotely comparable to an intellectual class among them" (Radin [1927] 1957:xii).

Contemporary readers might balk at the use of the term "class" with reference to aboriginal North America, but the point, if not the language, is surprisingly palatable. Radin used "class" in the conventional Marxist sense of an elite creating an ideology for the proletariat, arguing that philosophy was always an elitist sort of thing, a product of specialization in the social division of labor. Like science in contemporary Western society, it was unintelligible to the average person in the culture that devised it. Philosophers thought, if not lived, in ivory towers. Radin's argument was directed to the elite, the intellectuals, the academics of his own society—who must recognize themselves as having peers elsewhere. On the one hand, Radin sought dialogue, if not dialectic, of anthropologists and aboriginal philosophers "in the field"; on the other hand, he envisioned a less ethnocentric academy, humbled by its encounters with other societies.

The foreword to *Primitive Man as Philosopher* was written by John Dewey, educator, pragmatist philosopher, and maven of the Chicago school. The American pragmatists optimistically assumed that the world could be remade to correspond to human wishes and goals, with a lingering commitment to the Boasian-discredited notion of progress through social evolution. Dewey read Radin's argument as creating "an almost new field," previously unknown to the interdisciplinary social scientists. An outsider to Radin's discipline with considerable prestige in the academy of his time, Dewey explicitly acknowledged that anthropologists alone would fail to find the book's conclusions "contrary to the beliefs which are implicitly current" in the social sciences (Radin [1927] 1957:xii). For Dewey, anthropology's cross-cultural method based in firsthand fieldwork was crucial to the interdisciplinary mix.

In Dewey's rendering, Radin asserted the universal existence of "a definite intellectual class, proportionate in numbers and influence to the 'intellectuals' in any civilized group" who had "ideas on most of the themes which have long formed the staples of philosophical discussion" (Radin [1927] 1957:xii). These "themes" were, for Radin, the crux of the matter. Primitive man (Dewey, like Radin, accepted both "primitive" and the generic "man" as reasonable and unmarked) might be limited in ideas, which could appear "crude because of limitations of subject matter at their command" (Radin [1927] 1957:xviii); but within these limitations, there was no inherent hierarchy of intellectual potentiality. The primitive philosopher, in fact, proved "tough-minded" and realistic; both were highly valued attributes of interwar pragmatism (see Handler 1986 for the valorization of these values in the poetry of Sapir and Ruth Benedict). Dewey accepted Radin's contention that philosophers reasoning from other premises may have arrived at solutions to shared philosophical problems "sounder," at least in some cases, than our own (Radin [1927] 1957:xix).

The "primitive philosopher" had no difficulty dealing with the real world. Recapitulating a discourse long established in the work of Herder, Steinthal, and Humboldt, Dewey accepted Radin's argument that the "inner form" of such philosophical questions was stated explicitly by thinkers across cultures, while merely "expressed mythically by the mass" of members of primitive cultures (Radin [1927] 1957:xx); the same distinction, of course, could be applied easily to contemporary Western society.

Radin's new introduction argued: "There can be little doubt that every human group, no matter how small, has, from time immemorial, contained individuals who were constrained by their individual temperaments and interests to occupy themselves with the basic problems of what *we* customarily term philosophy" (Radin [1927] 1957:xxi; emphasis mine). He made no claim that "philosophy" existed cross-culturally as a discrete domain of inquiry. That was an empirical question to be answered anew for each society. Among the Native North Americans with whom Radin philosophized, however, the things that elders know formed a rich but unlabeled amalgam that included elements of what he was accustomed to label as culture, history, art, literature, religion, philosophy, and pedagogy.

Interestingly, Radin was less clear that "the languages at their disposal were adequate either in structure or in vocabulary for the formation of abstract and generalized ideas and philosophical concepts" (Radin [1927] 1957:xxi). Although he fancied himself something of a linguist, Radin interpreted the linguistic prong of the Boasian program as a fairly direct route to reconstruction of distant history through genetic relationship and in the absence of written records. His own identification in 1919 of a single linguistic family for all of North America was received uniformly as disastrous.

Radin was neither party to nor much persuaded by Boas's emphasis on the psychological or typological forms taken by particular American Indian languages (Boas 1911a). Nor did he become enamored of later explorations by Sapir and Benjamin Whorf of the intimate relationship of language, thought, and reality. In contrast Radin used Boasian diffusionist terminology to argue that grammatical categories had "secondary historical causes" that precluded identifying their origins. Moreover, the "mentality" and "interests" of a people were not constrained by "primitive" grammars. For Boas this proposition meant that similarities due to genetic relationship could not be reliably distinguished from more recent borrowings. For Radin it meant that the thinkers in "primitive" societies could adapt their languages to philosophical purposes.

What differed between so-called primitive and civilized, for Radin, was the existence of "integrated philosophical systems," which depended on "the presence of a certain type of social-economic structure" (Radin [1927] 1957:xxiv). Hymes (1966:126–31) presents a contemporary exemplar of the relative systematization of the cultures of the Crows and Hidatsas, known to be the same people until well into historic times. The Crows continued a nomadic lifestyle and individual-based knowledge tradition, while the settled Hidatsas moved toward cultural formalization. Across a range of cultural forms, expressive style remained characteristic and consistent with altered ecological adaptations. Integration and systematicity correlated with cultural elaboration.

In Radin's view, however, the "evolution of philosophy," perhaps even within the Western tradition, did not necessarily depend on formal integration into systems of thought but rather on the capacity to formulate philosophical problems (Radin [1927] 1957:xxv). No good (philosophical) reasons demonstrated that all thought "attempts to become like our own, as our own appears when we reflect upon it as 'thought'" (Radin [1927] 1957:xxvii); by implication most people in Radin's own society were not reflective in this way. Primitive philosophy did not distinguish between everyday thinking and systematic thought; to impose "the special kind of mentality for all but the Greeks and their cultural descendants" was, therefore, a distortion (Radin [1927] 1957:xxvi). Western philosophy, then, was an ethnocentric concept, unproblematic only for the intellectual heirs of its inventors.

Information in a society without writing was transmitted orally and "rarely given willingly" to local apprentices and would-be successors or to anthropologists (Radin [1927] 1957:xxviii). Its transmission depended crucially on "a very special kind of relationship . . . between the investigator and the investigated" (Radin [1927] 1957:xxix). Given the fieldwork ethics of Radin's day, the coercion implicitly acknowledged here caused him no particular anxiety. Benefits to science vastly outweighed the hesitations of the owners and custodians of the knowledge he aspired to document. Effective critique of the values of science from anthropology's traditional subjects was yet to come.

Radin thought that this relational element in philosophizing, the need for an "outsider" as interlocutor, was inevitable prior to the invention of writing (Radin [1927] 1957:xxxix). He privileged the dialogic intention of the anthropologist:

> Ideally the investigator's role should have been confined to seeking his philosopher, explaining to him what he wished and, having persuaded him to talk, to record what he said. That, however, would have required not only a native philosopher who was willing to give the information but an investigator who was a philosopher and who had neither prejudices nor preconceived notions as to the mentality of the people he was studying. Such investigators are extremely rare [but not nonexistent]. As a result the philosophies in question have, generally, been described either by the investigator himself or elicited, question by question. (Radin [1927] 1957:xxix)

It was methodologically unreliable to elicit explanations not offered spontaneously. The interpretations of outsiders "can be subjective to a dangerous degree. They must not under any circumstances be regarded as primary sources" (Radin [1927] 1957:xxx). Nor must they be confused with spontaneous or culturally standardized articulations of knowledge. Much of the cryptic quality of elders' teachings responds to the communicative incompetence of the anthropologist-as-learner (see Briggs 1986).

The value of direct questioning "depends upon the relationship between the investigator and his informant" [Radin [1927] 1957:xxxi). "Knowing the language" was a major factor creating the possibility that "this can become something analogous to a true philosophical dialogue" (Radin [1927] 1957:xxxi). The ability to establish communication, conversely, could be interpreted as "evidence of the existence of true philosophical formulations and systematizations" (Radin [1927] 1957:xxxi). Radin envisioned philosophy as Socratic, using dialogue as a method of teaching and transmitting knowledge; he was less interested in whether the resulting knowledge was systematic in form. This agenda, when transferred to the ethnographic site, entailed the primary role of the anthropologist as apprentice and learner. Ironically, however, the increase in sophistication was more on the Native side than on the anthropological!

Radin's rhetoric remarkably anticipates that of the recent "experimental moment" in ethnographic writing. An important difference in emphasis, however, arises from the dialogic and pedagogic method at the core of Radin's understanding of the very nature of philosophy. Contemporary experimental ethnographies often focus on the ethnographer's process of coming to know an "other," a "confessional" rhetoric (Van Maanen 1988) rarely explored by the early Boasians. Radin was more interested in what could be learned from the "other" than in his own role in the ethnographic encounter. His "method" as writer and theoretician consisted in offering relatively brief quotations of dialogue, poetry, song, story, and ritual from a variety of aboriginal societies and defending their status as genuine philosophy. Examples reflecting his own North American Indian fieldwork were supplemented by excerpts from Melanesia, Africa, and New Zealand. The Natives were permitted to speak for themselves, sometimes at reasonable length, albeit within Radin's interpretive context.

Many speeches and dialogues were obtained only because of the observer's presence. Radin hypothesized, however, that priests engaged in such speculation among themselves and that ideas were transmitted "as a unified whole" and by "formal teachings" despite considerable "difference of opinion" among experts within a given society (Radin [1927] 1957:xxxviii). To assume otherwise was a form of ethnocentrism. Radin's acceptance in principle of the legitimacy of intracultural variability remained in tension with the degree to which (Western) philosophy itself was understood as tending toward codification. Decoupling the posing of philosophical questions from systematic philosophy crucially grounded Radin's argument for the universal distribution of philosophers across cultures.

The West's history of itself, with a powerful tendency toward individualism, stressed "the intellectual class" and "the exceptional man." Ethnology, in contrast, usually put forward "group beliefs" to represent the height of philosophical thought, even though they were usually "the beliefs and customs of the non-intellectual class" (Radin [1927] 1957:4). To compare so-called primitive and civilized societies fairly, the philosophers of each tradition must be placed in direct contact. "Primitive cultures" should then be described "in terms of their intellectual class, from the viewpoint of their thinkers" (Radin [1927] 1957:5).

Philosophers found each other by a kind of gravitational attraction, even across boundaries of culture and language. Radin argued that the ratio of the philosophically inclined to the mass of persons in any society was constant, with the "same distribution of temperament and ability as among us." He insisted that he did not begin with this idea; rather, it was "slowly forced upon me" by observation and contact with primitive societies (Radin [1927] 1957:5). (This view counters Kroeber's a priori explanation of the uniform incidence of genius across cultures by technological innovation as valued within the Western tradition. Both, however, postulated universal distribution without empirical evidence or effort at sampling.) Radin came to respect the knowledge given to him by his Winnebago consultants and consequently reconsidered the premises of European superiority always implicit in anthropology. The content of philosophy reflected linguistic and cultural experience, but method and sophistication of thought were universal.

Indeed, the abyss between the man of thought and the man of action in both primitive and civilized society was far wider than the superficial distance created by linguistic and cultural background. Scholars, usually men of ideas, overvalued the role of thought in culture (Radin [1927] 1957:11). "The cultured ethnologist" sought out those of like mind (Radin [1927] 1957:13) and was rarely conscious of his habitual devaluation of the practical and the ordinary (Radin [1927] 1957:17).

Radin took his key, albeit without citation, from Carl Jung's 1923 *Psychological Types*. Margaret Mead recalled discovering this book in 1924 via Sapir, who reviewed it with the enthusiasm of a disciple, claiming he never before understood why people did not understand him or he them. Sapir and Lowie corresponded about how Jung's typology applied to their professional colleagues. This amusing parlor game acknowledged intracultural diversity dependent on "temperament" or "personality" (Darnell 1990a:139–43) and not restricted to the so-called civilized.

Jung valorized the "intuitive introvert"; most of his readers, certainly Radin and Sapir, saw themselves as falling into this desirable category. For Radin this type became the image of the "primitive philosopher," the antithesis of the mere man of reason. Radin's fondness for Jung's typological scheme illustrates the process of intellectual-seeking-out-intellectual that he envisioned between ethnologist and informant.

"The medicine man, the thinker, the poet" valued thought for its own sake (Radin [1927] 1957:21). The man of action, in contrast, "unhesitatingly accepts the form which the thinker has given to ideas" (Radin [1927] 1957:242). Those who separated the primitive from the civilized mind erred in expecting that "every analysis must be the work of the rational faculties" (Radin [1927] 1957:28). In fact, "the primitive" man was more likely than the civilized man to attain a truly integrated personality, recognizing alongside the rational, the "kaleidoscopic emotional reactions" tied to the experience of a moment (Radin [1927] 1957:40). Psychoanalysis had failed to cure the ills of North American society. Radin, like Sapir, longed for a more "genuine" culture, such as those he felt himself to have observed in his American Indian fieldwork.

The apparent integration of primitive cultures was a by-product of separation between the group and the individual (Radin [1927] 1957:52). The "interplay of participants and storytellers" (Radin [1927] 1957:48) precluded a single version of knowledge, again in the context of a particular moment and a dynamic progression of moments. Native Americans allowed freedom of belief: "That is my way of telling the story. Others have different ways" (Radin [1927] 1957:57). Such free thought was "a purely private concern." The price, however, was that "few coherent systems of belief have been obtained" (Radin [1927] 1957:57). This choice, itself a result of the philosophical predilections of particular societies rather than of absence of capacity for abstract thought, explained why philosophy was not everywhere systematic. Systematic thought was not necessarily valued beyond the world of the thinker. It "could be and was attempted, but it carried no validity, brought no prestige. It remained the expression of a particular man or, at best, of a particular group" (Radin [1927] 1957:57). Knowledge was different for each listener, uniquely and progressively constructed in relation to personal experience.

Because primitive philosophical speculation was primarily contextual, it met the "preponderantly practical needs of human intercourse" (Radin [1927] 1957:68). The investigator was dependent on texts applying philosophical speculation to behavior and social interaction. Such texts recorded "only statements made by the Winnebago themselves in accounts either actually written by themselves or contained in verbatim descriptions of the rituals obtained in the original Winnebago" (Radin [1927] 1957:64). Translation and accuracy were crucial issues of method and theory.

Philosophers, sages, seers, medicine men, moralists, and poets combined their insights. Just as American aboriginal languages lacked a single word for what Europeans call philosophy, English had no single word for what Radin called philosophy among primitives. The defining feature of this role was "a considerable degree of directed thought" (Radin [1927] 1957:276). The symbols attributed to whole cultures by ethnologists often appeared cliched; they were, however, "originally the interpretations of a specially gifted individual" (Radin [1927] 1957:211), perhaps like our own metaphors. Unlike most Western thought, however, this thought for its own sake was not divorced from everyday life (Radin [1927] 1957:321–22). It was simply how a certain type of individual saw the same world as cultural fellows of different temperament.

Radin even speculated that monotheism, correlated with a search for philosophical unity, characterized philosophers in all cultures, regardless of the common or official theology surrounding them (Radin [1927] 1957:365). Transformer and Trickster, creator and buffoon, were sides of the same question (Radin [1927] 1957:347). Explicit monotheism was rare among primitive peoples (Radin [1927] 1957:371), its spread dependent not on the nature or conclusions of philosophers but on sociological causes beyond the control of individuals (Radin [1927] 1957:372). The degree of formalization of a culture set implicit conditions enabling a primitive monotheist to sway the community to his position.

Radin claimed to have discovered "speculative philosophy and critical approach" among "representative primitive people" (Radin [1927] 1957:384); sampling was not addressed, and the original edition lacked an extended, individualized exemplar. The new appendix added the story of John Rave, a failed Winnebago visionary who became a successful curer, persuading himself that perhaps he held blessing after all; this primitive philosopher's life was dramatically restructured when peyote brought him "real" visions. The case study exemplified "An American Indian Religious and Philosophical Formulator" (Radin [1927] 1957:395–444). Like the new section on methods, its verisimilitude was methodological.

During the three decades separating the two editions of *Primitive Man as Philosopher,* the standards of ethnography changed, partly through Radin's own efforts. His work has renewed resonance today for the critique of representation, reassessment of linguistic relativity, and examination of the ethical implications of cross-cultural field research. Despite undeniable problematics in Radin's life history constructions (see Brumble 1988; Krupat 1996), this version of John Rave's story offered sustained consideration of the role of philosophical questions in the experience of a single individual; it included motivation and emotional investment in ideas and showed how peyote stimulated culture change at the level of an individual thinker and social actor. Such sophisticated examples were unavailable when Radin first argued, largely on faith, that his Winnebago comrades were potential philosophers in a way that could be meaningful to readers steeped in Western philosophical traditions.

The Individual in History

In *Method and Theory of Ethnology: An Essay in Criticism,* Radin attempted to unpack the Boasian paradigm, arguing that the quantitative distributional method "leads to overgeneralized, external, and patchwork histories of traits, in abstractly deduced time perspectives, rather than to specific histories of societies as experienced and created by their members" (Diamond 1981:85). His fellow Boasians had not taken the implications of the critique of evolution to their logical conclusion, as he had done in *Primitive Man as Philosopher.* Ethnology, as opposed to the whole scope of anthropology, was an unproblematic domain for Radin, defined by the culture of "those aborigines with whom the Europeans have come in contact since the fifteenth century" (Radin 1933:3). The discipline was a product of a specific historical context and its aftermath.

In Radin's view Boas had successfully challenged the evolutionary presupposition that ethnology should be a mere handmaiden to theory. Although evolution had "fortunately been relegated to oblivion, . . . its aftermath is still with us" (Radin 1933:4). Ethnologists still neglected the study of particular so-called primitive societies for their own sake because they were preoccupied with being natural scientists. Consciously or not, this led them to reify cultures studied, "as though we are dealing with a tabula rasa" (Radin 1993:5); "everything has to be proved anew" (Radin 1933:7). Science required the observer to treat phenomena as unknowns at the start of investigation. But the ethnologist's subjects "are nothing of the kind; they are *unknown cultures,* not simply *unknowns*" (Radin 1933:7; Radin's emphasis). Radin as historian privileged the concept of culture and revamped analysis toward interpretation rather than explanation.

In the absence of documentary records, trait distributions substituted for actual dynamics of aboriginal cultures. Boas stuck to documentation, "the type of factual presentation he manifestly prefers," with the "bare facts presented without comment" except about trait distribution (Radin 1933:8–9). Thus the facts he presented were "quite meaningless without annotation" (Radin 1933:65). Radin assumed, in contrast, that cultural facts did not speak for themselves as physical facts did. When Boas failed to comment on the facts as seen by the Kwakiutls, he inappropriately applied a quantitative scientific model to ethnological data. Emphasis on single-trait distribution even more dramatically limited the possibility of recognizing patterning within a single culture. Radin found Boas's scientism contradictory because he claimed that cultural and physical phenomena were different in kind and required different methods of study, then stopped just as "multiple causation" emerged. Despite Boas's explicit claims, therefore, his implicit theory was "certainly not a cultural historical one" (Radin 1933:11). Nonetheless, Radin qualified his critique: Boas's purported theoretical negativism merely manifested his scientific attitude, in itself a good thing.

The critical difference was the position of the observer; "we are part of the cultural facts we are describing" (Radin 1933:11). Scientific objectivity was "unattainable" precisely because historical facts consisted of "imponderabilia" rather than of "permanency and durability" (Radin 1933:12). Boas's so-called historical method equated the historical with the philological, comparing the distribution of static phenomena to attain a sequence of events. Radin believed Boas then turned sociologist, postulating inner local developments that remodeled foreign elements. Neither the sociological nor the linguistic method related to the method of the historian as Radin understood it.

Boas's "eclecticism," then, was fundamentally incoherent (Radin 1933:19). Radin deplored such crossing of the conventional methodological boundaries of sociology, psychology, science, and history, usually with short shrift to the latter. (He did not address institution or discipline boundaries, of little interest to the Trickster figure of Americanist ethnology.) Boas engendered "a certain ill-defined feeling of the nonimportance or nonsignificance, as such, of the specific history of a given culture" pervading "even the best of his monographs" (Radin 1933:27).

Because Boas trained "the vast majority of ethnologists in America," Radin set out to undermine his theory of history. The crux of his critique was that Boas excluded the individual from history by ruling out "the personal element in aboriginal culture" (Radin 1933:41). Radin accused Boas of withdrawing from using internal evidence of myths and rituals to secure "even a relative time sequence" (Radin 1933:50). Lowie followed suit, dismissing oral history because it mixed legend and fact. Kroeber, like Boas, was a naturalist at heart, while Sapir emphasized the stability of static linguistic patterns. Nonetheless, Radin acknowledged that Boas at least avoided the "analytical" extremes in delineating criteria for "distributions and clusterings" of traits practiced by Sapir and Clark Wissler (Radin 1933:28; cf. Payne and Murray 1983).

Boas's method was salutary in the early critique of evolution, but he failed to change his procedures after the enemy was vanquished. For Radin the distinction between so-called primitive and so-called civilized was a lamentable artifact of the age and area model of trait distribution. The "culture-area hypothesis" had produced a "deadlock," a failure to explain the history of cultures without writing. Yet Radin's fellow Boasians refused to give up "the only alternative . . . [to] chaos" (Radin 1933:30–31).

Radin defined his own usage of "historical": "What every historian means: the description of the culture in such a way that we feel we are dealing with real and specific men and women, with real and specific situations, and with a real and specific tradition. In addition, even if we realize that the history of a culture is unprocurable, no description ever carries conviction unless its recorder is convinced that it has had a history" (Radin 1933:177). As in *Primitive Man as Philosopher*, Radin used his own work on the "contemporary history" of the Winnebagos as exemplar. The ethnologist must "describe a specific culture as he finds it, without any reference to what has preceded or what is to follow" (Radin 1933:32). A footnote qualified "contemporary" to refer to the culture "as it existed three or four generations ago" (Radin 1933:34), that is, within the range of memory through oral transmission. Radin expounded at some length on the duration and intensity of fieldwork required to capture the Native point of view. Boas's work, by implication, was much more superficial.

Radin was unimpressed by "the somewhat compulsive urge to establish time sequences" (Radin 1933:52–53). The distributional method produced "a fictitious definiteness" of culture elements that "separated culture and culture growth from its vital connection with individuals" (Radin 1933:53). Sapir, normally "clear-headed," went to "compulsive" lengths to abstract methodological principles of time depth for preliterate cultures; in Radin's reading, however, Sapir ended with a disclaimer: "Everything depends upon the specific conditions of a specific problem" (Radin 1933:59).

Radin was most distressed by subordination of "the complete description of a culture" to other ends (Radin 1933:89). Emphasis on material culture and economic determinism led to inappropriately quantitative methods, which mired the work in method rather than in the ethnographic substance that was its proper raison d'être.

The "difficult and arduous" task of obtaining "the desired material in text" was the only way to produce an authentic and complete "picture of a culture" (Radin 1933:106). Radin had little to say about nontextual ethnography, insisting that folklore and literature were distinguishable stylistically, both within aboriginal cultures and in the analytic canon of anthropology. The Boasian textual method "is not, therefore, simply a piece of pedantry, . . . but a preliminary precaution for the attainment of accuracy"; commitment to accuracy also enjoined the ethnologist to provide "some information about the individuals from whom the texts emanate" (Radin 1933:108). We must know the information sources of informant and ethnologist, thus "keeping our record as clear from discernible personal distortions as . . . is humanly possible" (Radin 1933:114). Texts revealed nonliterate history: "The value of beginning with a document cannot be too strongly stressed. In elucidating culture we must begin with a fixed point, but this point must be one that has been given form by a member of the group described, and not by an alien observer. This is, of course, a truism to the historian" (Radin 1933:186).

Radin even proposed that a smaller number of "informants" would produce a better description. A complete description was always impossible, so the ethnologist must learn to concentrate, to seek out the "primitive philosophers." The whole question of the individual informant was subverted by those who "have preferred to make ethnologists out of their informants," training "their most promising collaborators" and retreating to roles of "arranging and editing," or "frequently, unfortunately, not editing, the data obtained by them" (Radin 1933:114). Radin included himself along with Truman Michelson and Boas among those who had taken this easy road. Philologists did better at maintaining textual integrity.

The ethnologist had a solemn obligation not to interfere with the textual records, which were "after all, in the same category as the archives of history. They may be dull, repetitious, uninspiring, dead. So, frequently, are the archives. Yet we have no right to touch them, even to the extent of rearranging them in the interests of clarity. They should undoubtedly be explained, rearranged, commented upon, and the breath of life be instilled into them. But this must be done apart from the records themselves" (Radin 1933:117). In this regard, Boas alone was fully consistent.

Every ethnologist aspired to "study an aboriginal culture as it presumably functioned before it had been seriously influenced or disturbed by contact with the major European and Asiatic civilizations" (Radin 1933:119). Among "the aborigines of North America," no group had fully functioned for at least three generations; the line between normal culture change and breakdown of culture was arbitrary and "somewhat delicate" (Radin 1933:122). Radin preferred "not to speak carelessly of a complete disorganization of the social order but, better, of a supplanting of one type of social organization by another to which the natives have not as yet become adjusted, but which enables them to live in security" (Radin 1933:123).

Methodological muddle was inevitable because "informants upon whom we have to rely" often spoke from hearsay and incorporated "their own generalizations and syntheses" (Radin 1933:125). Whatever the interest of the indigenous philosophical ideas, the ethnologist had to sort it out, moving between individual and culture. Radin's intent was not psychological. Explanation of John Rave's Winnebago texts in terms of his personality "would be entirely subjective," especially since Radin had failed to obtain his view of some of the events. Rave, however, "from my observation, was an extremely logical and ruthless thinker and very loyal where his feelings were aroused" (Radin 1933:209).

In Radin's view much of the apparent coherence of cultures resulted from the analytic imposition of sharpness and clarity. Few ethnologists were conscious that "cultures, on the whole, are rarely clear-cut and distinct, that it is only by a process of elimination and abstraction" that they come to seem so (Radin 1933:149).

Boas "dreads to visualize" ethnology "divorced from a rigorous logical and scientific method," fearing consequent inability to distinguish ethnology from belles lettres. The work of Margaret Mead or Malinowski nowhere included "an even approximately complete account of the people he [Malinowski] visited"; in the absence of texts, they were "simply impressionistic sketches" that could not be "critically controlled" (Radin 1933:173). Radin believed his fellow Boasians, in contrast, were "willing to forego the pleasures of surreptitious definiteness for one whiff of reality" (Radin 1933:168). Texts were the validity criterion for qualitative social science.

Radin's final chapter was titled "Theoretical Ethnology." For all his criticisms of then-contemporary theory, Radin acknowledged the impossibility of refraining from theory. Paradoxically, evolutionists and sociologists "frankly state that primitive peoples are not on a par intellectually and culturally with civilized nations," while anthropologists claimed to believe otherwise. Yet the theoretical significance of studying "primitive peoples" seemed to depend on their being qualitatively different (Radin 1933:256). Radin assumed "deep differences in initial presuppositions between ourselves and the primitives," realizing that "there was no easy way to study primitive society on its own terms" (Vidich 1966:xi). Radin denied the difference in order to explore the consequences of his position. The quantitative method erred in separating so-called primitive cultures from our own: "The analysis and description of Kwa-kiutl culture must be made according to the same principles as that of our own civilization" (Radin 1933:184). Civilization differed only in its progressive "en-largement of the sphere of awareness of the nature of our actions" (Radin 1933:167), what we would now call its reflexivity, in part due to knowledge of other cultures and their philosophers.

Method and Theory in Ethnology exposed Boasian internal squabbles to pub-lic scrutiny. Lowie's *The History of Ethnological Theory* in 1937 attacked Radin's penchant for rendering the reader "witness to an academically courteous form of clique warfare" (Vidich 1966:lii). Lowie, according to Arthur Vidich, rec-ognized that within Radin's strawman critique of Boas "there lurks a much deeper interpersonal drama in which the stakes are no less than the betrayal of the master, with all that implies for introducing self-doubt and consternation in the ranks of the loyal" (Vidich 1966:lii). Radin rejected Boas's habitual fail-ure to "tolerate theoretical or ideological differences in his students" (Radin 1933:xxv). In addition to being limited in his historical sense, Radin's Boas was personally rigid and disapproving. Lowie, in contrast, saw Boasian anthropol-ogy as fortunate in a leadership that produced gradual and cumulative increase in knowledge, that is, postrevolutionary normal science.

The Counterargument for Systematic Philosophy

Radin's insistence that anthropology should be history was not universally ac-cepted among his peers. Kroeber, for example, descried its dependence on the standpoint of the individual as an actor in history. In *Configurations of Culture Growth,* absence of writing motivated his dismissal of alternative systems of philosophy because "such efforts at philosophizing as there might have been previously, would be likely to be lost" (Kroeber 1944:789). *A Roster of Civiliza-tions and Culture* defined philosophy in the context of the limitations of cul-tural history:

> [Philosophy must be] something more than the occasional reflections of peas-ants, Eskimos, or any essentially illiterate peoples, shrewd and profound as these sometimes are. I would define philosophy as coordinated abstract think-ing on the nature of the universe, of being, of ourselves as men [sic], and of our knowing; with the employment of words in a consistent manner until some of them become essentially precise or "technical" terms, usable in the erection of

a systematic conceptual structure, which in turn is capable of enlargement or serving as foundation for further systematizing. (Kroeber 1962:81)

Kroeber's encapsulated and culture-specific definition particularly insisted on freedom of systematic philosophy from mysticism, magic, ritual, and religion—all threatening the rationality he took to be at the core of philosophy. The philosophies Kroeber considered legitimate arose virtually simultaneously in China, India, Iran, and Greece. Ancient Near Eastern nations, in contrast, had "philosophizings" but not "systematic philosophy" (Kroeber 1962:81). "It is also clear that no American people had achieved a systematic philosophy" (Kroeber 1962:82). Although Radin explicitly denied making a claim for systematic philosophy as a universal, Kroeber's impossibly high standard effectively insulated Western thought from contact with other traditions known to ethnologists (because they were preliterate rather than because they were non-Western).

Robert Redfield emphasized that preliterate societies explain things according to convention or custom, so that "the principles of rightness which underlie the activities are largely tacit. And they are not the subject of much explicit criticism, nor even of very much reflective thought" (Redfield 1953:14). For Redfield the "moral order" of ideas rather than the simple materialism that he equated with (much of his own) civilization reflected the "great theme of Western historiography and philosophic writing" (Redfield 1953:76). There was no room in this conversation for the primitive philosopher.

Practical knowledge was more important than philosophy, as Malinowski had demonstrated for the Trobriand Islanders. Expanding civilization might create an intelligentsia, but it would consist largely of unhappy marginal men (Redfield 1953:44). (Redfield referred here to culture change in Mayan villages rather than to the plight of the North American intellectual in the absence of a genuine culture.) The ancient Maya cities had their "literati who carried a folk tradition into a specialized, esoteric, and reflective form" (Redfield 1953: 59). Eventually, these specialists become "writers, and calculators, and thinkers" (Redfield 1953:64). But such philosophy was a product of the increasing complexity of the state, which produced statesmen and philosophers (Redfield 1953:65), rather than a property of human communities everywhere.

Redfield conceded Radin's observation that "to some degree among primitives and peasants" there was a distinction between "the reflective and the merely active" character; this "becomes very great in civilizations." Redfield described such a man:

I make a study of Maya Indians of Yucatan. One man of the village in particular is a thoughtful fellow; he really ruminates. When I ask him questions, his
mind seems naturally to arrange things into systematic wholes. I find it easy to
put down what he says, just because it is so well considered and makes such coherent sense. But does he really represent the other Indians who can say so
much less to me about the world they inhabit? . . . Then there is already, in
primitive society, at least some slight difference between the world view of most
people and the cosmologies of the more thoughtful. But, as civilization advances, the difference becomes greater. (Redfield 1953:88)

The task of the ethnologist, then, was to ignore philosophical speculations not
held in common by every member of a society—precisely the anthropological
blinder against which Radin railed! Indeed, given the nature of disciplinary
generalization, anthropologists were "fleeing for refuge among Indian or An-
damanese, where what one man thinks is not too different from what most of
them think" (Redfield 1953:89). Ethnologists were trained to document "the
usual and institutional, not what is unusual and creatively novel." Their efforts
to record culture influenced "the average native" to be "more systematic and
reflective . . . than is actually true" (Redfield 1953:114). Redfield dismissed Radin's examples of philosophical thinking because the purported philosophers
were already "affected by civilization." Native minds were "set in motion by a
civilized mind" (Redfield 1953:115).

This position removed "primitive man as philosopher" from the possibility
of anthropological investigation and assumed a now-untenable passivity of
aboriginal peoples in the face of European contact. Redfield qualified his critique somewhat, noting that twenty-five years had brought "no important ref-
utation" to Radin's book (Redfield 1953:115). Indeed, "in any primitive society
there are some people who make explicit systems out of looser traditional
ideas," especially cosmologies and origin myths (Redfield 1953:116). Redfield
conceded Radin's argument insofar as it was based on fieldwork: "Most ethnologists who have worked intimately with isolated, nonliterate people who
enjoy even a little time in which one might reflect find in such communities a
few people who do reflect" (Redfield 1953:117). Redfield simply doubted that
this was speculation for its own sake or that, in the absence of writing, the thesis of philosophical universality could be resolved.

Redfield also doubted that this reflection was systematic; further evidence
for the absence of genuine philosophy in "primitive" societies came from Mar-

garet Mead's description of the Mountain Arapeshes, whose "outlook on the universe is primarily affective, not cognitive," with "little intellectual systematization; the universe is very loosely structured" (Redfield 1953:94-95).

Alexander Goldenweiser, Radin's crony in many contexts, saw history as providing ethnological time depth, concluding that "critical thought and a sober outlook upon things is quite foreign to early man" who "does not think straight; at least not when it comes to explanations and hypotheses" (Goldenweiser 1922:156). For Goldenweiser, as for Kroeber, supernaturalism precluded philosophy. Moreover, "the early system of knowledge" was "highly pragmatic" and "semi-automatic," with expertise but "no critical thought" and "no professional addiction to investigation" (Goldenweiser 1953:157). The anthropologist functioned as the philosopher for the primitive. The only professional role Goldenweiser recognized in societies he had studied was that of "professional gossip" (Goldenweiser 1953:157).

Mankind must learn "through measurement and inquiry and criticism and the detachment of the individual, to evade the pitfalls of myth and ritual, the shrewdness of the priest and the magician, and his own craving for the impossible" (Goldenweiser 1922:234). Whatever this statement says for Goldenweiser's conception of philosophy in his own tradition, it is far from Radin's view of the importance of the individual and the uniformity of human capacities regardless of cultural complexity.

In sum, there was considerable lack of consensus among the Boasians about the proper relationship of culture to individual, history to contemporary society, and primitive to civilized.

The Closing of the Philosophical Mind

The legacy of American pragmatism has moved considerably beyond the cross-cultural curiosity with which John Dewey introduced the first edition of *Primitive Man as Philosopher*. Richard Rorty, perhaps the most persuasive contemporary advocate of a context-free philosophy without metaphysical foundations, argues, with disappointing ethnocentrism, that philosophy is always deeply grounded in culture, "because culture is the assemblage of claims of knowledge, and philosophy adjudicates such claims" (Rorty 1979:3). At first glance the argument sounds anthropological, but Rorty fails to address cross-cultural evidence. Systematic constructive philosophy should become edifying and therapeutic, a conversation, rather than a truth claim, situated outside history. No neutral analytic language is possible. Evaluation of alternative descriptions is a property of historiography rather than of things in the world (Rorty 1979:267–82). Without its conventional Enlightenment foundations, philosophy becomes merely history of science; Western philosophy can answer its questions only by reliving its past (Rorty 1979:33). Since objectivity is impossible, *Bildung,* self-realization, what Dewey called "aesthetic enhancement," becomes a more limited but attainable goal (Rorty 1979:13).

Philosophical argument transforms itself into a story in which conversation replaces confrontation of positions. Rorty reframes representational truth and objective reality in terms of social practices: "We need to turn outward rather than inward, toward the social context of justification rather than to the relation between inner representations" (Rorty 1979:210). The obvious next step would seem to be ethnographic exemplification—but Rorty retreats to introspection, a thought experiment about incommensurate Antipodeans (Rorty 1979:70–127). Rorty professes himself interested primarily in "why we have such a phenomenon as 'philosophy' in our culture" (Rorty 1979:229). Radin, as ethnographer, would have reformulated the question as "why does our culture have the kind of philosophy it does?" That question would be answered by comparison to philosophies arising from diverse cultural contexts.

For Rorty philosophy without foundations exploits philosophy's linguistic turn. He privileges a vocabulary specific to Western philosophy in which arguments depend on prior arguments within a continuous, albeit contested, conversation synonymous with the history of Western philosophy. Rorty is primarily interested in epistemology, defined in terms of familiar knowledge claims whose rationality may be assessed by their formal statement. Hermeneutics, in contrast, involves coping with the incommensurable, that is, the exotic, whether separated from ourselves by time, space, or cultural tradition. This is where cultural anthropology fits in, where "nothing save tact and imagination will serve," given that beliefs expressed in a philosophical language alien to them will always appear to be false, as, for example, are the witchcraft beliefs of the Azandes described by Evans-Pritchard ([1937] 1976). Commensurability, a requirement of doing (systematic) philosophy, entails rational agreement, defined as the construction of an epistemology involving "the maximum amount of common ground with others" (Rorty 1979:293, 316).

Relativism involves abandoning hope of commensuration. Rorty proposes that hermeneutic rationality implies to "refrain from epistemology, the expectation of a common vocabulary" and "to be willing to pick up the jargon of the interlocutor rather than translating it into one's own" (Rorty 1979:318). Radin, in contrast, insisted that ethnologists learn the language, including the philosophical language—and presumably learn to express their own ideas in it. In the more ethnocentric tradition of Western philosophy, however, the hermeneutic circle allows the investigator (assuming the process goes only one way) to change positions, thinking initially within the alien system (in the field) and later outside it (as translator). To take a hermeneutic position is to admit that we do not understand what is happening (Rorty 1979:321). Rorty does not find this interesting.

The best disambiguation device is "the discovery of an epistemology written within that culture" (Rorty 1979:346). Radin's texts from John Rave constitute such an epistemology, albeit outside the catchment of Western philosophy. Rorty acknowledges that one can function in an exotic language-game but remains skeptical about continuing to care "what sentence in our ordinary language-game is materially equivalent" (Rorty 1979:355). For him learning to cope in the field does not ensure an adequate stance for ethnographic reportage.

The same philosophical stance should apply to exotic cultures as to historical periods, scientific disciplines, and the "poetic activity of thinking up" things (Rorty 1979:356–60). Rorty, however, casually equates ethnography with other "alternative descriptions offered by poets, novelists, depth psychologists, sculptors, anthropologists, and mystics"; these are "not privileged representations," and ethnographies are merely "among the repertoire of self-descriptions at our disposal" (Rorty 1979:362). Attaining consensus across cultural boundaries cannot surmount the communicative gap: "All we can do is show how the other side looks from our own point of view. That is, all we can do is be hermeneutic about the opposition—trying to show how the odd or paradoxical or offensive things they say hang together with the rest of what they want to say, and how what they say looks when put in our own alternative idiom" (Rorty 1979:364-65). Rorty identifies this "polemical intent" with the deconstructionism of Heidegger and Derrida (Rorty 1979:365); but it would seem also to dismiss the thoughts of the philosopher-from-elsewhere, alongside those of ethnographers, as just-so stories.

Oddly enough, having buried cultural anthropology (in which he includes intellectual history), Rorty returns to praise it. But the praise consists in refusing to acknowledge the need for a natural history or a positivist science of knowledge claims (Rorty 1979:381). He fails to come to terms with how consensus and epistemological behaviorism (i.e., the new pragmatism) work within Western philosophy but not outside it. Yet, paradoxically, he proposes to study contemporary academic disciplinary boundaries, using ethnographic methods: "Such disciplinary matrices are studied by the usual empirical-cum-hermeneutic methods of 'cultural anthropology'" (Rorty 1979:385). For the group studied, "these subjective conditions" combine common sense "with the standard current theory about the subject" (Rorty 1979:385). The anthropologist or historian of ideas, in contrast, focuses on "the empirical facts about the beliefs, desires, and practices of a certain group of human beings" (Rorty 1979:385).

Despite the impossibility of standing in both positions simultaneously, Rorty sees no reason to "subsume the two in a higher synthesis": "The group in question may itself shift from the one point of view to the other. . . . But this is not a mysterious process which demands a new understanding of human knowledge" (Rorty 1979:386). In Radin's language Rorty acknowledges that practitioners of a scientific discipline may think as philosophers. A short step could extend this capacity to philosophers from other cultures. Indeed, Radin's willingness to make this move has enabled his Americanist successors to apply the train of thought formalized by Rorty to philosophers regardless of their historically grounded cultural backgrounds.

Rorty's later work revisits the question of what conversations can be like. The essays included in *Contingency, Irony, and Solidarity* are even more pessimistic about the feasibility or interest of ethnography. At any given moment, each individual and each culture has a "final vocabulary," an ongoing product of all previous experience. There is no criterion to choose among the "incarnated vocabularies" of persons or cultures: "So our doubts about our own characters or our own culture can be resolved or assuaged only by enlarging our acquaintance. The easiest way of doing that is to read books, and so ironists spend more of their time placing books than in placing real live people. Ironists are afraid that they will get stuck in the vocabulary in which they were brought up if they only know the people in their own neighborhood" (Rorty 1989:80). One thing the ironist (i.e., the philosopher without foundations) may read is ethnography. Meanwhile, Rorty seems to have given up on epistemological consensus even within his own tradition. His ethnographic ironist is locked in a prison set by categories, unredeemed by a relativism that descends into metaphysics.

Moreover, the anthropological search for universals is futile. Each topic of conversation simply produces another "redescription" (or reorientation in terms of a new vocabulary) incommensurable with previous alternatives (Rorty 1989:51). Radin's example was the "primitive" culture conquered by a more advanced one, in practice the European. Rorty expects "that one's self and one's world are futile, obsolete, *powerless*. Redescription often humiliates" (Rorty 1989:90). He sees the so-called primitive solely in relation to his own powerful postcolonial society.

Moving even further from the lessons of Radin's "primitive philosophers," Rorty proposes that philosophy is merely a private matter, the *Bildung* of an individual isolated from collectivity. "The perfect life [of the ironist] will be one which closes in the assurance that the last of his final vocabularies, at least, really was wholly *his*" (Rorty 1989:97). If the philosopher is also a theorist, she or he will restrict this assemblage of the past to "a particular, rather narrowly confined, literary tradition—roughly, the Plato-Kant canon, and footnotes to that canon" (Rorty 1989:97). Theory, then, "has become a means to a private perfection rather than to human solidarity" (Rorty 1989:96). It is a closed system. Neither Radin nor his Winnebago interlocutors would be likely to comprehend, much less embrace, this conclusion.

Rorty is prepared to concede claims to representation and thus to the very possibility of social science. Novels and ethnographies are equated in their capacity to "sensitize one to the pain of those who do not speak our language"; the solidarity at the basis of liberal democracy, for Rorty, is attainable only as "constructed out of [such] little pieces" (Rorty 1989:94). Ethnography remains, for him, a thought experiment:

> Imagine that I am forming such a theory about the current behavior of a native of an exotic culture into which I have unexpectedly parachuted. This strange person, who presumably finds me equally strange, will simultaneously be busy forming a theory about my behavior. If we ever succeed in communicating easily and happily, it will be because her guesses about what I am going to do next . . . and my own expectations about what I shall do or say under certain circumstances, come more or less to coincide, and because the converse is also true. She and I are coping with each other as we might cope with mangoes or boa constrictors—we are trying not to be taken by surprise. (Rorty 1989:14)

Radin's ethnographic texts recording actual philosophizings from other cultures underscore Rorty's failure to carry his concern for liberation from sterile representationalism to its anthropological application. The methodological appendix to *Primitive Man as Philosopher* incorporates both an optimism and an interpretive charity absent in Rorty's contemporary version of pragmatism.

Are the Alternatives Philosophies?

Radin's extension of the capacity to philosophize to some members of all human cultures was primarily geared to even out the power differential between the primitive and the civilized, to create a space for cross-cultural conversations. He lacked sufficient evidence to decide whether attention to what his own culture defined as philosophical questions would constitute a comparative domain across cultures. Because of the way in which he formulated the question, however, his successors have been forced to address it. Clearly, "they" do something interesting, in a variety of different ways, but it is less clear that "philosophy" is an illuminating cover term.

Stephen Tyler, perhaps the most extreme critique of the possibility of anthropological representation, suggests that, among the Dravidian Koyas of southern India, thinking, never mind philosophizing, is simply not a focus of attention. The Koyas prefer to report what people said, leaving the underlying thought process implicit. The person is passive in relation to something closer to emotion, desire, or opinion than to rational thought, with somewhat paradoxical results:

> All of this may lead us to conclude that when a Koya thinks, he has nothing in mind, which may well be correct from our point of view, but it is also the case that he hasn't much to say about it either, for thought and thinking are not major topics of discourse. The first Koya "Symposium" is yet to be held and what someone says, does, and desires is far more important than what he thinks about thought. In the commonsense world inhabited by Koyas, saying and doing—words and deeds—are far more important than thinking, and this is reflected in their linguistic habits. (Tyler 1987:166–67)

Dravidian languages avoid representation; most nouns related to thought are borrowed from Sanskrit and not used in everyday speech. Throughout India, things, substances, are considered illusory and constantly in flux. Insofar as it is useful to speak about rationality, its Dravidian counterpart would encompass "a way of feeling/knowing." Phenomenology, "only a disturbing afterthought" in Western philosophy, would form the core of Indian philosophy, as "another point of view" [Tyler's subhead] (Tyler 1987:167–68).

An alternative response to this other point of view toward a cross-culturally adequate concept of "thought" might treat the extreme rationality of Western philosophy as the aberration and seek a more sensorially and experientially based cover category. Tyler's own move from "representation" to "evocation" applies such a strategy to the tool kit of the social scientist. Perhaps a Koya philosopher and a Western anthropologist could productively negotiate the extent to which they were talking about the same things or could empathize with each other's need to talk about some things and not about others. Notably, Tyler does not even pause to panic over the oral character of what might or might not be Koya philosophy. As for Radin, writing is trivial relative to the posing of philosophical questions.

There are multiple ethnographically attested cases where people decline to articulate their cultural beliefs in words, much less systems of thoughts. For example, Jane Fajans revisits the frustrations of generations of ethnographers (including Gregory Bateson, whose description of a New Guinea ritual system [*Bateson* 1958] was arguably the first symbolic ethnography) at their inability to pin down in words the world of the Bainangs. Previous ethnographers erred, Fajans argues, not in their failure to capture something that was out there in the Bainang world, but in their failure to acknowledge that what was "boring" to anthropological outsiders formed the stuff of life for the Bainangs: "The Bainang, while friendly, accepting, and gentle, are neither inquisitive nor garrulous. Conversation is obsessively mundane. . . . Gossip is minimal. Very little information comes forth spontaneously. Even the few traditional narratives seem to elicit little interest. . . . Questions are usually met with a mixture of incomprehension, shyness, and passive disinterest . . . and people are loath to put themselves forward by answering questions" (Fajans 1997:5). Fajans concludes, somewhat anticlimactically: "The cumulative effect of these characteristics of Bainang culture, society, and personality" is "to strain the common assumptions and practices of anthropologists as participant-observers to the breaking point" (Fajans 1997:5).

Johannes Fabian (1998:102) problematizes Radin's argument in yet another direction. Philosophy, at least in the African societies most familiar to him, has been undemocratic, failing to think in terms of communal as well as individual well-being; further, the category of philosophy was imposed by colonialism. Fabian doubts that Africans will "be able to think their way out of their present predicament," not because they lack "either cognitive capacities or moral fiber" but because Western regimes of power remain outside their control (Fabian 1998:103). He is more concerned to establish the "presence" of African thought in global arenas than to document its existence, which, since Radin, can be taken for granted. Fabian turns to popular culture to "show what Africans have in mind when . . . they reflect on, and talk about, thought and thinking" (Fabian 1998:106). He seems to concur with Radin, moreover, that thinking/philosophizing need not be systematic when he describes his own fieldwork method in terms of thought and memory rather than of analytic objectivity (Fabian 1998:106). In contemporary Zaire, thinking and remembering invoke nostalgia as a powerful subversive technique of resistance (Fabian 1998: 107).

Interestingly, Fabian recognizes a philosophy most readily when he can locate an individual at the center of the syncretism between imposed missionary and traditional practices. The Jamaa gnostic movement, embodied in the charismatic figure of Placide Tempels, is a philosophy because it involves thought and a goal for society, both of which Fabian deems absent from the demoralized, introverted mysticism of the Christian charismatic renewal. He cautions that the surface forms of African philosophical systems will involve magic and sorcery as compatible with modernism and "critical emancipatory potential" (Fabian 1998:112).

Fabian is unwilling to leave aside the question of whether African philosophers are representative of their cultures, whereas Radin was willing to focus on an isolated individual thinking about things without feedback prior to the arrival of an anthropologist. Fabian argues that Jamaa teachings, despite their status as hermetic doctrine, deal with issues of everyday life that are widely shared, especially in urban areas. The terminology of the movement allows participants to talk about their experiences in the same way. Further, "thinking" is a broader term than in Western philosophy, incorporating dreaming and imagining and their historical consequences (Fabian 1998:122). This "epistemological realism" is based on claims to authority by witnesses or "compilers of testimony," both roles compatible with the traditional preoccupations of an anthropologist. Fabian's primitive philosophers are historians of a social constructionist bent with a political agenda.

In Search of Contemporary "Primitive" Philosophers

My own work with the Plains Crees of northern Alberta over the last three decades has become increasingly "philosophical," further removed from behav-

ioral observations and more dependent on conversations with elders and traditional teachers. I wrote fairly extensively about the premises of "interactional
etiquette" that underlie Cree performances across a range of content domains
(e.g., Darnell 1974c, 1979, 1981, 1984, 1985b, 1988b) without fully addressing
what the Crees might make out of my articulation of their implicit ways of
treating living beings (including human persons). I undertook to systematize a
set of formal principles codifying what I had been taught about how to behave
"like a Cree person" (*Nehiyaw*), a standard of behavior and understanding
open to persons of any ethnic descent. I came up with thirty-nine postulates,
and members of a largely non-Native conference audience added a few more.
Non-Native observers are all too prone to describe First Nations/Native American actions and interactions in negative terms relative to mainstream North
America, further entrenching cross-cultural miscommunication. Obviously,
no Cree person would state a series of postulates; they are my abstractions
from interactions and explicit teachings. Nor do they predict individual behaviors; rather, they codify normative assumptions about the evaluation of behavior and "the wish to look well in the eyes of others" (Darnell 1991b:90).

In relation to Radin's argument, I now wonder about the degree to which
this information is structured in a way commensurable with, albeit not identical to, Cree self-representations. The exercise involves cross-cultural empathetic imagination and claims validity for mutual resonance based on my own
fieldwork experience: "If a Cree person were going to write a series of postulates for language, its place in interaction, and the grounding of language and
interaction in the domain of power," the result might look like Table 1 (Darnell
1991b:91–101).

The interactional system summarized in these postulates entails reasonably
consistent answers to fundamental epistemological and ethical questions that
are also recognized in the Western philosophical tradition. These questions are
not usually raised in this form by Cree persons, however, because they consider
such matters part of what "everyone knows" and therefore not reportable.
Nonetheless, most Crees with whom I have discussed these matters agree that
the things I have singled out are true; moreover, they can cite examples of non-
Native people who do not know them and consequently behave disrespectfully.

The question of whether such implicit philosophical questions and their
culture-specific answers are the product of individual philosophers thinking
about things is more complex than whether the results are coherent or systematic. The answer, I believe, resides in how such things are learned. Many of the

Table 1. Postulates of Plains Cree Communication

---

1 / Interaction usually proceeds dyadically.

2 / Social occasions are defined by copresence rather than by talk.

3 / Under many conditions, the most respectful speech is silence.

4 / The personal autonomy of living beings precludes attempts to interfere with or control their behavior or opinions.

5 / Respect for autonomous persons precludes direct contradiction.

6 / Deniable strategies, often nonverbal, are preferable to confrontational talk.

7 / It is respectful to avoid eye contact.

8 / Face-to-facedness is incidental to effective communication.

9 / The participants in interaction are not interchangeable.

10 / The asymmetry of social relationships makes interactional control residual to the oldest or most respected person present.

11 / Initiative to structure the progress of an interaction is dangerous and to be avoided wherever possible.

12 / Knowledge is age-graded and those who know things are to be treated with respect.

13 / Questions should be phrased indirectly.

14 / Questions, direct or indirect, do not require a reply, although they remain on the floor and open to response at any later time.

15 / The ideal speech is a monologue, in which someone speaks who is culturally defined as authoritative, as knowing something important enough to convey to others.

16 / Eye-witness accounts based on personal experience are privileged over the theoretical, abstract, and second-hand.

17 / Old information is preferred over and subordinated to new.

18 / When people are together, they are assumed to be known to one another.

19 / Known persons express respect by assuming the on-going nature of their social relationship(s).

20 / Closure of topic shuts off further interaction; there should always be loose ends.

21 / Referential speech is less important than expressive speech; reference should be embedded in social relationship.

22 / Listening and speaking are equally active roles in communication.

23 / A listener must confirm his or her attention to the speech of another, signifying attentiveness but not necessarily agreement.

Table 1. *Continued*

---

24 / A thoughtful pause is necessary before any verbal response in an exchange of turns at talk.

25 / Spoken words are available for exegesis at any future time.

26 / Everyone present is implicitly addressed when serious words are spoken.

27 / A speaker needs an audience of at least one listener; others present may join in at their own will at any time.

28 / In storytelling or narrative, say as little as possible.

29 / Storytelling or narrative should be tailored to the situational context of a particular telling.

30 / Interpretation is open-ended and will differ across listeners.

31 / Formal verbal instruction is only necessary for things that cannot be conveyed in any other form.

32 / Someone who knows something is under obligation to pass it on to an appropriate successor who will use it wisely.

33 / Teaching is deliberately cryptic.

34 / The community of living persons is extended to the ancestors and to the animate powers of the natural world.

35 / Persons who have died and spirits are potential addressees and respondents.

36 / Personal knowledge, particularly in the power domain, must not be disclosed in detail except on the person's deathbed.

37 / Use of the future tense jeopardizes ongoing processes in the world of power.

38 / When a speaker moves between the secular and the sacred worlds, in either direction, a transition is necessary.

39 / Although genres of speaking are named and distinguished in principle, assignment to a genre is often problematic in practice.

---

postulates are about how to learn. Elders teach some of them verbally and explicitly, at least to anthropologists and children. Mentors will point out how people acted in a given situation (sometimes using a traditional story), calling attention to the consequences for a thoughtless or uninformed learner. One can ask someone (usually later) what is or was going on or what someone meant. When an elder has spoken, people talk about what she or he said and its meaning in terms of their various and overlapping experiences. Such occasions for philosophical conversation do not depend on cross-cultural experience or external inquirers. As Radin noted, some people are more eager to enter into such philosophical speculations than others, and some are more subtle in their reasoning. The corollary is that not any old Indian will do. There is no reason other than ethnocentrism, often manifested as failure to listen, to envision a culture in which such interactions fail to occur.

Jean Becker's unpublished M.A. thesis attempts to reconcile the habitual assumptions of a morally compromised positivist anthropology with her identity as an Innu woman who is also a scholar. She argues that some forms of anthropology are both ethical and deeply resonant with the principles of First Nations (Native American) interaction; commensurability with certain kinds of anthropology is possible and desirable: "I saw similarities between postmodern thought and Aboriginal values and beliefs and it occurred to me that a researcher with post-modern attitudes, concepts and assumptions might be able to create a different kind of relationship with Aboriginal people than the one which exists today; a relationship based on mutual respect and one in which the researcher recognizes and seeks to eliminate the power differential between herself and the research subject" (Becker 1993:2). Feminist standpoint epistemology is also commensurable with the ways of knowing that Becker learned as a child (Becker 1993:45–47). How such a position is to be put into practice remains to be clarified, but she believes that postmodern rhetoric points in a promising direction.

Becker's "distaste" for conventional anthropology centers around the offensive experience of being objectified (Becker 1993:3–4). Social relations, for First Nations peoples, are supposed to be nonhierarchical (Becker 1993:39), which poses a serious paradox for the aboriginal researcher in conducting interviews and imposing interpretations on the views of others. Postmodernism changes the old relationships primarily through its capacity to transform the consciousness of the anthropologist, which in turn should transform the products of her or his ethnographic writing (Becker 1993:36).

The "cultural misrepresentation" imposed by positivist anthropology is, for Becker, indistinguishable from cultural genocide (Becker 1993:42), the antithesis to a "vehicle that finally will allow you to interpret yourselves for us and allow us to interpret ourselves for you" (Becker 1993:43), that is, a dialogue. Like Radin, Becker envisions the production of ethnographies requiring "the skills of communal rather than individual achievement" (Becker 1993:53). The thinker, whether anthropologist or consultant/interlocutor, will act individually but with reference to the group or community.

Becker concludes that she can retain her anthropological identity as long as she gets to define the anthropology, but the needed transformation of anthropological consciousness has so far remained elusive:

> I have not found any indication in post-modern theory of the central, most vital aspect of the Aboriginal world-view—the spiritual dimension. In addition I find no evidence of the Aboriginal concern with the natural environment and no understanding of the relationship between human life and other forms of life. I regard the absence of these components from post-modernism as serious flaws in the theory rather than evidence that spiritual and environmental concerns do not belong with intellectual pursuits. From an Aboriginal viewpoint, the false separation of mind, body and spirit is the paramount and most dangerous error of the Western world-view. (Becker 1993:55–56)

The epistemology of positivist science "calls for a disintegration of the integrity of the person that is inappropriate for Aboriginal people" (Becker 1993:76). We need not cling to a rigidly materialist science to know and to share knowledge. It is appropriate, at least some of the time, to talk to outsiders, to draw on more than one knowledge tradition, as long as it is done reciprocally and respectfully. Indians are not the only ones who speak from a grounded standpoint.

The kinds of principles derived from First Nations' answers to basic philosophical questions seem, even to the outsider, well adapted to the oral traditions and small, isolated, face-to-face communities of their origins. But they continue to be applied as guides to everyday life by contemporary aboriginal people, both in cities and on reservations (called reserves in Canada), who unproblematically appropriate new communications technologies of writing, radio, television, and telephone to maintain the quality of life characteristic of the home communities "from times immemorial," in the idiom of the traditional oral cultures. Despite the intensity of recent culture change, there is no reason to suppose that people have not always had philosophers who self-consciously adapted tradition to contemporary realities.

Fieldwork may well be the most theoretical of the things anthropologists do, because it forces us to reflect on the premises of our personal traditions, both culture-of-origin and professional. The work we produce is constrained from two powerful directions: first, from the theory of anthropology, and second, from the theories of those with whom we interact in the course of our fieldwork. Alongside Jean Becker, I acknowledge that aboriginal forms of knowing have colored my understanding of interdisciplinary theory in the social sciences and humanities and clarified my view of anthropology's potential contribution to that series of philosophical conversations.

Congruencies between postmodernism and various Native American philosophies do not imply that either forms a single coherent system of thought or that they arise from similar contexts. Native philosophers, in contrast to many postmodernist skeptics, do not worry about paradoxes, ambiguities, relativities, and open-endednesses; rather, they assume the world is complex and cannot be modeled in any simple or linear way, at least from the standpoint of a human philosopher. Their philosophizing takes a rhetorical form because culture itself is a symbolic form and identity a social construction conveyed through communication.

A final point requires emphasis: The person most often disoriented by the fragmentation of truth as situated knowledge seems to be the visiting postmodernist anthropologist who expects ethnographic subjects to operate with a modernist respect for positivist coherence, while she or he alone constructs the world in more fluid terms. Radin's legacy rejects a distinction in kind among persons who think merely because of the cultural tradition in which their thinking is grounded. The privilege of philosophizing across cultural boundaries is reciprocal and universal. The philosophers with whom anthropologists engage in other cultures have history, tradition, and authorial authority in the same sense that we claim it for ourselves.

BENJAMIN LEE WHORF

CHAPTER 5

Linguistic Relativity and Cultural Relativism

Benjamin Lee Whorf has become an icon in the histories of North American anthropology and linguistics, his life-work consequently reduced to the single idea of linguistic relativity, the relation of mutual entailment among language, culture, and reality. Dis-ease about his purported lack of rigorous method has alternated with a wistful hope that language might indeed claim a pivotal role in the constitution and integration of the human sciences. That there would be no such relationship is counterintuitive; to demonstrate its precise nature, however, has remained an elusive prospect for Whorf's successors. Icons are difficult to frame relative to everyday disciplinary work. Whorf has been the most controversial figure in Boasian inner circles—complex, intriguing, thoroughly misread. Protégé and sometime student of Sapir, Whorf is remembered as a linguist whose work, which seemed to some to consist of equal parts science and mysticism, spanned anthropology, linguistics, and psychology. Debates continue, intensified by the 1997 centennial of his birth, as to whether Whorf was right or wrong about the relationship of language, culture, and reality; contemporary cognitive science is, at best, ambivalent.

I want to sidestep this question temporarily and situate Whorf first in relation to the cadre of students around Edward Sapir and second in terms of the "psychological" language of Ruth Benedict's *Patterns of Culture,* which appeared in 1934 just as Whorf was formulating his own ideas about the study of language in anthropology. Whorf's argument, like Benedict's, was about relativity (a powerful metaphor in the science of the day) and its moral consequences for the individual (primarily in modern Western society). Benedict and Whorf shared a profound distaste for the directions in which their own society was moving and hoped cross-cultural evidence from anthropology could provide a better direction.

If Whorf is the Boasian about whom his intellectual heirs have been most ambivalent, then Ruth Benedict is surely the one whose place alongside Boas was most secure. She was the first woman (of many who followed her) to attain distinction among Boas's students. After brief forays into social work, teaching, and feminist writing, she rejected the conventional roles of marriage and family to enroll at the New School for Social Research in 1919, seeking to come to terms with the maelstrom caused by the First World War and the sterility of her marriage. Her teachers, Alexander Goldenweiser and Elsie Clews Parsons, soon introduced her to Boas, and she received her Ph.D. in 1923, after three semesters at Columbia (Mintz 1981:144), where she settled into the core of New York anthropology as Boas's second-in-command (often also his mediator to younger generations of students). In the intense intellectual ferment of Columbia University in the 1920s, Benedict wrote poetry under the name of Anne Singleton and became particularly intimate with Edward Sapir and Margaret Mead.

Benedict's work formed a bridge between the scientific and the humanities poles of Boasian anthropology, particularly through the transition from the trait diffusion model of her dissertation research on the guardian spirit quest in North America to the holism of *Patterns of Culture* eleven years later; the latter work brought the psychological fit of individual and culture and the aesthetic contrast among ethnographically known cultures to the forefront of Boasian theory. Benedict, Mead, and Sapir would develop this perspective into what later came to be known as culture and personality.

Although Benedict attempted to characterize cultures as wholes, like Sapir she was passionately interested in the role of individual choice and creativity. Along with Boas she wrote lyrically about race and the rise of Nazism, insisting on "the study of culture as a way to explain" (Mintz 1981:154). Her later work, including a study of Japan "at a distance" (Benedict 1946), employed the critical perspective of cultural relativism, understanding things in their own terms before employing them to focus attention on the consequences of diverse cultural patterns in North American society. Virginia Young (MS) suggests that "beyond relativism" is the key term in Benedict's later work; in this cross-culturally sophisticated comparative phase of the anthropologist's work, Boasian anthropology would prove its worth in the public sphere as well as among the academic disciplines.

Benedict and Whorf, then, were similar in their insistence that anthropology (including linguistics) alone provided modern Western society with a method to see itself clearly and act upon that knowledge. This reading suggests that, in one sense at least, the so-called Whorf Hypothesis has very little to do with language except as exemplar. Rather, the argument rests firmly on the Boasian dichotomy between history and psychology as the alternative explanatory modes of anthropology. History, for Benedict, meant the Boasian trait diffusion model, whereas Whorf elaborated Sapir's historical inference from linguistic evidence (see Figure 2, Chapter 1). Both Whorf and Benedict reflected the Boasian turn to psychology, although Benedict emphasized the individual personality constrained by culture and Whorf sought the cognitive underpinnings of the human capacity for language.

Benjamin Lee Whorf as Core Sapirian Linguist

To reach beyond the inherited stereotype of Whorf requires placing him in the social and intellectual context of his own times. That context was the first Yale School of Linguistics that developed around Edward Sapir in the 1930s (Hymes 1971; Hymes and Fought 1975).

At Yale, Whorf, the self-trained gentleman scholar who never quit his day job as an insurance adjuster, found himself for the first time among peers, appreciated rather than singled out for having a single obsessive idea. His best-known paper on linguistic relativity, "The Relation of Habitual Thought and Behavior to Language," appeared only in 1941, the year of his death, in a memorial volume for Sapir.

The influence of Sapir on Whorf was, however, more complicated than a dyadic mentor-student relationship. John Carroll, in his introduction to Whorf's posthumous selected writings, emphasized Whorf's "contact with a small but earnest band of Sapir's students" at Yale as the beginning of his career as a professional linguist (Carroll 1956:16). But Sapir was the sole source neither for Whorf's professional network nor for his commitment to cross-linguistic work. Even before Sapir moved to Yale, where he was easily accessible from Whorf's home base in Hartford, Connecticut, Alfred Tozzer, Herbert Spinden, and Sylvanus Morley, his Harvard mentors in Mayan and Aztec archaeology, encouraged Whorf to contact Sapir and Boas. Harvard, in the museum tradition established by Frederick Ward Putnam in the late nineteenth century, specialized in the early twentieth century in archaeology and physical anthropology, leaving Boas free to direct his attention to cultural anthropology and linguistics. Harvard was both alternative to and competition for the Boasian program centered at Columbia University. The Harvard archaeologists sent their protégé to Sapir because he was Boas's most distinguished linguistic student.

Whorf's Harvard mentors had considerable stake in providing him with respectable credentials in the cutting-edge linguistics of the day. Whorf had worked extensively on Mayan and Aztec cryptography and iconography. The archaeologists needed him, or someone like him, to help them interpret their archaeological data. Because Middle American civilizations were literate, archaeologists had to deal with inscriptions that, if they could be deciphered, would shed light on strictly archaeological materials. Linguistics, for most anthropologists, was still primarily a tool for ethnological reconstruction. They didn't care how the answers were arrived at; they just wanted to plug them into puzzles of prehistory. Linguists were convenient magicians, frequently suspected of sleight-of-hand. Both Sapir's classic essay on "time perspective" in 1916 and his 1921 six-unit classification of American Indian languages should be interpreted in this framework. The glottochronology of his student Morris Swadesh in the 1950s, designed on analogy to radiocarbon dating, further extended the linguistics-as-handmaiden-of-prehistory tradition. Charges of intuition, genius, and poetry came more from linguists than from the anthropologists who easily adopted such borrowed linguistic frameworks. This widening gap reinforced dismissal of the First Yale School and its work, both during Sapir's lifetime and over the ensuring two decades.

Oral tradition identifies Sapir as the crucial catalyst in what would eventually become the Whorf hypothesis of linguistic relativity. Moreover, the sometime addition of Sapir's name implies that Whorf merely elaborated, perhaps exaggerated to the point of caricature, the ideas of his prestigious mentor. Rollins (1980:62) characterizes Whorf's views as "mystical," arising from his lifelong interest in theosophy, as though no one could do trustworthy linguistics while holding such beliefs; Sapir's view, in sharp contrast, was read as "secular." Linguistic relativity per se thus entails neither mysticism nor scientific secularism. Accurately noting that Sapir was a nonpracticing Jew, Rollins valorizes his ostensibly positivistic, nonreligious approach. Nonetheless, Sapir remains for him an ambivalent scientist, "delicately poised between science and art" (Rollins 1980:66).

That Sapir was "intuitive," a "poet," and a "genius" encouraged dismissal of what he said about linguistic form. If such disclaimers of scientific authority could be applied to Sapir, they even more thoroughly disenfranchised Whorf from consideration as a serious linguist. Sapir did not share this dichotomization of science and humanism. He used "the dangerous term 'genius'" in reference to Morris Swadesh (Sapir to Kroeber, 17 June 1935, UCB) and described Stanley Newman's grammar of Yokuts as "beautiful" (National Research Council minutes, 1935). Newman's Yokuts was acknowledged by Zellig Harris (1943-44:197–98) as the prime exemplar of the Sapirian process grammar. To the extent that linguistic relativity was grounded in the commonsense, taken-for-granted linguistic worldview of Sapir and his students, if Whorf had not elaborated the implicitly shared concept of linguistic relativity, one of the others might well have done so.

The ascendancy of (neo-)Bloomfieldian structuralism brought a dramatic semantic reversal of the adjectives that could be applied to linguistic work. The humanistic tenor of the mentalist and configurational linguistics that Sapir and his students valued in one another's work made them highly suspect to many of their immediate successors; behaviorism imposed new standards of rigor and replicability that effectively excluded meaning or culture. Whorf shared the vision of cross-cultural linguistics that characterized the First Yale School.

Whorf's degree in chemical engineering from M.I.T. served him well in his lifelong employment as a fire insurance claims adjuster. He did not separate this scientific training from his work in linguistics. Indeed, he was wont to employ representative anecdotes from his work to the relationship of linguistic categories and real-world experience. There was nothing mystical about his belief in the real world. Best known is his cautionary tale of the "empty" gasoline drum, treated as no longer dangerous because of a misleading linguistic label. Whorf did not, however, claim that this experience from his fire insurance work led him to formulate the linguistic relativity hypothesis—any more than the metaphysical correlation of Hopi grammatical categories with relativity physics would lead a Hopi, without Western scientific training, to revolutionize physics.

Ironically, Whorf, trained as an engineer, knew more about science than did any of his fellow Boasians. He read widely in the physical sciences, habitually (and accurately) applying scientific metaphors to linguistic questions. Einstein's relativity was the formative scientific discovery of Whorf's generation; he followed its technical details and linked it metaphorically to the superficially incommensurable thought-worlds entailed by different languages. In the M.I.T. *Technology Review* in 1940, Whorf exhorted scientifically educated readers to follow his own progression from Einstein's physics to linguistic form: "We are thus introduced to a new principle of relativity, which holds that all observers are not led by the same physical evidence to the same picture of the universe, unless their linguistic backgrounds are similar, or can in some way be calibrated" (Whorf 1956:214). "Calibration" was a highly congenial method of scientific investigation for Whorf; linguistics was supposed to be a science.

Whorf was not alone in his fascination with the physics of relativity. (Boas faced the same dilemma in the psychophysics of the color of seawater, which began his path to ethnology as a proper domain of relativity as observer effect.) As early as 1924, Sapir had explicitly identified "the relativity of the form of thought" grounded in the "incommensurable analyses of experience in different languages" (Sapir 1949:158). This was "not so difficult to grasp as the physical relativity of Einstein," despite blinders imposed by "our naive acceptance of fixed habits of thought" (Sapir 1949:159). Sapir's flirtations with linguistic relativity, however, were received with less skepticism than were Whorf's. The sheer magnitude and quality of his other work allowed him to be taken seriously, as Whorf never was.

Commentators have consistently failed to acknowledge the integration of Whorf's position, what Penny Lee characterizes as "the Whorf theory complex" (Lee 1996:30): Whorf was interested in "linguistic thinking," in "patternment," "configuration," or "linkage;" he believed that language sustained mental connections in a "linkage" or "rapport" comparable to Sapir's "points in the pattern" (i.e., phonemes). "Isolates of experience" were selectively elaborated into "isolates of meaning"; "the salience of such patterns abstracted from experiential data was one of the cognitive functions of language." Each language "fosters in its users" selections among possible linguistic forms, producing a characteristic "picture of the universe" or "view of the world." An implicit or unconscious "calibration" of such forms created "agreement" about meanings; conscious "multilingual awareness" sharpened the precision of language use to formulate theories about language. This cross-culturally sophisticated linguistics was a core human capacity. Respect for other logics and pictures of reality freed the linguist from illusions about reality created by habitual language use; the necessary tolerance and reflexivity should operate on a planetary scale.

In the eyes of his immediate successors, Whorf's comparisons of Hopi and what he called Standard Average European (SAE) were thoroughly unscientific.

Whorf did not claim, however, that his pronouncements should be interpreted literally or that they resulted from controlled scientific comparison of the two languages. Despite their skepticism toward anything that suggested "mind," the Bloomfieldians and neo-Bloomfieldians expended considerable energy trying to reformulate the Whorf hypothesis in terms amenable to unambiguous testing (e.g., Hoijer 1954). The Southwest Project spearheaded by John Carroll remained inconclusive (Murray 1994:195–96).

The shift in tenor of North American linguistics after the untimely deaths of Sapir in 1939 and Whorf in 1941 applied to writing grammars as well as to reception of the linguistic relativity hypothesis; they were sides of the same coin. The Second Yale School that coalesced around Leonard Bloomfield and Bernard Bloch was self-consciously, for most of its participants, discontinuous from its Sapirian roots (although Charles Hockett consciously tried to blend the Sapirian and the Bloomfieldian legacies).

(Neo-)Bloomfieldian rereadings of the tradition associated with Whorf portrayed linguistic relativity as radical and undemonstrated. In fact, however, its distinguished and conservative intellectual genealogy is more accurately rendered as the Herder-Humboldt-Boas-Sapir-Whorf hypothesis (Bunzl 1996; Darnell 1990a; Koerner 1992). In the context of the 1930s, Sapir's process grammar and phonemics were far more radical than linguistic relativity. But neither Whorf nor Sapir was around to defend, qualify, or elaborate the linguistic relativity hypothesis—and that made all the difference.

During the 1930s there was an increasing divergence between the Boas camp in New York and the Sapir camp in New Haven. The primary bone of contention was phonemic vs. phonetic transcription and orthography. Sapir's innovative phonology allowed the First Yale School to produce abstract statements about sound systems that reflected their "psychological reality" (Sapir 1933) for native speakers. Boas and his students, however, thought the new approach distorted the essential character of unwritten languages studied in the field. Since these languages were rapidly disappearing, it was by implication unethical to fail to record them with the greatest technologically possible detail and accuracy. Feelings still run high: I recently witnessed a lively debate between two of my own former teachers, trained in the Columbia and Yale camps respectively. For a Columbia-trained ethnologist, accuracy and respect for the detail of sound systems unique to each language far outweighed the loss of generalization in a literal phonetic orthography. For a Yale-trained anthropologist, in contrast, the atomism of a nonphonemic orthography belied the all-important search for psychological reality, the world as it appeared to members of culture. The abyss lay between the Boasian anthropologists, for whom linguistics was part of an ethnological enterprise, and the linguists around Sapir, who increasingly thought of themselves as professional linguists rather than as linguistically specialized anthropologists.

Historiographic evidence supports the "group" identity of the First Yale School. In 1931 Whorf's newly acquired peers were not naive students; most of them were what we would now call post-docs, who had followed Sapir from Chicago to New Haven. Mary Haas retrospectively observed that nothing permanent came through for any of them during Sapir's lifetime, predictably in the heart of the Depression (Murray 1998). She did not blame Sapir, who tried to support them all on a series of piecemeal research and fieldwork grants. Sapir himself assessed the job market as more sanguine in ethnology than in linguistics, encouraging any student who expressed interest in ethnology to pursue it and do linguistics on the side (Sapir to George Peter Murdock, 8 August 1938, YUDA, with reference to Charles Hockett).

Few of the linguists who professionalized their discipline as autonomous from either anthropology or language and literature were based in departments of linguistics. Most of the founders reflected the general decline in emphasis on classics and the resulting shift to synchronic study of languages; few were anthropologists. Despite the founding of the Linguistic Society of America and its journal, *Language,* in 1925, academic institutionalization of linguistics continued to lag behind even such late arrivals on the academic scene as anthropology. This failure to coalesce into a single homogeneous paradigm partially reflects the marginalization of so-called exotic languages, typified by those of aboriginal North America, relative to Indo-European languages with their comfortingly familiar veneer of "civilization" (Andresen 1990). Studying with Boas or Sapir entailed Americanist fieldwork. Even Margaret Mead did a much-detested summer stint among the Omahas. Until the late nineteenth-century professionalization of American science, Americanist linguists and ethnologists were amateur data collectors whose work was interpreted elsewhere by European armchair scholars. The prestige of Boas and Sapir, in ethnology and linguistics respectively, mitigated this dismissal of evidence for human culture in all its variants.

When Boas died in 1942, soon after Sapir, the Americanist linguistic mantle passed to Leonard Bloomfield, an Indo-Europeanist by training and professional practice and employment. Despite the apparent hiatus foregrounded in the oral histories of anthropology and linguistics, Bloomfield also shared most of Sapir's program. The distinctive features of the First Yale School were: to develop methods of structural description and "to test their application in the analysis of both exotic and well-known languages"; to develop linguistics as a discipline; to record disappearing languages; to continue work on the genetic relationship of American Indian languages; and to connect linguistics to other disciplines and to practical affairs (Hymes and Fought 1975:997).

Although Bloomfield tried to mentor the students stranded by Sapir's death, the post–World War II Yale School of Linguistics moved increasingly away from its Americanist roots. During the 1930s, however, the group around Sapir at Yale seemed destined to constitute the core of professional linguistics. Sapir was at the center, but important work was already being done by Morris Swadesh, Stanley Newman, Mary Haas, George Trager, George Herzog, Zellig Harris, later Carl Voegelin, Charles Hockett, and, indirectly, Joseph Greenberg. There were further ties to Sapir students employed elsewhere—Harry Hoijer remained at Chicago after Sapir left, and Fang-Kuei Li created a job for himself in his natal China after Sapir's Athabascan/Na-dene synthesis disintegrated (Darnell 1990a).

Because the young linguists around Sapir were living on short-term grants, they traveled a lot to the field and back, and they learned to work collaboratively. Especially after Sapir's first heart attack in the summer of 1937, Whorf, who lived in nearby Hartford, held down the home front. Whorf's papers at Yale confirm that "Ben" was the glue keeping the group together through the periodic dispersals of its core members during each summer field season. He ensured that the round-robin letters made their full rounds and often decided what Sapir, who needed to conserve his energies, would or would not be told.

The oral history of dismissing Whorf and his supposedly monolithic hypothesis has made much of Whorf's failure to hold an academic appointment—as though that failure meant he did not deserve one. In the context of the Depression, however, Whorf was fortunate to have a position that supported him and his family and allowed him to pursue his linguistic avocation. John Carroll refers to "several offers or academic or scholarly research positions . . . during the latter years of his life," which Whorf refused because he already had "a more comfortable living and a freer opportunity to develop his intellectual interests in his own way" (Carroll 1956:5). There is no direct evidence of such offers. His only teaching was as what we would now call a sessional lecturer, as a sabbatical replacement for Sapir. Whorf did fieldwork on his vacations, supported by prestigious Social Science Research Council grants, and worked on Hopi in New York City with Ernest Naquayouma. Moreover, some of his work was published in unconventional journals, directed to engineers or theosophists, aimed at making technical linguistic material accessible to non-professional audiences (also the goal of Sapir's only book, *Language*, in 1921).

At this stage Whorf's peers at Yale didn't hold academic appointments either; he died before they did so. That Whorf never earned a Ph.D. in linguistics is only superficially an index that he was not as fully professional as others in his cohort. Most of them came to Yale with doctorates and considerable fieldwork experience. Whorf's prior experience with Mayan and Nahuatl placed him at a comparable stage of his career. Whorf pioneered in applying the insights of phonetics to Mayan script, treating it as "the visual form of spoken Maya" (Coe 1992:268).

Whorf achieved much during his Yale years. Sapir wrote about him to Kroeber: "Whorf is an awfully good man, largely self-made, and with a dash of genius. He is sometimes inclined to get off the central problem and indulge in marginal speculations but that merely shows the originality and adventuresome quality of his mind. . . . [He] is one of the most valuable American Indian linguists that we have at the present time" (Sapir to Kroeber, 30 April 1936, UCB). At Yale, Whorf became a convert to Sapirian consolidation of American Indian linguistic stocks, ironically at a time when Sapir himself was moving away from such questions. Whorf aspired to do for Uto-Aztecan what Sapir had done for Athabascan (and Bloomfield for Central Algonquian) (Whorf to Oliver LaFarge, 3 January 1933, YU). Kroeber strongly supported this work, urging Whorf to release a provisional classification useful for ethnology (Kroeber to Whorf, 5 June 1935, YU). Although enthusiastic about the classificatory methodology itself, Whorf remained cautious about the adequacy of the database: "There are still too many little known languages lying around and perhaps concealing facts that might materially affect my views" (Whorf to Kroeber, 20 August 1935, YU).

Around 1937 the Yale group attempted a collective historical synthesis, largely independent of Sapir except for inspiration. According to George Trager (1946:3), he and Whorf were the key figures in modifying the old, baseline Sapir classification (Sapir 1921a, 1929) and its accompanying map. The Yale map was used locally but never published. The major substantive breakthrough of this new classificatory work was the linking of Trager's work on Tanoan with

Whorf's on Uto-Aztecan into a superphylum, following up on "Sapir's intuitions" (Haas to Whorf, 16 February 1937, YU).

Sapir thought sufficiently highly of Whorf's phonemic work to encourage him in an epistolatory debate with Prague School linguist Count Nicolaj Trubetzkoj on the number of vocalic phonemes in Hopi. Sapir emphasized the decisive importance of native speaker judgments "even if they express themselves amateurishly" (Sapir to Whorf, 4 October 1938, YU). "General principles" could not decide the question. By implication Trubetzkoy was forced to rely on such general principles because he had not done fieldwork. European linguistics was necessarily somewhat spurious from an Americanist standpoint.

Here Sapir restated the principle of fieldwork with native speakers that links Whorf's work on American Indian grammars to the linguistic relativity hypothesis. Whorf was the only contributor to the Sapir memorial volume *Linguistic Structures of Native North America* (Hoijer 1946) to author two grammatical sketches, of Milpa Aztec and of Hopi. This is the work with which Whorf's peers identified him. His ideas on linguistic relativity and habitual thought appeared not in linguistic periodicals but in the ethnological memorial volume edited by Leslie Spier, A. Irving Hallowell, and Stanley Newman (1941) alongside work by Sapir's anthropology students, for whom linguistics was primarily a tool for culture history. Whorf alone contributed to both projects.

The linguistic relativity question, insofar as it was about language rather than about culture, revolved around the notion of grammatical categories. Whorf saw lexicon and sound system as merely substantive features of language. Grammatical categories, in contrast, selected some features of the world for emphasis and elided others, a process lurking just outside habitual consciousness. The logic parallels that of Ruth Benedict describing each culture's selection from a larger set of human potentials. Because Whorf's successors tested his linguistic relativity hypothesis largely based on lexical materials, his own conception of the critical influence of grammar on thought has yet to be decisively investigated. Dell Hymes suggests: "[Grammar] is relatively more stable, both through time and across dialects, than vocabulary and phonology often are; because it contains features that are relatively more general and fundamental, since, unlike individual words and sounds, they 'must be expressed' [quoting Boas]; and because the concepts associated with grammatical features often pertain to general categories that find a place in metaphysics—

space, time, act, person, thing" (Hymes 1964:115). That is, the interdependency of language and logic could be explored through the attested diversity of grammars. What Whorf called "calibration" transcended such diversity through "general taxonomy and description," implying a kind of metalanguage—known to the linguist on the basis of familiarity with many languages—in which all particular distinctions could be expressed (Hymes 1964:119).

The Boasian manifesto on grammatical categories, the introduction to the *Handbook of American Indian Languages* (Boas 1911a), had articulated the principle that grammatical categories adopted from the civilized languages of the Old World were useless for Americanist work. Accurate analytical categories could only be derived from the languages being studied. The *Handbook* sketches intended a psychological [i.e., typological rather than genetic or historical] overview. For Whorf as well, psychological selection motivated the diversity of attested grammatical categories.

Sapir and Swadesh's "American Indian Grammatical Categories" provided the long-promised generalization of Boas's argument. Sapir's posthumous paper, completed from his notes by Swadesh, chose illustrations from the "structural transformations" of the English sentence "He will give it to you" in six languages on which he had personally done fieldwork. The empirical particularity of the exemplar was firmly in line with the tenor of the *Handbook* sketches, but the call for an Americanist philology was more general: "It would be naive to imagine that any analysis of experience is dependent on pattern expressed in language. Any concept, whether or not it forms part of the system of grammatical categories, can be conveyed in any language. If a notion is lacking in a given series, it implies a difference of configuration and not a lack of expressive power" (Sapir and Swadesh 1946:106).

During Sapir's sabbatical in 1936–37, spent in New York City recovering from his first heart attack, fellow Boasian ethnologist and acting anthropology department chair Leslie Spier hired Whorf to teach Sapir's courses. Spier reported to Sapir that he had urged Whorf to package the technical linguistic material for Yale anthropology graduate students with limited enthusiasm for studying linguistics by emphasizing its correlations to ethnology (Spier to Sapir, 30 June 1037, YUDA). Whorf was avidly delighted at the opportunity to teach a broad course in American Indian languages: "I realize that . . . the students will have, for the most part, only the haziest notions of linguistics, and my idea would be to excite them in the linguistic approach as a way of developing understanding of the ideology of other peoples" (Whorf to Spier, 4 August 1937, YUDA) Spier acceded to this strategy, writing to Dean Edgar Furniss that Whorf "has a very stimulating way . . . and I would like to take advantage of his interest in hooking up language and ethnology, for I think it would take with many of our students. They might thus be encouraged to give serious attention to linguistics, when a 'straight' linguistics course might leave them cold" (Spier to Furniss, 6 August 1937, YU).

Whorf wrote to John Carroll that the link of language and ethnology would have "a psychological direction"; he intended to examine "the organization of raw experience into a consistent and readily communicable universe of ideas through a medium of linguistic patterns" (Whorf to Carroll, 19 August 1937, YU). These documents conclusively demonstrate that the linguistic relativity hypothesis emerged out of Whorf's determination to "translate American Indian linguistics in the Sapirian framework for nonlinguists" (Darnell 1990a:381). It was a construction for pragmatic purposes, firmly grounded in principles shared by Whorf's peers in the First Yale School.

The Linguistic Relativity Hypothesis

The concept of relativity, both cultural and linguistic, is seminal to the systematic program of Boasian anthropology, a program Jane Hill and Bruce Mannheim (1992:385), in reviewing recent work on language and worldview, suggest involved a fundamental category error, an unjustifiable equation of subject matter (language, culture, or individual personality) with academic discipline (linguistics, anthropology, or psychology).

Relativity is an issue of wider-than-disciplinary scope, a metaphor for the epistemology of Western science that percolates across the natural sciences, humanities, and social sciences. Boasian anthropologists were influenced dramatically by trickle-down effects from the physics of Werner Heisenberg and Albert Einstein. The relativity metaphor was duly generalized, albeit with another fundamental category error: acceptance of the everyday commonsense meaning of relativity that "anything goes."

This reading is superficially rigidified into nihilism both by some contemporary deconstructionist theoreticians (most extremely Derrida, Baudrillard, and Rorty). Philosopher Richard Bernstein (1991:14) suggests that the modernist preoccupation of Friedrich Nietzsche with relativism as a form of nihilism fails to resolve the crisis of how we can know that we know anything (that is, of how we can have a falsifiable social science). Indeed, the "entire range of the human and social sciences" has produced "a questioning that reveals cracks and crevices in what had been taken to be solid and secure" (Bernstein 1991:3–4). The "rush to embrace various forms of relativism" applies across substantive domains including "the nature of science, or alien societies, or different historical epochs, or sacred and literary texts." We can no longer appeal to universal standards of rationality to adjudicate competing claims to reality and "we are limited to our historical context and to our own social practices" (Bernstein 1991:3–4). This fashionable "malaise" frequently produces "cynicism and a growing sense of impotence" (Bernstein 1991:3–4). The "endless playfulness of interpretation" wars with the intuitive certainty that there is a world "independent of our beliefs and fancies" (Bernstein 1991:3–4).

This dichotomy of nihilism vs. relativism has too often been attributed to so-called postmodernist anthropology by its critics (e.g., Knauft 1996; Kuznar 1997). Few anthropologists have actually suggested that cross-cultural comparison and evaluation of cultures are impossible or undesirable. Willful or otherwise, this conclusion is a misreading of what the Boasians meant by their core concept of relativity. For Benedict and Boas, as for Sapir, Whorf, and Radin, relativity is not about the absence of absolute standards, or about the incommensurability of apples and oranges, but about standpoint or the position of the observer. In physics the location of a particular particle could not be specified simultaneously in time and space. In culture one could focus on overall pattern or on individual actors within it, but one could not hold both perspectives simultaneously.

For the social sciences the matter was further complicated by the capacity of human subjects for reflexivity. From the standpoint of a single observer, the grammatical categories of a given language or the social norms of a particular culture appeared as absolutes, natural rather than culturally constructed. Relativity theory, in the social sciences, had to get beyond the single standpoint. Thus Whorf talked about "multilingual awareness" and Benedict about becoming "culture-conscious." Alongside their relativism was an equally fundamental commitment to rationalism, an analytic stance grounded in anthropology's characteristic method of cross-cultural comparison (Darnell 1974b).

The implicit covert critique of North American society for Whorf and Benedict involved a moralistic, Puritan streak consonant with American pragmatism. The cold WASPs of New England articulated the romantic enthusiasms of the warm but alien Jews of the earliest Boasian cohort. The Boasians were moralists who believed that their comparative disciplines, whether cross-cultural or cross-linguistic, allowed the scientifically trained observer to transcend the limitations of standpoint. They further believed that the salvation of modern Western civilization lay in the use of such cross-cultural and cross-linguistic data. These data were understood, insofar as possible, in their own terms—relativizing the observer's view, thereby creating awareness of new social forms inconceivable within the shackles of (our own) tradition.

Principled tolerance for diversity was the necessary first step to self-awareness, what we would now call reflexivity. Conversely, tolerance was impossible without awareness of the existence and depth of cultural and linguistic diversity. Tolerance so grounded would lead not to uncontrolled proliferation of incommensurable cultures or grammars, but to an empirical search for universals or near universals. Relativity was the initial stage in a double hermeneutic. The fieldworker must suspend the categories and expectations of her or his natal language and culture and learn to think from the standpoint of other local knowledges. Only then could the analyst step in to draw the moral(s). Standpoint epistemology established the starting point for ethics, defined as the possibility of effective cross-cultural and cross-linguistic communication. For the Boasian moralists, the very future of Western civilization was at stake.

The concept of "the primitive," however distasteful it appears today, provided a convenient relativizing "other" for the civilization that had produced Western science. Utopian nostalgia lay at the core of what Stanley Diamond (1960:v), introducing a memorial volume for Paul Radin, glossed as the "retrospective" tradition in anthropology. More recently George Stocking has characterized the "anthropological sensibility" in terms of "romantic motives" (Stocking 1989). Diamond's exemplar for this romantic tradition was "Culture, Genuine and Spurious," especially Sapir's powerful juxtaposition of the emotional anomie of the modern North American telephone operator and the idealized harmony and integrity of the simpler societies known to fieldworking anthropologists. Such "genuine" cultures, despite the influences of European contact, provided their members with routes to personal self-fulfillment, the *Herzenbildung* of the German romanticism Franz Boas imported to North America (Bunzl 1996; Liss 1996; Müller-Wille 1998). In the language of Sapir's later musings about linguistic relativity, "grooves" or even "ruts" both constrained and enabled the relations of individuals to culture. Sapir chose his examples from the Native North American societies he knew best. He deployed them to capture the price of civilization, the rather widespread post-World War I sense that civilization had come at high cost. Sapir was not convinced that it was a good bargain. The apparent spuriousness of modern life reflected the anxiety of intellectuals disconcerted by blatant failures of the prospectivist notion of progress.

Linguistic Relativity and Analytic Philosophy

Whorf's linguistic relativity principle links him less to the mainstream of North American linguistics than to the turn to language within analytic philosophy. For Whorf and Sapir, as for Boas (1911a), linguistic relativity invalidated any method based on imposing the grammatical categories of one language upon another. For Sapir this interdisciplinary tradition of relativism was mediated through *The Meaning of Meaning* (1923) by Charles Kay Ogden and Ivor Armstrong Richards. Sapir had also read Bertrand Russell (Joseph 1996: 382), but Ogden and Richards was the source through which he began to think about meaning in relation to his own linguistic work. He reviewed the book in *The Freeman* mere months after its publication and sporadically corresponded with Ogden over a period of eleven years (Gordon 1990:1).

The infatuation, however, was not mutual. Based on their reading of *Language: An Introduction to the Study of Speech* (Sapir 1921b), Ogden and Richards (1923:7, 8, 101, 260) criticized Sapir's approach to meaning as a question of linguistic form. They dismissed Sapir's proliferation of subcategories of concepts, subsuming both material objects and abstract ideas under concepts, and using grammatical categories as though they reflected something in the world (Gordon 1990:2). The last point is inaccurate: "Sapir and Whorf share with the analytic philosophers a fundamental belief in a transcendent, universal logic which no 'natural' language captures perfectly" (Joseph 1996:394).

Sapir took the initiative, writing to Ogden (3 July 1923) that their positions were not so far apart (citations to this correspondence are taken from Gordon 1990 and Joseph 1996); his own "concepts" were "no ambitious universals nor do they lay any claim to forming an introduction to a science of knowledge." Rather, they were "categories that have seemed useful to me from a strictly linguistic standpoint." He was aware that such grammatical categories might "confuse types of referents and methods of referring." But the fault lay in the phenomena of diverse linguistic forms rather than in the absence of method: "My scheme intentionally parallels the helter-skelter functioning of language itself." Moreover, Sapir agreed with Ogden and Richards that a theory of reference was quite different from a "philosophy [of the form and functioning] of language." He apparently conceded the necessity of a distinction between thoughts, words, and things (Gordon 1990:2). Sapir, however, was more interested in how language mediated between symbol and referent; his was an unmitigated mentalism, grounded in culture as well as in language.

Sapir did not normally take public criticism well; nonetheless, his review was extremely positive: "Every intelligent person knows that words delude as much as they help. And yet few accept with due cheer and conviction the notorious failure of a given universe of speech-symbols, a language, to correspond to the universe of phenomena, physical and mental" (Sapir 1923:572). No philologist had ever been quite as articulate about "why an understanding of the nature of speech is a philosophic essential" (Sapir 1923:572). Sapir took this concept as an invitation to apply cross-linguistic data.

John Joseph attributes Sapir's "otherwise surprising enthusiasm" for Ogden and Richards to his inspiration that the relevance of language could be grounded in what Joseph calls the "metaphysical garbage" position underlying analytic philosophy (Joseph 1996:392). That is, language gets in the way of expressing concepts clearly and unambiguously; it must be purged of semantic fuzziness.

Sapir first articulated his distaste for the correspondence theory of meaning in so-called primitive languages in his critique of the appendix to *The Meaning of Meaning* on "The Problem of Meaning in Primitive Languages" by Bronislaw Malinowski; an anthropologist of the British functionalist school was a much more direct competitor. The appendix was "a very bad piece of work" (Sapir to Ogden, 29 April 1930). Neither the authors nor Malinowski "do full justice to the . . . purely formal trends in language"; these required "a far more powerful and subtle psychology than we yet possess" and were "vastly more determinative of linguistic phenomena than the rather crude cultural and psychological factors that Malinowski so enthusiastically singles out" (Sapir to Ogden, 3 July 1923). Sapir's criticism could have applied equally well to the whole volume.

Sapir conceded with Ogden and Richards that many if not most grammarians descended to a morass of "technical exercise of strictly limited scope, instead of the inspiring study of the means by which truth is acquired and preserved" (Sapir 1923:572). Words brought only "pitfalls and illusions"; it was "the task of Grammar to prepare every user of symbols for the detection of these" (Sapir 1923:572). But when Ogden and Richards went on to ask rhetorically: "How many grammarians still regard their science as holding the keys of knowledge?" (Ogden and Richards 1923:261–62) Edward Sapir would undoubtedly have responded resoundingly: "I do!" That is, he saw himself as the exception to the charges made by Ogden and Richards and accepted their challenge to revitalize the scientific study of language. Indeed, he was already engaged in such an enterprise.

For Sapir the key to transcending the pernicious distortional effects of habitual linguistic categories in Western philosophy (i.e., the metaphysical garbage position) lay ready at hand, in the cross-linguistic research of the Americanist tradition. In "The Grammarian and His Language," a year after his review of Ogden and Richards, Sapir acknowledged that the linguistically naive philosopher was often "the dupe of his speech-forms," that "the most hard-headed thinkers" had been "cajoled" into linguistic category errors and proposed his own solution: "Perhaps the best way to get behind our thought processes and to eliminate from them all the accidents or irrelevances due to their linguistic garb is to plunge into the study of exotic modes of expression. At any rate, I know of no better way to kill spurious 'entities'" (Sapir 1949:157). Genuineness, in this context, involved recognizing the arbitrariness of signs—virtually impossible to grasp when the analytic vocabulary was drawn from the language being analyzed (an impasse that has plagued generative semantics in our own time).

Sapir's foray into "the meaning of meaning" was far from a momentary aberration. In 1931, he proposed that the "tyrannical hold" of linguistic categories could be broken by comparing "languages of extremely different structures" (Sapir 1949:528). In case his readers could not think of any, Sapir provided an exemplary list, adding to the familiar Indo-European languages of his own initial training the American Indian and the African; he had worked firsthand on all of these languages.

Sapir liked Ogden and Richards because 1) they emphasized the symbolic and emotive functions of language, 2) they grounded linguistic theory in the psychology of intentionality (thereby legitimating Sapir's abiding interest in the relationship between culture and the individual), and 3) they derived meaning from interpretation (i.e., communication) rather than from correspondence to external reality (Darnell 1990a:275). Such intentionality fit well with the creative individual as the locus of culture, the perspective that Sapir was developing as he moved from linguistic analysis to culture theory. So Sapir read Ogden and Richards against the grain, as a pungent critique of the metaphysical garbage position. His alternative "magic key" view, derived primarily from the Humboldtian conviction that language expressed the essential identity and integrity of a people or a culture, would rescue the philosophers from their bind (Joseph 1996). Sapir's version of the magic key added linguistic form to romanticized nostalgia.

Sapir expressed his unease over Ogden and Richards's theory of signs (Sapir to Ogden, 3 July 1923); neither Ogden nor Malinowski understood the decisive power of linguistic categories. Respect for the integrity of *form* was something only a linguist could contribute to the philosophers' debate. Joseph notes Whorf's parallel distaste for scholarship by "trained men of other disciplines . . . with an essentially parochial viewpoint" of equating language in general with English in particular (Joseph 1996:384). Sapir and Whorf agreed that the philosophers would not get anywhere until they relativized their standpoints by incorporating cross-linguistic data. Sapir, in contrast, wanted to engage this audience with his own version of cross-culturally sophisticated linguistics. His position was both mentalist and symbolic: "It is an illusion to think that we can understand the significant outlines of a culture through sheer observation and without the guide of the linguistic symbolism which makes these outlines significant and intelligible to society. Some day the attempt to master a primitive culture without the help of the language of its society will seem as amateurish as the labors of a historian who cannot handle the original documents of the civilization which he is describing" (Sapir 1949:161–62).

Ruth Benedict and the Arc of Cultural Selection

Returning to what the interwar Boasians meant by "the primitive," Stanley Diamond, in a remarkably outmoded formulation of the position, argued that "civilized men have always and everywhere been compelled by the conditions of their existence to try to understand their roots and human possibilities," while "primitive societies" (not even the individual "men" within them) have no "systematic" idea of civilization (Diamond 1960:v). The "primitive person" would not ask the same kind of questions: "Therefore, it is only a representative of our civilization who can, in adequate detail, document the [cultural] differences and help create an idea of the primitive which is necessary to the self-consciousness of [our] civilization" (Diamond 1960:xvii).

Ruth Benedict, whom Diamond presumably considered to share Radin's position on "the primitive," in fact accepted it only in the most trivial sense. She agreed that modern North American society was ethnocentric (and temporocentric, with the present state of affairs unproblematically standing for all time). The same attitude underlay the anthropologist's "ethnographic present" and failure to grant coevalness to the so-called primitive. Although anthropologists were products of their own cultural contexts, their discipline was founded on the refusal to substitute "the study of one local variation, that of western civilization," for the diversity of human cultures (Benedict 1934b:21). "World-wide cultural diffusion" ("colonial hegemony" in more contemporary terms) has the unfortunate "psychological consequences" of protecting us "from having to take seriously the civilizations of other peoples" (Benedict 1934b:21). Despite the cross-cultural evidence available to anthropology, "we have failed to understand the relativity of cultural habits" (Benedict 1934b:25). Anthropology could surmount the blinders of this inherited worldview, although for Benedict the argument was not tied to analytic philosophy, as it was for Sapir.

Benedict parted company with the homogenization of the category of the primitive in the primitivist tradition. Modern society was too complex to constitute a social laboratory, in either Durkheim's idealization of the primitive as noncomplex or Kroeber's culture as superorganic senses (Benedict 1934b:202), although its (sub-)cultures were units comparable to those of the geographically isolated communities traditionally studied by anthropologists. She was adamant that we must study the patterned integrity of primitive cultures, in the plural. "The study of cultural behavior, however, can no longer be handled by equating particular local arrangements with the generic 'primitive'" (Benedict 1934b:56).

Diamond argued that British functionalism erred in applying the cultural relativist assumption of "the legitimacy and human adequacy" of primitive cultures to "civilized, increasingly totalitarian states" (Diamond 1960:xxvii). His moral stance thereby circumvented his nonrelativist position regarding Hitler and the Holocaust, but at the cost of perpetuating the primitive-civilized divide. He posed a scientific or a sociological question about the basic minimum form that would prove to be universal. The core Boasians, in contrast, took a humanistic position based on an attestable, in principle finite, number of alternatives and declined to entrench an insurmountable gulf.

Hill and Mannheim note that Sapir coined the term "linguistic relativity" for the "cross-cultural epistemology of the Boasian tradition" (Hill and Mannheim 1992:383). But this relativity was not "formulated . . . as a discontinuity" between primitive and modern thought. Here, they argue, Americanist anthropologists alone draw a moral lesson for their own society from the legion of alternative known and knowable cultural and linguistic forms; theirs was not a binary or an exclusionary system (at least by intention). (Even in phonology Sapir's sense of pattern, with its emphasis on "psychological reality" from the standpoint of the native speaker, was more gestalt-like and less feature-oriented than the Prague School version, which was formulated more or less simultaneously.)

The case for a continuum from "primitive" to "civilized" is clear in Benedict's cultural relativism (the term most commonly used today, although the 1930s favored "cultural relativity," which is more directly parallel to "linguistic relativity" with its connotations of hard science). Benedict's "arc of cultural possibilities" was drawn directly on the analogy of linguistic relativity. In *Patterns of Culture* she grounded her concept of cultural relativity in phonology rather than on the "grammatical categories" most obviously associated with the linguistic relativity hypothesis: "In cultural life as in speech; selection is the prime necessity. . . . But each language must make its own selection and abide by it on pain of not being intelligible at all" (Benedict 1934b:34). A linguist might quarrel with the "unlimited" number of potential speech sounds. More significant than Benedict's limited understanding of the analogy in linguistic terms, however, is her rhetorical reliance on it: "A culture that capitalized even a small proportion of these would be as unintelligible as a language that used all the clicks, all the glottal stops, all the labials, dentals, sibilants, and gutterals from voiceless to voiced and from oral to nasal. Its identity as a culture depends upon the selection of some segments of this arc" (Benedict 1934b:35).

Benedict had internalized the concept of "alternating sounds" (Boas 1889) but remained less interested in "the form-feeling of social actors" inherent in Sapir's formulation of the concept of the phoneme (Sapir 1925) and its "psychological reality" for at least some native speakers (Sapir 1933). In Sapir's terms, Benedict, like the analytic philosophers, failed to understand the formal character of the selections made by each language and their structural interdependence within it. The patterns of concern to her were more formless and less (phon-)emic; the analyst would categorize personality types favored by socialization in specific cultures.

For Benedict integration (as opposed to variability) of cultural patterns involved a conventional anthropological exploration of the implications of the culture element diffusion paradigm. Boas's brief introduction to *Patterns of Culture* emphasized that cultural traits must be interpreted in their specific cultural contexts in order to "grasp the meaning of a culture as a whole," a language consistent with the Humboldtian "magic key" view of Sapir and Whorf (Joseph 1996), "a deep penetration into the genius of the culture, . . . of the attitudes controlling individual and group behavior" (Boas 1934:xiv).

Boas did not expect this approach to elucidate the relationship of culture and the individual; that was Sapir's problematic. It was Benedict's only insofar as she worried about the fate of the abnormal individual stigmatized by the ideal forms selected by his or her culture (Benedict 1934a). She was powerfully affected, for example, by the plight of a Zuni man whose creativity would have been valued in her own society but who, before European contact, would undoubtedly have been executed as a witch. Boas's introduction used the term "relativity" only in relation to normality or abnormality "when viewed from the standpoint of our civilization" (Boas 1934:xv).

Boas emphasized that Benedict chose "extreme cases" of unfamiliar "configuration" (Boas 1934:xv; cf. Wolf 1999). Her cases were extreme in two senses: first, in the degree to which each was "permeated" by a single "dominating idea," and second, in the oddity of the selections from the arc of cultural possibilities. Benedict explicitly defended her lack of attention to sampling: "A few cultures understood as coherent organizations of behavior are more enlightening than many touched upon only at their high spots. . . . We must hold ourselves to the less ambitious task, the many-sided understanding of a few cultures" (Benedict 1934b:61). It was not a question of counting or of randomness but of integration or consistency. Few ethnographic descriptions were sufficiently "thick" to invite such exegesis. However limited her participation, Benedict had lived among the Zunis and abstracted the pattern of their culture from her experience.

The cost of pattern consistency, however, was to gloss over intracultural variability, treated statistically or otherwise. Benedict was unimpressed by Sapir's epiphany over James Owen Dorsey's report that "Two Crows denies this" (Sapir 1949:568-77); Two Crows, a perfectly respectable Omaha, disagreed with equally respectable fellow Omahas precisely because each individual uniquely embodied the culture of which she or he was a member. It was left for Wallace to provide a methodology for shifting psychological anthropology from a Benedictine "basic" personality type shared by all members of a culture, what he calls "replication of uniformity," to a "modal" personality type, implying a more socially realistic "organization of diversity," with considerable variability of social roles within each cultural unit (Wallace 1961: chapter 2). Alternate models of cultural analysis could also be read at the level of individual "maze-way" synthesized in unique biographical experience.

Ruth Benedict was the key figure in moving the Boasian program from the study of cultural traits to their articulation into cultural wholes (Darnell 1977a), a shift most clearly marked by her dissertation on the guardian spirit quest (Benedict 1923). Sapir praised Benedict's view of "how the particular elements crystallized into the characteristic pattern" and proposed that she consider an explicitly psychological model, thereby exploring the relationship of culture to the individual—advice that she ignored (Sapir quoted by Margaret Mead 1974:22–23). The level of analysis that interested Benedict was an autonomous one, very close to the superorganic concept of culture espoused by Kroeber but with a supplemental attention to group psychology approached via socialization.

Benedict was adamant that the book's title remain exclusively in the domain of the cultural, thus avoiding facile psychologizing. She was uninterested in the categories of individual psychology. Rather, her strategy was to generalize her professional experience and expect colleagues to supply additional cases. Sapir, in contrast, preferred to proceed by extending his own individualized creative consciousness ("agency" in more contemporary terms) to the so-called primitive. Benedict was not about to let Sapir stampede her into consideration of the individual qua individual.

The guardian spirit paper contrasted the Apollonian Pueblo ethos with that of the Dionysian Plains, the former known to her through fieldwork and the latter through the work of Boasian colleagues, especially Lowie and Wissler. In *Patterns of Culture* Benedict expanded her nascent cross-cultural typology to encompass two more cases, though each of the four remained a separate and independent selection from the arc of cultural possibilities. The Dobuans had been studied by Mead's second husband, Reo Fortune, and the Kwakiutls by Boas; Benedict was intimately familiar with both ethnographic corpuses. She wrote to Mead in 1932 of the "reworking of raw material" from her own Pueblo fieldwork and from Boas's descriptive textual ethnography. Fortune's material, in contrast, was already "in shape" (Mead 1974:39).

Benedict avoided providing a typology of the kinds of patterns that could be selected out of the arc of cultural potentials. Mead, however, liked typologies, showing particular enthusiasm for Jung's psychological types. When Mead inquired about how many "configuration classifications" there were, Benedict insisted that hers was an "open system" in which terms could be borrowed from the abnormal psychologists without implying any theoretical orientation (Mead 1974:42). Although she aspired to capture the uniqueness of each integration rather than to classify integrations across cultures, the argument has not been read as Mead claimed that Benedict intended it to be.

The core of Benedict's standpoint was the need for modern North American tolerance of cultural difference. Nonetheless, all cultures were not equally valuable or equally integrated. Rather, she presented "thematic set-pieces imposing a moral coloration on a system of practices," intending to "disconcert" the reader; the Zunis evoked "reproach," the Kwakiutls "caricature," and the Dobuans "accus[ation]" (Geertz 1988:113). Benedict was far from a naive realist. To claim that every culture was "genuine" in Sapir's terms would be to cede the cross-cultural analyst's claim to moral authority. Although Benedict carefully specified that terms from abnormal psychology did not imply insanity, she did not think the competitive paranoid schizophrenic Dobuans were happy campers, with or without the clinical burden with which psychologists endowed these descriptive terms. The Dobuan selection from the arc of cultural possibilities was remarkably consistent but hardly one to be emulated.

Regardless of the value of any particular "other" alternative, Benedict moralized primarily for the benefit of her own society. The megalomania of the Kwakiutl "will to superiority" reminded her of the egoism of North American males and the competitive culture of the business world at the height of the Great Depression. Nonetheless, the various patterns could not be compared: "They are travelling along different roads in pursuit of different ends . . . [that] cannot be judged in terms of those of another society because they are incommensurable" (Benedict 1934b:196). Only by analogy and awareness that pattern resulted from cultural selection [i.e., choice] could North American society learn to critique itself.

Cultures could fail to achieve integration (presumably always valued from their own point of view) because different parts of the culture, for example, religion and economics, were organized on different principles. A tribe could move away, stay at home, or live on the boundary of two culture areas—all factors compatible with the Boasian element diffusion method of historical reconstruction. Benedict anticipated Kroeber's failure a decade later to find among literate civilizations patterns that held across domains of cultural achievement.

Benedict also allowed for "a genuinely disoriented culture" (Benedict 1934b: 196). Moreover, previously integrated cultural patterns could be broken, as for the Digger Indians of California in the proverb that began *Patterns of Culture:* "In the beginning, God gave to every people a cup of clay, and from this cup they drank their life . . . They all dipped in the water . . . but their cups were different. Our cup is broken now. It has passed away" (Benedict 1934b:xvi, 33). Configurational elements depended "on history as well as upon psychology" (Benedict 1934b:203), that is, the poles of the Boasian program were drawn into American anthropology's turn to psychology. History, based largely on culture traits or elements, continued to precede psychology, based on configuration or integration of those elements, in both the logic and practice of Benedict's anthropology. For Benedict the history that Radin argued had no room for the individual retained its relatively autonomous superorganic level of explanation.

Benedict was a relativist because she asked her readers to respect the variety of attested cultural selections. Margaret Caffrey's biography suggests that, prior to the publication of *Patterns of Culture,* most Americans equated relativity with "uncertainty, the potential for chaos" (Caffrey 1989:210). Benedict made relativity seem positive, consistent with "the old goals and values of American society" (Caffrey 1989:210). Using Benedict's own terminology, the anthropological concept of relativity was to be integrated within an existing North American configuration.

Benedict's antirelativism (Geertz 1984) arose when she turned to the fate of an individual temperament that is alien to its cultural setting, arguing that normality and abnormality were necessarily relative to the eye of the beholder. Thus applying local norms of evaluation, a friendly Dobuan would be dismissed as a simpleton and an aggressive Zuni tried as a witch. If there were a single value from the standpoint of the "culture-conscious" anthropological sophisticate, it would be tolerance of apparent abnormality (see also Benedict 1934a), especially in the creative individual (where Benedict finally drew closer to Sapir's position). In this moralistic context, Benedict's citation of Sapir's humanistic critique of North American society in "Culture, Genuine and Spurious" rather than his work on linguistic form makes sense.

We can now return to the question of whether linguistic relativity achieves a consistent position in its underlying tension with the potential for a metalanguage of rational thought. Not only does Benedict's implicit "mirror of nature" (Rorty 1979) logic contradict the relativity principle, but Whorf sometimes appears willing to decide which languages come closest to that universal logic. I agree that such a theory of reference is characteristic of analytic philosophy. However, when Whorf waxed ecstatic over tense-aspect relations in Hopi, he was squarely grounded within the Benedictine mode of moralizing to an educated North American readership. If that readership already spoke Hopi and were unfamiliar with any Indo-European language, I suspect that Whorf would have reversed the direction of his valorization. The question of conceptual adequacy of grammatical categories, in what Whorf called Standard Average European (SAE) as well as in Hopi, was resolved in the affirmative for all human languages. At least in some contexts, Whorf subsumed this linguistic question to the "multilingual awareness" that more than one categorization was possible only for the linguist working cross-linguistically.

Like relativity in physics, therefore, linguistic relativity finally came down to standpoint, the position of the observer. The social sciences added the possibility of alternative standpoints and the need for a matrix to enable selection among them in full awareness of the social costs of each selection. This vision of relativity was shared by interwar Americanists on the basis of their cross-cultural and cross-linguistic fieldwork, their intimate encounters with the recently primitive.

Relativism by itself is an impossible stance for the moralist. Cultural relativism has the capacity to "degenerate" into "silliness" when "freed of its original context" of antiracism (Daniel 1996:195). The opposite extreme, antirelativism, however, encapsulates and valorizes ethnocentrism. Boasian "anti-anti-relativism" (Geertz 1984), then, refused ethnocentrism in its commitment to see things first in their own terms, from the Native point of view, and only later to draw the morals in a more global context. Benedict and Whorf could not predict the future of Western science, but their concept of relativism was sufficiently robust to persist alongside complexity, the unintended consequences of interacting variables that increasingly threaten chaos (in the colloquial sense). The interaction of so-called primitive and so-called civilized refracts the same pattern at different scales, each allowing the other to enlarge the standpoint from which a global system is constructed by cultural selections from an arc of possibilities reflexively accessible to the choosers.

The complexity of Benedict's position on cultural relativism was not always well understood even among her contemporaries. Redfield, for example, was startled by the hermeneutic sophistication she took for granted: "Ruth Benedict was a cultural relativist who told us that cultures are equally valid. Nevertheless, in reading some of her pages, one doubts that she found them equally good" (Redfield 1953:150). He cited the "social waste" she noted in the competitiveness of both the Kwakiutls and the residents of Middletown, U.S.A. (Lynd and Lynd 1929); she concluded that rivalry was "notoriously wasteful. It ranks low in the scale of human values." After quoting Benedict, as though the question would not have occurred to her, Redfield asked "Whose scale?" (Redfield 1953:151). In his view Benedict both assumed an undefined universal scale and considered its application to her exemplars unproblematic; social waste "includes a poor choice of desired behavior traits, human suffering, and frustration" (Redfield 1953:151). At least in the case of modern Middletown, Redfield envisioned Benedict employing a kind of "scoring," a quantitative index to the mental health of whole cultures. Whereas Benedict muddled the distinction between "description and evaluation," Redfield sought a way to "compare and evaluate" (Redfield 1953:151).

But Redfield also knew it wasn't that simple: "It is that disturbing fellow, the living human individual, who makes trouble for the scientist's stern principle of perfect objectivity. Whenever the anthropologist looks at him, something human inside the anthropologist stirs and responds. It is easy enough to be objective toward objects; but the human individual refuses to be only an object" (Redfield 1953:151–52) In fieldwork, in the course of talking to particular individuals, the anthropologist "is apt to feel for that native while he is trying to describe him objectively" (Redfield 1953:152). Indeed, the "field ethnologist" usually favored a cultural pattern that "keeps men's lives in directions that they find good" (Redfield 1953:152), that is, she or he responded to what Sapir called a genuine culture. Redfield suggested that the anthropologist had an obligation to communicate "the human warmth of an exotic scene" (Redfield 1953:152), presumably so that readers might undertake the characteristic Benedictine move beyond relativism with which Redfield failed to credit her.

Radin read Benedict in terms of his valorization of the Boasian commitment to ethnographic verisimilitude: "We are all willing to forego the pleasures of surreptitious definiteness for one whiff of reality" (Radin 1933:168). It was impossible for him to go beyond "simply impressionistic sketches" without "a body of texts," a "presentation of the facts in such a way that they can be critically controlled" (Radin 1933:173). Margaret Mead's sociological leaning toward "the acquisition of case histories" failed to meet this standard. Radin acknowledged that Benedict shared his own distaste for quantitative generalization: "Her whole temperament is that of a culture historian to whom the history of a specific group has significance and validity. Her difficulties lie in the fact that she is trying not to be one" (Radin 1933:179). She sought "a succinctness of characterization that fails because it is too refined" (Radin 1933:179). In his view she left out "unpalatable facts" that didn't fit her patterns; the "distilled syntheses" of her Apollonian-Dionysian contrast (Benedict 1923) might hold for individuals but certainly not for whole cultures or culture areas (Radin 1933:180). Moreover, her poetic style precluded explicit statement of method (Vidich 1966:lxxvi), despite the unmistakable clarity of "her profound rejection of Western institutions and values and her personal involvement with the rhythm and poetry of primitive life" (Vidich 1966:cxii).

Cognitive Science vs. Grammatical Categories

Contemporary readings of Whorf by cognitive scientists have surprisingly little to do with the terms in which Whorf himself formulated the question of linguistic relativity. This unacknowledged selectivity has precluded attention to Whorf's intellectual genealogy from Boasian anthropology and German romanticism. It is an honorable genealogy, deeply enmeshed in the moral imperative of North American anthropology, which steered between relativistic tolerance for diversity, whether of language or culture, and the obligation of the anthropologist as public intellectual to bring the fruits of cross-cultural investigation back to the critique of his or her own society.

Recent decades have seen considerable realignment of cross-cultural cognitive studies toward a search for universals, often to the extent of permitting only trivial variability (e.g., Shaul and Furbee 1998). Only historiographic retrieval can recapture the emphasis on differences in linguistic and cultural particulars that motivated Whorf and his First Yale School contemporaries.

John Gumperz and Stephen Levinson retain Whorf's characteristic phrase "linguistic relativity" in the title of their edited collection on the state of the art in cognitive science, while simultaneously asserting that the concept needs "rethinking": "Readers will find that the original idea of linguistic relativity still live[s], but functioning in a way that differs from how it was originally conceived" (Gumperz and Levinson 1996:2). The tone of most papers and the introductory discussion is firmly revisionist.

Levinson, the volume's most articulate advocate of a new cognitive science synthesis, emphasizes his differences from Whorf's position. Whereas Whorf was interested in cultural and linguistic diversity, cognitive science assumes a species-wide, wired-in explanation for cross-culturally attested similarities in the processing of linguistic and other communicative information. Levinson characterizes the contemporary search for psychologically and biologically grounded universals as rationalist, with Whorf's contrasting position relegated to the status of mere empiricism. The realism of cognitive science further contrasts with the idealism of Whorf (that is, the mentalist concern with what was going on in people's heads, by implication to the exclusion of attention to the real world outside linguistically conditioned human minds.) "In this light, the Sapir-Whorf hypothesis [in its original form] seems uninteresting" (Gumperz and Levinson 1996:177). Anthropology, Levinson suggests, "Remains largely outside this current of thought: viewed from cognitive science it is a reactionary output of empiricist ideas with an outmoded stress of human ideational difference and the importance of environmental learning [i.e., socialization into a particular culture and language]" (Gumperz and Levinson 1996:134). Levinson dismisses the Boasian historical particularist emphasis on unique grammatical categories of each human language, arguing by implication that the anthropological concept of culture is an unproductive strategy, given what we know today about universal cognitive structures. Extensive fieldwork with particular informants to produce native language texts becomes a waste of time if their underlying structure is known in advance. Whorf, in contrast, took ethnographic particularity for granted. Universals of linguistic form would be arrived at by a comparative methodology seeking similarities across many languages. Levinson's strategy would presumably have appeared to him as an instance of the premature generalization that Franz Boas habitually deplored, evading the empirical question of how we distinguish the universal from the culture-specific.

Levinson calls for "a sophisticated theory of the co-evolution of mind and culture" (Gumperz and Levinson 1996:141) to approach the pragmatic inseparability of language and culture. Sapir, in contrast, switched between standpoints: culture and the individual (or culture and personality) understood as "sides of the same coin." The agency and creativity at the core of his theory of culture have no obvious place in the rhetoric of cognitive science. Even more fundamentally, Boas, based on his critique of evolution as applied to culture, would not have discussed evolution in the same breath as diversity of linguistic or cultural forms. The biological overtones of Levinson's desiderata remain unacceptable in an Americanist anthropology that continues to separate culture from biology and to privilege the former.

When Levinson turns to his own data on spatial expression in Tzeltal, a Mayan language, he deplores the unintentional ethnocentrism of semantic analysis based on unproblematized Indo-European categories. This formulation of the uniqueness of a particular set of categories would have made sense to Boas, Sapir, and Whorf alike. Levinson's claim to discontinuity therefore applies to setting new priorities to carve out disciplinary space for a cognitive science, for which Americanist anthropology is an unlikely home base. In this "intermediate position," the cognitive synthesis considers "such diversity . . . within the context of what we have learned about universals" (Gumperz and Levinson 1996:3).

John Lucy, in a more nuanced version of the rejection of Whorf's methods and conclusions, praises Sapir's intuitive genius and insists that Whorf tried to test his ideas empirically. (Indeed, they have yet to be tested formally in the ways Whorf himself understood the empirical problem, but to do so is not Lucy's project). Lucy argues that Whorf successfully produced "the nucleus of a procedure for establishing a neutral basis for the comparison of language-reality relationships" by playing Hopi and SAE against one another without privileging either of them (Lucy 1996:43, 1992). Moreover, Whorf fell within a moral framework for linguistics "which placed the science of language at the center of all efforts to advance human understanding" (Lucy 1996:64); this is the Boasian-Benedictine moralism explored in the previous section.

It is possible to arrive at something like cognitive science by routes other than Whorf's Boasian one and thus to rely less on a rhetoric of discontinuity to justify contemporary innovations (Murray 1994). For example, Maurice Bloch, whose work integrates British social anthropology with French structuralism, argues that contemporary anthropology is being torn apart by a dichotomy between, on the one hand, "the hermeneutic and literary dimensions of ethnography" and, on the other hand, by an "aggressively naturalist" insistence on the realism of the world as the grounding for mental constructs (Bloch 1998:40). Bloch views these frequently oppositional strains of anthropological theory as "two fundamentalisms" that have "developed in the work of anthropologists who identify with only one side of this dual heritage and who consequently wish to 'purify' anthropology of the other orientation. We are therefore faced with two movements which have in common their rejection of the hybrid character of the discipline" (Bloch 1998:40). Anthropologists, especially in North America, have permitted their quest for "scientific credibility" to erode the discipline's traditional reliance on the ever-continuing cross-checking of theory against data emerging from participant observation fieldwork; they have, he argues, simply accepted what their informants tell

them about their worlds as authoritative and ceded their own obligation to analyze and compare (Bloch 1998:41). Americanist roots have been elided.

Bloch argues persuasively that cognitive science provides a way out of the
respective fundamentalist impasses because it informs ethnographic practice
with some hope of objectivity in dealing with the traditional core subject
matters of anthropology, in his view social structure, political organization,
and ritual (Bloch 1998:43). Unlike Levinson, at least in his rhetorical mode,
Bloch insists that the particularism of ethnography is crucial to testing cognitive schemas in cross-cultural contexts. Anthropologists inevitably employ
psychological theories in their efforts to interpret the behavioral patterns of
other societies. Cognitive psychology offers more valid and replicable ways of
interpreting alterity than does an unreflexive folk psychology (which, in any
case, is usually applied naively) (Bloch 1998:43–44). Although Bloch's position
provides a plausible rationale for the ethnographic application of cognitive
science, its internal concerns are less with discovery procedures for fieldwork
and more with universal constraints on human thought across cultural and
linguistic communities. His argument may persuade anthropologists to attend
to cognitive science, but it is less clear that the reverse is true.

The Gumperz and Levinson collection provides a useful straw person for the
contemporary status of linguistic relativity debates because it includes contributors from multiple disciplinary and theoretical backgrounds. Although not
all contributors directly address continuities or discontinuities from cognitive
science back to Whorf, those most sympathetic to the Whorfian position are
fieldworking anthropologists whose approach is usually subsumed under the
rubric of ethnography of speaking.

Dell Hymes's "Two Types of Linguistic Relativity" (1966) suggested that
Whorf's emphasis on variations in linguistic structure entailed glossing over
variability in favor of an assumed uniformity of social function within each
speech community. Reversing Whorf's argument but retaining his preoccupation with nontrivial relativity, Hymes identified a second kind of linguistic relativity, in the use of language. He predicted that language functions would
prove to be universal, although they would take dramatically different surface
forms in particular societies. Moreover, "the ethnography of speaking" and
"the ethnography of communication" were virtually interchangeable for
Hymes, reflecting his commitment to explore ethnographically the structure
of nonlinguistic modalities and their relative positions in a given communicative economy. This formulation of the Whorfian ethnolinguistic tradition in

Americanist anthropology is not necessarily incompatible with the rationalist and universalist agendas of cognitive science. Whorf, like Sapir and Hymes, sought a critical methodology to study linguistic relativity.

In sum, the Whorf who is cited as an ancestor or precursor to cognitive science is not a Whorf who would have been recognized in his own time. As Levinson astutely observes, the intellectual climate changed in the 1960s, allowing for the reworking of continuities of the Boas-Sapir-Whorf position with a renewed focus on the qualitative: culture as a mentalist and symbolic construct, psychological reality, individual creativity, and appreciation of cultural and linguistic difference for its own sake. The contemporary challenge is to retain these insights. At the same time, however, we must come to an increased understanding of the cognitive, rationalist, universal mechanisms that underlie diverse cultural and linguistic expressions, yet we must do so without disintegrating into biological determinism or mechanistic quantification. Such a synthesis is yet to be attained.

ELSIE CLEWS PARSONS

CHAPTER 6

The Challenge of Life Histories

Variable Uses of the Life History

The relationship between life history documents of various kinds and the genre of ethnographic writing was problematic and contested in North American anthropology through most of the twentieth century. Life history documents undoubtedly formed part of every anthropologist's field notes. Fictional representations of Indians also often adopted a pseudobiographical format. In Boasian publication, Kroeber's "Ethnology of the Gros Ventre" (1908) and Radin's "Personal Reminiscences of a Winnebago Indian" (1913) set scientific parameters for the individual life as a window into culture. Radin's *Autobiography of a Winnebago Indian* (1920) was the first book-length life history. This chapter examines three exemplars, moving from a groundbreaking collaborative experiment to a textbook mode of introduction to the discipline to redefinition of the interdependence of "informants" and anthropologists.

In the first case Elsie Clews Parsons, aided and abetted by Alfred Kroeber, used a life history format to combine the methods of anthropological science with a more humanistic, interpretive, and accessible view of culture as it might be experienced by an individual or individuals within it. The "typical" life cycle had long been part of the standard organization of the ethnographic monograph, but Parsons invited her collaborators to undertake presentations that would draw nonprofessional readers into an empathetic relationship with the plights of particular individuals in a variety of American Indian societies. Techniques of fiction—tending to melodrama in the 1920s—could be adapted to the purposes of anthropology in its role of cultural criticism, that is, the critique of North American society.

A quite different but widely circulated collection of cross-cultural life histories by anthropologists was edited by Joseph Casagrande in 1960. This collection was directed to undergraduate teaching of anthropology rather than to the North American public. Contributions portrayed specific individuals known to the anthropologists-as-authors through fieldwork, without inventing characters on whose experiences one might hang ethnological facts. Literary writing techniques were largely subordinated to social science language. By 1960 it was far from inevitable that North American anthropologists would work with American Indians. The geographical diversity of the twenty sketches reflected American postwar expansion of access to and interest in a more global geographic and political perspective. University growth further intensified the need of a small and little known discipline for textbooks attractive to students.

In the third instance a number of volumes could reflect the changes in the relationships between anthropologists and their "informants," a process reflected in part by increasing discomfort with the traditional disciplinary label of "informant" for those who agreed to work with anthropologists. The collection edited by Margot Liberty in 1978 elaborates the concept of the American Indian intellectual developed by Paul Radin. Interestingly, however, most of the portraits deal with dead Indian elders rather than with contemporary philosophers engaged in ongoing dialogue with anthropologists and, by extension, with North American society.

The dialogic potentials of life history discourse are considerable, although the genres of ethnographic production that develop them have moved, in practice, beyond life history in the narrow sense. Contemporary Americanists reflect teachings from multiple Native specialists, emphasizing sharing and transmitting of knowledges rather than narrative authority jealously guarded by the anthropologist. Let me cite two recent examples.

Anthropologist Robin Ridington and Omaha tribal historian Dennis Hastings collaborate in telling the story of the sacred pole of the Omaha nation, personified as Umon'hon'ti, "the Venerable Man" or "the Real Omaha." The association of Umon'hon'ti with the Omaha people goes back before what white people call history. Ridington and Hastings (1998) document the return of Umon'hon'ti to his native land and the Omaha people after a century of exile at the Peabody Museum of Harvard University (where Ridington met him in 1962 as a student of anthropology). The narrative interweaves past and present Omaha experiences: their world before written records, the loss within the contemporary community of knowledge and confidence about respectful treatment of the pole, and the partial recovery of such knowledge that resided in the collaborative ethnography of anthropologist Alice Fletcher and her Omaha adopted son Francis LaFlesche in the early part of the twentieth century (Fletcher and LaFlesche 1911). In a cycle moving across generations of intermeshed rituals and stories, both Omaha and anthropological, Ridington and Hastings negotiate a present that encompasses the past; the understandings and absences of one period supplement and complete those of another.

Sarah Hill's (1997) exploration of the four basketry traditions of the eastern Cherokees dissolves the abyss separating anthropologist-as-outsider and cultural-member-as-expert in a different way. Continuing the tradition in which Franz Boas insisted upon getting the story that accompanied an object of "material culture" (the very term implies that material things objectify underlying or ideal constructions of meaning), Hill illustrates individual art objects; her photos also include the living makers of baskets who shared with her their adaptations of tradition. Hill's exploration of the meaning domain of basketry leads her from the Cherokee story of the origin of the world through the history of contact and removal to contemporary environmental and social degradation. Like Ruth Bunzel, once a secretary in the Columbia department of anthropology and encouraged by her mentor Franz Boas to become a full-fledged anthropologist, Hill attempted to learn basketry traditions in practice as well as in theory. *The Pueblo Potter* (Bunzel 1929) set the precedent for going beyond abstract verbal representation of cultural knowledge; its subtitle, "A Study of Creative Imagination in Primitive Art," drew no principled distinction among Pueblo pottery, Greek pottery, and then-contemporary modern art.

The heritage of the life history genre inheres in these and other contemporary works in which individual lives, experiences, and specialized knowledges bring initially alien cultures to life for readers of anthropological accounts. Usually the individual or individuals are permitted by the conventions of the genre to speak for themselves, at least some of the time. Usually the anthropologist foregoes the textual invisibility of the omniscient narrator to reveal the character of human relationships arising from her or his fieldwork. Various genres of life-history-like ethnographic writing have persisted in aspiring to represent the quality of individual experience in an unfamiliar setting rather than restricting themselves to generalization at the cultural level. Contemporary experiments build on a consistent tradition of recording American Indian lives arising from Boasian culture and personality studies (e.g., Dyk 1938; Simmons 1942).

The methodological individualism of such projects, which involve intense collaboration between subjects and recorders, is deeply and, for some, prob-lematically embedded in Western social science as well as in the expectations of readers, be they professional colleagues, students who may or may not be-come anthropologists, or members of the general public (an amorphous cat-egory, albeit frequently invoked by academics trained in the 1960s and retain-ing something of a populist streak) who want to transcend surface barriers of cultural diversity and marginalization on the basis of race, ethnicity, class, gender, sexual orientation, and so on. Whether individualism as a strategy to create identification with the "other" would be effective for members of most of the communities anthropologists study is another matter altogether. Brum-ble (1988) argues that autobiography is an artificial genre in Native American cultures, since such documents exist only by virtue of anthropological inter-vention.

Elizabeth Cook-Lynn argues that American Indian intellectuals must re-claim the right to represent their own cultures according to local standards of "tribal realism" (Cook-Lynn 1998:132). Native American representations are, in her view, far too dependent on university support and on the priorities of outsiders to Native communities. The life history genre is particularly danger-ous because of its inherent individualism, reinforced by the prominence of mixed-blood Native writers whose tribal experience is often limited. The "post-colonial story" of these bicultural Native Americans may be attractive to postmodernist literary studies (Cook-Lynn 1998:125); it does not, however, re-flect either Native expressive conventions or Native control of Native intellec-tual property. Anthropology has yet to address this challenge fully, although it has reached disciplinary awareness by way of life history methodology and the interactions between Americanist anthropologists and particular "others."

The Baseline: *American Indian Life*

The baseline text for systematic early Boasian interest in the life history genre is *American Indian Life* (1922), edited by Boasian ethnographer, feminist, activ-ist, and philanthropist Elsie Clews Parsons (see Deacon 1997; Hare 1985; Zum-walt 1992). It is an ultrarich text, speaking differently to successive profes-sional generations. At the beginning of my career, I read the Parsons anthology in relation to culture and personality, then in the latter days of its theoretical ascendancy. After about 1910 the central theoretical problem of Boasian/ Americanist anthropology shifted from historical reconstruction of particular tribal histories to the relationship of culture to the individual, or as Edward Sapir preferred to put it, "the impact of culture on personality." Boas's own paradigmatic text, *The Mind of Primitive Man* (1911b), set the tone for the explorations of his various students. A few years later, Paul Radin (1927) argued for primitive man more as philosopher than as inarticulate savage. American Indian life histories enlivened these theoretical arguments by presenting individual interpretation of experience.

Thirty odd years later I turn to this same text to explore changing fashions of ethnographic representation. What fascinates me now about Parsons's collection is that "life history" did not yet constitute a monolithic textual genre. The authors approached their assigned task in diverse and surprisingly characteristic ways. I am left with several nagging historiographic questions: Was genre of ethnographic writing an issue for the founding Boasians? Were they willing to participate in this experimental project only because it was directed to the general public rather than to a professional audience? What did they think was the popular appeal of life histories?

"Mrs. Parsons" (as she was inevitably formally addressed by her contributors) was a force to be reckoned with in American anthropology in the period around World War I. Elsie Clews Parsons was a committed feminist, pacifist, and social critic, who often embarrassed her wealthy and socially prominent family. She advocated free love and trial marriage, yet paradoxically thought women needed further education to prepare them for the vote, depended on the support of ceremony and conventions, and had a duty to have children (Friedlander 1989:284–85). She received a Ph.D. at Columbia in sociology in 1899; by 1915, however, "she decided that empirical anthropology provided the best methods for studying the ways social forces within society checked self-expression" (Friedlander 1989:286). Already in her forties, Parsons began her intensive fieldwork in the American Southwest, on two occasions accompanied by Boas. She pioneered in studying the interconnection of Spanish and Indian cultures, working also in Mexico for comparative purposes. Boas persuaded Parsons to collect black folklore throughout the New World, and she in turn encouraged others to this work. In 1940 she became the first woman president of the American Anthropological Association.

In addition to her personal research, Parsons was important for her financial support of institutions and fieldwork by Boasians, particularly women, in the interwar period. Boas lacked a ready source of fieldwork funds for himself and his students after he broke with the American Museum of Natural History in 1905. It would be more than a decade before the Rockefeller Foundation began to fund the interdisciplinary social sciences, including anthropology. Even then Columbia remained outside the new synthesis; the anthropology under Boas's control in New York had already settled into its canonical form within its own disciplinary boundaries (even though these were broad in scope). Not until after World War II were government research grants available.

During the hiatus, "Mrs. Parsons" provided vital support for the activities that allowed Boas to function as an institutional leader, not merely as an intellectual one. For example, she underwrote secretarial expenses for his work and for the *Journal of American Folklore* during Boas's editorship. Further, her funding and moral support encouraged women to carry out ethnological fieldwork, thereby facilitating Boas's well-deserved reputation for welcoming women to study anthropology at Columbia.

Parsons believed that the North American public had little reliable material available with which to learn about Indians; readers were caught between the "forbidding monographs" of the professional anthropologist and the "legends of Fenimore Cooper" (Parsons 1922:1). Moreover, she insisted that anthropologists had never intended to make their works inaccessible to an audience beyond their technical specialization: "Appearances to the contrary, anthropologists have no wish to keep their science or any part of it esoteric"; she reasoned that public interest in the discipline would produce enhanced "facilities for the pursuit of anthropology" (Parsons 1922:1).

Parsons echoed Boas's emphasis on the urgency of the documentary project. Many "tribal cultures" would disappear before anything was learned about them. Therefore, "the white man's traditions about Indians," regardless of their intrinsic interest, "have been disregarded" in favor of an effort to capture the Native point of view (Parsons 1922:2). In a remarkably contemporary-sounding passage, Parsons acknowledged that few—even among anthropologists—were able to transcend their "own cultural bias or habits of mind." She noted explicitly her lack of faith in the objectivity of existing ethnographic reports, worrying whether "the writers have not read other traditions from their own culture into the culture they are describing" (Parsons 1922:2). The resulting accounts could be "quite misleading," if only because they tended to focus on phenomena differing from the observer's culture or interesting in contrast to other cultures the observer had studied as an anthropologist. No account could avoid the standpoint of its author. Because of such cultural and professional blinders anthropologists failed to see "the foreign culture as a whole, noting only the aspects which happen to interest us. . . . Hence, our classified data give the impression that the native life is one unbroken round [of the pattern described]. . . . The commonplaces of behavior are overlooked, the amount of 'common sense' is underrated, and the proportion of knowledge to credulity is overlooked" (Parsons 1922:2). The view from outside was necessarily piecemeal. An important variant of anthropological holism was inextricably bound to the attempt to capture the Native point of view. Unless tied to the standpoints of particular individuals, the accounts of anthropologists would remain forever normative and lifeless, failing to convey the satisfactions of a genuine culture. The more superorganic holism favored by Kroeber and Benedict could also be depicted, however, in relation to individual experience of it.

Indian "tales" in the form that they were habitually told to anthropologists exacerbated problems of observer bias because their brevity lent them a "necessarily impressionistic character" (Parsons 1922:2). The "impressions" were inevitably those of the anthropologist. Parsons believed her volume could sidestep the technical problems of psychology and historical reconstruction—we would now say of representation and voice—which constituted the twin pillars of Boasian theory, because the format was ostensibly transparent, merely "a book of pictures," easily accessible to nonprofessional readers (Parsons 1922: 3). Contemporary visual anthropologists, of course, would be less sanguine about the transparency of such representations to depict the Native point of view.

For readers interested in more extensive anthropological evidence, the appendix of *American Indian Life* noted "how the problems are being followed up." Parsons made no effort to claim that her experimental work would supersede more conventional ethnographic genres; "realist" ethnographies (Van Maanen 1988) would retain their value for a professional audience. Despite her insistence on the proximate target of imbuing a general audience with increased awareness of and tolerance for cultural diversity, Parsons further hoped to increase popular respect for anthropology as a discipline capable of producing materials for such cultural instruction. "If the pictures remain pictures for him [the hypothetical reader], well and good; if they lead him to the problems, good and better. Anthropology is short on students" (Parsons 1922:3). Parsons was straightforward that an important secondary motivation of the life history genre was professional recruitment.

The stature of the project within anthropology increased dramatically when

Kroeber agreed to write the introduction. For him the primary issues it raised were professional: genre experimentation illustrated the descriptive and expressive potentials of the new Boasian ethnology. Boasian control of the North American discipline was consolidated during the early 1920s (Darnell 1998a) and its core participants saw themselves as spearheading a scientific revolution of considerable magnitude. Most of the early Boasians produced textbooks in this period, among which Kroeber's *Anthropology* (1923) was a prime exemplar.

Despite his close personal relationship with Parsons at the time, Kroeber supported the project for his own reasons, demonstrating little interest in the usefulness of *American Indian Life* for a popular audience. Rather, he emphasized that the old "speculative" ethnology (which "thought out a formula . . . then ransacked the accounts of travellers, missionaries and residents among primitive tribes for each bit of evidence favorable to his [*sic*] theory") had been replaced "in full swing" by a new "inductive" science of anthropology (Kroeber 1922:5). Only in "non-scientific quarters" did the old [comparative evolutionary] methods of "theory fabrication persist" (Kroeber 1922:5). The experimental ethnographies of the 1920s were part of the Boasian critique of evolution. Particularism and local context countered the assumption that all societies shared the same progressive evolutionary history and established the scientific credibility of the Boasian paradigm. Readers, Kroeber implied, would want to attune themselves with the new ethnology. Contrary interpretations of the past remained dependent on the "method of ignoring [the] context" that was meticulously provided in the sketches for this volume (Kroeber 1922:5). The new ethnology "modestly grew up" by putting facts in their "natural order, sequence, geographical relation and degree of association": "The whole culture of the group must be more or less known before the history and meaning of an institution can become intelligible. Detached from its culture mass, a custom reveals as little of its functioning as an organ dissected out of the living body" (Kroeber 1922:5). A solid ethnographic database necessarily preceded cultural integration or explication of the meaning of personal experience.

In conventional Boasian fashion, Kroeber emphasized the "heavy significance" of geographical distribution. This substituted for the history of "primitive peoples" and provided "rather reliable insight" into the past, sometimes even into origins (Kroeber 1922:7). Kroeber envisioned aboriginal American culture history as "a flow of things of the mind . . . of culture, not of populations" (Kroeber 1922:10). People thought about things and elaborated ideas initially borrowed from their neighbors. A "series of culture centers" developed in succession along a "ladder of cultural development," which constituted "a real sequence of history," albeit undated. Kroeber had recently become intrigued by seriation of Zuni pottery and its possible implications for relative chronology (Sapir's "time perspective") in aboriginal American cultures, leading him to reassess the potentials for historical understanding implicit in the ethnographic study of contemporary cultures.

Kroeber went on to characterize some of the major culture areas of the continent. The North Pacific Coast mostly "went its own way," independently developing cultural features that elsewhere diffused from Mexico. On the "treeless Plains," elements from further south were "remodeled" into "a little civilization of their own," with a brief efflorescence of buffalo hunting (Kroeber 1922:13). Among the Eskimos "stern necessity forced a special inventiveness on the mechanical side" (not precisely the absence of environmental determinism Boas argued for as a result of his Baffinland fieldwork). The culture areas were units for the unique historical interaction of peoples in each area. The Eskimos, for example, remained open to continuing Asian influence.

Kroeber emphasized that "many small items of ethnic knowledge" became significant once "antiquarian fragments" gave way to systematic specialized anthropology. The assembling of sufficient facts for an overall scientific description of the Indians required several generations and could not be accomplished by any single person (Kroeber 1922:12). In fact, context was so crucial that each anthropologist investigated thoroughly only one tribe (or at the most, two or three). Studying a culture in "the field," the new ethnologists entered into "as close relations as possible with its most intelligent or authoritative members [Radin's 'primitive philosophers']" (Kroeber 1922:12). At least *qua desideratum,* survey fieldwork had been superseded by a more intensive and interpretive brand of ethnography. Practical limitations continued to be imposed, however, by limited fieldwork funding and summer field seasons organized around an academic calendar.

"The final outcome is a monograph—a bulky, detailed, often tedious, but fundamental volume, issued by the government or a scientific institution" (Kroeber 1922:12). Kroeber suggested that as "a by-product" of such "intensive" studies, there arose a popular literature less rigorous in its adherence to actual ethnographic contexts. Moreover, this "psychology of the Indian" usually came from untrained observers less well informed than anthropologists but not—in the rhetoric of today—reticent to appropriate aboriginal voices.

Kroeber extolled the life history genre within the new ethnology because it provided anthropologists with a forum for speculative or intuitive insights that did not fit well within the scientific monograph as conventionally conceived. Monographs were supposed to stick to "objective facts" even though the "mental workings of the people whose customs are described are subjective . . . and much more charily put into print" (Kroeber 1922:13). Although such insights usually remained unpublished, "every American anthropologist with field experience holds in his memory many interpretations, many convictions as to how his Indians feel" (Kroeber 1922:13).

Kroeber's reference to each anthropologist's having "his Indians" is an anachronism that should not be judged by contemporary standards. Relative to the "untrained observers" for whom he expressed such disdain, Kroeber and his fellow Boasians attributed considerable agency to the members of cultures they studied. They believed that ethnographic intuition was real, trustworthy because of the anthropologist's deeply ingrained reflexivity about his or her own subjectivity. The Boasians identified with their subjects and defined themselves professionally in relation to them.

In Kroeber's view the originality of the volume rested precisely in the reliability of the "stories" told by the anthropologists. They had been there. They were scientists, trained observers able to control the biases embedded in the cultural and idiosyncratic subjectivities that worried Parsons (who held a doctorate in sociology, a discipline more inclined to worry about such matters). Even the project's contributors learned something from the exercise about their own epistemological premises and interpretive practices: "To many of us, the writing of our tale has been a surprise and of value to ourselves. We had not realized how little we knew of the workings of the Indian mind on some sides, how much on others" (Kroeber 1922:13).

Parsons, as the volume editor, had "devised" the "fictional form of presentation" and allowed her colleagues the "freedom to depict" such thoughts and feelings: "In fact, it incites [the author] to active psychological treatment, else the tale would lag. At the same time, the customs depicted are never invented. Each author has adhered strictly to the social facts as he knew them. He has merely *selected* those that seemed most characteristic, and woven them into a plot around an imaginary Indian hero or heroine. The method is that of the historical novel, with emphasis on the history rather than the romance" (Kroeber 1922:13; emphasis mine). Method was crucial; it permitted appropriate selection of facts and fictionalization of circumstances. Literary techniques could be borrowed without abandoning anthropology's commitment to science.

The only disciplinary precedent Kroeber cited was Adolphe Bandelier's *The Delight Makers* ([1890] 1971) (but see also George Bird Grinnell 1892). Bandelier's successful novel presented "a picture of native American life," with "the intensive and special coloring of each tribal civilization" (Kroeber 1922:14). The "facts" hung together differently for each tribe. In this way "the common elements of Indian culture are brought out most truthfully, even though somewhat indirectly" (Kroeber 1922:14). Kroeber used the analogy of "composite photographs," a seeming precursor of a fabricated product simulating authenticity, simulacrum without an original. These stories could be truer than actual events and persons. The product, resulting from fieldwork by professionally trained observers, was "social science, not merely literature" (Kroeber 1922: 14). Artistic license was successfully constrained by reality. Kroeber did not pursue the relationship of such composite construction of ethnographic reportage to the methodological conventions of the social sciences, though most of us would doubtless do so today.

In Kroeber's view the literature on American Indians disproportionately emphasized religion, with relatively little known about economic and political institutions. For many of the things ethnologists wanted to know, it was already too late because of the rapid disintegration of traditional cultures; but some forms of culture were reliably remembered longer than others. "Ritual and ceremony follow exact forms which the native is able to relate with accuracy from memory, long after the practices have become defunct" (Kroeber 1922:14). In fact, the generic Indian (Kroeber did not distinguish among particular groups in this reflection) enjoys these conversations, once "his confidence is gained." Often the interaction involved an element of nostalgia, with the anthropologist the only audience willing to listen, the last link in a disappearing chain of knowledge transmission. Kroeber did not pursue the question of the authenticity of knowledge so gained; there was no alternative. Nor did he explore the ethics of encouraging reticent "informants" to reveal tribal secrets.

Culture change demonstrated the plasticity of the "social usages" that were being "profoundly modified." Although Kroeber's definition of culture was interpretive, symbolic, and capable of verbal articulation, he was also fully cognizant of ongoing social behavior and its relation to the transmission of traditional knowledge through oral tradition. In other contexts Kroeber was often oblivious to the ethics of communication between Native communities and "their" anthropologists, as well as to culture change as such. But the work required "tacit coordination of Indians and ethnologists to explore the vein of most vivid productivity" (Kroeber 1922:14). Again uncharacteristically, Kroeber presented the ethnographic encounter as a collaboration, in which the "informant" and his anthropologist [ownership was reciprocal!] decided what should or could be recorded. In practice ethnographic fieldwork was dialogic.

Religion also dominated the existing literature because the "average Indian" devoted more time to religion than, for example, to warfare. Economic and political forms were "first to crumble on contact" and "lack[ed] the definition of ceremonialism" for the cultural reconstruction (Kroeber 1922:15) that was the aim of Boasian historical particularism. From the Native point of view, economic and political matters could be taken for granted and therefore were deemed less reportable.

"[W]e [anthropologists] have done much better" at describing the "daily life, personal relations, and the ambitions and ideals of the individual born into aboriginal society" (Kroeber 1922:15). Daily life provided an entrée to culture for the anthropologist as for the (presumably more naive) reader. Life cycle, abstracted from the experience of any particular individual, was already a staple of the generic ethnographic monograph. In fact, the "exhibit of the workings of the Indian mind which these tales yield in the aggregate" produced "a surprising degree of insight and careful accuracy" into the phenomenological reality of life in a "foreign" (interestingly, not a "primitive") culture (Kroeber 1922:15).

Kroeber noted some of the rhetorical devices contributing to successful representation of the Native point of view, including the "elusive" quality of humor, the conveyance of which "presupposes a feeling for the exact psychic situation of the individual" as well as "the finest nuances of his cultural setting" (Kroeber 1922:16). A mere "reconstructor" should not aspire to convey humor. At best, he [sic] might manage to touch "the bounds of irony"; of necessity "we scientists [are] novices in the domain of fiction" (Kroeber 1922:16). Anthropologists must take care not to overestimate what they know.

Who, then, were the selected participants? Surprisingly, for a self-professed feminist dedicated to applying ethnological perspectives to the institutions of love, marriage, child rearing, and the family in then-contemporary American society, all of Parsons's invited contributors were men. Several of them, including illustrator Grant LaFarge, had been her lovers (Deacon 1997). There were certainly fewer women in professional anthropology in 1922 than a decade later. The overwhelming maleness of the contributors and Parsons's failure to mention this one-sided representation as a problem seem, at the very least, to indicate that she did not attempt to redress gender imbalance among them. It is tempting to speculate that, for all her avowed feminism, she did not like women, or at least enjoyed being the *only* woman in a group.

Parsons's gender biases in her representation of life at Zuni are intriguing as well. She described socialization for both sexes by means of what we might now call negative ethnography: The girl was not initiated like her brother, whose initiation was then described as the cultural pattern. Parsons asserted at some length that women were unimportant in "ceremonial management." We eventually learn that "the couple rather than the individual is the Zuni unit" (Parsons 1922:164). She did not seem to notice that half of every such couple was a woman. Her account also de-emphasized the agency of Zuni persons: "The differentiation of the sexes follows lines of least resistance" (Parsons 1922:164). Apparently, getting outside the cross-culturally attested pattern of greater visibility of men in ceremonial contexts would require women to defend their potential equality quite forcefully (which they were disinclined to do). Parsons concluded: "Household work is confining" (Parsons 1922:164). This remark presumably reflected little of the Zuni point of view.

All but two contributors, one a coauthor with Parsons, were professionally employed in anthropology. She identified herself in the table of contents merely as "a member of the Hopi tribe." The list of contributors (see Table 2) reads like a map of the institutional structure of the profession around 1920— that is, universities and museums, with only Alfred Tozzer maintaining a dual affiliation. The apparent continuing dominance of museums at a time when Boasians already held major academic positions is largely attributable to the inclusion of sketches from Mexico, a research field dominated by Harvard-trained and museum-based archaeologists. Significantly, the only anomalies in professional affiliation are attributable to Parsons herself; they focus in the Southwest culture area where her own work centered after about 1915.

Parsons' male colleagues apparently considered it politic not to refuse her invitation to contribute to *American Indian Life*. Like it or not, and some did not, her control of scarce financial resources put her in a position to enforce her wish for colleagues to contribute to a volume accessible to the public.

The volume added additional scientific context to the rather disembodied stories with a map of Native American groups, arranged according to the cul-

Table 2. Contributors to *American Indian Life*

University-employed:

University of California, Berkeley	Alfred Kroeber
	Robert Lowie
	Paul Radin
University of Pennsylvania	Frank Speck
New School for Social Research	Alexander Goldenweiser
University of Washington	Leslie Spier
Harvard University	Herbert Spinden
	Alfred Tozzer ($^1/_2$)
Columbia University	Franz Boas

Museum-employed:

American Museum of Natural History	Clark Wissler
	Pliny Goddard
	N. C. Nelson
Milwaukee Public Museum	Alanson Skinner
Museum of the American Indian, Heye Foundation	John P. Harrington
	T. T. Waterman
Brooklyn Institute Museum	Stewart Culin
Field Museum of Natural History	John Alden Mason
Carnegie Institute of Washington	Sylvanus Morley
Peabody Museum (Harvard)	Alfred Tozzer ($^1/_2$)
Division of Ethnology, Geological Survey of Canada	Edward Sapir
Bureau of American Ethnology	Truman Michelson
	John Swanton

Anomalies:

Member of the Hopi tribe	Elsie Clews Parsons
Student, Hampton Institute	T. B. Reed (with Elsie Clews Parsons)
Sometime resident among the Hopi and Navajo	A. M. Stephen

---

ture area concept widely used by the early Boasians and formalized by Clark Wissler in *The American Indian* (1917) (see Table 3).

The age and area method codified the historical pole of Boasian theory. Its organizing function, both for the volume and for North American anthropology as a whole, was attested by the carefully systematic geographical coverage. Boas, although most of his own fieldwork was done on the Northwest Coast, covered the Eskimos; alternative contributors were easily available for the Northwest Coast.

Each contributor interpreted the assignment idiosyncratically, with products ranging from the generic lackluster descriptions of Alanson Skinner on Ojibwe Mide initiation and Truman Michelson on child rearing to much genuinely dramatic writing. The style of many pieces, however, was peppered with disclaimers of ethnographic authority: "let us say," "may have," or "we may suppose."

Romantic rhetoric reached its peak with the archaeologists, who were in the particularly awkward position of having no texts elicited in the field or field notes reflecting conversations with contemporary aboriginal philosophers to serve as the basis of their narratives. There is an inverse relationship between the availability of texts in the words of native speakers and rhetorical flourishes reminiscent of the flowery novels of James Fenimore Cooper that served Mrs. Parsons as rhetorical straw figures for the project. She envisioned more accurate and less sentimental portraits of contemporary American Indian life.

John P. Harrington, a linguist, resorted to a time machine to bring alive his Lenape Delaware burial site from an unspecified past time; his alter ego returned to his own society only reluctantly. Although he had worked with speakers of many aboriginal languages, Harrington located the viable culture of interest to general readers in the romanticized precontact past. The archaeologists who worked in Mexico also imagined themselves in the times of their excavations. They did not date their stories, leaving the impression that human sacrifice, for example, was a contemporary practice. Such a bizarre practice would titillate the general reader because it seemed impossible, from a Western standpoint, that the sacrificial victim could be a voluntary participant. Although tragic endings were well established in the short-story conventions of the period, their frequency in the contributed life histories perhaps also suggests jaundiced authorial acceptance of the public expectation that bizarre customs would produce unpleasant consequences (presumably thereby reinforcing the moral order of the readers' own society). Anthropologists of the period often shared the public belief that the Indians were rapidly disappearing, adding urgency to the recording of their cultures. Personal tragedy thus aesthetically mirrored historical inevitability.

The anthropologist appeared as an actor in several stories. J. Alden Mason reconstructed the skeptical position developed by an heir to traditional belief. This skepticism underlay his willingness to sell the artifacts he had inherited from a shaman who expected him to continue the ritual practice. Stewart Culin described visiting his friend Frank Cushing at Zuni, thereby characterizing both of them as ethnographers in relation to that place. Clark Wissler portrayed himself serving as scribe for a Blackfoot shaman; at least on the surface, narrative authority was shared, and the shaman was enabled to speak for himself.

Other generic plots imagined by the anthropologists for the edification of the unsuspecting public included star-crossed lovers, arranged marriages, and war or sacrifice as disrupting an otherwise promising life. The life histories emphasized the domestic, understood to be the domain of the individual, over the political. Shamans, visions, and the supernatural added spice.

Many of the stories were highly dramatic, even though the genre encouraged stock plots and stock characters. Robert Lowie told of a shaman who was old and blind but whose rival survived after his family was killed off; it was impossible to decide who had won the power contest between them. Lowie also described a kidnapped wife subjected to false accusation of infidelity, who, according to tribal custom, could not be reclaimed honorably by her husband; pathos was enhanced by telling the story in the frame of a story told to a skeptical child by an old woman filled with nostalgic regret for the lost love of her youth. Frank Speck dramatized the dilemma of a young woman compelled to choose a spouse. One suitor excelled in traditional hunting and the social obligations that went with it, while the other chose to live by the white man's trade in furs. Alexander Goldenweiser's tale depicted the social destruction of an Iroquois matron who was forced to depose her own son. Kroeber's hero grew into his dreams, well on the way to becoming an important shaman, but died in battle before he had a chance to realize this potential; his talents were then lost to his people. Lowie's ambitious would-be warrior rejected an alternative dream-mandate for his life, against the advice of a shaman, and thereby chose, according to local understanding, to die in battle. T. T. Waterman's rendition of "trouble on the Klamath" showed how "all goes back to" events of the distant but well-remembered past.

Table 3. Culture Areas Represented in *American Indian Life*

Plains:

Crow (3)	Robert Lowie
Blackfoot	Clark Wissler

Middle West:

(Chippewa/Ojibwe)	Alanson Skinner
Winnebago	Paul Radin
Meskwaki	Truman Michelson

Eastern:

Montagnais	Frank Speck
Iroquois	Alexander Goldenweiser
Lenape	John P. Harrington
Tulsa	John Swanton

Southwest:

Apache	Pliny Goddard
(Hopi and) Navajo	A. M. Stephen
Zuni	Elsie Clews Parsons
Zuni	Stewart Culin
Havasupai	Leslie Spier
Mohave	Alfred Kroeber

Mexican:

Tepecano	John Alden Mason
Tezcatlipoca	Herbert Spinden
Maya	Sylvanus Morley
Toltec	Alfred Tozzer

Pacific Coast:

Mutsun	N. C. Nelson
Klamath	T. T. Waterman
Nootka	Edward Sapir

Northern Athabascan:

Chippewyan	Robert Lowie
Ten'a (Alaska)	T. B. Reed and Elsie Clews Parsons

Eskimo:

Eskimo	Franz Boas

The moment of first contact was a powerful locus of the anthropological imagination. For the popular audience, contact with Europeans was inevitably presented without dates. The time of first contact, of course, shifted across the continent, rendering a consistent temporal framework elusive. John Swanton described a Tulsa sage who understood that he taught a successor who would live in a changing world with different truths. N. C. Nelson depicted a cultural innovator who sought change and whose death seemed to reestablish traditional ways, ironically just at the time Europeans were appearing nearby; the conservative forces had won only a transitory victory. T. B. Reed and Parsons constructed a secondhand story told by a young man who did not know many things about his traditional culture because he had spent four years in boarding school; the irony of this forced assimilation was not noted in their recording of what was still remembered. A. M. Stephen presented a narrative of how biomedicine proved itself superior to traditional curing at St. Michel's Mission in Navajo country. Parsons and her southwestern collaborators more clearly favored assimilation than did the core Boasians, who tended to sympathize with traditional cultures.

Boasian Explorations of the Arts

By the time of Parsons's project, reexamination of the canons of ethnographic writing was already well underway in Americanist anthropology. Anthropology was far from isolated from the world of belles lettres. Various Boasians, of whom Sapir and Ruth Benedict were best known, wrote poetry. I have argued elsewhere (e.g., Darnell 1986b, 1990b) that the respect for individual creativity entailed in poetic production fed back into the ethnography of Sapir, Radin, and Goldenweiser in particular. Beginning around 1917 Sapir contributed poems and reviews to various small literary magazines. His interest in the individual Indian was not unrelated to his insistence on the uniqueness in his own culture, what he came to call "the locus of culture" in each individual.

Sapir agreed with Parsons that conventional ethnographies did not make good reading, writing to Ruth Benedict: "I am afraid that the boldly impersonal point of view we have all gone in for is good for still-born works only. I almost feel it needs a semi-literary outsider to do our writing for us. We know too many facts and are too proud of our field techniques and erudite negativism" (Sapir to Benedict, 15 April 1923, Sapir family documents). Sapir was less concerned about being a scientist than were many of his fellow Boasians. He also worried about the imposition of anthropologists' categories on Native consultants. At the Hanover Conference (the Rockefeller Foundation-sponsored think tank of the interwar years) in 1926, he noted: "You can get satisfactory responses to build up a fine monograph if you ask certain questions that more or less force a certain kind of answer. If you are honest, you find at certain stages you are prejudicing the whole thing, you are projecting your previsaged concepts on the people you are discussing" (quoted by Leeds-Hurwitz and Nyce 1986:502). The best source of unbiased data was elicitation of grammatical categories and cultural texts from native speakers, who were the final arbiters of acceptability.

In the proceedings of the American Psychological Association, Sapir explored the implications of holistic ethnographies based on reconstructions, themselves based on texts obtained from "a few old men and women"; although "you get what looks like a unified account," it "has to be weighted differently at different points as far as the realities of life are concerned" (quoted by Leeds-Hurwitz and Nyce 1986:502-3). Sapir was unequivocal that "the cultures so carefully described in our ethnological and sociological monographs are not, and cannot be, the truly objective entities they claim to be. No matter how accurate their individual itemization, their integrations into suggested structures are uniformly fallacious and unreal" (Sapir 1949:593). No Native person would undertake such a presentation. Sapir's concept of pattern or integration in culture appears to have emerged as a subjective result of fieldwork experience, intuition, and the acknowledged constructedness of the ethnographic account. A particular anthropologist could only report relationships as she or he perceived them. "The culture," therefore, did not exist in the cultural practices themselves or even in reports of them.

Life history had the considerable potential advantage that the genre would/could allow the "other" to speak, thus moving it toward the genuinely dialogic anthropology for which Dennis Tedlock has long called. Tedlock and Mannheim are pessimistic, however, about the actual achievements of life history writing as illustrated in *American Indian Life;* "a typified, consensus view of society reappears in the margins of the life histories of individuals" (Tedlock and Mannheim 1995:12). Their honorable exception to Boasian generic homogenization of texts is the dialogue among peyote religion founders in Radin's *Method and Theory in Ethnology* (1933). Nonetheless, Tedlock and Mannheim's concern with the possibility of cross-cultural dialogue has longstanding precedents in the Americanist tradition. In the preface to his student

Walter Dyk's *Son of Old Man Hat,* Sapir suggested the covert origins of efforts to portray individuality in life histories, "partly under the cover of orthodox ethnology, partly in unconcern of it" (Sapir 1938a:vi–vii). "One discovers that a 'primitive' can talk, often prefers to talk, about his personal memories even where they do not seem to give the ethnologist chapter and verse for some important rubric in his filing cabinet" (Sapir 1938a:vi–vii). In life histories, as in culture and personality work in general, the anthropologist must listen attentively to the speaker.

Sapir's contribution to the Parsons compendium first appeared a year earlier in *The Queen's Quarterly* in Ottawa (1921d). A poetic version, "The Blind Old Indian Tells his Names," was published in *The Canadian Bookman* in the same year (1921c). This chronology suggests that Sapir probably was considering the expressive premises underlying experimental ethnographic writing *before* Mrs. Parsons drew him into her project. Certainly the piece for her volume was not an isolated product. This is the period in Sapir's life when he was most active in writing poetry and in participating in Ottawa literary circles (Darnell 1986b, 1990b). What Parsons *may* have done for him, however, was to cement his conviction that such explorations *need not be separate* from his ethnography. This result, ironically, was the reverse of Parsons's stated intention to move Boasian anthropology toward a nonprofessional public audience rather than to revise professional canons or genres of writing. She had unleashed something that, in retrospect, is much more interesting, as her colleagues experimented with ways to carry out their ambiguous assignment.

Sapir's paper for *Queens Quarterly* aimed at "a reliable conception of the typical West Coast tribe but in a form that is definitely less technical than the ordinary scientific paper. At the same time, the paper attempts to steer clear of the usual sentimental kind of thing that is generally published in popular journals on the Indians" (Sapir to Ferguson, 14 July 1920, NMM). Parsons, of course, shared his concern for the reliability of what was portrayed as typical as well as for avoiding sentimentality.

Sapir and Benedict aimed at a modernist "hardness" in their poetry, in opposition to mere sentiment (Handler 1986). The modernist social sciences evinced a parallel anxiety for the status of science in their quest for "objectivity." Sapir argued that the "realist monograph" (Van Maanen 1988) was boring. Many of its goals, perhaps the most important ones, could be met just as well by the convenient fiction of individual experience in a biographical or autobiographical genre.

Parsons wrote to potential contributors (e.g., to Sapir, 16 January 1920, NMM), explaining what she had in mind. A "general framework" intended to "give uniformity" to the volume. Grant LaFarge's illustrations, frontispieces to each story, would "bridge the gap for the reading public between our esoteric monographs and shall we say, Fenimore Cooper." These instructions were repeated in her preface to the published work: "*We* are proposing to get out a popular book on American Indians to be written jointly by anthropologists . . . each contributor to deal with the story of the life of a fictitious male or female member of the tribe he has visited" (Parsons 1922:1; emphasis mine) Most of the male contributors, however, chose to depict the life of a male subject (see Table 6). Male bonding seems to have been integral to the ethnographic encounter. Male ethnographers may have had limited access to Native women, but they also assumed the primary significance of male activity in cultural description. This trend is only partly mitigated in later collections.

The "we" of the prospectus is intriguing. Tellingly, Parsons reported the origin of the project among "our New York lunch club" (Parsons to Sapir, 16 January 1920, NMM). Thus she had already co-opted Boas, Kroeber, Goddard, Nelson, Goldenweiser, Spier, Lowie, and, of course, herself. That is, at least eight of the potential contributors were based in or passing through New York. The Columbia anthropologists of the immediate post–World War I period had not ventured far from Boas's home bailiwick. The project, therefore, was fait accompli even before the nonlocal contributors were officially invited to participate.

Whatever his actual feelings, Sapir responded politely that he would be pleased to participate in principle but did not understand Parsons's intentions for editorial uniformity (Sapir to Parsons, 20 January 1920, NMM). He may well have resented her coming up with what he felt to be *his* idea. Almost certainly, he considered himself the harbinger among the Boasians of integration of ethnography and belles lettres (Darnell 1986b, 1990b). There was, however, a world of difference between the two visions. Parsons apparently meant quite literally what she said in the prospectus quite literally. Her own sketch of Zuni was a lifeless generic life history. The only other contributors who so restricted themselves, Michelson and Skinner, were both peripheral to the critical mass of core Boasians at the center of the project.

Sapir elaborated the multiple experimental possibilities he foresaw in Parsons's exercise, wondering "whether a genuine short story, that is fiction, is required, or a popularized ethnological sketch of the life of an individual. Of course, the two ideas are absolutely distinct. In the former, ethnographic material could be brought in accidentally. In the latter, the ethnological material is the point" (Sapir to Parsons, 20 January 1920, NMM). Parsons responded that she envisioned a distinction between "fiction" and "a popularized ethnological sketch of the life of an individual" (Parsons to Sapir, 22 January 1920, NMM). She wanted the latter, readable objectivity, and failed to address Sapir's query about the factuality of the life selected for description. Potential appeal to a broad audience mattered more than accuracy of ethnographic detail.

Sapir's review of *American Indian Life* praised the volume's effort to provide the public with "some idea of the strange yet always intelligible life of our natives" (Parsons 1922:297), a position fully consistent with his developing theory of culture (Darnell 1997a; Darnell, Irvine, and Handler 1999), in which ethnography involved removal of the exotic to reveal the underlying sense making of other cultural worlds, in principle no different from our own. The reader would absorb ethnographic "facts" in their appropriate experiential context, identifying painlessly with the characters and the social contexts of their interactions.

Sapir's review in 1922 shows that he had moved considerably beyond Parsons's conception of the project, musing as to whether such a form might "penetrate into the vitals of primitive life," thereby "fashion[ing] for ourselves satisfying pictures on its own level of reality" (Sapir 1949 [1922b]:570). He wondered whether it was ever really possible to reason from the Native point of view. The constructedness of the ethnographic account might be destined to impose an external reading regardless of generic experimentation.

Nonetheless, Sapir's review acknowledged that Parsons's volume included some potentially seminal experiments that began to "capture the spirit of the primitive" by "transcribing, either literally or in simple paraphrase, personal experiences . . . written down or dictated by natives" (Sapir 1949 [1922b]:570). He was concerned more with the effect on the audience than with accurate representation of the native speaker as storyteller. It was acceptable to put words into the mouth of the generic Indian. Self-consciousness about dialogue with Native narrators and about rhetoric of ethnographic representation were singularly absent (cf. Clifford and Marcus 1986). Implicitly, however, Sapir recognized the potentially ambiguous relationship of the Boasian text tradition (bound to what particular Native persons actually said) to mainstream genres of ethnographic writing.

Unfortunately, "bare recital of details of any mode of life" (Sapir 1949 [1922b]:570) was not automatically intelligible, in fact quite the contrary. Parsons attempted to address the gap. Ethnographic notes were required to help the reader make the transition. These notes, plus references and a map, appeared in appendices. The notes followed a standardized format cataloging location, population, language family, and basic bibliography.

The way was now cleared for Sapir to muse on how biographical experience might be organized by members of [other] cultures. This possibility is, I think, the crux of Sapir's fascination with Sayach'apis or Old Tom, the Nootka trader to whose experience he repeatedly returned as a rhetorical figure (Sapir 1921d, 1922a). Ceremonial activities centering on transmission and inheritance of names, songs, and other symbolic property were the key events of an individual Nootka life. This cultural fact emerged from analysis by Sapir as ethnographer, but by implication these were also the key biographical events of Old Tom's self-image of his life, although Sapir unabashedly presumed to speak for him and to attribute emotional intention to him. Tom's persona, as animated by Sapir, centered on aesthetically satisfying or "genuine" memories of past glory attained through the ritual distribution of wealth he had acquired as a successful entrepreneur and trader. Sapir was careful to specify that Tom was *not* what Radin called "primitive man as a philosopher." He was a pragmatist, a man of action rather than of ideas. Perhaps for this reason Sapir felt it *his* task to appropriate Tom's voice, to speak for him at a level of generalization that the subject himself would doubtless have found unintelligible, if not actively offensive.

Lowie also appropriated Native voice, with a self-confidence that now seems both naive and arrogant. He wrote to Sapir that he had based his sketch for the Parsons volume quite directly on a "prototype" from his 1918 Crow myths: "You'll notice that I embody some of the concrete details practically as recited to me, but flatter myself that I have presented the Crow-Hidatsa spirit *more accurately* than it is portrayed in this particular narrative of my informants" (Lowie to Sapir, 28 March 1921, NMM; emphasis added). This attitude is hardly reflects a strategy of liberating the voice of the Native as agent and theoretician! Nonetheless, the questions are posed, though not answered, in terms entirely intelligible today.

The limitations of Sapir's position are characteristic of the period. Although the solutions are only marginally satisfying today—aesthetically, ethically, or methodologically—experimentation with ethnographic genre by Sapir and his colleagues laid the groundwork for later, more dialogic efforts. Historicism is crucial here, lest we efface the continuity of this tradition.

In sum, the Parsons collection juxtaposed a series of sketches with quite diverse formats and left the reader to draw the comparisons. In characteristic Boasian fashion, conclusions were implicit rather than spelled out. Even for the general public, premature generalizations were to be avoided.

Transmitting Disciplinary Wisdom: *In the Company of Man*

By 1960 North American anthropology had arrived at a new location. Postwar expansion of the academy was particularly intense in anthropology. The experience of returning veterans contributed to the disintegration of isolationism. The result was a greater awareness of cultural diversity, increased involvement with colonial and postcolonial societies around the globe, and growing emphasis on anthropologists' ability to create tolerance of alternative lifeways, despite surface exoticism.

There was a need for textbooks, summarizing the disciplinary perspective and recapitulating the codification of the Boasian paradigm between about 1910 and 1925 (Darnell 1998a). As anthropology expanded, it became less a family of professionals known personally to one another. Textbooks became increasingly important in presenting the fundamental standpoint of the discipline to wider audiences. How to think like an anthropologist was a problem to be addressed at an impersonal scientific distance, in writing rather than through immersing each convert in his or her own fieldwork. Only traces of firsthand experience remained for the reader, who was even less likely than his or her teacher to have firsthand contact with the ethnographer as writer/reporter.

Moreover, the societies studied were increasingly exotic and removed from the likelihood of direct experience. Whatever cross-cultural generalizations might be drawn, the anthropologist as interpreter strove to convey the quality of the experience, the particular mystique of the discipline "in the field." Once these experiences were interpreted or translated into familiar functional patterns with behaviors and ideas merely combined in novel ways, the reader would find "the primitive" individual pretty much like people back home. Just below the diversity of surface forms, there was a commonality of human experience, of human nature even, that kept anthropology from flying off into diversity unlimited.

In this context Joseph Casagrande edited a new collection of life histories from societies studied by his postwar colleagues. *In the Company of Man* (1960), although quite dated in such matters as the absence of gender-inclusive language, moved far beyond the collage of genre constructions of the Parsons collection. Twenty "portraits of anthropological informants" described specific named individuals whose photographs accompanied their life stories.

Only two women appeared among the subjects (see Table 6). Casagrande argued that this lack of female representation did not constitute bias because he had sought more sketches of women (Casagrande 1960:xiv). (It is tempting to compare Clifford's (1986) assertion that feminist scholars had not contributed much to the experimental moment heralded by *Writing Culture*.) On the other hand, there were more women among the contributors than among the biographical subjects (Margaret Mead, Cora DuBois, Ethel Albert, Laura Bohannan); none of these women, however, were Americanists. Gender, at least in this case, registered in professional credentialization before it did so in ethnographic representation.

Although each contributor retained authorial control, all of the pieces reflected an implicit dialogue between the key informant and the anthropologist. There was a newly human face to the ethnographic account, "a side of the discipline seldom touched upon in more technical anthropological writings" (Casagrande 1960:xiii), which played well in the classroom.

The geographic scope of the volume (see Table 4) reflected expanding horizons of American political hegemony after World War II. All of the Parsons sketches were from North or Central America. Casagrande, in contrast, presented six from the Pacific (not surprising as the American role there mushroomed), three from Asia, four from Africa, one from South America, and six from North America. Despite growing globalism, in anthropology as in North American society, the American Indian had hardly disappeared; almost one third of the reports were still Americanist, although, interestingly, they were located at the end of the volume.

Casagrande wrote with a rhetoric of continuity, portraying the anthropologist as the biographer of a culture, whose methods "have evolved from this work with the simpler groups" but were being applied increasingly to complex societies. Fieldwork was "at heart a collaborative enterprise," one "necessarily done in the company of man" (Casagrande 1960:x). Anthropologists were not (primarily) book-learning people. Casagrande acknowledged the impossibility of this "audacious undertaking" without the "often freely given" cooperation

Table 4. Contributors to *In The Company Of Man*

Anthropologist	Affiliation	Location
PACIFIC		
Raymond Firth	London School of Economics	Tikopia
Thomas Gladwin	National Institue of Mental Health	Truk
W. E. H. Stanner	Australian National University	Australia
Harold C. Conklin	Columbia University	Hanunoo (Philippines)
James B. Watson	University of Washington	New Guinea
Margaret Mead	American Museum of Natural History	New Britain
ASIA		
Cora Du Bois	Harvard University	Javanese-American
John T. Hitchcock	UCLA	India
David G. Mandelbaum	University of California, Berkeley	South India
AFRICA		
Ian Cunnison	University of Manchester	Bagga Arabs (Sudan)
Victor W. Turner	University of Manchester	Northern Rhodesia
Ethel M. Albert	University of California, Berkeley	Ruanda-Urundi
Laura Bohannan	Northwestern University (trained Oxford University)	Nigeria
SOUTH AMERICA		
Charles Wagley	Columbia University	Brazil
NORTH AMERICA		
Edmund Carpenter	University of Toronto	Eskimo
Robert H. Lowie	deceased; emeritus, University of California, Berkeley	Crow
Clyde Kluckhohn	Harvard University	Navaho
Joseph B. Casagrande	Social Science Research Council	Ojibwa
John Adair	Cornell University	Pueblo
William C. Sturtevant	Bureau of American Ethnology	Seminole

of informants like those foregrounded in the volume's twenty chapters: "Let it be admitted, too, that the successful outcome of field research depends not only on the anthropologist's own skills, but also on the capabilities and interest of those who teach him [sic] their ways" (Casagrande 1960:x).

The role of Radin's primitive philosophers was acknowledged. For the anthropologist, fieldwork differentiated individuals as separate personalities, varying in roles, expertise, and willingness to enter into friendships and collaborations with the anthropologist. No longer were they cardboard "ethnic prototypes" (Casagrande 1960:xi). Nonetheless, Casagrande's position reads today as remarkably naive by virtue of the absence of attention to the power relations of the larger society, which necessarily loomed between the anthropologists and their favorite informants.

The intention, however, was not to provide "full biographical detail" but to "profile":

> The authors' aim has been to reveal the unique personality, to delineate the individual as a credible human being seen against the background of his own locale and culture, and to show him [sic] in the context of his social roles rather than simply to chronicle a life. While the native subjects are the central figures, we have written as well about our relationships with those we have sought to portray, about our personal relations to people and circumstances, and about the way we have gone about our work . . . [T]hese chapters are thus also in some measure autobiographical accounts. They could not but be. (Casagrande 1960:xiii)

A dialogic or confessional quality dominated the enterprise, even though Parsons's intention to present ethnographic information through the personal story also remained powerful.

Casagrande suggested that the exercise was rather like the relationship between psychiatrist and patient in that depth and intimacy constantly warred with the effort at objectivity. In the final analysis, the focus of the anthropological imagination in the building of cross-cultural bridges was without parallel in the undertakings of the other social science disciplines.

The anthropologist's "capacity for entering into the life of another people," however, was easily obscured in "most anthropological writings" (Casagrande 1960:xii). The genre of "personal memoir" aspired to return the humanistic quality of fieldwork to the ethnographic account. The individuals remembered by the anthropologists would serve as "prismatic lenses" for understanding the cultures in which their lives unfolded (Casagrande 1960:xii).

Casagrande suggested that the focus of ethnographic fieldwork had changed. Explicit attention to culture change supplanted memory culture at the center of the new accounts. Cultural conflict replaced homogeneity; individuals foregrounded in the sketches often had lives including much "personal tragedy" (Casagrande 1960:xv). The political correctness of the day specified the "individuality and personal worth," the "exceptional" if not "admirable" quality of each informant, and the (almost certainly unrealized) ideal of the subjects as "full partners in the study of man" (Casagrande 1960:xv).

Whatever the literary qualities, and these are generally less impressive than in the Parsons collection, "each sketch is firmly grounded in fact" (Casagrande 1960:xvi). Lowie's posthumous sketch made him the only contributor to both projects; his pieces are quite different. In describing his Crow interpreter Jim Carpenter, Lowie emphasized their disagreements, illustrating the vicissitudes of personal relationship through Jim's letters to him. Lowie honored Jim's "feeling for the ancient Crow life" (presumably the "memory culture" that Casagrande claimed had receded from professional attention) and his paradoxical combination of skepticism with respect for the traditional ways of his people: "Jim continued to revere tradition even when he did not accept its basis. He himself did not worship the sacred rocks of his seniors, yet he hated to see their sons sell them to shopkeepers in nearby towns. It outraged his sense of decency. . . . Though not quite ready to part with his father-in-law's bundle of sacred arrows, he intended to bequeath it to some museum; to do otherwise would be disrespectful to the old man's memory. . . . Jim showed [respect] in many ways that others considered old-fashioned" (Casagrande 1960:435). In the context of this project, Lowie avoided the fictional artistic style of his three powerfully written sketches in the Parsons collection. This time his chosen character was a "primitive philosopher," not a "typical" Indian.

Casagrande's own sketch depicted Ojibwe "primitive philosopher" John Mink, a shaman (or sorcerer, depending on one's point of view) and Midewiwin Medicine Lodge Society priest, both roles that traditionally "codified native learning" and provided "a natural attraction for a strong personality of intellectual bent" (Casagrande 1960:474). The recalled events that structured John Mink's understanding of his own life story were "encounters with the spirits," both formal and informal; nonetheless, knowledge and confidence were waning in his culture and he never practiced skills he knew, for example, shaking tent conjuring (Casagrande 1960:480). Casagrande stereotyped John Mink as "something of an anachronism" (Casagrande 1960:487), combining old and new, often preferring the former. A lingering nostalgia still linked the anthropological imagination to a static concept of traditional culture.

American Indian Intellectuals Relegated to Ethnohistory

Margot Liberty's collection of 1978 consciously updated Radin's notion of the "primitive philosopher." The thinker among the formerly primitive had become an intellectual rather than a more or less systematic philosopher, exploring cognitive or rational formulation of cultural knowledges and political agendas. Politicization of the life-history genre is the most notable change. Liberty suggested that most of the life-history subjects were "bridging the gap between Native American peoples and their alien invaders from the East" (Liberty 1978:52). This rhetoric of alignment with Native political positions was absent from both previously considered collections. The ethnological value of the subjects' research on their own traditions, moreover, was equated explicitly with the professional work of anthropologists. Loretta Fowler, for example, suggested that Northern Arapaho tribal historian Bill Shakespeare was an "oral historian or ethnologist" among his own people (Liberty 1978:227); Marjorie Halpin emphasized the "injustice" of the usual anthropological dismissal of Tsimshian ethnologist William Beynon as merely an "informant and interpreter" (Liberty 1978:141).

The sixteen biographical subjects (see Table 5) were not dependent on anthropologists for their identity; authors took pains to emphasize the role of each intellectual within his or her own community. Only two of the sixteen subjects were women, although seven of the authors were women, the same professionalization pattern vs. field practice found in Casagrande (see Table 6).

American Indian Intellectuals moved from the "Indians-I-have-known" model of making anthropology more broadly accessible toward an ethnohistoric focus. All but one of the subjects were born in the nineteenth century; all but two were deceased before the volume appeared, although many of the contributing anthropologists had worked with the individuals they described. Authorial voices were formal and distanced for the most part. The ethnographic focus, for whatever reasons, was restricted mostly to the Plains peoples and the

Table 5. Contributors to *American Indian Intellectuals*

Anthropologist/Affiliation	Intellectual	Nation
Elizabeth Tooker Temple University	Ely S. Parker (1828–1895)	Seneca
Catherine S. Fowler University of Nevada	Sarah Winnemucca (1844–1891)	Northern Paiute
Margot Liberty University of Pittsburgh	Francis La Flesche (1857–1932)	Omaha
David Reed Miller Indiana University	Charles A. Eastman (1858–1939)	Santee Sioux
Douglas R. Parks Mary College	James R. Murie (1862–1921)	Pawnee
Raymond J. DeMallie Indiana University	George Bushotter (1864–1892)	Teton Sioux
Rennard Strikland & Jack Gregory Tulsa/Arizona State University	Emmet Starr (1870–1930)	Cherokee
John C. Ewers Smithsonian Institution	Richard Sanderville (ca. 1873–1951)	Blackfoot
Hazel W. Hertzberg Columbia Teachers College	Arthur C. Parker (1881–1955)	Seneca
Marjorie Myers Halpin University of British Columbia	William Beynon (1888–1958)	Tsimshian
Annemarie Shimony Wellesley College	Alexander General (1889–1965)	Cayuga-Oneida
William N. Fenton SUNY, Albany	Jesse Cornplanter (1889–1957)	Seneca
Hugh A. Dempsey Glenbow-Alberta Institute	Long Lance (1891–1932)	Catawba-Cherokee (adopted Blackfoot)
Garrick Bailey University of Tulsa	John Joseph Mathews (1894 –)	Osage
Triloki Nath Pandey University of California, Santa Cruz	Flora Zuni (1897 –)	Zuni
Loretta Fowler City College of New York	Bill Shakespeare (1901–1975)	Northern Arapahoe

Table 6. Gender Distribution of Anthropologists and "Informants"

Parsons (1922)		Casagrande (1960)		Liberty (1978)	
Anthropologist	Informant	Anthropologist	Informant	Anthropologist	Informant
Lowie	M	Firth	M	**Tooker**	M
Lowie	F	Gladwin	M	**Fowler**	F
Lowie	M	Stanner	M	**Liberty**	M
Wissler	M	Conklin	F	Miller	M
Skinner	M	Watson	M	Parks	M
Radin	M	**Mead**	F	DeMallie	M
Michelson	F/M	**DuBois**	M	Strickland	M
Speck	F	Hitchcock	M	& Gregory	
Goldenweiser	F	Mandelbaum	M	Ewers	M
Harrington	M	Cunnison	M	**Hertzberg**	M
Swanton	M	Turner	M	**Halpin**	M
Goddard	F	**Albert**	M	**Shimony**	M
Stephen	M	**Bohannan**	M	Fenton	M
Parsons	F	Wagley	M	Dempsey	M
Culin	M	Carpenter	M	Bailey	M
Spier	M	Lowie	M	Pandey	F
Kroeber	M	Kluckhohn	M	**Fowler**	M
Mason	M	Casagrande	M		
Spinden	M	Adair	M		
Morley	M	Sturtevant	M		
Tozzer	M				
Nelson	M				
Waterman	F/M				
Sapir	M				
Lowie	M				
Reed & **Parsons**	F				
Boas	F/M				

Bold = female anthropologist

Iroquois. The volume included documentation of the broad call for papers by Margot Liberty and William Sturtevant of the Smithsonian Institution, documenting that this imbalance was not deliberate.

Triloki Pandey (in Liberty 1978:217) portrayed Flora Zuni's story of her life as an artifact of anthropological obsession, because the Pueblos themselves lacked a genre of autobiography, eschewing the "confessional introspection" that formed the heart of such accounts in the West. This piece prefigured a new kind of intersection between life history and autobiography, anthropology and literary studies. David Brumble (1988), for example, has explored the kinds of telling of life histories in oral tradition that appear to have been indigenous in North America. Plains counting coup and boasting about successes in war, however, lacked introspective focus. Accounts more popular among Western readers proved both more romanticized and more influenced by the anthropological amanuensis. A similar train of thought was followed by Arnold Krupat (1992) in his discussion of what he called "ethnocriticism," the evaluation of narrative texts by members of the society from which they come. These excursions into exegesis suggested a relinquishing of authorial control to the autobiographical subject, thereby reinserting agency in dialogue.

Numerous contemporary life histories focus on the narrative authority implicit in oral tradition (Cruikshank 1990, 1998; Milliken 1997; Wolfart and Ahenakew 1992, 1993, 1997). Barry Milliken and Freda Ahenakew are themselves aboriginal people with training in ethnology, linguistics, and Native studies. The narratives edited by Millekin and Cruikshank are told in English, albeit an English highly colored by traditional language patterns ranging from grammar to discourse to interactional etiquette (Darnell and Valentine 1991, 1994; Darnell, Valentine, and McDougall 1997). Significantly, many of these narratives foreground the experience of women and focus on the traditions still practiced during their childhoods and not otherwise passed on to their descendants. Unconventional technologies of tape recording, video recording, written books, and radio and television provide for the continuity of traditional knowledge and practices associated with oral transmission alongside innovative technologies adapted to traditional purposes. Because First Nations/Native American narrators have insisted on the experiential basis of legitimate knowledge and knowledge transmission, life history has moved onto new foundations that are often surprisingly independent of anthropological intervention yet highly conditioned by the tradition of Americanist anthropology within which the life-history narrative has evolved during the twentieth century.

A. IRVING HALLOWELL

CHAPTER 7

Blurred Genres of Ethnography and Fiction

Fieldworking anthropologists have always struggled to find effective ways of presenting the results of their research to an audience without prior experience of an unfamiliar cultural context. Elsie Clews Parsons was not the only Boasian to embrace the life history as the most personal and accessible genre of ethnographic presentation. Many ethnographers experimented with narratives and anecdotes that brought alive the experiences of individuals despite cultural barriers. Among the distinguished early innovators with form and style of ethnographic writing in order to convey the Native point of view was A. Irving "Pete" Hallowell, whose studies of the Berens River Ojibwes during the 1930s remain canonical.

This popularizing strand of Boasian ethnography, aimed at making the results of cross-cultural research available to students and to a wider general audience geared toward the critique of North American society, has mushroomed since Hallowell's day. Although Hallowell was certainly attuned to the humanities heritage of Americanist anthropology, his successors turned even more overtly to literary techniques of representation.

Such work is highly controversial in the current positivist backlash against postmodernism. To many who long for the authorial certainty of Malinowski, Evans-Pritchard, or even Boas, interpretivism seems to have run amok. Boundaries between ethnography and fiction appear increasingly permeable in light of postmodernist obsession with rhetoric and the inevitable constructedness of texts, even scientific ones. Contemporary ethnographers have been forced to defend their claims of producing reliable and valid, albeit situated, representations.

It seems to me that the validity and reliability of ethnographic portraits depend on knowing their context and evaluating the qualities of the construction. A work of ethnography claims to describe the world; authorial artistic license is limited by what was actually observed. At the other extreme, a novel or poem evokes an impression of another cultural reality that may be more or less accurate in feeling or tone; evaluation of such accuracy depends, as does that of ethnography, on the access and sensitivity of the recorder, be that person an insider or outsider to the culture.

Those who want to know about other cultures are no longer restricted to reading technical monographs by professional anthropologists. Rather, a range of genres has become available. Anthropologists have been joined as reporters by members of the societies they formerly studied on the basis of information from "informants." Members of a culture are not always concerned with social science standards of truth but rather with those of spiritual connection between author and audience. Traditional genres are indeed blurred by this cornucopia. And yet the standards for ethnography across the lines of fiction and fact remain firmly grounded in Americanist ethnographic practice.

This chapter postulates a continuity of intention and method extending from Hallowell's ethnography to the work of contemporary Native American writers to the anthropologically informed science fiction of Kroeber's daughter Ursula Le Guin to generic experiments by humanistically oriented contemporary anthropologists. Each of these exemplary works, like Hallowell's pioneering Ojibwe ethnography, requires considerable interpretive skill of readers as they defamiliarize the everyday and familiarize the exotic, employing the stereoscopic lens of intense cross-cultural experience. Anthropologists these days attack difficult subjects and standpoints (e.g., Cynthia Mahmood's (1996) empathetic interviews with Sikh terrorists or Val Daniel's (1996) sensitive exploration of the ethnic violence, the "charred lullabies" of his strife-torn Sri Lankan homeland. Such projects retain continuity to Boasian roots.

Psychology and Culture in the New Ethnography:
A. Irving Hallowell among the Ojibwes

Conventional ethnography faces the same rhetorical tasks explored in self-consciously experimental contemporary works. The Americanist text tradition, the creativity of the individual in culture, and the fascination of alternative lifeways are the very stuff of ethnography. The Ojibwe fieldwork of A. Irving Hallowell provides an exemplary body of ethnographic evidence with ongoing repercussions for the ethics and epistemology of cross-cultural representation.

Hallowell came to anthropology by a roundabout route, taking graduate courses in sociology while working as a social worker in his native Philadelphia. His fellow fraternity member, Boasian Frank Speck, persuaded him to join his energetic revitalization of anthropology at the University of Pennsylvania. Hallowell went up to New York to work directly with Boas and received his doctorate (on the basis of a trait study of circumpolar bear ceremonialism) from Pennsylvania in 1924, where he taught almost continuously until his retirement in 1962 (Brown 1992:xiv).

Hallowell made seven visits to the northern Ojibwes between 1930 and 1940 (Brown 1992:xi). He was particularly intrigued by the contingency and culture-specificity of Western categories. Terms like "human," "animal," and "supernatural" inevitably distort the thought-world of the Ojibwes. Such apparently obvious distinctions as dream vs. reality become meaningless in the Ojibwe worldview. Hallowell's exegesis of such concepts as time, space, mapping, travel, measurement, and spirits of the dead were all explored in relation to what he called "the behavioral environment of the self," which included the adaptation of Ojibwe culture to its local environment. He further concerned himself with culture change, attempting to measure it geographically on a continuum of acculturation across a series of Ojibwe communities. This potent combination of ethnography, psychological reality, and history was virtually unique among early Boasians (Hallowell 1955, 1976, 1992).

His interest in culture and personality alternated between the role of the individual in culture, based on the work of Speck's close friend Edward Sapir, and an effort to measure the cognitive organization of worldview. The Rorschach techniques available to Hallowell are now thoroughly discredited, but his efforts to access psychological universals in culture-specific forms was key to both his theory and his ethnography; in practice he applied the Rorschach results to elicit patterns of thought and to enhance his ethnography. He further pioneered the study of human adaptation and evolution, combining the cultural and biological sides of Boasian four-field anthropology, a perspective that very few among his contemporaries were open to exploring.

Jennifer Brown has recently edited Hallowell's previously unpublished overview of his Berens River Ojibwe ethnography in a textbook format (Hallowell 1992) that has been widely adopted, especially in Canada. Brown, a historian, and Maureen Matthews of Canadian Broadcasting Corporation (CBC) Radio have returned to northern Ontario to retrace Hallowell's fieldworking footsteps and interview the people who remember him or have heard him discussed. This long-term project has involved them in learning to speak Ojibwe from a contemporary elder, Roger Roulette. Matthews and Roulette (1996) describe the project in a volume coedited by Jennifer Brown on Native history as "reading beyond words," building on oral traditions and cultural interpretive conventions. The updating of Hallowell's canonical early ethnography (Hallowell 1955) has brought the contemporary Berens River Ojibwes a voice in the representation of their own history, both oral and written.

Hallowell was meticulous in letting the Ojibwes speak for themselves. He was a master of the representative anecdote. Generations of students, including me, recall that stones are grammatically animate in the Cree language because Hallowell reports strolling down a road with an Ojibwe friend and asking if all stones are alive; "No," he was told, "but some are." Stones, it seems, have the capacity to connect human persons to the world of the spirit—and some of them actually do so. In another instance Hallowell recounts sitting on the porch with an elderly couple, watching a storm, when the old man asked his wife, utterly casually, if she caught what the thunder said. There was nothing mysterious to the old man, but he had not been attending closely enough to understand the message directed to him. Hallowell went on to muse about how intimately integrated "other-than-human persons" are within the everyday experience of the Ojibwes.

Hallowell recapitulates the matter-of-factness with which the Ojibwes embody the cultural structures of their imagination, a technique that draws the reader or listener into also taking them at face value. Judgment is suspended by this application of cultural relativism to ethnographic reportage. Yet the results are far from impressionistic. The following narrative by Hallowell's friend, collaborator, and interpreter Chief Willie Berens firmly grounds cultural description in textual evidence:

> As I was going about hunting, with my gun in my hand, I came to a lake. A steep rock rose from the lake shore. I climbed up this rock to have a look across the lake. I thought I might sight a moose or some ducks. When I glanced down towards the water's edge again, I saw a man standing by the rock. He was leaning on his paddle. A canoe was drawn up to the shore and in the stern sat a woman. In front of her rested a cradle board with a baby in it. Over the baby's face was a piece of green mosquito netting. The man was a stranger to me but I went up to him. I noticed that he hung his head in a strange way. He said, "You are the first man (human being) ever to see me. I want you to come and visit

me." So I jumped into this canoe. When I looked down I noticed that it was all of one piece. There were no ribs or anything of the sort, and there was no bark covering. (I do not know what it was made of.)

On the northwest side of the lake there was a very steep rock. The man headed directly for this rock. With one stroke of the paddle we were across the lake. The man threw his paddle down as we landed on a flat shelf of rock almost level with the water. Behind this the rest of the rock rose steeply before us. But when his paddle touched the rock this part opened up. He pulled the canoe in and we entered a room in the rock. It was not dark there, although I could see no holes to let in any light. Before I sat down the man said, "See, there is my father and my mother." The hair of those old people was as white as a rabbit skin. I could not see a single black hair on their heads. After I had seated myself, I had a chance to look around. I was amazed at all the articles I saw in the room—guns, knives, pans and other trade goods. Even the clothing these people wore must have come from a store. Yet I never remembered having seen this man at a trading post. I thought I would ask him, so I said, "You told me that I was the first human being you had seen. Where, then, did you buy all of these articles I see?" To this he replied, "Have you never heard people talking about *pagitcigan* (sacrifices)? These articles were given to us. That is how we got them." Then he took me into another room and told me to look around. I saw the meat of all kinds of animals—moose, caribou, deer, ducks. I thought to myself, this man must be a wonderful hunter, if he has been able to store up all this meat. I thought it very strange that this man had never met any other Indians in all his travels. *Of course, I did not know that I was dreaming.* Everything was the same as [if] I had seen it with my eyes open. When I was ready to go I got up and shook hands with the man. He said, "Any time that you wish to see me, this is the place where you will find me." He did not offer to open the door for me so I knew that I had to try and do this myself. I threw all the power of my mind into opening it and the rock lifted up. Then I woke up and knew that it was a dream. It was one of the first [i.e., there were more] I ever had [emphasis mine]. (Hallowell 1955:97)

It takes the non-Ojibwe reader some time to realize that this narrative tells about a dream; for an Ojibwe listener, anomalous details would have made this fact immediately obvious. The Ojibwes report dreams matter-of-factly and concretely. Hallowell says his informant "narrated this dream as the equivalent of many other personal experiences he had told me about that were not dream experiences." W[illiam] B[erens] added to the above narrative that he later found the precise location on the Berens River that he had visited in his dream. Because he was a Christian, however, he never called upon the dream spirit who had invited him to do so.

Ironically, some descendants of Willy Berens acknowledge his spiritual authority in the traditional belief system and seek to reclaim the knowledge he rejected but allowed Hallowell to record (cf. Ridington and Hastings 1998). In any case Hallowell based generalizations about Ojibwe worldview on consecutive narratives in Ojibwe voices, presenting them to the reader so as to make clear which words were his and which were those of Ojibwe persons.

One potential measure of the effectiveness of communicating the results of the anthropologist's fieldwork is the degree to which his or her major "informants" become known persons in the discipline itself. Within the Americanist text tradition, major "informants" are all too often identified briefly in terms of age, sex, and linguistic experience. The intensity of the collaboration necessary to produce such texts is informally understood more often than acknowledged in published works. By convention, text volumes were deemed to be authored by the anthropologist/linguist even if a single narrator was responsible for all of them. Yet any Americanist moves instantly from Hallowell's Ojibwe ethnography to Willie Berens, from Sapir's Wishram texts to Louis Simpson, from Boas's Kwakiutl texts to George Hunt, from Alexander Goldenweiser's Onondaga ritual text to Chief John A. Gibson. Early volumes of the *American Anthropologist* contain obituaries of a few such collaborators. Today they regularly appear in the newsletter of the Society for the Study of the Indigenous Languages of the Americas (ssila). This inclusion is one index of the increasing collaboration that has replaced earlier, more exploitative encounters. Achievements of the amanuensis pale next to those of the narrators.

Because the ethnographic record often contains extensive texts from the same narrator, it is possible to return to materials in the literature for reanalysis, reconstruction of the style and artistry of particular speakers. For example, Melville Jacobs and Dell Hymes have both provided exegesis of the style and psychological focus of the Chinookan texts of Victoria Howard. Linguists and anthropologists who recorded such texts have too often been insensitive to variability of knowledge and narrative artistry, considering their texts as concrete and more or less objective records of cultural facts. Yet exemplars exist. To the extent that the form inheres in the text itself, philological analysis can recover its structure even after the language has ceased to be spoken.

Dell Hymes, in *In Vain I Tried to Tell You* (1981), has pioneered in structural analysis of such texts as "Native American ethnopoetics," his subtitle. Although his work on the various Chinookan dialects is, at first glance, forbiddingly technical to the nonspecialist, the method parallels that which the literary critic habitually applies to more familiar languages. (Indeed, Hymes taught seminars in English as part of the professorship from which he recently retired at the University of Virginia).

Hymes documents stages in his analysis of the same materials over a period of years, highlighting the complexity of the structure implicit in the texts he works with. One clear result of his work and that of others who have followed his lead is that the expertise, both in knowledge and in the manner of its expression, of native speakers of Indian languages, is laid bare and can no longer be ignored. He has enjoined all anthropologists, not just linguists, to maintain the same meticulous respect for philology in Chinookan or Algonquian that would be taken for granted in Chinese or Arabic or Indo-European. In the words of Sapir: "The goat-herd of Assam walks hand-in-hand with the philosopher of Macedonia" (Sapir 1921b:234). To acknowledge the pejorative character of the traditional term "informant" is inadequate. Native consultants must be recognized as skilled and highly creative poets in an oral tradition. They are the individuals who bring their culture to life and transmit it to another generation, sometimes even including members of another culture, our own.

This is a peculiarly anthropological approach to texts. Colleagues in the other social sciences are less concerned with individual variability and creativity. Each discipline carries considerable cultural baggage into its life histories. For example, sociologists are socialized to avoid individual agency as explanation. Even autobiographies of sociologists, for example, W. I. Thomas, the paramount theoretican of the Chicago School, do not deal with the role of the individual in creating and maintaining disciplinary culture. Sociologists are accustomed to generalizing about groups rather than about individuals. They do not, at least in a professional capacity, delve into the personal experiences that produce a unique individual. Rather, multiple autobiographies are amassed from a subculture or community in order to compare them.

Americanist anthropologists are socialized to ask different questions about a biographical subject. We tend to take for granted the school of thought, that is, culture, and ask about the subject's integration of interests, his or her networks of contact to colleagues, the way her or his ideas came to their canonical form—in short, to explore individuality. These questions emerge naturally from the experience of doing fieldwork in another culture; they are anthropological questions. To answer them, however, requires techniques that often are borrowed both from the natural sciences and from the humanities.

What Is That Coyote Up to Now? Native Writers and Anthropological Stereoscopy

Writing by Native North Americans, much of it fiction rather than ethnography in the narrow sense, draws on many of the same conventions of documentary ethnographic genre employed by anthropologists like Hallowell. Native writers produce more fiction than ethnography in the social science mode because academic prose fits uneasily with the aesthetic premises of indigenous expression. Much of this fiction is autobiographical; the anthropological life history provides a continuous model.

This growing body of literature strikes a viable contemporary stance toward the last five hundred years of American history through the perspective offered by the Trickster. Manifestations of the Trickster vary across the continent, but the essence is standpoint, an aesthetic response to structural ambiguity and personal ambivalence. Trickster is a shape-changer.

Allen Ryan (1999) explores Trickster themes in First Nations art across Canada, moving fluidly between visual and verbal productions. Photographs and analysis of art productions range wildly in surface genre but share this edge, a critique of the society that engulfs contemporary aboriginal peoples; these visual elements are juxtaposed with interview excerpts in which artists speak for themselves about their visions and intended audiences. Ryan cites Native American poets, especially Gerald Vizenor, alongside the artists. Trickster is a way of seeing, a lens rather than a being who can be pinned down to a single form or meaning. Much is left to the interpreter, as is respectful to those who see or listen.

Green Grass, Running Water (1993), a novel by Native writer and professor of literature and Native studies Thomas King, elegantly replicates the cyclicity and repetition inherent in the myth-stories of First Nations traditions. The adventures of his characters cross and recross one another, albeit without consciously understanding the larger patterns within which they act. Transitions pick up the movements of water and the shape-shifting of race, gender, time, and place. Trickster vision reigns as four old Indians, characters who seem mostly to be men but sometimes also women, periodically escape from benign custody to "fix" things in the human world and successfully change the ending of a John Wayne movie so that the Indians win. And in Blossom, Alberta, the human spirit regenerates itself. (The CBC Radio adaptation of King's fictional world, *Dead Dog Cafe,* has attained near-cult status in Canada, its ironic Trickster humor communicating across cultural boundaries.)

Cree playwright Tomson Highway also plays recurrently with permutations of the Trickster form. In *The Rez Sisters* (1988) seven women conspire to win the biggest bingo in the world, in Toronto; their Trickster is always male, sometimes a bird, death, a welcome companion, the bingo master. In the companion piece *Dry Lips Oughta Move to Kapuskasing* (1989), seven men from the same community reel in shock as the women invert the social order by establishing their own hockey team; the script explores sexual violence and community disorder through a female Trickster also appearing in multiple guises. Highway's autobiographical first novel, *Kiss of the Fur Queen* (1998), describes the idyllic, preresidential-school childhood of two brothers; the boys grow up under the fickle protection of a beauty queen who rewarded their father, Abraham Okimasis, with a kiss when he won the great dogsled race just before the birth of Champion, Highway's alter ego, and before that of his younger brother. The boys are destined to be artists, isolated from their far northern home but linked to it by the ties of Trickster vision.

The Trickster figure insists things can't be pinned down to a single meaning. Native American storytelling passes down its collective wisdom to new generations, so they can make sense of the stories in their own lives. Storied content cannot be separated from the knowledge and experience of the storyteller or from the circumstances of the telling to an outsider recorder, who becomes thereby a partial insider. There is no omniscient narrator.

King and Highway tell their own stories, life histories, in order to apply them to the predicament of aboriginal peoples in general. The concrete experience of the part stands for the whole. In *Keeping Slug Woman Alive* (Sarris 1993:7), university professor Greg Sarris, whose heritage is Coast Miwok, Kayasha Pomo, Filipino, Jewish, German, and Irish (and the last is the most awkward for discourse across cultural boundaries), describes his efforts to learn and record the stories of Cache Creek Pomo medicine woman Mabel McKay. The project is social science; the genre is narrative and dialogic.

Sarris has to reconsider almost everything he thinks he knows, even, or perhaps especially, how to peel potatoes; he begins in the frame of a story, which is his own as well as Mabel's:

> I was sitting at the kitchen table listening to Mabel McKay tell about a man she had known when she was a young girl, around ten or so. It was Mabel's eighty-second birthday, and I had driven Auntie Violet Chappell to Mabel's place so we could visit and celebrate. Despite her recent trouble with arthritis, Mabel looked bright, alert. . . . She was near the head of the table, as always. I was sitting next to her, busy taking notes. I was a graduate student at Stanford University preparing a dissertation on the life story of Mabel McKay, renowned Cache Creek Pomo Indian basketweaver and medicine woman, whom I had known since childhood. No part of the project had been easy. Mabel didn't present her stories in chronological sequence. Her stories moved in and out of different time frames and often implicated me as a listener. Of course this was always my experience with Mabel. Still, I wanted to get the pieces of her life in some order so that I might grasp it for others, and when she started talking . . . , I quickly found a pencil and paper. It was something I hadn't heard before. (Sarris 1993:1)

There is a recursive quality to the hearing and retelling of stories that operates over generations in oral tradition. Mabel, in quintessential Trickster fashion, refuses to interpret her stories, that being the work of the listener: "Don't ask me what it means, the story. Life will teach you about it, the way it teaches you about life" (Sarris 1993:5). For Sarris, a scholar steeped in postmodernist literary theory, the challenge was to present the story as a series of interacting relationships, to "interweave a myriad of voices with autobiography and theoretical discourse to create a document representing exchanges that open the world people share with each other" (Sarris 1993:6), to write an ethnography.

Mabel speaks in English, and Sarris professes uncertainty about how "traditional" her performances are. His description, however, suggests that Mabel's traditionalism lends itself well to the reflexivity and open-endedness of postmodernist theorizing. Her responses to questions are "maddening" precisely because she refuses to respond in academic style or categories (Sarris 1993:17). Mabel's daughter muses on the meaning of tradition: "But she left us a tradition, something to keep thinking and talking about in our lives, something to carry through all time. But it's up to us to do it. And this is the next step. You see, we're sitting here and talking about it, about prophecy, about the teachings. We're knowing who we are" (Sarris 1993:64).

Mabel rejects the tape recorder, insisting on remaining present in her words. Sarris leads the reader to follow Mabel's path of teaching with him, insisting that scholars must be "vulnerable" (Sarris 1993:29) to challenge of their assumptions about the organization of knowledge, about the cultural structures of imagination. This remains true for Sarris even though he ends by (artificially) writing down his learning experience.

Trickster stories, intersecting with individual life histories, provide a wedge against intolerable chaos. Karl Kroeber, son of Alfred and professor of English, says: "The possibilities opened up by Trickster are liberative and healing qualities because they derive from acceptance of the possibility that reality may be chaotic. 'Chaotic' here means not incoherent but so complexly interdependent as to be irreducible to simple, unchanging principles of cause and effect. Chaotic reality, then, is not merely a mess; rather, it is constituted of diverse systems of coherence whose irregularities of interaction exceed the organizing capabilities of Western logic" (Kroeber 1998:228). Trickster motifs are an organizing device for life histories whether employed in oral performance, in conventional ethnography, or in adaptations to the written medium by Native writers.

Anthropologically Sophisticated Literature:
The Science Fiction of Ursula K. Le Guin

I was in the audience in 1991 when Ursula K. Le Guin, daughter of Alfred Kroeber and one of my favorite writers, received the American Anthropological Association's media award for her public representations of the discipline. She spoke with considerable grace of finally understanding what her father was doing when he went off to "the anthropology meetings" in her growing-up years. But the citation on the plaque presented to her disturbed me by its failure to explore the anthropological insights that permeate her writing. The abiding question of the science fiction genre—"What would a world be like if . . . ?"—is an anthropological question: Le Guin as ethnographer explores shaman's power in the Earthsea trilogy (1968, 1971b, 1972a), political resistance in *The Dispossessed* (1974), gender in *The Left Hand of Darkness* (1969), human nature in *The Lathe of Heaven* (1971a), ecology in *The Word for World Is Forest* (1972b), and the conflict of Dionysian and Apollonian cultures and the construction of an ethnographic account in *Always Coming Home* (1985). Moreover, her constructions of "fiction" seek intelligibility in an initially unfamiliar world (scene), unfolding in its own terms through dialogue (revealing character and agency) and the course of events (the plot). Her insight derives as much from cross-cultural sophistication as from Aristotelian poetics.

(Ursula Le Guin is also the daughter of Theodora Krakow Brown Kroeber Quinn, whose evocative portrait of *Ishi: The Last of the Yahi* [1961] employed elegiac rhetoric to condemn the racism and violence of the extermination of many California Indian tribes.)

Le Guin describes her work as "thought experiment," claiming that only "comparative ethnology" can provide more concrete evidence (Le Guin 1989: 9–10), that is, evidence from the real world. She problematizes the multiple truths inherent in a single story in terms of her personal experience of anthropologists:

> There may be some truth in that story, that tale, that discourse, that narrative, but there is no reliability in the telling of it. It was told you forty years later by the ten-year-old [Le Guin] who heard it, along with her great-aunt, by the campfire, on a dark and stormy night in California; and though it is, I believe, a Plains Indian story, she heard it told in English by an anthropologist of German antecedents [Kroeber]. But by remembering it, he had made the story his; and insofar as I have remembered it, it is mine; and now, if you like it, it's yours. In the tale, in the telling, we are all one blood. (Le Guin 1989:29–30)

For Le Guin, the story is enriched by recontextualization in successive tellings, removed from its original ethnographic context. Although she acknowledges that the anthropological problem is more complex, because many of the stories belong to people and communities, her impulse is to pass on the stories she has learned and imagined, through whatever involuted routes.

Le Guin worries about pinning down what anthropologists know that others do not. For example, "the non-urban peoples of the Americas" lacked history "properly speaking"—"therefore [they] are visible only to the anthropologist" (Le Guin 1989:84). Historians can only get at this unwritten history insofar as "they [the formerly primitive] entered into white history." Anthropologists, on the contrary, are trained to extrapolate history from the cultural record accessible through fieldwork. The complacency of the historian is a "dangerous . . . organized forgetting" of cultural genocide and dehumanization

(Le Guin 1989:84). Le Guin's version of the anthropological standpoint is (meta)historical as well as political and moral. Anthropologists, mostly Americanist, are the authorities for her personal political agenda of resistance to the utopias of unrestricted growth and the dominance of rationality in Western civilization. "I am not proposing a return to the Stone Age. My intent is not reactionary, nor even conservative, but simply subversive" (Le Guin 1989:85). The Benedictine inherent moral force of the cross-cultural is unmistakable in the anthropological lessons Le Guin has internalized. The possibility of doing or thinking things differently destabilizes the way things have always been done, especially within the mainstream cultures from which most contemporary anthropologists and writers of fiction come.

Le Guin adopts the subversive Native American Trickster voice of Coyote and aspires to preserve California as a noneuclidian space, with the minimally onerous price of exclusion from world history (Le Guin 1989:94). Lévi-Strauss's "beautiful piece of anthropological thinking" about the contrast between hot and cold societies, reminds us that "surviving primitive societies" project alternatives to the progress engendered by the Industrial Revolution, without being "antagonistic to the human condition" (Le Guin 1989:91). In her father's *Handbook of California Indians* (1925), they refuse to draw maps in euclidian space; rather, places are named and storied in relation to human cultures (cf. Basso 1996). For Le Guin as for Ruth Benedict, the anthropologist as moralist sets the stage for reassessment: "If we listened to the anthropologists we might hear them telling us, with appropriate [i.e., respectful] indirectness, that the White West is not the center. The Center of the world is a bluff on the Klamath River, a rock in Mecca, a hole in the ground in Greece, nowhere, its circumference everywhere" (Le Guin 1989:97–98).

Le Guin explores literary genre through anthropological models. If, for example, we are to identify and valorize the poetic core in every oral or written expressive tradition, we must redefine poetry "as independent of verse"; she identifies Dell Hymes and Dennis Tedlock as paramount among the "scholar-poets" who force the literary disciplines to acknowledge the ethnocentrism of their and our canon (Le Guin 1989:106). The efforts of anthropological poets to translate across linguistic as well as cultural boundaries lead Le Guin to envision writing within a single language as also an exercise in translation. The "other text, the original" is not in any transparent way accessible to the writer, translator, or poet. Le Guin aspires to compose without distinction between poetry and prose (Le Guin 1989:113). Cross-cultural translators work "across the widest possible gaps, from an oral, performed text in the totally alien language of a radically different culture, into written English," thereby rendering our own literary tradition "alive, unfixed, on the move, defying definition" (Le Guin 1989:113).

Anthropologists did not, however, always get it right. Boas, for example, turned his texts into prose, itself an artifact of writing; Boas's first transliteration "is actually not prose, nor poetry, nor drama, but *the notation of a verbal performance*" (Le Guin 1989:182; emphasis in the original), quite a different thing. Le Guin's critique of anthropological texts is that of an insider. She applies that critique in her fiction.

The most explicitly ethnographic of Le Guin's novels, at least in its surface structure, is *Always Coming Home* (1985). Her intentions adapt the performance vein of which Boas was, in her view, inadequately conscious (Le Guin 1989:186–87). The Kesh, "a non-existent Californian people" somewhere in the future (but very like the Indians of her own childhood experience), refuse to choose between written and oral literature. Anyone could be a poet, and poetry was understood "not as masterpiece but as life-work" (Le Guin 1985:167). Poetry, regardless of its quality, was at the center of Kesh life, an attitude Le Guin specifically associates with women, presumably in contrast to male professors of English devoted to new criticism.

The second problematic of the text is Le Guin's "rash attempt" to imagine a world in which the Hero and the Warrior are stages in maturation rather than ends in themselves and the parent-child relation is constructed from the point of view of a child who will become a mother whose own child will have a standpoint of her own, in an iterative succession of generations (Le Guin 1989:229).

Always Coming Home is a genre experiment, with ethnographic appendices sideshadowing and partially paralleling the table of contents of a conventional anthropological monograph. The core narrative is the tripartite life history of a woman who in mature life took the name of Stone Telling. Le Guin notes that "many people in the Valley" of the Kesh told their life stories. Both biographies and autobiographies were written and presented to the kin group "as an offering, as a gift of life"; they formed a "'hinge' or intersection of private, individual, historical lived-time with communal, impersonal, cyclical being-time" (Le Guin 1985:263). Individual stories were repetitions on common experiences and themes, not valued or preserved as what we would call historical documents. The value was the individual choice to tell her or his story.

The story of Stone Telling in particular and Le Guin's fascination with life history in general reiterate (and perhaps resolve through the telling of experience) the central Boasian problematic of the inevitable and irresolvable tension between culture and the individual, between the social order and the particular personalities of social actors. The purported champions of the polar views, Kroeber and Sapir, in fact denied their opposition and refused to reduce either core construct to the other. This emphasis on the individual as actor and creator of culture, the psychological as opposed to the social, most clearly distinguishes the Americanist tradition from its counterparts in Britain and on the Continent. For Le Guin, whose muse was steeped in anthropological imagination, this emphasis should come as no surprise.

Eight short life stories provide a "chorus" around the story of Stone Telling, expressing contrastive standpoints of gender and age. A culture has more than one member; the position of each individual must be specified by thinking (at least some of the time) from the personality and/or standpoint of one individual at a time. These brief life histories simultaneously foreground the uniqueness of the central autobiographical narrative; they are life histories as Sapir intended them to be used. As the Archivist explains to Pandora, the invasive outsider with the assumptions of a "hot" society, "we have lived [up until now] in the Dream Time" (Le Guin 1985:172). The experience of Stone Telling with the Condor, the warlike people of her father, with whom she lived for a time, nearly as a slave by Kesh standards, is a story "as near history as we have come." The Archivist, an insider grieving for the changes that have come to the Valley, hopes that "history" will again leave the Kesh in peace (Le Guin 1985:172). The arrow of time has become irreversible and history an elegy for the dislocation of the Kesh present.

Stone Telling ends her own narrative with similar sentiments favoring the "cold" society: "So there is no more history in my life after that; all that I could bring into the Valley from outside I have brought, all that I could remember I have written; the rest has been lived and will be lived again. I have lived in this place until I have become [taken the name] Stone Telling, and my husband Stone Listening, and my quail [daughter] has become Shining; and in this house Acorn and Phoebe have made me the grandmother weaving at the loom" (Le Guin 1985:376). Le Guin's title metaphor, "coming home," is both about Stone Telling, who names herself "Woman Coming Home" (Le Guin 1985:358), and about the Kesh's understanding of how things come full circle, of how they come home (Le Guin 1985:404). The cultural pattern is recapitulated in individual experience.

Pandora, alter ego of the anthropologist and more ambivalently of Le Guin as author, is the foil for the stability of the Kesh world. "Worrying about what she is doing," Pandora "addresses the reader with agitation" over the cost of her decision (Le Guin 1985:147). The Promethean act of opening the box was an attempt to "give them time" rather than history, presumably time to make choices and decide how to encounter the outside world. The biggest difference, she concludes, is that "there are not too many of them" (Le Guin 1985:147); stability constitutes a viable option with sufficient resources to support the population and its cyclical, noneuclidian culture. The tragedy of our own society's uncurtailed commitment to progress is the burden it places on conquered and displaced peoples.

Pandora's predicament, the cost of her hindsight, precedes her encounter with the Kesh. Even as she finds her way into the Valley, she "worries" (as most fieldworking anthropologists also do) about the implications of intervention (Le Guin 1985:239). The Archivist explains to Pandora that it is difficult to decide what to throw away: "It's arbitrary, unjust, and exciting" (Le Guin 1985: 314). Annual secret destruction ceremonies constitute "a kind of orgy. A fit of housecleaning . . . unhoarding" (Le Guin 1985:315). Books die, in the Archivist's view, because they are not about the information they contain, but about the relationships of people, which do not matter once those people are gone. This is the logic of an oral tradition small enough to function in face-to-face relationships.

The Kesh have their "scholars," who give highly situational and context-sensitive advice (Le Guin 1985:297). They give "no reason or justification whatever" for their customs, "neither religious, nor genetic, nor social, nor ethical." They simply accept "the way people are: that is how human people behave" (Le Guin 1985:427). Despite Pandora's efforts, the Kesh do not want to be social scientists (or "primitive philosophers" for that matter).

Containment of power is more important to the Kesh than the preservation of "historical" or personal documents, although the Archivist implies that these might otherwise have some value. More importantly: "How do you keep information yet keep it from being the property of the powerful?" (Le Guin 1985:316). The Kesh are consistent. Despite her frustrations, Pandora acts as ethnographer for the "gentle reader" and asks questions unimaginable from within the Kesh world (Le Guin 1985:339). In the end Pandora is "no longer worrying" because she "dances with her friends" as Le Guin shifts from the Valley to her own acknowledgements as author (Le Guin 1985:506). The ambiguity of the anthropological standpoint as that of the outsider and powerful "other" dissolves into collective experience, the possibility of conversation across a deep divide. Pandora/Le Guin has imagined the Kesh in words accessible to others. She has embraced the anthropologist's métier in another medium.

At a level of great interest to our inquiry, *Always Coming Home* is a treatise in anthropological method. Le Guin has explored systematically what constitutes an adequate description of another culture in its own terms and what the ethnographer must tell the reader from an alien society in order for that portrait to make sense. Le Guin has also addressed the question of the role of the writer/ethnographer's voice in that description and the power relations she or he cannot avoid. Readers are virtually forced to address the Kesh as if they were a "real" society, existing outside the pages of a novel, that is, as in an ethnography. It is as easy to forget that this is "fiction" as it is to remember its evocation of the world of California Indians before the unwelcome advent of the Condor, the white intruder, the predator intimations of something called history.

On the Anthropological Applications of an English Degree

Literary concerns intersect with the way in which at least some of us do anthropology. Postmodernist attention to experimental writing and reflexive ethnography has brought to the fore matters of rhetoric, the aesthetic quality of writing, and the inevitability of ethnographic artifice. The field of cultural studies has done much to politicize the science of culture, that is, anthropology. Literary critics have borrowed from the social sciences, while many anthropologists of my generation retool the liberal education of our youth and question the need for impermeable boundaries between the social sciences and the humanities. It is perhaps the sixties generation coming of professional age (see Rosaldo 1989), whatever that might portend for the longevity of the present turn.

Back in 1959 Alfred Kroeber talked about the "personality of anthropology" in terms of an uneasy ambivalence between its equally legitimate roots in the natural sciences and in the humanities. Even among the already somewhat bastardized social sciences, anthropology's ancestry was distinguished by its "two-pronged impulse to apperceive and conceive at once empirically and holistically" (Kroeber 1959:400). Anthropology was further characterized by its fixation on fieldwork, defined as "an opportunity, a privilege, and a professional cachet. We want the face-to-face experience with our subjects" (Kroeber 1959:400), and we think that gets us beyond nature loving, bird watching, and mere antiquarianism (i.e., the natural science side of things). What Kroeber called "primitive ethnography" (Kroeber 1959 passim) was the particularism of time, place, and imagination, to wit, the humanities heritage.

Things have changed considerably since Kroeber's time. The Gulbenkian Commission on the Restructuring of the Social Sciences, for example, suggests that "shifts in viewpoint in all fields seem to be moving more toward than away from the traditional standpoints of the social sciences" (Wallerstein et al. 1996:69). "The tripartite division" between natural science, social science, and humanities "is no longer as self-evident as it once seemed" (Wallerstein et al. 1996:69). Moreover, "the social sciences are no longer a poor relative" polarized between the two prongs of their heritage; "rather, they have become the locus of their potential reconciliation" (Wallerstein et al. 1996:69).

Anthropology has a particularly salient role in this integrative reconciliation. In the present intellectual climate, even the natural sciences have begun to consider the irreversibility of "the arrow of time," of history, while literary critics have discovered theory ("theorizing is not what literary scholars used to do" [Wallerstein et al. 1996:69]). The "culture" of cultural studies is increasingly politicized (Wallerstein et al. 1996:68). The Gulbenkian Commission identifies three themes, all of which engage the cross-cultural interpretive skills of anthropology: 1) a non-Eurocentric study of social systems, 2) a hermeneutic turn to locally situated histories, and 3) an assessment of values alternative to those arising from the Western obsession with technological progress (Wallerstein et al. 1996:65). These are thoroughly Boasian and Americanist objectives. More problematic, however, is the undocumented assertion that ethnography has "lost its commanding role" within anthropology in favor of the study of "the forgotten peoples of modernity" (Wallerstein et al. 1996:65), who indeed have much in common with the formerly primitive. The commission has failed to register that ethnography provides the most viable method for all three investigations. Method, rather than an outmoded emphasis on the so-called primitive, must be (re)claimed as our peculiar province and expertise.

Qualitative social science is deeply implicated in the humanities side of Americanist professional genealogies. While it would be perverse to claim that my personal experience is typical or even normative, I use it here to frame the kinds of literary methods and techniques that can be brought to bear productively on the solution to more or less conventional anthropological problems reconfigured by their encounter with the aesthetic, the evocative, and the persuasive or rhetorical. Some years ago a former English professor wrote me, expressing appreciation for something I had written and regret that I had left English after my undergraduate degree. I reacted indignantly, perhaps even self-righteously, that I had not "left," that much of my career as an anthropologist had applied skills grounded in the reading and critique of literature. After all, I had written and published ethnographic poetry, explored the semantics of both culture and grammatical categories in the Algonquian language family, translated texts from Cree into English, sought semantic regularities carried over from Algonquian and Iroquoian languages into English, lobbied for persuasive and aesthetically engaging writing as foundational to the ethnographic enterprise, and explored culture from the aesthetic as well as epistemological point of view of the "other."

In the thirty-five years since I completed my double major in anthropology and medieval English literature at Bryn Mawr, the two disciplines have moved closer together. Back then, in the heyday of the new criticism, interpretation was supposed to be restricted to internal properties of the text. The intention of the author and the literary quality of the work were paramount for assessing a canon inscribed in stone. Perhaps I exaggerate but not much. The social sciences also have changed. The first person singular has replaced the "royal we" of the omniscient scientist abstracting from mere experience. Standpoint, frequently acknowledged these days, facilitates open-ended reader interpretation and multiple layers of (re)contextualization. To write well, in those halcyon days when Truth seemed simpler to access, was sometimes more embarrassment than advantage.

At the time I did not understand fully that I was writing anthropology papers for my English courses, that my anthropological training had shifted the focus of my literary work, without conscious reflection on my part, from text to context and social milieu, that is, to culturally construed *Weltanschauung* (worldview) as analytically prior to *Lebenswelt* (the life world of the individual). Captivated by the mystique of fieldwork, I chose graduate work in anthropology, where I imagined a professional life outside the ivory tower, learning from people as well as from books. I was not yet sufficiently confident to proclaim myself a "writer."

The real world turned out to be much more complicated than the simple dichotomy I had constructed between the unmediated experience of the anthropologist and the mere regurgitation of what someone else had said, which was presumably superior in the first place since it had already entered the literary canon. Many of the methods that I have come, in the course of professional socialization in anthropology, to think of as ethnographic now seem, with the benefit of hindsight, to have arisen—at least for me—from literary roots. I developed the habit of looking for internal consistency in behavior and text through literature, if not literary theory per se. "Suspension of disbelief" is a powerful concept in cross-cultural experience as well as in reading; it precedes any analysis that is just and accurate to its text. Anthropologists do essentially the same thing when they accept the validity of the world as perceived by someone from a different culture and attempt to untangle the way it makes sense from the everyday world of that individual. Such work is compelling because it could not have emerged from the thought or culture of the observer/reader. To be fascinated rather than threatened by alternative worldviews is, I believe, the essence of literature as well as of ethnography.

In the initial experience of the reader, I see minimal difference among genres usually understood to have different relations to truth conditions in the world, for example, the historical novel, contemporary fiction, and the well-written ethnography. The "culture" can never be precisely that of the reader. "Our" society is a complex and manifold entity, if an entity at all, such that native intuition of it is at best problematic, at worst illusory. The challenge for the author, including the anthropological one, is to render an unfamiliar world believable and normal, to depict a world in which ordinary individuals pursue everyday activities with motivations and intentions identifiable as particular forms of more general patterns that characterize humankind as a whole. Again, good literature and good ethnography share these properties.

On second reading, however, there is a vast difference between literature and ethnography. At the level of analysis, the social scientist applies a criterion of replicability. Anthropological wags regularly quip that Malinowski's description of the Trobriand Islanders, which set the standards for modern ethnographic practice, would be justifiably significant in disciplinary history *even if the Trobrianders had never existed*. Most anthropologists, however, care whether Malinowski was "right" in his analysis of this previously obscure Melanesian people. Contemporary intensive attention to the subjectivity of ethnographic writing aspires to transcend it, to draw generalizations that do not distort the particular. However problematic the referents of the pronouns may become, it is disciplinary credo that "they" are out there in the world and that "we" can figure out what "they" are up to. Therein lies the anthropological challenge to which neither fiction writer nor literary critic is bound.

This position is so fundamental that we must spell out its implications. On first glance the claims of relativism and realism in the epistemology of cross-cultural research appear incommensurable, operating in competition. Nonetheless, most anthropologists continue to insist that cross-cultural research is possible, that cultural boundaries are surmountable through the immersion of fieldwork (with subsequent translation), that communication across such boundaries is desirable (in part because it illuminates the epistemological stances of Western analytic philosophy). Anthropologists have concerned themselves with two sets of knowledge claims—those of their own discipline and those of the initially exotic cultures they study.

The enterprise of translating across cultural boundaries would be unsustainable without a claim of realism about the world. If only at a pragmatic level, we must proceed as though there is something out there that is accessible to our inquiries. Such an operating assumption makes sense because regularities of social order have emerged across time and space. At the same time, however, the variability of cross-cultural categories and expressive forms suggests that we must be irrealists about the possibility of knowing the world independently of culturally situated knowledge, including our own expert knowledge of diversity in language, culture, race, class, gender, ethnicity, and biographical experience.

Our traditional disciplinary commitment to cultural relativism requires only that we refrain from judging whether more or less commensurable realities are true of the world, or whether some are more true thereof than others. Ours is a moral position, taken on political grounds and held as a tenet of belief. It entails systematic tolerance for diversity of race, language, and culture—along with an obligation to convey that belief to the larger society of which anthropology is a part and out of which it has arisen.

It is probably impossible and perhaps undesirable to aspire to construct a complete or finite description of any cultural world. This does not, of course, preclude attempts, ranging from the heroic to the dogged, to include evidence from voices within other cultures about how the world is constructed within them. Moreover, multiple versions of a culture exist within it, each distinguishable from the voice of the ethnographer, whose task is to respect and empower this plurality, this dialogic heteroglossia.

Understanding, of the intuitive variety, *verstehen,* operates outside realism, through relativism and suspension of disbelief. It is the necessary epistemological stance for the fieldworker as participant in another culture. To remain fully within a relativist frame, however, is to deny the validity of the observation in our participant-observation, indeed to reject the very possibility of social science. Realism doesn't go away. In a logically subsequent stage, the anthropologist must stand apart from the experience of another culture and its ways of being in the world to compare, to analyze, to formulate in alternative terms a translation that will make sense out of the original experiential context. Cross-cultural understanding entails a double hermeneutic and embraces it as methodological breakthrough rather than crippling tautology (as it appears to the philosophers).

The comparative method that, from its beginnings, has characterized anthropology as an identifiable form of inquiry depends on triangulating the "real" world in relation to its differential construction by a multiplicity of cultural lenses. The overlap among such cultural constructions illuminates the properties of the world, phrased in terms of cultural universals or near universals. The more cultures that produce interpretations of the world and how human persons interact with it, the more likely are its fundamental properties to be disclosed; the role of the anthropologist, then, is to ensure that encapsulated local knowledges are communicated and shared. Consensus ideally enables assessment of the relative validity of alternative representations. The epistemology of doing anthropology, therefore, leads directly back to the ethics of incorporating the objects of study as cosubjects of interpretation. That we have not always succeeded in this incorporation should be read in the context that we, alone among the social scientists, have posed the question in these terms.

Ours is far from the methodology conventionally privileged by Western philosophy, in which one reasons from introspection, by the construction of thought-worlds. I worry that such worlds are necessarily ethnocentric, in ways not easily subject to correction. It is not so much that philosophers are prejudiced as that contrastive evidence by definition is absent. For a social scientist such evidence is available in the world through descriptions of the speculations of philosophers in other cultures, whose thought-worlds are distinguishable from our own and reflect different histories and experiences. So far, the fact that these speculations are transmitted from elsewhere, largely through oral tradition, has hindered their active engagement with the mainstream of Western philosophy. Nonetheless, ethnographers regularly discover in the

field ideas arising from other minds, ideas that are far too complex and historically particular to be accessed merely by introspection or imagination.

The relativist pole of the ethnographic imagination depends on empathetic
capacity, suspension of disbelief, and at least provisional acceptance of phenomena called into existence by alternative assumptions (e.g., witchcraft, see
Lindahl 1999). The standard of truth is coherence rather than correspondence
with an external world. In this mode ethnography is closer to literature than to
natural science. Many anthropologists, indeed, resist the label of scientist because they want to evade imposing judgment about truth.

Ethnography, however, is only part of what anthropologists do. We move
back and forth between the epistemologies of experiencer and theoretician.
Indeed, everyday behavior and ordinary language involve a parallel epistemological alternation. Only in degree and systematicity does the anthropologist
transcend the strategies of common sense. Anthropologists need a high tolerance for ambiguity and cognitive dissonance. Postmodernist disquiet about
nihilism without ultimate rationally grounded truth strikes the cross-cultural
researcher as utterly impoverished. The relativist stance sometimes appears to
require a self-conscious leap into absurdity. But proponents argue that the diversity of contextually legitimate interpretations of the world that arise from
different cultural and epistemological premises provides conceptual tools with
which to think, to theorize, to philosophize. Lévi-Strauss had it right for Western society as well as for the so-called primitive when he decreed that myths
are things to think with, counters in a system of classification, culture-specific
in detail and universal in that something like them exists in every viable human culture.

What if the Ethnographer Writes Well?
Reading the New Ethnographies

The question of artifice is perplexing. If replicability of ethnographic writing is
a priority, then aesthetic complexity of ethnographies might obscure the purported objectivity of reported observations. On the other hand, literary artifice
is a potential device to facilitate communicating the reality of the "other";
moreover, the "other" can only be understood in relation to the "self." In the
first instance, the self is the ethnographer. But the reader, a yet more distant
other, must finally be implicated. Ethnographers who worry about the techniques with which they write about other cultures also tend to care about the

words (and communicative economies more generally) in which members of other cultures express themselves. The result is a dialectic, a multilogue, in which the culture, the "informant," and the ethnographer are logically as well as pragmatically interdependent.

In anyone else's hands, Dennis Tedlock's *The Spoken Word and the Work of Interpretation* (1983) might have been a disorganized book. It alternates papers about two societies related only by Tedlock's fieldwork in each—the Zuni and the Quiche Maya. Most of the essays previously appeared elsewhere. But Tedlock (who holds a chair in English at SUNY Buffalo and is a poet and playwright as well as an ethnographer) frames and counterpoints his material to give it aesthetic unity. The voice of the narrator begins and ends the volume. There is a progression from specific to general, from transcription and translation to poetics, then to hermeneutics and dialogue; in each case the Zunis and the Quiches approach the issue differently, theorizing it in culture-specific terms. The world that ethnographic method aspires to delineate in its comparative dimensions transcends the binary "us" vs. "them."

Interestingly, given that the same charge has been laid frequently against Boas, although perhaps for different reasons, Tedlock largely fails to state his theoretical position for the reader. Rather, the theoretical unity of the book and its approach to text are implicit in the arrangement and mode of analysis. Read as a scientific text, the book would be unintelligible. The interpretive techniques of literature must be applied both to the author's voice and to his portrayal of ethnographic others. Sadly, it is still relatively startling for an anthropologist to demand such sophistication of his or her readers.

Confessional and impressionist ethnographies (Van Maanen 1988) range from the entertainingly anecdotal to the philosophically reflexive and dialogic. None are fictional, although each is crafted, constructed, and thereby grounded in the scholarly and cultural contexts of its production. A small but persistent minority of anthropologists have been concerned with these issues (e.g., Bandelier [1890] 1971; Parsons 1922; Tedlock 1991). The initial impetus to explore genres of ethnographic writing came in poetics, where to read one's own poetry at the annual meetings of the American Anthropological Association became something of a bandwagon for a few years in the mid-1980s. Although there was no stipulation that the poetry have anything to do with anthropology, most of it did. Anthropological poets instinctively used the medium to explore issues about their professional experience, particularly of fieldwork, in ways that didn't fit into traditional ethnographic formats. In contrast, most of the poems read at the Linguistic Society of America meetings during the same years could have been written by anyone; most were poetry first and linguistics second, if at all. Surprisingly, however, the linguists retained an annual poetry reading much longer. Over the last several years, the Society for Humanistic Anthropology has devoted its sponsored sessions to readings of poetry and ethnography, calling wider disciplinary attention to the fact that some anthropologists take their writing seriously.

Iain Prattis edited a collection of poems and commentaries about the experience of fieldwork, the profession's obsession and integrating experience. *Reflections: The Anthropological Muse* was published in 1985 by the American Anthropological Association. Several of the poems, including my own, experimented with taking one voice from another culture and putting into its mouth things that the original "informant" would not say, producing a paraphrase, usually an expansion, designed to be intelligible to an audience accustomed to different expressive conventions.

The unpublished poem "High School Math" (Darnell 1982c) elaborates a casual conversation with a young Indian man who regretted never finishing school. The expansion proceeds in terms of cross-cultural miscommunication, of voices speaking past one another, put into words by the poet but inexpressible in the everyday idiom of an ostensibly pluralistic Canadian society. The young man's reflexivity about his teacher's disappointment came only years later, after he too had become a teacher.

I.

I find it so frustrating to teach
these classes of Indian students.
They seem to speak English adequately,
to understand the words I use. Yet
I always feel my meaning eludes them.
They do not seem to share the value
I place on education, as the only route
imaginable out of their poverty, alienation.

Occasionally, though, a good student.
There's one in my math class this year.
I know he understands the underlying
logic, symmetry, beauty of numbers.
Last fall I had such high hopes

for this young man. A teacher needs
to see a change in some of those lives.
I was sure he would help me face other years.

Gradually though, I lost the rapport
with this one student who understood.
I wanted him to show the class
that this stuff was possible to learn.
More and more I knew I had lost
most of these placid, tuned-out souls.
The worse it got, the more he asked
questions at the level of the worst.

I didn't know what to do. It hurt.
After class, I could no longer talk to him.
I couldn't believe he wanted to learn
when his questions were so elementary.
And he asked the same questions
over and over again, with smiling patience.
He must have understood. Why did he
torture me with endless repetitions?

How can I go on teaching this way?
I try to ask him why. He smiles
and tells me he likes my class, likes math.
It seems he cannot understand my hurt,
cannot tell me why this impossible impasse.
Yet I feel he knows, and pities me.
I didn't become a teacher for this.
I can't go on like this, year after year.

II.
I feel sad sometimes, because I never
really got a decent education.
I wasn't a bad student actually.
I think I would have been good
at math. I liked it anyway.
I remember one high school teacher,

a white lady of course, who tried
her best to teach me what she knew.

But the rest of the class didn't
learn from the way she explained it.
And I was a member of that class.
They were the kind who drop out
the day they turn sixteen, with relief,
and escape to the bush or a job,
never learn to cope with a white world.
Public education is for us all, them too.

So I asked questions, simple questions,
patiently repeated until the last one
knew what that teacher meant.
I was the only one who could ask
because I was the only one who understood.
They were all afraid, not wanting
to show ignorance, most not even
knowing what questions to ask.

Looking back now, I guess I realized
I was driving that teacher crazy.
But I thought she should've known
I asked all those questions for them.
I guess she was ready to give up
on most of that class and just teach me.
But I had no right to learn that way,
at the expense of my fellow students.

I guess it must have been hard for her
to face those blank faces day after day.
Her culture says you gotta show off
if you know the answers, and try
to achieve beyond the level of the class.
It didn't make sense to her that I cared
about the others. I couldn't explain it then.

It hurt when that teacher rejected me
because of something I had to do.
And I was sorry not to learn math.
Well, I didn't finish high school either.
I suppose she thinks that I'm just like
all the others. But I wanted to learn.
There just wasn't a place for me
in that white man's school.

The poem depicts in microcosm the dismal and all-too-frequent failure of cross-cultural communication, leaving the reader to imagine a way out of the impasse.

Dennis Tedlock's *Days from a Dream Almanac* speculates that the "poetics of fieldwork" is the weirdness "of being a stranger twice over," the second time on return from the field: "The usual way of dealing with strangeness is to write it into a general descriptive account, or into translations and interpretations of texts and artifacts collected in the field, or into a personal memoir of the field experience, or into poems that evoke that experience. All these ways of writing start from deliberate attempts to call strangeness to mind, and all of them treat it as if it existed only in the field" (Tedlock 1990:xi). In contrast Tedlock begins his poetic text with the premise that strangeness crosses the boundaries between here and there, home and field. Indeed, "the simple matter of wondering what today's date is" enmeshes the ethnographer returned from the Quiche Mayas in a profoundly non-European world calendar that "reverences" the earth in all its "roundness" (Tedlock 1990:88). The day-name combinations of this Mayan calendar refuse to stay within their boundaries, enticing the reader across worlds, spaces, cultures, languages. Indeed, "the poetics of fieldwork . . . cannot take place within just one language, nor can it leave the poet's native language untouched" (Tedlock 1990:88).

Tedlock's culture is far from homogeneous. His cultural experiences do not come in static packages. Interpretations are situated in individual, unique experiences. Readers make what they can of such images. The "dream almanac" is hardly realist ethnography—but it is certainly about the ethnographer at work.

Danger, at least insofar as the claim is to represent alternate views of the world, lurks in directing to the reader a language of evocation that is not that of the individual subject or culture depicted. Is it reasonable to restrict artistic license that wouldn't make sense to the people who shared their stories and experiences with anthropologists? Robin Ridington self-consciously emulates the story-creating style of the Omahas themselves: "The oral traditions of many First Nations code information in a way that is analogous to the distribution of visual information in a holographic image. Each story, like each piece of a hologram, contains information about the entire structure of which it is a part. Stories function as metonyms, parts that stand for wholes. Stories in the First Nations traditions with which I am familiar are part of a highly contextualized discourse which assumes familiarity with biography and shared experience" (Ridington 1999:19). Every repetition, every recurrence forms a spiral pattern of necessity inherent in the patterns of relationship. The anthropologist-as-writer is, in part, amanuensis and medium.

In a "narrative ethnography" the writer describes, and by describing interprets, his or her own experience of another culture. The voice is that of the narrator/anthropologist at the time of the experience. The result, for example, Barbara Tedlock on Zuni (1992) or Robin Ridington on Dunne-za [Beaver] (1988), reads like a novel with the anthropologist as protagonist if not hero; but it is nonfiction, with the goal of an accurate ethnographic portrait. Any resemblance to raw field notes is superficial. Understanding of what events mean comes with reflection, often over years following return from "the field." In literary convention the narrator reports, interprets, and speculates as though captured in the time warp of the narrative; this Native strategy parallels the "ethnographic present" of more conventional realist ethnography.

It is yet unclear what audience such works will attract, either in anthropology or in literature. But they allow anthropologists to apply and convey parts of what they know about other cultures that have traditionally been relegated to prefaces and acknowledgements, casual anecdotes, or scientific footnotes—or forgotten altogether. Such works must be read differently from traditional ethnographies.

The premise that a fictional genre may be truer than an ethnography is further justified in terms of the need to protect individual anonymity, especially in the case of individuals who cannot speak analytically for themselves or to the purposes of scholarship. For example, Michael V. Angrosino's *Opportunity House: Ethnographic Stories of Mental Retardation* (1998) adapts particular cases to imagined and imaginatively unified stories to convey the underlying meaning rather than the precise factual details of his encounters over long-term fieldwork. Writing fiction for ethical as well as aesthetic reasons, Angrosino lays claim to the mantle of social science, albeit in its qualitative mode, by framing his stories with methodological conversations. His naive interlocutor, a student, provides a trope, allowing him to articulate the premises of his work. Trusting his own intellectual and translational capacities, Angrosino emphasizes that "meaningful stories" can be told "even through highly unconventional forms" reflecting the thought-worlds of those with mental deficits (Angrosino 1998:37). He focuses on form rather than on content, placing himself firmly within the narrative as the perceiving intelligence that integrates and guides the reader through the stories. He explicitly disclaims narrative omniscience: "The reader can do what the ethnographer does—immerse him- or herself in the particulars and try to figure out what it all means" (Angrosino 1998:41). The reader might come to different conclusions than the ethnographer, and that would be a good thing. "Narrative cogency" is more important than "a fully objective account" (Angrosino 1998:267).

Indeed, redefining objectivity is one of the most intriguing challenges of contemporary theory. The Gulbenkian Commission suggests that objectivity is "the outcome of human learning," representing "the intent of scholarship and the evidence that is possible" (Wallerstein et al. 1996:92). Scholars achieve a kind of objectivity through their attempts to persuade one another to accept interpretations. Coherence, replicable methods, open presentation to peer judgment, and utility in explaining data are all non-arbitrary criteria for assessment of competing knowledge claims. Consensus engages "the intersubjective judgment of all those who do research or think systematically about the particular subject" (Wallerstein et al. 1996:92). Although there is certainly need for further rigor, continued vigilance, and "strengthening the organizational underpinnings of the collective effort," the commission is optimistic that social science has not been "reduced to a miscellany of private views, each equally valid" (Wallerstein et al. 1996:92). They call for "a meaningful degree of objectivity" as preferable to distortion inherent in a rigid standard of objectivity.

Another permutation of ethnographic voice that appears in the poetic efforts of anthropologists is a (usually self-conscious) strategy of reporting on culturally sensitive information without compromising the integrity or feelings of the "informant"/consultant. That which the ethnographer presents as firsthand experience does not place responsibility for the interpretation on any member of the culture described or evoked. Dramatic tension is sustained because it could have been otherwise, less happily. For example, in "My Grandmother, the Bear" (Darnell 1985a), the anthropologist as poet describes a superficially mundane encounter with a mother bear and her cubs and interprets it in light of Native American understandings of the vision ties between individual human persons and spirit beings, usually animal. Most of the poem, with the refrain "I am your grandmother, the bear," adopts the voice of the bear speaking to the human female who invades her domain. The voices then reverse, as the poet confirms acceptance of the spirit link by the repetition of "You are my grandmother, the bear."

Because of the strong taboo against speaking about contacts with the world of power, most Americanist anthropologists know more about such subjects than they are willing to say publicly. Poetry, then, becomes a medium for the anthropologist to speak in her or his own voice without implicating others. There is still danger, conceived as a misuse of power links. Native individuals vary considerably in their opinions about this issue, but it is a danger that the anthropologist as speaker, narrator, or poet takes upon herself or himself. There is no violation of confidence. Implication and indirection leave interpretation to the reader; the writer explicitly uses techniques to convey information and knowledge, particularly about culturally serious subjects, that are widely characteristic of Native American discourse. Poetic technique is deployed as ethnographic method (Darnell 1991a) with both descriptive and explanatory adequacy.

Anthropologists have even used poetic techniques to explore the history of their discipline. For example, Robin Ridington, in a volume of essays on anthropological uses of poetry edited by Ivan Brady (1991), argues cogently that Benjamin Lee Whorf's theory of linguistic relativity (the relationship between language, thought, and reality) has been blatantly, though not necessarily deliberately, misread by more behavioristically inclined successors as quasi-objective science. In contrast Ridington arranges some of Whorf's most lyrical passages (about the force with which grammar structures habitual thought) into poetic lines. Whorf's use of language calls for sensitive ethnographic explication rather than rigidly experimental tests of whether a particular relationship exists between language and thought. Read poetically rather than scientifically, Whorf's work need not be judged simplistically as either true or false but rather as a suggested approach to universal human meaning as encoded by a range of languages and cultures.

Although the theoretical issues raised by the productive combination of such manipulation of "ethnographic genre and poetic voice" (Darnell 1991a) are intelligible in literary theory, their strongest roots are in Americanist anthropology. That is, anthropologists employ literary forms primarily for reasons internal to their own professional preoccupations. That they borrow forms from the humanities, usually without overt acknowledgment, does not mean they have become literary scholars. The standards of evaluation differ profoundly.

Dell Hymes's introduction to the Prattis volume emphasizes that, if anthropologists choose to use literary forms, they must expect to be judged on aesthetic as well as on ethnographic grounds. Whatever their anthropological importance, Hymes finds these poems somewhat lacking in artistic quality. This I do not dispute, despite having been a contributor. But I wonder if the reverse case is not more interesting, anthropologically at least. I recall a colleague who praised the ethnography of one of my poems, noting that it was "really" prose arranged in poetic lines. I was certainly not offended, given that for me poetic form is primarily a means to an anthropological end. Anthropological poets perhaps can afford to be second-rate poets (after all, not all second-rate poets are anthropologists) as long as they are excellent ethnographers. (Alternatively, perhaps such experiments are not "poetry" at all. We may also question, moreover, how many anthropologists are adequate judges of poetic or literary quality.)

The term "new ethnography" was used in the 1960s to describe attempts to reflect categories used by members of culture. Experiments in methods of writing ethnography in the present context, then, would be the *new* new ethnography. The experimentalists must educate an audience within their own discipline. One approach is to do so through ties to existing disciplines that have already developed methods of textual analysis, intertextuality, and cultural description. Rapprochement between some literary critics and some anthropologists has, indeed, already begun; for example, Brian Swan and Arnold Krupat (Swann 1992; Swann and Krupat 1987) have collaborated with anthropologists and linguists to produce texts in translation for an audience that is in great part literary. Despite these fine exemplars, however, the boundaries between literature and the oral traditions recorded by most Americanists still resist cross-fertilization.

What has been recorded is all too accidental, each set of texts "primarily a history of lucky intersections between generous and gifted Native American oral poets and patient, skilful scribes" (Bringhurst 1998:15). Poets in an oral tradition are no less individuals than their counterparts who write. "Whether we learn their names or not, no two are interchangeable" (Bringhurst 1998:13). In *A Story as Sharp as a Knife: The Classical Haida Mythtellers and their World,* Bringhurst translates the texts of Skaay, the cripple, and Ghandl, who was blind, putting permanently to rest the idea that oral tradition is anonymous:

> [These texts] are typical in that they are subtly constructed and intricately balanced. And they are typical in that they link stories of poignant human emotion to the structure of the cosmos. . . . The mythworld is structured like a forest or an animal. It wakes and feeds and sleeps and dreams and changes. And it is made of separate parts that live and die. The poems, when they were oral, did the same. The poems themselves were ecological components of the world they describe. Properly speaking, what we have here are the fossils of poems, the transcripts, and not the poems themselves—not the living bodies that exist in a flourishing oral tradition. (Bringhurst 1999:133)

The story of these classic Haida poets is interwoven with that of John Swanton, the young Boasian who recorded the texts in 1900-1901, as well as with the story of Bringhurst as poet and translator.

In a full circle, literature and ethnography meet productively around the shared experiences and productions of Native Americans and anthropologists. The experimental ethnographic formats discussed in this chapter have in common a commitment to document and revitalize the knowledge traditions and expressive forms recorded by Boasian ethnographers like Hallowell and Swanton as well as the contemporary work in both anthropology and literary studies that builds upon them. We must become more sophisticated readers of a variety of genres of ethnographic reporting and become accustomed to evaluating them in terms of what each attempts to accomplish. The new forms, far from being radical, are deeply grounded in the ethnographic writing of Boasian anthropologists and in the collaborations they established with Native American communities and individuals. This is one of the most productive sites of energy within the contemporary Americanist tradition.

CLAUDE LÉVI-STRAUSS

CHAPTER 8

Will the Real Americanists Please Stand?

Rhetorics of Continuity and Discontinuity

Discussion of contemporary instantiations of the Americanist tradition rapidly becomes mired in debates about the seemingly amorphous interdisciplinary movement loosely glossed as poststructuralism or postmodernism. I suggest that postmodernism has a place in anthropology, although the nature of that place remains one of the salutary but unresolved side effects of the heterogeneous critiques so labeled (cf. Lemert 1997). But I also want to frame the critique of postmodernism in anthropology as one of several interpretive paradigms of the late twentieth century, all tracing back in part to the Boasian Americanist tradition. These contemporary paradigms do not lend themselves to a single mainstream consensus, although interpretivism itself seems destined to remain vibrant.

The choice of figures to represent the overlapping and competing strands of this heritage from Boasian roots cannot help but be somewhat arbitrary. I have chosen to focus on the symbolic, interpretive, and postmodernist or reflexive positions, represented respectively by Claude Lévi-Strauss, Clifford Geertz, and contributors to *Writing Culture* (Clifford and Marcus 1986). Other choices might have been made and indeed have been made by others (most recently Kuper 1999).

Lévi-Strauss's version of structuralism has been freely adapted to Anglo-American conventions of empiricism, particularly by British social anthropologists, in line with their commitments to social structure, political organization, and ritual as the core of anthropology. But Rodney Needham, Edmund Leach, and Mary Douglas are decidedly not Americanists; the Lévi-Strauss of their reading is not the one influenced by the Americanist ethnographic and cultural historical tradition and by his wartime experience in the United

States. Moreover, Lévi-Strauss's French disciples have employed his analytic method without acquiring his Americanist overlay; meanwhile, the French ethnographic establishment proceeds largely independently of structuralist allegiance. Lévi-Strauss's overlap with Boasian models, then, stands alone, although his work as a whole has tendrils of connection to other national traditions.

Although Clifford Geertz is the anthropologist best known to theoreticians from the humanities, Victor Turner's anthropology of performance attracts an audience in the performing arts, and Marshall Sahlins's symbolic historicism enjoins historians to reconsider the mechanistic ethnocentrism of their conventional interpretations. Both are powerful contenders for center stage.

Victor Turner is a hybrid in terms of national traditions, having been trained at the University of Manchester under British social anthropologist Max Gluckman; but he moved to the United States to teach and rapidly adopted many Americanist assumptions about culture and meaning. His early work on Ndembu ritual explored liminality and rites of passage as antitheses of static structure. Later, Turner identified a liminoid ritual status in contemporary complex societies; not all complex societies were derived from western European Judeo-Christianity. Turner pioneered in exploring the ritual character of everyday life. His "anthropology of performance" sought universals in myth, ritual, and drama, emphasizing transformation of individual consciousness, intensity of performance, interaction of performers and audience, transmission of performative knowledge, and evaluation of performance (Turner 1990). Culture was to be interpreted as performative text, always emergent and subject to exegesis.

Marshall Sahlins came to interpretivism as an about-face in midcareer. He began as an avowed Marxist and neoevolutionist, attempting to reconcile Julian Steward's cultural specificity with the universal generalizations of Leslie White. In the late 1960s Sahlins moved into Lévi-Straussian structuralism, embracing its mentalism but not its relegation of ethnographic evidence to theoretical exemplar. His third productive career turned to "mythopraxis," in which myth is simultaneously interpretation and cause for unique events that in the West are called history.

Neither Marxism nor neoevolution had provided satisfying explanations for historical events, which were constructed by participants and (later) observers on the basis of deeply ingrained cultural assumptions. Sahlins's reading of the ritual murder of Captain Cook in Hawaii has proved highly controversial because of a challenge by Sri Lankan–born anthropologist Gananath Obeyesekere, implicitly based on his ability to understand the Native point of view, even though he has not worked in Hawaii, and Sahlins has (Obeyesekere 1992; Sahlins 1985, 1995). Both parties to the dispute, however, agree that symbolic interpretation of culture as text is the core of the anthropologist's task. Their shared assumptions are fundamentally Americanist.

Adam Kuper, who has written extensively on the history of British social anthropology (1983, 1988), recently turned his hand to what he describes as an international critique of the Americanist concept of culture, which he considers to embody a pernicious and "pervasive idealism" alongside "its handmaiden relativism," producing "a growing if motley collection of aesthetes, idealists, and romantics agreed that Culture Makes Us" (Kuper 1999:19, 20). Kuper attributes his hostility to his South African roots, where he sees the theory of culture as having justified apartheid; he fails to acknowledge, however, the influence of British anthropology's focus on society rather than on culture. Indeed, the Americanists went wrong, in his view, when Talcott Parsons persuaded Boasian Clyde Kluckhohn that anthropology, in the postwar interdisciplinary synthesis that created the Harvard Department of Social Relations, would restrict itself to studying culture; the individual went to psychology, while Parsons's sociology retained social action (instructively, the stuff of British social anthropology that Kuper covets).

The excesses of postmodernism seem to Kuper no less compromised than more modest versions of interpretivism: "By and large, they [anthropologists] have switched their intellectual allegiance from the social sciences to the humanities, and they are likely to practice interpretation, even deconstruction, rather than sociological or psychological analysis" (Kuper 1999:x). He proposes to avoid the "hyper-referential" word culture and jettison the Americanist project altogether.

Despite this thinly veiled distaste, Kuper succeeds in outlining the work of three contemporary theoreticians of culture: Clifford Geertz, David Schneider, and Marshall Sahlins. These are legitimate choices, although one might question the single lineage from Harvard Social Relations to Chicago; as we have demonstrated, the Americanist tradition on which all of these folks draw is much more broadly constructed, in both past and present. Whatever the legacy of Parsons, these scholars are all also latter-day Boasians. David Schneider is among those who, though not Americanists in the narrow sense, acknowledge their diffuse intellectual debt: "Yes, I beat the culture drum. Geertz beat the culture drum. . . . Indeed we were Boasians; if not directly from Boas, we were Boasians partly through Kroeber and Kluckhohn and Parsons, but partly also because that was the general climate of anthropology in America, in which we grew up and participated" (Schneider 1995:203).

The choice of Schneider seems to me most perverse, at least from the standpoint of the Americanist culture theory that underlies all contemporary interpretivisms. Schneider's importance for Kuper appears to be that he rejected ethnography as the necessary database for anthropological theory because of the inherent limitations of local knowledge in sociological generalization (Kuper 1999:99). The study of American kinship, however, owes at least as much to Ward Goodenough and Anthony F. C. Wallace as to Schneider. Goodenough, who, like Schneider, also pioneered in both Pacific and American kinship studies based on Native semantic categories, relied heavily on Trukese ethnography (producing a massive bilingual dictionary that was simultaneously a specification of cultural knowledge and presupposition); at the same time, he attempted to retain the comparativist perspective of his own Americanist lineage at Yale's Institute of Human Relations, the home of George Peter Murdock's Human Relations Area Files (Darnell 1998b). Wallace, trained at the University of Pennsylvania by Frank Speck and Hallowell, explored kinship systems in terms of variability across members of the same culture and sought the psychological reality of analytic models; like Schneider he attempted to ground human cognition in biological capacities. Goodenough, Wallace, and their linguistic colleague Dell Hymes developed at Penn a more meaning-oriented, ethnographically based interpretivism than the Chicago version. There are choices of genealogy, even within a national tradition.

The anthropological response to postmodernism is still in progress, making it difficult to isolate a single figure for emphasis. It is not yet clear whether a canonical position will ultimately come to stand for the current body of work. What is of interest to the Americanist tradition, however, is the trajectory of this Americanist/postmodernist train of thought—particularly its reliance on cross-cultural exemplar and ethnographic methodology. This anthropological stance potentially resolves some of the thornier representational, epistemological, and ethical problems of contemporary interdisciplinary theory.

The distinguished scholars singled out above represent three successive generations of anthropological theorists, suggesting that the "experimental moment" touted by Clifford and Marcus relies more on rhetorical flourish than on substance or historicist engagement with the work of predecessors. Interpretivist continuities, then, must be rescued from their present invisibility and contextualized in terms of their intentions and audiences.

Interestingly, those most clearly associated with the purportedly new anthropology that crystallized after 1986 (Clifford and Marcus 1986; Marcus and Fischer 1986), have not consistently identified themselves as postmodernists. From within the in-group loosely defined as the contributors to *Writing Culture*—in addition to the coeditors: Mary Louise Pratt (the only woman, wife of another participant), Vincent Crapanzano, Renato Rosaldo, Stephen Tyler, Talal Asad, Michael Fischer, and Paul Rabinow—there are varying degrees of commitment to experimentation and considerable differences in defining how radical this experimentation should be. "Reflexive" anthropology avoids some of the backlash that has surrounded the very term postmodernism.

Regardless of the protestations of its contributors over blanket application of the postmodernist label, *Writing Culture* has become widely known for its rhetoric of discontinuity (Murray 1994) to the anthropological past and concomitant rejection of much that previously had been considered crucial to the definition and continued existence of the discipline. This rhetorical stance has asserted hegemony over postmodernism in anthropology, as though it were the only possible articulation of anthropology's history and present condition. Critics within the discipline charge that the new gurus have conceded their claim to realism, that is, to the existence of a world external to the anthropologist as author. More conventional ethnographers have claimed that the experimental ethnographies, of which a very few (especially Marjorie Shostak's *Nisa* (1981) and Vincent Crapanzano's *Tuhami* (1980)) were cited repeatedly in 1986, revealed far more about their anthropologist authors than about the peoples purportedly described. There are many more exemplars now.

Adding to the sense of disciplinary crisis, critics from the humanities and cultural studies tended to read internal critiques of representation as undermining anthropological authority in all study of the "other," not just among those experimenting with postmodernist rhetoric and representation. For at least some of the new critics, this rhetoric was read literally and projected widely.

The rhetoric of discontinuity adopted by the core group fueled acrimony, implying that those who did not jump on the bandwagon were old-fashioned, boring, or just plain wrong—a rhetoric reminiscent of the reaction to ethnoscience in the 1960s (Berreman 1966) when most of these scholars were graduate students. In well over a decade since the furor erupted, there has been no resolution. Certainly no Kuhnian scientific revolution has unambiguously established a new paradigm to which a critical mass within the discipline has shifted allegiance. Things are not as they were before, but neither has consensus emerged.

Exclusions from the new experimental synthesis created by the rhetoric of discontinuity are striking. Clifford, for example, justifies the omission of feminist anthropology on the grounds that it has "not contributed much to the theoretical analysis of ethnographies as texts" (Clifford and Marcus 1986: 19-20). This cavalier dismissal incensed many anthropologists, both female and male, for whom feminist scholarship (particularly standpoint theory) is pivotal to the anthropological critique of modernity. With the exception of an occasional reference to the work of Dennis Tedlock or Keith Basso, moreover, the Americanist tradition of studying text and discourse at the intersection of anthropology and linguistics is ignored. Linguistic anthropologists have been particularly active in expanding conventional genres of ethnographic writing (see Chapter 7).

The potential inclusion of linguistic anthropologists, feminist anthropologists, and others is elided by this telescoping of continuity to previous work. The rhetorical claims to an absolute innovation through which such telescoping is effected are oddly incongruent with the premises of the postmodernist critique as applied to other paradigms. Something that comes after modernism must surely have roots therein.

Despite its emphasis on rereading the ethnographic canon, the Clifford and Marcus collection contains surprisingly few references to the work of predecessors; it is as if contributors began reading around 1980. The impasse between the self-styled innovators and everyone else has been exacerbated by a rhetoric of disempowerment leveraged atop that of discontinuity. This rhetoric identifies the core group as a social and intellectual network; conversely, perhaps even perversely, they argue that this identity excludes them from nonconfrontational collegial acceptance by more conservative or traditional colleagues. At least in the "corridor talk" at professional meetings, anthropological postmodernism portrays itself as beleaguered and endangered in professional advancement (e.g., Marcus and Fischer 1986:xii). By dire implication graduate students who affiliate themselves with the new dispensation risk not getting jobs or tenure (as if anyone could take either for granted over the last fifteen years). The opposing rhetoric, then, must retain considerable vitality if it can stonewall the new critics and their disciples.

A rhetoric of continuity (see Murray 1994) is more likely to produce nuanced historicist understanding of the relationship between postmodernism, the Americanist tradition, and anthropology in North America. It is not necessary to claim that Boas and his classic early generation of students were postmodernists ahead of their time, only that their characteristic trains of thought continue to be refracted through contemporary experiments.

In another sense, however, Boas himself may be interpreted as a precursor of postmodernist dis-ease with grand theory. The experimentalists have ignored or dismissed Boas's "five-foot shelf" of Kwakiutl ethnography, arguing that its constructedness is largely implicit, buried under a mere compilation of undigested data. The Americanist textual tradition is represented by these critics as the rhetorical antithesis of interpretive or postmodernist anthropology. Arnold Krupat (1990), for example, attempts to rehabilitate Boas as theoretician by exploring "ironic" dimensions of his career-long oscillation between the rigors of deductive science and the subjectivities of historical or cosmological reasoning. According to Stocking, "Boas's scientific life may be seen as a transvalued and dichotomized *Kulturkampf;* on the one hand, as a struggle to preserve the cultural conditions of the search for universal rational knowledge, and on the other, as a struggle to defend the validity of alternative cultural worlds" (Stocking 1992:97). Boas's failure to resolve this fundamental dichotomy constitutes for Krupat an unintended irony, leaving Boas's successors to privilege the strengths of reflexive subjectivity in ethnographic production. Unfortunately, in this reading it is the new critics who are ironic, not Boas.

So Boas remains—for the new experimentalists as for the neoevolutionists, the techno-environmental determinists, the respectful former students, and the structuralists—an ancestor relegated to the past by cursory acknowledgement. By virtue of how he wrote (or did not write) about theory, his role is seen by some as hindering contemporary theoretical agendas. Perhaps this is the inevitable fate of a figure writ so large in the history of a discipline that his or her influence must be denied in order to establish the identity and autonomy of positions derived more or less directly from the mentor/teacher (cf. Clifford Geertz and his former students today). Sufficient time now has passed that historians of anthropology are enjoined by historicist canons of evidence to restore the visibility of continuities and to question the rhetoric in terms of which ideas are put forward as "new."

Claude Lévi-Strauss as Self-Incorporated Americanist

At first glance the Lévi-Strauss whose structuralism dominated French intellectual life in its heyday during the 1960s (persisting into the 1970s in North America) has little to do with Americanist anthropology and the tenets of Boasian historical particularism. Geertz, for example, refers to "my own admitted skepticism toward the structuralist project as a research program and my outright hostility to it as a philosophy of mind" (Geertz 1988:27). Anglo-American anthropologists characteristically have been unnerved by the a priori character of Lévi-Strauss's theory of mind and by the absence of context in his citations of ethnographic evidence. Nonetheless, Lévi-Strauss did do fieldwork, in South if not in North America. The majority of his theoretical exemplars of structuralist method employ data drawn from Americanist ethnographies. Although he does not claim to be an Americanist, he praises the grand tomes produced by the Bureau of American Ethnology as well as the work of the Boasians, particularly Robert Lowie and Alfred Kroeber, with their respective leanings toward social structure and superorganic culture. Lévi-Strauss adapted Boasian culture trait comparative method to answer new questions.

Contemporary experimental ethnographers have ignored Lévi-Strauss's ethnographic oeuvre, citing him primarily for his elegiac, partially autobiographical *Tristes Tropiques* ([1955] 1975), published more than two decades after the fieldwork on which it was based. Geertz considers it a tour de force, combining multiple genres: travelogue, ethnography, philosophy, "reformist tract," indictment of Western civilization, and "symbolist literary text" structured around an encounter with superficially chaotic sensory imageries (Geertz 1988:39, 41). Arguably the first postmodern confessional ethnography, it focuses more on Lévi-Strauss in the tropics than on any South American tribe. Susan Sontag (1961) aptly characterized the narrative itself as a myth of quest with the anthropologist as hero.

The fieldwork (by contemporary standards rather superficial safaris into the Amazon jungle) was carried out on academic holidays from the University in São Paulo. Without question, however, the fieldwork experience functioned as a rite of passage, transforming Lévi-Strauss's view of the gulf between civilized and primitive. In *Tristes Tropiques,* virtually alone among his voluminous writings, he recorded his alienation from the civilization he knew and his despairing compassion for the poignant plight of cultural loss suffered by the oppressed and impoverished aboriginal peoples of Brazil. Lévi-Strauss wrote as a man suffering from profound culture shock.

Fieldwork allowed Lévi-Strauss to teach in Brazil while simultaneously distancing himself from French sociology, dominated by the legacy of Emile Durkheim. Going to the field was anthropological work rather than exile from France, where Lévi-Strauss could not get a job. Nonetheless, his ethnographic contribution was substantial, given how little was known about interior South America in the 1930s. His stature as an Americanist in this descriptive sense is demonstrated by his extensive contributions to the *Handbook of South American Indians,* edited by Boasian Julian Steward (1946–59).

Long before Lévi-Strauss became an anthropologist, he was the quintessential outsider. Born in Belgium, he became a passionate convert to French intellectual culture. Although he rarely constructed himself as a Jew, his grandfather was a rabbi. After his self-imposed exile in Brazil, Lévi-Strauss escaped the Second World War in New York, cementing what Marianna Torgovnick calls his "transcendental homelessness" (Torgovnick 1990:218). Lévi-Strauss emphasized the liminality of his shipboard interlude, possibly leading him to identify for the first time with the lower class, feeling himself "subject to extermination" as were the primitive tribes he had met in Brazil (Torgovnick 1990:212). Torgovnick hypothesizes Jewish exile as a mediating term between endangered primitive and endangered modern European intellectual; Lévi-Strauss aspired to transcend the particulars of history and his own personal alienation (Torgovnick 1990:288, 214). This tendency toward transcendence became his signature.

Lévi-Strauss thereafter privileged a disengaged authorial position, leaving behind his nostalgic primitivism in face of the helplessness of aboriginal Brazilians to avert cultural genocide and environmental degradation. Although he never personally became an advocate for preservation of viable alternative lifeways in the contemporary world, *Tristes Tropiques* has provided an effective rallying point for others with political commitments closer to the surface of their anthropology, humanism, and activism.

Arriving in New York in 1941, Lévi-Strauss quickly established common cause with other newly transplanted European intellectuals fleeing Hitler's Europe as well as with the less recently immigrant Boasians (of whom the majority in the early cohort were German and/or Jewish). Boas himself helped many of these émigrés to settle in the New World. In retrospect, Lévi-Strauss has claimed that his preference for Americanist rather than for British or French anthropology preceded this arrival.

Lévi-Strauss was drawn immediately into the New York art scene. "The surrealists were attuned to the irrational and sought to exploit it from an aesthetic standpoint," while the anthropologists clustered around Boas at Columbia were "part of the decor of avant-garde art and writing" (Clifford 1988:266, 243). The atmosphere blended with Lévi-Strauss's ongoing efforts to distinguish his position from that of the Durkheimians back in France. His emergent rationalist notion of structure, adopted from the linguistics of Ferdinand de Saussure, assumed an external analyst's insights from comparative data inaccessible from within a given culture.

This argument paralleled Boas's argument for the diffusion of folklore elements on the Northwest Coast, with the Native point of view obscuring past historical events because of what Boas called "secondary rationalization." Only an outsider/analyst could reconstruct past histories of borrowing, which were not psychologically real for members of the culture(s) in question. Although Lévi-Strauss was less interested in history than in what the cultural evolutionists had called "the psychic unity of mankind," his methodology drew freely on the analyst's position of Boasian historical reconstruction.

The four ambitious volumes of *Mythologiques* ([1964] 1969b, [1966] 1973, [1968] 1978, [1971] 1981) and *La Voie des Masques* (*The Way of the Masks* [1975] 1982) compared abstract versions of the same myth, one that appeared widely across South and North America. But Lévi-Strauss did not work with his voluminous appropriated data in an Americanist way. The Boasians drew on texts in the words of native speakers of aboriginal languages. Lévi-Strauss, despite an occasional foray into literary criticism, professed utter disinterest in linguistic form or expressive style, in a manner alien to the spirit of text collectors and text narrators alike. He wanted to extract myth elements and plot structures for comparison across time and space. Meaning, from anything like the Native point of view, was engulfed by the analytic language of structural oppositions.

Each of Lévi-Strauss's books trained "the constant, unchanging, structuralist gaze on one or another domain of anthropological research; a huge rotating searchlight, lighting up first this dark corner, then the next" (Geertz 1988:31). Conventional text-based ethnography in and of itself can be opaque; Lévi Strauss aimed to "restate the thought of those societies in another language which is intelligible to us" (Pace 1983:143). Walter Benjamin's "The Task of the Translator" (1968) evokes similar resonance of a superlanguage toward which all languages aspire. In Lévi-Strauss's version, "the vocabulary of relational thought," borrowed from linguistics, explored "the role of unconscious mental activity in the production of logical structures" (Lévi-Strauss and Eribon 1991:43).

A very un-Americanist project resulted, intensified by the shift of Boasian anthropology toward the study of cultural pattern, individual personality, and culture change after about 1910 (and after World War II to area studies). Lévi-Strauss, in retrospect, constructed his structuralist edifice more as *bricoleur* than as engineer. Crucial components of his vast theoretical structure, however, came directly from his exposure to Americanist anthropology: its symbolic definition of culture, its text tradition of ethnography, its use of diffusion to reconstruct patterns beyond the conscious awareness of cultural members. Yet Lévi-Strauss grafted these borrowed materials to his own purposes, rooted in a quite different tradition of inquiry.

The "symbolic" character of Lévi-Strauss's structuralism is perhaps the most important thing he shared with the Boasians. He defined the entire gamut of cultural forms as symbolic, encompassing language, marriage rules, economic exchange patterns, art, science, and religion (Lévi-Strauss [1950] 1987:16–17). In a conversation with Didier Eribon, moreover, Lévi-Strauss admitted the possibility of premature generalization implicit in this symbolic definition of cultural structures: "The idea that structural analysis can account for everything in social life seems outrageous. . . . [I]n this vast empirical stew . . . where disorder reigns, are scattered small islands of organization" (Lévi-Strauss and Eribon 1991:102). Boas would have applauded the methodological caution—the avoidance of metanarrative, in updated jargon. To the extent that there is a Boasian metanarrative, it is about refusal of metanarrative.

For Lévi-Strauss as for Boas, meaning intersected with the substantive forms of culture. In *La Voie des Masques,* for example, Lévi-Strauss argued that masks were like utterances in language, "each one does not contain within itself its entire meaning" (Lévi-Strauss [1975] 1982:56). Versions of a myth or types of masks formed interrelated series "functionally bound together" in complementary distribution with "other real or potential masks that might have been chosen in its stead and substituted for it" (Lévi-Strauss [1983] 1985: 57, 144). "Logical operations" rather than plastic or verbal surface forms were at stake (Lévi-Strauss [1983] 1985:147). For Boas also, the masks and the stories explaining them were inseparable, one meaningless without the other (Rohner and Rohner 1969:38).

Lévi-Strauss's North American sojourn constituted a second stint of field-work far from the center of French intellectual life. In *Le Regard Eloigne,* the third volume of his collected papers (*The View from Afar* [1983] 1985), Lévi-Strauss described "New York in 1941." It was as alien to him as the Brazilian jungle, "an anthropologist's dream, a vast selection of human culture and history," a city evincing rare "moments of intelligible human order and transformation surrounded by the destructive, entropic currents of global history" (Clifford 1988:237). His culture shock gave way to a kaleidoscopic "redemptive metahistorical narrative" of civilization (Clifford 1988:215). Rhetorical flourishes aside, this is a different Lévi-Strauss than the one who avoided overgeneralization with nearly Boasian intensity.

In New York, Lévi-Strauss felt like Alice stepping through the looking glass, with "immense horizontal and vertical disorder attributable to some spontaneous upheaval of the urban crust" (Lévi-Strauss [1950] 1987:261). His "sense of oppression every time I revisit New York" warred with its exoticism and the "curious shapes" of "beauty" within it (Lévi-Strauss [1950] 1987:258). Clifford argues that Lévi-Strauss envisioned the human mind as "implicitly surrealistic" in its capacity to encompass chaos and diversity (Clifford 1988:140). An outsider to the culture of New York, which epitomized North America for him, Lévi-Strauss defamiliarized his briefly adopted country as a fieldwork site, providing further grist for his structuralist mill. He was curiously caught up in the art museums, libraries, and curio shops, the material forms of New York's complex cosmopolitan culture. Clifford reads this obsessive absorption of the alien as an émigré chronotype for "modern art and culture collecting" (Clifford 1988:236), an encapsulation of the so-called primitive apart from the mainstream of modern life, aestheticized, as it were.

Lévi-Strauss's American fieldwork was not, however, as isolated as that he did in Brazil. His American experience was filtered through intensive contact with refugee colleagues who shared his exile, temporary though it turned out to be. Foremost among these were André Breton, Georges Duthuit, Max Ernst, Roman Jakobson, André Masson, and Yves Tanguy. They were not Americans. In fact, Lévi-Strauss had virtually nothing to say about his interactions with Boasian anthropologists in New York. His identity remained firmly grounded in Europe.

An alternative—more opportunistic and less Americanist—reading of Lévi-Strauss's structuralism is possible (Darnell 1995b). Lévi-Strauss often underplayed the structuralist elements in Durkheimian sociology so as to distinguish it from his own position. Yet he was steeped in the sociological tradition leading from Montesquieu to Rousseau to Durkheim (see Gurvitch and Moore 1945). His title *Les Structures Elementaires de la Parenté* (*Elementary Structures of Kinship* [1949] 1969a) explicitly paralleled that of Durkheim's *Les Formes Elémentaires de la Vie Religieuse* (*Elementary Forms of Religious Life* [1912] 1961), and *Le Pensée Sauvage* (*The Savage Mind* [1962] 1966) evokes Lucien Lévy-Bruhl's ([1923] 1966) flirtation with the nature of "primitive mentality". Lévi-Strauss's introduction to the works of Marcel Mauss ([1950] 1987) expresses notable filial piety. Moreover, the incipient structuralism embedded in the work of Durkheim and Marcel Mauss laid the groundwork for Lévi-Strauss's seminal appropriation of structuralist methodology from Prague School linguistics. When Lévi-Strauss and Jakobson met in New York in the early 1940s, the former was ideally positioned to extend the method beyond language to all symbolic systems constituting culture.

Lévi-Strauss was wont to wax ecstatic over Americanist ethnography, when he mentioned it at all. "The Work of the Bureau of American Ethnology and Its Lessons," included in the second volume of *Anthropologie Structurale* (*Structural Anthropology* [1973] 1976), eulogized the "sacrosanct volumes" of bulletins and annual reports purchased from a New York collector. These works preserved the "fundamentals of mankind" from irretrievable loss "when the last primitive culture will have disappeared from the earth" (Lévi-Strauss [1973] 1976:50, 51). This passage invoked the rhetoric of *Tristes Tropiques:* its intent meshes well with the romantic motives of Boasian urgent ethnology and linguistics. Lévi-Strauss was exposed to this Americanist preoccupation between his Brazilian interlude and writing his complex, reflexive ethnographic memoir; his reworking of fieldwork experience undoubtedly drew upon his subsequent American sojourn.

Interestingly, Lévi-Strauss failed to distinguish the work of the Bureau of American Ethnology from that of the Boasians (some Boasians, of course, published in the BAE). Although the contest for institutional and theoretical control of North American anthropology devolved to the Boasians (Darnell 1998a) two decades before Lévi-Strauss arrived in North America, war-time Boasians were convinced that the dominant Americanist paradigm of their day was the culmination of a successful scientific revolution. Boas's death in 1942 encouraged participants to emphasize discontinuity from previous Americanist work. The enduring documentary value of prior work was eclipsed thoroughly in the rhetoric of the period.

For Lévi-Strauss, because he was not in the narrow sense an Americanist, these differences were relatively insignificant (as they perhaps increasingly appear in our own time). Americanist ethnography was grist for his theoretical mill, illustrative of structuralist principles. His appropriated database "would form the authentic ethnographic material from which structuralism's metacultural orders were constructed" (Clifford 1988:245).

Because French structuralism came of age in anthropology through Lévi-Strauss, it introduced North American anthropology to interdisciplinarity, lending it an unaccustomed "sense of intellectual importance" because of its "wholesale invasion of neighboring fields" (Geertz 1988:25). Anthropologists were used to thinking of themselves as among the smallest and least fashionable of the social and human sciences, a mind-set that briefly gave way to delusions of disciplinary grandeur. French anthropologists, in contrast to interdisciplinary structuralists, persisted in an ethnographic program largely independent of this theoretical maelstrom: "Many of them find it curious and amusing, if not retrograde, that American and English anthropologists accord such great importance—based on superficial understanding—to such a prickly group of 1970s French intellectuals from other fields who understand or sympathize little with anthropology's traditional concerns" (Knauft 1996:300). Referents could range from Jean-Paul Sartre to Jacques Derrida, Michel Foucault, and Gilles Deleuze.

Structuralism was international as well as interdisciplinary, encompassing in France (in addition to Lévi-Strauss) Foucault, Roland Barthes, Louis Althusser, and Jacques Lacan. Ferdinand de Saussure was Swiss; Roman Jakobson, Mikhail Bakhtin, and Nikolaj Trubetzkoj were Russian; Louis Hjelmslev was Danish; Charles Peirce and Edward Sapir were American. In addition to anthropology, the home disciplines of these core scholars included philosophy, philosophy of science, literary criticism, psychoanalysis, and linguistics. Of these, only psychoanalysis and linguistics were familiar to most Americanist anthropologists when structuralism rose to prominence in the 1960s and 1970s. Connections forged there persisted into poststructuralism or postmodernism, permanently shattering the relative isolationism (despite its German romanticism via Boas) of North American anthropology's formative professional period.

In sum, then, Lévi-Strauss both is and is not an Americanist. He shares the Boasian symbolic definition of culture and appropriates to his own purposes the database assembled by the Boasians and their predecessors in the Bureau of

American Ethnology. Further, he links the mentalism of the Americanist and French traditions in contrast to the behaviorist empiricism of British social anthropology. His own compatriots were far from converts, at least after his political conservatism in May 1968; the British social anthropologists systematically misinterpreted his insistence on reasoning from universals to ethnographic exemplars, while the Americanists emphasized the cultural and interpretivist strands of his thought. In this sense, Lévi-Strauss remains within the interpretivist continuity of Americanist invisible genealogies.

Clifford Geertz as Nuanced Americanist

Virtually all of the self-styled postmodernists acknowledge Clifford Geertz as teacher and/or mentor. But they make no move to include him in their ranks. Indeed, these anthropologists claim that their experimental stance (which they conflate with postmodernism in its anthropological guise) is generationally based. Graduate students of the politically self-conscious 1960s have now attained sufficient academic seniority and professional security to experiment with inherited forms of ethnographic representation (Marcus and Fischer 1986:xii; Rosaldo 1989).

The "sixties generation"—to the extent that there is such a thing—undoubtedly now wields increasing institutional power and theoretical influence. But their coming to maturity is insufficient explanation for this particular brand of theory, given that others of the generation have theorized in other ways, using other rhetorics (e.g., a rhetoric of continuity pervades the collection that Lisa Valentine and I edited, *Theorizing the Americanist Tradition* [1999]; feminist theoreticians have taken a variety of stances toward the articulation of their work with mainstream anthropology).

A cynical observer might suggest that his former students do not want to share center stage with Geertz. For example, Steven Sangren charges that "young critics can undercut the authority and prestige of established scholars (note the patricidal treatment of Geertz in some of the essays in *Writing Culture*) while appropriating their best insights and at the same time inoculate themselves against criticisms of the same order" (Sangren 1988:422). A more charitable reading might emphasize that Geertz's interpretive anthropology takes a less extreme and more affirmative stance than the no-longer-very-young Turks would prefer. The label postmodernist, however, is reserved by the rhetoricians of discontinuity for the skeptical variant. Moreover, they reject the interpretivist intellectual genealogy, which I have argued is, in good part, Americanist. Thomas de Zengotita complains, for example, that Geertz "lectures" "the brood" of his protégés, and is "still essentially modernist, still innocently ironic." He dismisses Geertz as a "late modernist" (Zengotita 1989: 117, 118, 119).

Insistence on dividing the genealogy between late modernism and postmodernism, between Geertz and his former students, depends on anthropologists' self-perception of a dichotomy that actually masks considerable continuity. Whether or not he is a postmodernist, whether or not it matters, Geertz's position is more complex and less static than his critics imply. His Harvard Social Relations training in Parsonian quasi-evolutionary functionalism and modernization has undergone dramatic transformation.

Geertz, however, emphasizes the interdisciplinarity of his own intellectual genealogy rather than national anthropological traditions. He began in literature. Teaching anthropology at the University of Chicago throughout the 1960s, Geertz (like Edward Sapir before him) professed himself repelled by the "positivist social science" legacy of British social anthropology in the person of A. R. Radcliffe-Brown; "I just didn't believe it" (Geertz 1991:607). But Boasian anthropology seemed to him "undertheorized." In an otherwise non-Americanist, consciously articulated genealogy, however, he acknowledged his debt to the most humanistic among the Boasians, Edward Sapir and Ruth Benedict, for some of the foundations of what would become his own version of interpretive anthropology. This Americanist alternative, which surfaces periodically throughout Geertz's work, sets the stage for the turn to postmodernism spearheaded by a core group led by his own former students at Chicago.

Geertz anticipated many of their arguments. In his early view, "anthropological writings" were characterized as second- and third-order "interpretations" already considerably removed from events observed in the field. Ethnographies "are, thus, fictions fashioned by ethnographers as writers" (Geertz 1973:15). That such fictionality reflects "scholarly artifice" rather than "social reality," however, does not in itself threaten the "objective status of anthropological knowledge" (Geertz 1973:16). "Appraisal" rather than verification is the goal of interpretation. Geertz exhorts anthropologists to become "self-conscious about modes of representation (not to speak of experiments with them)" (Geertz 1973:16). Thirteen years were to pass before Clifford and Marcus laid claim to a new "experimental moment" along precisely these lines.

Geertz did not claim ethnographic evidence as privileged representation. Its utility was less one of objective documentary record than of "another country heard from" (Geertz 1973:23). Closure should not be expected in ethnographic work, although writing and theorizing could become increasingly sophisticated. The ethnographic reality presumed to lie behind the writing and the theory would remain elusive. Yet Geertz was concerned to avoid subjectivism and to connect his interpretations with "the hard surfaces of life" (Geertz 1973:30). His method rested on a metaphoric textualization of culture itself: "The anthropologist strains to read [cultural texts] over the shoulders of those to whom they properly belong" (Geertz 1973:452–53) (ownership being taken for granted, as for the Boasians).

Geertz's interpretivism has received considerable attention from philosophers of science, who characteristically take it to represent the knowledge claims of all anthropologists. James Bohman, for example, argues that "textual ruses" at the basis of ethnographic authority do not invalidate (unspecified) "forms of interpretive adequacy" as long as there is an epistemological potential for "dialogue with others"—what Geertz calls "conversation"—and a moral responsibility "to interpret others correctly" (Bohman 1991:131–32). Nor is Bohman worried about the inevitable ethnocentricity of the anthropologist, which "in no way precludes the possibility of valid knowledge" arising from her or his views (Bohman 1991:139). The contingency of local knowledge gained in the field can be specified empirically, moving it beyond the "merely contingent" (Bohman 1991:140). An interpretive ethnography, however, must be falsifiable. Skepticism is avoided by the reflexivity of the ethnography (Bohman 1991:147). At stake, both for Geertz and for the philosophy of science, is the claim to realism, that the world exists outside the ethnographer and can be described meaningfully, if not uniquely.

The anthropological postmodernists are more skeptical. Clifford, for example, delimits ethnography as a "mutual construction" or "multiple interpretation" (quoted in Bohman 1991:150–51). In Bohman's view neither ethical responsibility nor scientific accuracy should be conceded so readily to "uncommitted and ultimately apolitical and aesthetic multiplicity"; Geertz was correct to seek "better, epistemologically and morally justified" interpretations relying on "dialogue and mutual criticism," including criticism of the interpreter's own beliefs (Bohman 1991:151).

Inescapable ethnocentrism is pernicious only when it expects or coerces convergence of other views with its own, thereby restricting awareness of and dialogue with difference. Indeed, "benign ethnocentrism" may begin with the interpreter's background experience and assumptions but aspire to transcend them in a "critical pluralism" (liberal democracy plus multiculturalism) allowing multiple "acceptable" interpretations, all of which are congruent with scientific standards (Hoy 1991:156–59). To acknowledge such a pluralism does not, in David Hoy's view, preclude the interpreter's preference for his own views.

These contemporary philosophers of science seem prepared to trust the ethnographer to a remarkable degree (at least from the point of view of a practicing anthropologist with qualms resulting from having done fieldwork). For Hoy the anthropologist's authority to control an ethnographic discourse rests on having mastered both the tribal language and his or her own. He is prepared to agree that "tribal" peoples, a designation few would accept these days, are by definition more insular than the anthropologists who study them.

Geertz, who has done considerable cross-cultural fieldwork, expressed massive disquiet nearly two decades earlier; he was, in fact, reluctant to claim that he fully understood anything or that his claim to knowledge was different in kind from those grounded in the culture(s) he studied. More recently, he suggested that fieldwork is "a matter of living out your existence in two stories at once" (Geertz 1995:94). Its paradox rests in simultaneously being a familiar figure in the local scene and one who functions in larger political hegemonies (as do many members of the societies studied). Indeed, "it has become harder and harder to separate what comes into science from the side of the investigator from what comes into it from the side of the investigated" (Geertz 1995: 135).

Having established his interpretivist framework, with substantial continuity to Boasian work, Geertz turned to theorizing the undeniably Americanist concept of cultural relativism as foundational to anthropology as he understood it (Geertz 1984:264–65). "Anti-anti-relativism" responds to the climate of "philosophical disquiet arising everywhere around," two years before the publication of *Writing Culture* and before the label postmodernism was widely applied to anthropological theory. The spiritual entropy of a world without certainties does not preclude a moral stance of opposing racism, ethnocentrism, or provincialism; in fact, Geertz argues lyrically that anthropology can proudly proclaim a unique position among the human sciences:

> Looking into dragons, not domesticating or abominating them, nor drowning them in vats of theory, is what anthropology has been all about. At least, that is

what it has been about, as I, no nihilist, no subjectivist, and possessed, as you can see, of some strong views as to what is real and what is not. . . . We have, with no little success, sought to keep the world off balance. . . . [W]e hawk the anomalous, peddle the strange. Merchants of astonishment . . . [S]uch an affection for what doesn't fit and won't comport, reality out of place, has connected us to the leading theme of the cultural history of "Modern Times." For that history has indeed consisted of one field of thought after another having to discover how to live on without the certainties that launched it. (Geertz 1984:275)

Geertz's reformulation of long-cherished Americanist cultural relativism asserts that, by virtue of their cross-cultural experience, his colleagues already know how to think about relativity, and do so without inducing the crisis of intellectual foundations that appears to have paralyzed the more ethnocentric of the Western sciences. This affirmative claim of anthropology's relationship to postmodernism, then, arises from the Americanist anthropology that motivated Geertz to think about cultural relativism and cross-cultural experience in the first place.

Geertz's subsequent formulation of interpretive anthropology as engaging the "local knowledge" of particular communities reflects his increasingly far-flung interdisciplinary forays over the decade between his collections of theoretical essays in 1973 and 1983. "Local knowledge"—some variant of which by definition belongs to everyone, regardless of culture or circumstance—has considerable advantage over portraying the anthropologist as self-appointed arbiter of others' cultural knowledges by virtue of more extensive experience (even granting that we have progressed beyond a racist evolutionary claim of intrinsic Western superiority). Anthropology is "preadapted to some of the most advanced varieties of modern opinion. The contextualist, antiformalist, relativizing tendencies . . . , its turn toward examining the ways in which the world is talked about, depicted, charted, represented—rather than the way it intrinsically is. . . . [A]nthropology, once read mostly for amusement, curiosity, or moral broadening, plus, in colonial situations, for administrative convenience, has now become a primary arena of speculative debate" (Geertz 1983:45). Anthropologists, at least in relation to their own society, provide defamiliarized contrastive contexts for reading audiences without cross-cultural experience. Geertz's revamped cultural relativism retains a lingering and characteristically Americanist commitment to modernist representation. Whether our own or theirs, local knowledge can be framed by the anthropologist-as-translator to a "cosmopolitan intent" that extends the contexts within which that knowledge can be understood by nonlocal audiences. Alone among the social sciences, anthropology retains the "epistemological self-confidence" to produce a potentially universalist "social history of the moral imagination" (Geertz 1983:8–9).

This Americanist version of cultural relativism is deeply ethical; it is "the merest decency" to see members of other cultures as sharing our own nature (Geertz 1983:16). The next and more difficult move is to reframe our own local knowledge as merely one possibility among an indefinite number of possibilities. Johannes Fabian argued that anthropology, as a product of Western society, has failed to extend "coevalness" of individual and community agency and of historical context to those peoples until quite recently called "primitive." Ethnography—"the direct, personal encounter with the 'Other'"—is "the indisputed rule" that preserves anthropology from the fate of "becoming a hallucinatory discipline about an Other of its own making" (Fabian 1983:148). Such localized ethnography is the basis of the anthropological claim to ethical integrity, insofar as such a claim can still be made. Perhaps it cannot, according to contemporary reflexive sensibilities among some anthropologists. On the other hand, we may at least claim ethical superiority to those who fail altogether to consider such questions.

In any case, the anthropology that Fabian and Geertz espouse leads the social sciences in resisting, on ethical, political, and epistemological grounds the "constant temptation" toward "synopticism" (Fabian 1983:117–18), that is, movement from local knowledge to overstated or premature generalizations (a caution also characteristic of Boasian theorizing). Both historical particularism and cultural relativism are theoretical positions arising from within Americanist anthropology. Both continue to shape the ethnographic productions of the majority of anthropologists trained in North America, whether or not they work with the aboriginal peoples of the continent. (Geertz [1995:102] was engrossed in reading the Navajo materials of the Harvard values in five cultures project when the opportunity arose to go to Java; so there was an unfulfilled "moment" at which he might have become an Americanist in the narrow sense as well as in the more general one depicted here.) Geertz links this continuous general tradition to anthropological postmodernism in its North American guise.

When he turns from ethnography to history of anthropology, Geertz ostensibly applies the same methodological relativism to his fieldwork in the culture(s) of anthropologists. *Works and Lives: The Anthropologist as Author* (1988) identifies and explicates four distinctive, possibly incommensurable, strategies of ethnographic writing. Geertz claims that it is no more necessary to judge schools of disciplinary thought as better or worse than to rank the cultures of humankind in unilinear sequence (something we don't do anymore). The final position he treats is that of Ruth Benedict, who used ethnographic data to turn the North American gaze back upon itself, hoping to ameliorate the society from which she herself came. The rhetorical implication of ending with Benedict (who is less "contemporary" than his other subjects—Lévi-Strauss, Malinowski and E. E. Evans-Pritchard) is Geertz's vision that the West, learning from the fine-honed skills of fieldworking anthropologists, will come to see itself more clearly by virtue of understanding that its own cultural practices are choices holding no special privilege among many possible alternatives, from what Benedict (1934b) called the "arc of cultural possibilities." Plenitude in contemporary cultural variability motivates anthropologists to describe cultural practices and to offer the results for public consumption.

Geertz denies interest in individual biography or historical context, while acknowledging that the ethnographic genre itself rests upon a paradox: "the oddity of constructing texts ostensibly scientific out of experiences broadly biographical" (Geertz 1988:10). Yet his strategy fails to explore the process of getting from one to the other through the history of anthropology. This strategy isolates his subjects-cum-colleagues in a timeless ethnographic present that Fabian would doubtless characterize as denying coevalness to ethnographers of diverse persuasions and generations.

In the context of disciplinary history, Geertz worries about whether relativism will prove "corrosive" because his own ethnographic gaze might undermine the authority of anthropological knowledge claims (Geertz 1988:9). To undermine the knowledge claims of the "other" presumably does not carry the same reflexive potential to modify the terms of possible representation or to endanger the basic standpoint of the discipline of anthropology. That is, as Geertz moves from ethnography to history of science, he is inconsistent in equating the reflexive knowledges of other cultures (and their consequences) with anthropological knowledges.

In practice most writers of ethnography have disguised their rhetorical strategies in order to deflect their own anxieties about subjectivity—or those attributed to potential readers. Geertz's reading privileges the rhetorical grounding of ethnographic writing, the inevitable gap between writing and the fieldwork on which it is based, and the need to experiment. He unapologetically urges readers toward his own version of interpretive social science, albeit his conclusion is consonant with that of his postmodernist intellectual descendants and critics: "'the move toward meaning' has proved a proper [scientific] revolution: Sweeping, durable, turbulent, and consequential" (Geertz 1995:115).

The Illusory "Experimental Moment" of *Writing Culture*

The self-proclaimed revolutionary experimentalism of the Clifford and Marcus volume masks substantial underlying continuity. Geertz was not the only predecessor to have approached ethnographic writing through reexamination of the canon of classical ethnographies. For example, James Boon compared "isms and eras (really *epistèmes*) to culture" (Boon 1982:231). His symbolic history of anthropology moved between things in the world ("the tribal") and rhetorical practices ("the scribal") (Boon 1982:235). In fact, Marcus and Dick Cushman (1982) reviewed a substantial literature on the textuality of ethnography four years before the appearance of the much-touted paradigm statement (see also Strathern 1987).

The changes were incremental and ongoing. In 1987 Stephen Tyler argued for poetics as a crucial ethnographic textual innovation. The canonical statement of 1986, therefore, must be interpreted as a crystallization signaling public recognition rather than an actual point of origin for the new ethnography and ethnographic writing. The most sustained exploration of the implications of deconstructing the inherited anthropological standpoint, Clifford's *The Predicament of Culture: Twentieth Century Ethnography, Literature, and Art* (1988), combines ethnography, literature, and art, thereby focusing on the place of anthropological discourse among other Western cultural discourses.

Clifford's introduction to *Writing Culture,* titled "Partial Truths," claims that anthropology has been paralyzed by the inherited ideology that ethnographic representation must be transparent and fieldwork experience immediately interpretable. Positions shared by the conference participants claim to theorize anew the practice of ethnography and ethnographic writing, perhaps to theorize them for the first time. Clifford identifies the (surprisingly Americanist) shared assumptions (see Introduction for distinctive features; the position is closest to Sapir's alternative to Kroeber's theory of culture [see Chapter 3] and Benedict's critique of North American society [see Chapter 5]):

1 / **Culture is equated with the study of "contested codes and representations"** (Clifford 1986:2). Culture is no longer assumed to be knowledge shared among all its members. Conflict and change are inherent in culture, whether it be exotic or familiar, local or global. Nonetheless, culture is in people's heads rather than solely observable in behavior.

2 / **The subtitle of the volume asserts the inseparability of poetics and politics, of aesthetics and engagement.** Rhetorical form is privileged in ethnographic writing, in part as a means of cultural critique. Forms of local expression, as in Americanist texts, matter.

3 / **Science, traditionally positivist science, is to be contextualized by history and by language of expression.** Science can no longer be assumed to transcend the situated perspective of the scientist. "Standpoint," indeed, is a technical term in Boasian writing, used much as it is used today by feminist theoreticians in application to the nature of science (e.g., Haraway 1988; Harding 1991; see Chapter 2).

4 / **Genres of representation cannot be assumed to be separable and distinct.** All ethnographic writing has a constructed or fictional dimension (see Chapter 7). Conversely, much ethnographic fiction has a realistic intention. The same anthropologist may choose to report his or her field experience in dramatically different rhetorical formats, each of which should be taken seriously as ethnographic representation (e.g., Wolf 1992).

5 / **Ethnographic writing is "experimental and ethical"** (Clifford 1986:2). Experimentation enables the anthropologist to take a political stance in a world inhabited jointly by the fieldworker and her or his research subjects. Experimentation is deemed ethical because rhetorical diversity privileges complexity, reflexivity, and multivocality.

Based on this set of distinctive features, the "new" ethnography positions anthropology at the center of a wider discourse (loosely postmodern, although Clifford does not use the term). As a set the papers proceed from an unquestioned assumption of "crisis within anthropology," a discontinuity from its established, presumably positivist, conventions of ethnographic research and writing (Clifford 1986:3). This pessimism contrasts sharply with Geertz's suggestion that people live in "a sense-suffused world" in spite of anthropologists' worries "about the sheer impossibility of anyone, insider or outsider, grasping so vast a thing as an entire way of life and finding the words to describe it. Anthropology, or anyway the sort that studies cultures, proceeds amid charges of irrelevance, bias, illusion, and impracticality. But it proceeds" (Geertz 1995: 43).

Clifford's critique of positivism entails the fictional character of the new ethnography. "Fiction" encompasses both partiality and human construction, the latter in the sense of literary creation rather than of falsehood. Relativism is the only appropriate response to cultural diversity in the aftermath of colonial empires. Clifford, though not an anthropologist by training, worries more, in an insider's way, about this ethico-political challenge than about the possible collapse of standards for verification of ethnographic representations. Disciplinary confidence is highly vulnerable to undermining by alternative epistemologies derived from the knowledge systems of those studied. Particularly in the humanities and cultural studies, Clifford and Marcus are assumed to have radically rejected realism.

Clifford calls for "new" histories of "local practices" that are contingent, political, and processual (Clifford 1986:10). His rhetoric parallels that of Geertz in 1983. Clifford welcomes the increasing permeability of anthropology's disciplinary boundaries, which shade into "sociology, the novel, or avant-garde cultural critique" (Clifford 1986:23). Experimental forms, including poetry, are "not limited to romantic or modernist subjectivism: [they] can be historical, precise, objective" (Clifford 1986:26). Clifford warns that the status of ethnography as literature can never be ignored; despite these literary qualities, however, it retains a claim to truth about something in the world.

Claims to participation in the "experimental moment" are remarkably intertextual. For example, Vincent Crapanzano, himself the author of a so-called experimental ethnography (1980) widely and enthusiastically lauded by his fellow conference participants, also produced an earlier Americanist life history (1972) that remains invisible in this volume. Crapanzano critiques Geertz's canonical description of the Balinese cockfight for its ingenious "interpretive virtuosity" (Crapanzano 1986:53). In his reading, Geertz's rhetorical strategies blur his own subjectivity. Dialogue with readers is more salient than that with the Balinese. Emotions and motives are attributed to the Balinese without evidence or individuation. Geertz's "illusion of specificity" becomes, in effect, sleight-of-hand (Crapanzano 1986:70–76).

A more charitable reading might emphasize the historical importance of Geertz's essay in expanding the rhetorical strategies available to interpretive ethnographers, thereby laying the groundwork for the present "experimental moment." Crapanzano avoids such interpretive charity, perhaps because he was more interested in advancing his career by dissociating himself from Geertz than in addressing the historicist continuity from Geertz's interpretation of the Balinese cockfight to his own experiments in ethnographic writing.

The only contributor to *Writing Culture* acknowledged by his peers as fully postmodern is Stephen Tyler, whose description of the postmodern ethnography, therefore, may be taken as canonical:

> A post-modern ethnography is a cooperatively evolved text consisting of fragments of discourse intended to evoke in the minds of both reader and writer an emergent fantasy of a possible world of commonsense reality, and thus to provoke an aesthetic integration that will have a therapeutic effect. It is, in a word, poetry . . . by means of its performative break with everyday speech, [which] evokes memories of the *ethos* of the community . . . [and] thereby provokes hearers to act ethically. . . . Post-modern ethnography attempts to recreate textually this spiral of poetic and ritual performance. (Tyler 1986:125–26)

Whatever this description may "evoke" for the reader, Tyler's claim to retain "a form of realism" remains problematic. Descriptions of the world are "mimetic" (i.e., representational), creating mere "illustrations of reality, as in the fictional realities of science" (Tyler 1986:137). Tyler declines to spell out what remains of the traditional anthropological commitment to represent alternative cultural worlds (without science, never mind anthropology). The retreat from "representation" to "evocation," however, inevitably leads to loss of verifiability.

Paul Rabinow, following Rorty (1979), suggests that "edifying conversation" can be based on "knowledge without foundations" (Rabinow 1986:136). Anthropologists accomplish this more readily than do postmodernists from other disciplines because they are already accustomed to the idea of diverse social practices. Conversation is to be grounded in historical, cultural, and political contexts as well as in discursive practices. A gap remains, however, between the critical study of decolonization and an armchair concern with academic politics as ways of changing the world. Rabinow somewhat naively proposes an "interpretive federation" to lead anthropologists, their formalist critics, their political subjects (the fictive "others"), and all "critical, cosmopolitan intellectuals" (the interdisciplinarians) away from the ivory tower (Rabinow 1986: 252–53), presumably back to a politics of postcolonial engagement.

Maintaining the familiar rhetoric of discontinuity, Rabinow worries that "longer, dispersive, multi-authored texts" might not "yield tenure" (Rabinow 1986:243). Marcus emphasizes the "disarray" of grand theory and the consequent need for experimentalism. "Anthropological careers" are intimately connected to the fate of the putative "experimental moment." Indeed, "every individual project of ethnographic research and writing" is potentially experimental (Marcus and Fischer 1986:ix). Innovation resides more in anthropologists than in the ethnographies they produce. The common attribute of such ethnographers is that they are "deeply implicated" in the forms of representation they employ (Marcus and Fischer 1986:109). This agenda must be pursued diligently, lest it be overwhelmed by forces of positivist conservatism—a bizarre position, given its continuity with mainstream interpretive anthropology.

The "emergent post-modern world" requires anthropology to address a diversity of "political, historical, and philosophical" disciplines (Marcus and Fischer 1986:vii); the core contributors have volunteered as spokespersons. In a partial move back to the anthropological mainstream, the various pronouncements of Clifford, Marcus, Fischer, and others reiterate the need for commitment to realism in ethnography and ethnographic writing. Marcus and Fischer (1986:117) emphasize the embedding of multiple local cultures within a global economy. The poles of their rhetorical strategy are demarcated by poetry and politics; a "fundamental descriptive realism is what makes ethnographic techniques so attractive" to cultural critics across the disciplines. This cultural critique is "discovering diversity in what appears to be an ever more homogeneous world" (Marcus and Fischer 1986:133).

That such critiques have been around in anthropology for some time is dismissed within the rhetoric of discontinuity. Geertz, in spite of saying much the same thing about ethnographic representation and politics, is accused of producing a mere "afterthought" (Marcus and Fischer 1986:145). Dell Hymes's reader, *Reinventing Anthropology* (1969), is deemed irrelevant because it was directed toward a "temporarily radicalized" academic audience in the 1960s and was "immoderate and ungrounded in practice" (Marcus and Fischer 1986:34–35)—a startling claim in that most of the experimentalists were part of the intended audience. Intellectual genealogies may be chosen (and others rejected) to highlight innovation rather than to provide accurate historicist critique.

The Rhetoric of Normal Science

The paradigm statements of 1986 inspired a routinization of the rhetoric of postmodernist anthropology, a normal science in the terminology of Kuhn (1962). A few examples will suffice:

The potential chaos of alternative styles of ethnographic representation is typologized by John Van Maanen, not an anthropologist but a sociologist in a management department, in an explicit effort to theorize the expansion of attention to voice in writings by ethnographers, regardless of discipline. Traditional ethnographies are "realist tales." "Confessional tales" demystify the process of fieldwork and rectify some of the "most embarrassing" of realist conventions (Van Maanen 1988:73). Although the confessions respond to postmodernist revisionisms, they are less valued and tend to be published subsequent to realistic efforts by the same ethnographers (Van Maanen 1988:81). "Impressionist tales," "the backstage talk of fieldwork," are usually not published at all (Van Maanen 1988:96); they depict the experiential chaos suppressed in conventional genres of ethnographic reportage. The rhetoric of discontinuity and establishment opposition is adopted despite the mainstream textbook character of the volume. Van Maanen implies that anthropologists still haven't figured out how to produce truly impressionist, that is, postmodern, ethnographies; his third alternative, the dialogic, is almost entirely programmatic.

Paul Atkinson (1990), in contrast, emphasizes the continuity of revitalized ethnography with the long established symbolic interactionism of Chicago sociology, which adopted the participant-observation fieldwork methodology of anthropology, applying it to subcultures and communities in the city of Chicago, defined as a convenient laboratory for the social sciences (see Murray 1986). Modernist anthropology is explored as a baseline for postmodernist innovation in Marc Manganaro's edited collection (1990); innovations build on continuous research traditions. The same year, Roger Sanjek edited a volume that explored the origins of ethnographic production in field notes, moving the rhetorical constitution of ethnographic writing one step further back. These three sophisticated historicist attempts to fill in the rhetoric of the 1986 paradigm statements invite more than the original in-group to identify with the new directions.

Five years after *Writing Culture,* the School of American Research in Santa Fe sponsored another conference to update the insights of 1986. Richard Fox's *Recapturing Anthropology: Working in the Present* steers a careful course "between taking the critique of representation seriously but at the same time salvaging the role anthropology can play in providing an understanding of other cultures" (Lindahl 1999:284). Contributors focused on situating the anthropologist in relation to academia rather than to ethnographic subjects and on the uses of ethnographic representation in the political arena of the anthropologist's world. Writing is an ethical as well as a political enterprise because its reception can never be innocent. For example, Lila Abu-Lughod (in Fox 1991:140) highlights the uncomfortable positioning of the non-Western anthropologist who crosses insider-outsider boundaries. The inevitable displacement disrupts the seamless narrative of cross-cultural communication and questions the very legitimacy of anthropology itself (see Said 1978).

Feminist scholars have attacked *Writing Culture* for its inadequate attention to the politics of representation. *Women Writing Culture,* edited by Ruth Behar and Deborah Gordon in 1995, directly addresses the omission of feminist concerns from the 1986 project, focusing on the problem of multiple voices, both those of anthropologists and of their ethnographic subjects, repressed by conventional representational genres. Michaela di Leonardo (ed. 1991) argues that postmodernist decentering of the self still disenfranchises women by removing the ground for objective analysis of their structural marginalization. Like the contributors to Fox's volume, she wants to remove any excuse for avoiding identity politics.

Loosening the conventions of ethnographic representation has even affected writing on the history of anthropology. George Stocking's (1991) "antihistory" of British social anthropology speculates about the uncompleted works of four major figures. Imagining the roots of scholarly impasse is a peculiarly postmodernist preoccupation, unsurprising considering Stocking's Chicago professorship and the close association of the core group with the University of Chicago. The interpretive historicism Stocking (1968) defined three decades ago now reasons "against the grain," merging history with theory in a new relativization of representation. Despite the apparent success of the strategy, such a position may concede too much to fashion and rhetoric in its effort to create an audience for the history of anthropology alongside the critique of ethnographic representation, writing, and rhetoric. As in the case of ethnographic representation, there is, I believe, something out there in the disciplinary past that retains its own context and internal integrity.

Interdisciplinary Misreadings of Anthropology

Lamentably, interdisciplinary postmodernists have given short shrift to the complexity of anthropological engagements with the shifting intersections of relativism, realism, and ethnographic representation. Many appear to have read only one book, *Writing Culture,* and one theoretician, Clifford Geertz. The stereotype suggests that rhetorical techniques of representation borrowed from literary criticism make it impossible to distinguish an ethnography from a novel. Because there can be no single authoritative representation, critics outside the discipline often assume representation to be arbitrary. Geertz, Clifford, Marcus, and so forth make no such simple claim, although their ethnographic authority is certainly emergent rather than static and monologic. Other internal critics modify their skepticism, albeit with ambivalence and internal contradiction. Why, then, are the self-identified postmodernists in anthropology systematically misread?

The discourse initiated in *Writing Culture* is directed largely to an audience of North American anthropologists. Insofar as the contributors intended to speak to a wider interdisciplinary audience, they were careless in specifying disciplinary assumptions, both methodological and epistemological, that are far from self-evident outside this essentially Americanist shared framework. Literary critics, historians, psychoanalysts, philosophers, and such are not trained in cross-cultural analysis and participant-observation fieldwork. Consequently, they panic when confronted with the shifting standpoints that are commonplace tools of the trade among cultural anthropologists. Every additional complexity recorded causes certainty to recede into a morass of unexplained and perhaps ultimately inexplicable variability and lack of epistemological groundedness, creating the very anxiety that inspires many critics to fear the nihilistic potentials of skeptical postmodernism.

At precisely this point, I would argue (following Geertz) that anthropology offers a unique approach to the impasse of the interdisciplinary discourse. Anthropologists are rarely subject to premature panic attacks. Coping with ambiguity and cognitive dissonance is what we do for a living. We go to the field because what we find there is profoundly unimaginable from the armchair. The thought experiments of philosophers or the suspension of disbelief of readers of fiction cannot approach the heady sensation of learning something one could never have dreamed into being by introspection. Postmodernists in other disciplines are far more constrained in what they can imagine. They turn to anthropology seeking powers of representation otherwise unimaginable within the Western *episteme*. They want us to have tidy answers to fit unproblematically into their own discourses; our answers, to their dismay, are often hedged with the contingencies of our ethnographic intuitions and qualified, highly contextualized, generalizations.

Yet at the very moment when anthropologists are situated to resolve interdisciplinary postmodernist quandaries, whether intentionally or not, anthropologists are communicating that they have no more to offer than a novelist or a philosopher of language. Anthropologists who pursue postmodernist experiments first must reclaim their own expertise to hold conversations among a diversity of alternative "forms of life." Contemporary anthropology has rejected, rightly in my view, its traditional role of purveyor of the exotic in favor of a triangulation of worldviews, from the largest possible number of angles; or, to shift sensory modalities, stereoscopic vision allows multiple voices to blend into a larger view than any one alone could provide. The method is consistent with many of the tenets of interdisciplinary postmodernism, although the challenge still remains to teach nonanthropologists what we have known all along because we enter into conversations across cultural boundaries.

A few examples of readings and misreadings will illustrate the need for more accurate and sanguine articulation of the anthropological method and its potentials, one in which critical reflexivity is a strength rather than a cop-out from the fundamental principles of social science.

Art historian Marianna Torgovnick (1990) treats material objects, literary productions, and ethnographies in parallel terms to critique the moral and aesthetic valence of the concept of the primitive in Western culture. The ethnographic claim to realism, albeit situated in multiple perspectives, is never addressed, presumably because she has no stake in it. Yet her argument is more accessible to an interdisciplinary audience than Clifford's (1988), which is framed for an anthropological audience.

Pauline Rosenau (1992), a North American political scientist with limited patience for postmodernism in the social sciences, values the role of anthropology within the interdisciplinary discourse because she thinks it protects "local primitive cultures" from Western hegemony (Rosenau 1992:7), whether or not it contributes to the resolution of questions of representation. She rejects skeptical postmodernism (what Murray [personal communication] calls "scorched earth postmodernism") in favor of a more "affirmative" version consonant with the American pragmatist optimism of John Dewey and Will James; the social sciences can make a difference in the world. Her modernist postmodernism proposes to revitalize the social sciences without conceding conventional realist assumptions. So far, the anthropology is in sympathy.

Rosenau's reading of postmodernism in anthropology, however, excludes the discipline from her affirmation on the basis of Clifford's challenge of ethnographic authority (Rosenau 1992:27) (aligned largely with what she defines as Continental skepticism). Experimental ethnographies allow postmodern readers to become anthropologists, to join "in on the dialogue between ethnographer and subject," to "interact directly with exotica itself" (Rosenau 1992:27) But the putative "crisis" of representation remains her preoccupation: "Post-modern anthropologists disclaim all modern anthropological truth and theory. Truth, in anthropology, considered mere invention, is constantly being reinvented. Post-modernists contend that modernist anthropology creates the very phenomena it seeks to study. . . . All that can be offered . . . is narrative, fragmented fantasies, one person's stories. Anthropology is, in this view, 'persuasive fiction'" (Rosenau 1992:40, 87–88). This inaccurate attribution marginalizes anthropology, eroding its claim to represent realities across cultures.

For Rosenau, anthropology can be valid only insofar as it produces "accurate description" that corresponds to the external world. The "internal turmoil" of "post-modern anti-representational views . . . implies a clear relinquishing of professional authority" (Rosenau 1992:106). Anthropology is trivialized by her characterization of a retreat to postmodernist "storytelling," presented to more conventional colleagues as merely literary (Rosenau 1992:107). Anthropological modernism cannot be trusted either, because it has created the phenomena it studies. Inheriting the phenomena created by modernism, postmodernism disowns its own genealogy in a refusal of responsibility for ethnographic practice (as well as for acknowledging historicist continuity). The impasse is resolvable by a reflexive historicism familiar to anthropologists but not considered by Rosenau.

Careful reading of debates internal to North American anthropology compels a more complex and optimistic reading. Many critics of traditional ethnographic authority are attempting to devise increasingly adequate representations that do not concede realism to relativism. They do so in continuity with the established realist tenets of Americanist anthropology as well as with qualitative methods more general to the social sciences. For example, Clifford (1997) contrasts the equally valid portrayals of aboriginal traditions in four Northwest Coast museums differing in size, groundedness in local cultures, and intended audiences. In valorizing the interactiveness of such museum traditions with various audiences, Clifford seems to take Canadian multiculturalism as commensurate with social cohesion; Canada perhaps becomes his ethnographic "other."

The history, philosophy, and praxis of ethnography are in urgent need of explication to interdisciplinary audiences. Whether or not it is read correctly, there *is* a postmodernist anthropology in North America; it is becoming more respectable, at least in many circles. The rhetoric of discontinuity succeeded in calling attention to new perspectives in the initial stages of revisionism. But it is now giving way to a more inclusive normalization of the postmodernist reformulations, which potentially recovers previously rejected continuities. As participation increases, radical skepticism is increasingly subsumed within a rhetoric of continuity and a return to realism alongside relativism. The bridges, I suggest, are Americanist in more than merely rhetorical ways. The internal critical debate now underway promises to strengthen North American anthropology's input to the larger interdisciplinary discourse around postmodernism.

• • •

In sum, several strands of contemporary interpretive theory draw on Americanist roots and lead North American anthropologists into interdisciplinary discourses that engage the most fundamental assumptions of cross-cultural inquiry. Claude Lévi-Strauss's unique amalgam of French, British, and Americanist traditions drew on American Indian data and Boasian perspectives in the study of culture from a modernist structuralist position. Clifford Geertz fine-tuned the argument for contingent and contextualized interpretation through "thick description" based on cross-cultural fieldwork; although he did not work with Native North Americans, his position resonates with Americanist standpoints. Among his contemporaries, Victor Turner, Marshall Sahlins,

David Schneider, Ward Goodenough, and Anthony F. C. Wallace are all implicated in similar interpretivist inquiries. Despite the rhetoric of discontinuity
employed by George Marcus, James Clifford, and others, the engagement of interpretivism with postmodernism reveals deep and abiding roots in the Americanist tradition. The Americanist genealogies remain, for the most part, invisible, below the surface of awareness.

MARGARET MEAD

CHAPTER 9

Reconstructing the Metanarrative of Anthropology

The image of anthropology, both in the academy and in the public sphere, leaves much to be desired for those who think our disciplinary past has contributed positively to the making of today's world and that we have developed distinctive intellectual resources to engage the future. From within anthropology as I know it, the perspectives highlighted in this chapter seem so obvious as scarcely to need mention; anthropologists are accustomed to internal critique. Lamentably, however, what may be dead horses within Americanist anthropology appear to thrive elsewhere. Despite the urgency of reconstructing our heritage, few of our own number have ceded the value of the anthropological project (although many are understood by interdisciplinary audiences to have done so).

Anthropologists must accept considerable culpability for this misrepresentation in public discourse. Most of us believe that there is much to rehabilitate, and that it has been there all the time. Having examined some of the seminal ideas that have dominated the "Boasian century" (Boddy and Lambek 1997) with a view to revitalizing them, we have documented what anthropologists have actually been up to and attempted to reclaim continuities within our own history. Whether or not the label "anthropology" continues to be useful—and some have argued that it is not—the epistemological and moral position implicit in Americanist anthropology is urgently needed in our contemporary world. Let us now revisit the simplistic history of anthropology that we have inherited and enliven it with the energy and commitment of contemporary work.

Deconstructing "Us" and "Them"

Despite decades of anthropological fieldwork in modern, urban, complex societies, and communities, other social science colleagues are still wont to stereotype our discipline in terms of the so-called primitive. Our protestations to be more than purveyors of the exotic have gone largely unattended. No longer are anthropologists the unchallenged experts on weird corners of the globe; colleagues in sociology, economics, political science, history, and cross-cultural psychology now also visit the isolated communities that once fell within our exclusive purview, resulting in considerable attenuation of our previous disciplinary authority. While other disciplines have modified their intellectual programs, anthropology continues to be dismissed as frozen in its colonial and evolutionary past. The challenge to anthropological legitimacy has produced a variety of internal responses.

First, anthropologists claim to study both the formerly primitive and the complex in a different way from their colleagues in other disciplines. Participant-observation, as a method based on face-to-face interaction, developed out of fieldwork in small-scale societies. Cultural relativism, at least in its weak form of respect for alternative lifeways as a prelude to comparison and evaluation, is taken for granted by most practicing anthropologists, as a nonnegotiable ground of professional socialization. "Extreme cases" need not, however, go unremarked (Wolf 1999 after Benedict 1934b); Kwakiutl economic wastefulness, Aztec sacrifice, and Nazi genocide all raise questions of sustainability and quality of life. Our traditional concept of culture broadens the context for understanding the range of human behaviors and beliefs.

Second, the personal engagement of anthropologists in their fieldwork often leads them to become advocates and translators for individuals and communities where they work. Although remaining members of Western society, they also identify with the interests and perspectives of those they come to know elsewhere—in purported contrast to academics from other disciplines, politicians, missionaries, and the countless representatives of the power structure within which both anthropologists and their subjects/consultants necessarily operate. In practice, of course, anthropologists are co-opted, sometimes without their awareness, to factions within larger communities, a process that is too often elided in ethnographic accounts.

Contemporary political constraints of anti-intellectualism, corporatism, and economic retrenchment have placed escalating degrees of stress on a mature professional generation with political and social attitudes formed in the 1960s in a climate of apparently inexhaustible academic expansion and social optimism. Our views of the "other" and of the responsibility of mainstream culture toward them are not always popular when we expose "the face of power within the masks of cultural difference" (di Leonardo 1998, cover blurb).

Use of the term "primitive" without qualification is no longer acceptable, in or out of anthropology. Ironically, although this change arose in great part from the lessons Boasian anthropology brought to North American public culture, we who led the way are now the only ones thought to retain the patronizing asymmetry of primitivism. The critical problematic, then, is to disentangle the now distasteful, indeed immoral, concept of "the primitive" from the historical roots that produced anthropology as a discipline. In a potentially radical challenge to anthropological legitimacy, British social anthropologist Adam Kuper in *The Invention of Primitive Society* (1988) argues that the whole notion of "the primitive" was a category error, an unacknowledged carry-over into functional-structuralism of the evolutionary paradigm that buttressed and rationalized colonialism. Kuper appears remarkably unperturbed by this conclusion; moreover, his historical analysis proposes no alternative program for an anthropology without the illusory "primitive." But surely deconstruction of the canonical conceptual apparatus of a professional discipline has consequences in the real (or at least the academic) world! We must somehow reflexively reconstitute forms of alterity appropriate to a contemporary global community that, like anthropology itself, remains contaminated by inequities arising from our suspect imperialist heritage (e.g., Anderson 1983; Appadurai 1996; Asad 1973; Gupta and Ferguson 1997; Said 1978, 1993). Kuper's persuasive rereading of British social anthropology goads anthropologists, including Americanists, into reconsidering the ethical and epistemological basis of contemporary praxis in light of disciplinary history. Our disciplinary "dark ages" were a way station to elsewhere, on a journey still in process.

One buzzword of disciplinary reflexivity is "rethinking," for example, of anthropology (Leach 1961) or of psychological anthropology (Bock 1980). By implication anthropology was thought through in the first place and is not simply a haphazard product of random external influences; anthropologists have exercised agency all along. Another favored metaphor for internal critique is "re-invention" (Hymes 1969; Kuper 1988); in practice, "invention" has produced more radical critique than has "thinking."

There have been a few calls to ground contemporary theoretical debate in disciplinary history (Stocking 1968; Darnell 1974 ed., 1977b, 1982b), lest we carry with us the conceptual muddles of the past. Bob Scholte noted presciently: "Neither the possibility nor the desirability of a transcendent, purely scientific anthropology can or should be taken for granted. We must first subject anthropological thought itself to ethnographic description and ethnological understanding" (Scholte 1969:437). The professional socialization of individual anthropologists has traditionally established generational continuity through articulation to existing traditions as embodied by mentors and colleagues. Professional gossip has had its part in personalizing the history of anthropology; science operates through a network of peers who know one another as well as through its theories, methods, and institutional contexts. The present rhetoric of discontinuity threatens to eclipse such socialization (see Lewis 1999).

A student's question in a history of anthropology seminar some years back led me to formulate a critical convergence of anthropological effort to dissolve, or at least to reorient, our inherited dichotomy between "us" and "them." Such a critique has proceeded relatively independently from at least three directions:

1 / Anthropologists study "our society," either past or present, using techniques developed in the study of other societies; we bring the exotic home (di Leonardo 1998).

2 / Anthropology in neocolonial national traditions involves the study of what used to be called "primitive" societies by their own members (and in the course of studying themselves, they also sometimes study "us").

3 / Postmodern reflexive anthropology blurs the boundaries between "us" and "them," ideally creating dialogic interactions that allow "them" to help "us" understand both "them" and ourselves.

In each of these three lines of contemporary research, something remains that practitioners, historians, and theoreticians alike might call (and want to call) anthropology. The variety of intellectual traditions worrying about this issue strongly suggests that the discipline is responding to a widely and consciously acknowledged hiatus between the traditional conceptual apparatus of anthropology and the altered conditions of its current praxis. This convergence outside the traditional dichotomy between "the West and the Rest" raises some hope that "we" and "they" may meet without coercion as coevals (Fabian 1983).

1 / The Study of "Our Society"

Anthropologists have never restricted themselves to studying exclusively the "primitive," small-scale, or preliterate. In practice, however, stereotypical prim-

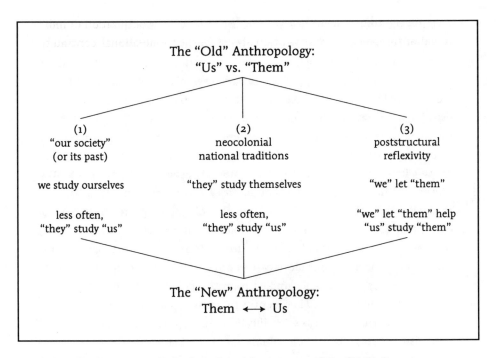

Figure 3. Changing Anthropological Standpoints toward the "Other"

itiveness has proved surprisingly difficult to separate from an equally stereo-typed modernism or civilization. Urban research in "traditional" field sites, of which Redfield's (1930, 1934, 1941, 1950) continuum of acculturation across four Mayan communities provides an early exemplar, problematized the dis-creteness of folk, peasant, and urban cultures. "Urban" communities certainly exist outside what we loosely call "our society." Eric Wolf (1982) argued that a global network of trade and contact encompasses all human communities, not just those with written histories. "We" have no monopoly on urbanity or mo-dernity. Both "we" and "they" are contemporary peoples.

The fuzziness of community boundaries has long preoccupied urban an-thropologists. Participant-observation methodology entails a relatively bound-ed unit of face-to-face interaction. Urban social and ethnic communities, however, often lack spatial boundaries for their interaction with cultural in-siders and outsiders. Ethnic identity has been problematized even for the kinds of communities traditionally studied by anthropologists. Michael Moerman (1965), for example, defined Lué identity in terms of whatever the Lués say it is, a politically correct as well as scientifically accurate progression beyond the old positivisms of geographic boundednesses.

In practice face-to-face interaction has successfully identified determinate boundaries in complex field sites even when anthropologists move among multiple and overlapping communities (e.g., Tsing 1993). "Anthropological lo-cations" can be anywhere (Gupta and Ferguson 1997). Our "research imagi-nary" has room for "multi-sited ethnography" that problematizes space as community, time as history, and voice as structure (Marcus 1998:10 ff.). Mar-cus worries that marginalization of conventional exotic fieldwork has caused anthropology to lose its sense of a central, shared discourse about its own iden-tity but concludes that "Nothing has as yet displaced ethnography" (Marcus 1998:249, 231). The centrality of ethnography could be read easily through the history of anthropology, although Marcus does not make this move.

Although at first glance these difficulties appear primarily methodological, they have generated dramatic theoretical reconsideration. Urban anthropol-ogy, in at least some of its manifestations, has self-consciously rejected the simple stereoscopy of studying a seamless "other." Moreover, anthropologists are no longer homogeneous, although the WASP ethnic identity has too long stereotypically been assumed to characterize an increasingly diverse North American society.

The participant-observation method has proved far more robust than the "primitive." Habits of cultural relativism acquired in studying more diverse "others" are sufficiently embedded in the psychic integration of anthropologists to carry over to the study of the anthropologist's own society. Native intuition potentially supplements or replaces cultural contrast as a way of sensitizing the observer to the nature of groups and communities. This is fortunate, since we could hardly imagine a social science without the possibility of transcending the standpoint of membership in one's own social group. Social scientists do study, and should study, societies beyond their own.

Sociologist and symbolic interactionist Erving Goffman used to hang around with anthropologists, haranguing the graduate students in ethnography of communication at Penn that we could not, on the basis of cross-cultural fieldwork, produce insights as sophisticated as those he derived from studying his own society by member intuition. Although most of us had not yet done our own fieldwork, the ethos we later brought to it could be read as a desire to prove Goffman wrong (which may well have been what he intended all along); the papers in Bauman and Sherzer (1974) presented detailed evidence about "ways of speaking" from cultures other than those of the investigator's socialization.

Goffman was not, in any simple sense, studying his own society. He was neither homosexual, mentally ill, nor a compulsive gambler; yet his descriptions of these subgroups of "our society" are legitimately acknowledged as foundational in several disciplines, including anthropology (Winkin 1988). Reduced to absurdity, the privileged insight from native intuition (also shared by Chomskian linguistics) implies that introspection rather than social investigation is the preferred method of analysis. Few anthropologists would go so far.

Although Goffman was fond of claiming that anthropology and sociology were virtually inseparable at Chicago in his day, potential convergences of method and theory produced little documentable overlap of intellectual or social networks (Murray 1986; Darnell 1990a). Nonetheless, Chicago School sociologists cited ethnographic data from so-called primitive societies and carried out "fieldwork" in the city of Chicago, modeled as a naturally occurring laboratory of social relations. Participant-observation methods were shared with anthropology, albeit without expectation that the investigator be an outsider to the community studied. For example, W. I. Thomas was intrigued by cross-cultural comparisons but dismayed by the impressionistic methods of the anthropologists (Stephen Murray, personal communication).

Moreover, the alterity that forged anthropology out of the Age of Discovery involved a fundamental blurring of the self-other distinction (Hodgen 1964). John Rowe (1965) argued persuasively that spatial or geographical expansion of European consciousness was paralleled by enhanced temporal perspective resulting from the rediscovery of classical manuscripts in Renaissance Italy, an "othering" of Europe's view of itself. Anthropology arose from this modern consciousness. In a similar mélange of temporal difference and spatial continuity, mid-nineteenth-century German Romanticism welded cultural and linguistic relativity with comparative folklore and dialectology to legitimize nascent nationalism (Bunzl 1996).

"They," the European peasant "folk," were an earlier stage of "us," the modern citizens of European nation-states. As a by-product of rationalizing modern sociopolitical units, the continuity of folk and urban effaced the dichotomy between "primitive" and "civilized." Although "the folk" might be naive and backward, as well as pure and original, they were never "primitive" in quite the old evolutionary sense of absolute alterity. These folks had the capacity to reach the pinnacle of civilization, demonstrated by the present status of their descendants. Europe imagined itself as a community with a long past (Anderson 1983). This concept of "the folk" remained more evolutionary than relativist: "They" are inevitably engulfed and superseded by modernity. Franz Boas imported much of this conceptual package to North American anthropology (Stocking 1996).

Evolutionary associations of the inferiority of cultural difference became less tenable when "they" were continuous with and only partially distinguishable from "us." The psychic unity of mankind could be taken for granted when the mankind in question was the ancestor of the investigator as well as the intended audience for the ethnographic report. The German tradition, however, still does not link such folklore studies with the more exotic subject matter of an ethnology closely tied to the fortunes of colonial empire ("anthropology" conventionally refers only to what North America calls "physical anthropology"). Although considerable ethnographic work was done in Germany's African colonies, folklore continued to be foregrounded relative to ethnology. (The processual dynamic of this colonial ethos also applies to the internal colonialism affecting the aboriginal peoples of North America.)

Evolutionary, diffusionist, functionalist, and structuralist models uniformly took for granted that the culturally diverse subjects of study were not members of "our society." Yet Boas never suggested that differences of method were required when moving from the study of so-called primitive societies to folk traditions within Western society; his methodological strictures (e.g., Boas 1887) were reserved for distinguishing the human and natural sciences. Although he did not himself study Western folklore, Boas practiced what he preached: During his editorship of the early *Journal of American Folklore,* papers were fairly evenly divided between literary studies of Anglo-American (including Afro-American or Franco-Canadian) and American Indian folklore.

In a sophisticated contemporary exploration of the inextricability of folklore and ethnology, Michael Herzfeld (1987) interweaves the stories of Greek thought in the historical emergence of the West, Greek national identity in the modern world, the anthropological study of Greece by outsiders, and the possibility of an anthropology constituted from within Greece itself. Despite labyrinthine style and absence of resolution among his competing narratives, Herzfeld reveals the complexity of situated perspective. The clear opposition of "us" and "them" dissolves in its complementary construction by modern Greeks, other Europeans, and (non-Greek) professional anthropologists.

In sum, there is an honorable tradition in which the study of the historic past of the investigator's own culture proceeds with methods partially derived from ethnology, thereby reconstituting a well-established link between ethnographic folklore and exotica.

2 / Neocolonial National Traditions in Anthropology

Increasing diversity in the demographic structure of anthropology also contributes to dissolving the dichotomy between "us" and "them." Despite occasional efforts at training nonmainstream anthropologists to study their own societies, few have moved beyond the status of glorified "informant." For a generation socialized to speak of "consultants" and "collaborators," however, the change should become more than cosmetic or euphemistic.

Anthropologists can document the ethnocentrism of the culture that produced anthropology with cross-cultural evidence. Ken Hale's collaboration with Albert Alvarez (Hale and Alvarez 1972) to analyze Papago grammar in Papago (now known as Tohono O'odham) provides a rare exemplar (appearing in a volume edited by the late Alfonso Ortiz, himself an anthropologist as well as a Tewa). English equivalents for Papago grammatical terms are hard to come by. This project is particularly courageous given the 1970s preoccupation of post-transformational grammar with universal constraints and its privileging of English as the analytic language of choice.

Around the globe contemporary anthropology is producing an increasing number of national traditions no longer subservient to the American, British, French, and German (or at a more general level of contrast, Anglo-American vs. Continental). Nationals now study groups that "conventional" anthropologists studied as "other"—the groups and their boundaries remain as they were but the position of the observer has shifted dramatically (Herzfeld 1987).

When I attended a conference on national traditions in anthropology sponsored by Wenner-Gren in 1968, the participants included representatives from a number of nation-states outside the core homelands historically constituting anthropology as a discipline (e.g., Italy, Greece, the former Soviet Union, Panama, India, China [represented by an American who had done fieldwork there], Japan, the Philippines). Most participants grounded their anthropological commitments in the tradition of the country where they received their training, usually Britain or the United States. The Scandinavian countries, however, retained ties to German museum-based diffusionist theory at least until after World War II. No one argued that indigenous national contributions to the definition and integration of anthropology were to be expected, that the peripheries could influence the center. It seemed reasonable then that study by an outsider was anthropology and study by an insider was sociology; "otherness" defined the anthropological position.

We have made substantial progress on this front. Adam Kuper's editorials in *Current Anthropology* around 1990 predicted the increasingly ethnonational and regionally diverse character of the discipline, despite growing global homogenization. So-called Third World countries, conventionally restricted to anthropological roles as objects for analysis, would increasingly appropriate analytic subject roles relative to cultural units within their own boundaries, responding to local interests independent of a theoretical center elsewhere. If only by sheer numbers, the relationship of anthropologist and people studied seemed likely to alter dramatically, whether the rhetoric of the realignment was one of continuity or of revolution.

In any case the dominant anthropological traditions of the Western worldview can no longer expect to remain the sole arbiters of what is anthropology or who are its proper subjects. To incorporate the findings of counterparts from less traditional or long-established centers of anthropological research into a shared mainstream remains the challenge of the postcolonial future.

3 / "Us," "Them," and Postmodernist Reflexivity

Contemporary interdisciplinary critique of the concept of culture has produced a third strand of dichotomous dissolution. There is something new here,
despite clear continuities, that is far more satisfying than the justifiably transcended dichotomy of "us" and "them," self and other. Perhaps the most
enduring contribution of these interrelated critiques is to challenge the reductionism of cherished metanarratives in conventional academic disciplines.
Meaning comes to be situated in particular contexts from which it cannot
be disentangled; the perceiving subject moves out of the center of meaning
construction. Experience is textual; a single context-free interpretation is impossible.

The inherent relativism of the postmodernist position, however, is unnerv-
ing to a commonsense, pragmatic approach to the world through positivist
science. Unsympathetic responses from established scholars have been exacerbated by the postmodernist rhetoric of discontinuity. For most people, relativism is not a comfortable intellectual position. Anthropologists, however, are
not most people. We are professionally trained to wind our minds around
someone else's way of structuring reality and to find the process intriguing
rather than threatening. Respect for ways of being different is deeply ingrained
in us (although the other side of this coin is the potential moral pitfall of con-
descension).

Anthropology's versions of postmodernism articulate with work, largely in
France, in disciplines as diverse as literary criticism, political science, philosophy, linguistics, and psychoanalysis. The turn to writing and representation
rather than participant-observation fieldwork as the problematic core of the
anthropological project has produced experimental ethnographies that worry
about the relation of ethnographer and subject. "Us" and "them" are ideally
separable only in terms of who is speaking at a given moment. The possibility,
if not certitude, of voice reversal remains (though all dialogic approaches raise
the question of why "they" would want to speak to "us" on "our" terms—as
well as whether the result can reasonably be considered dialogue).

Reflexivity is the key to postmodernist reexamination of the subject-object
relation inherent in fieldwork. It makes explicit the contextualized relationship of investigator and subject (rather than object) as source of information.
The reflexive investigator acknowledges her or his necessarily colored percep-
tion of what is going on; "data" are contingent, situational, and ideally negoti-

ated by all parties to cross-cultural interaction. Paul Rabinow's (1977) confessional ethnography, for example, illustrates the biographical character of his coming to know Moroccan society through several of its articulate individual members; critics, however, have charged that one learns more about Rabinow than about Morocco or Moroccans. Reflexivity coupled with dialogue (Van Maanen 1988) lends itself well to the life history method of getting at culture as experienced (e.g., Shostak 1981; Crapanzano 1980), the phenomenological relation of the individual to her or his culture that problematizes whether shared knowledge is an appropriate criterion for defining culture.

In addition to genre explorations of "narrative ethnography" (Tedlock 1992; Ridington 1988) and poetics (Brady 1991; Tedlock 1990), the literary side of the Americanist tradition has produced a virtual cottage industry of Native American autobiography as narrative genre, cultural voice, and counterpoint to traditional anthropological privileging of "our" voices over "theirs" (Swann and Krupat 1987; Swann 1992; Brumble 1988; Krupat 1989, 1992, 1996). Genre experiments by anthropologists and exploration of genres discovered elsewhere through fieldwork deliberately subvert traditional impositions of voice, which dominate individuals and cultures by the inscription of difference (see Bahktin 1981; Boon 1982). Despite myriad impositions of Western literary conventions on native speakers as narrators, Native aesthetic forms and the personal dignities of speakers have often been preserved. In ways not always obvious to collectors and editors of American Indian autobiographies, "the savage strikes back" (Lips 1937).

Despite considerable sympathy with the aims of reflexive postmodernist anthropology and its textual, interpretive goals, I am concerned by concomitant readings of our own disciplinary history and praxis. We must retain the possibility of finding one interpretation to be a good one and another execrable, epistemologically as well as anecdotally. Unfortunately, the textual approach encourages practitioners to read "against the grain" of the historically constituted intentionality of actors, from whichever side of the cultural fence. Synchronically, postmodernist anthropologists consider situated perspectives and contexts of action. But as historians of science, the same thinkers are apparently willing, in principle as well as in practice, to read in terms of contemporary concerns without distinguishing the two standpoints. Historicism and presentism may be sides of the same coin, but there remains a methodological necessity of distinguishing them at any given moment.

Cross-citation has been surprisingly rare between postmodernist critique of the discipline and work in genre and poetics arising from the Americanist tradition. Although dialogics and impressionism potentially resolve the excesses of disciplinary confession that overwhelm the cultures and individuals described, this literature fails to cite Dennis Tedlock's cogent linking of dialogue to the dialectics of being in the field and trying not to appropriate the voices of conversational partners in other cultures. Tedlock (1983) and Hymes (1981), in related projects, explore ways to empower voices traditionally rendered mute by our disciplinary habit of speaking for "them" to our own theoretical issues. Boasian use of texts and focus on language provide ample models for Native speaker articulation of *Lebenswelt* and *Weltanschauung* as essential to the definition of culture itself.

. . .

What is left of anthropology postdissolution? "They" are out there somewhere, in something we assume to be a real world, albeit known to us only through particular situated positions, and "we" can learn from and with as well as about "them," even returning to convey something of our experience to fellow members of "our" society who haven't been there. On the question of the real world, ethnographic experience suggests that, despite the subjectivity of the relationship between "informant(s)" and fieldworker(s), interpretations can be tested against other ethnographic experience; by judicious use of ethnographic intuition, we can aspire to more accurate, elegant, and complex interpretations. Such an anthropology is not merely literary criticism. It distances itself from the defeatism about the possibility of knowledge that sometimes seems inherent in the postmodernist position. In writing fiction there is no reality check. Authorial intention is irresolvable because of hesitation to privilege the author's often post hoc interpretation over others' interpretations.

More voices are heard in postmodernist ethnographies. Their cacophony provides fodder for multiple perspectives that are neither equal, interchangeable, mutually reducible, nor illegitimate. The complexity of polyphony or heteroglossia (Bahktin 1981) facilitates construction of contextualized interactive discourse in a world outside the observer (although no observer's version can be finally privileged without distortion of alternative voices). However chaotic a surface model for cross-cultural method and theory, heteroglossia is an effective model for the practical business of doing anthropology, based on texts (written or oral) from particular individuals under particular cultural circumstances.

When, in the manner of Lévi-Strauss in the Amazon, we have inscribed and made intelligible the commonsense reality of the exotic, we discover that "they" are very little different from ourselves. In the immortal words of Pogo, "We have met the enemy and he is us." Unlike Lévi-Strauss, I conclude that the exotic made comprehensible is more rather than less interesting, producing valued diversity rather than blandly egalitarian plurality, reflexive contextualization rather than sterile and narrowly judgmental humanism, interpretive verisimilitude rather than the absolutes of positivist science.

Anthropology has, at least in the realm of theory, dispensed with its albatross dichotomy, releasing its potential to move beyond stereotypic and discriminatory evaluation of very real and deep-lying cultural difference. In Ursula Le Guin's *The Lathe of Heaven* (1971a), the dreaming-into-reality of a world without racial conflict creates a place in which everyone is gray—it is an ugly, boring, and inhumane world. Anthropology, like the best science fiction, celebrates cultural difference as productive tension between the culture-specific and the universally human.

No human society, including the one in which anthropology has emerged and flourished, has attained "equality." Nonetheless, it is widely acknowledged as a right in the public sphere and a condition of "genuine" interaction in the private domain. Despite lip service to the political dimension of contemporary global society, in practice postmodernist anthropologists have concentrated almost exclusively on microanalysis of the private and interactional dimensions of reflexive fieldwork.

Politics, however, occurs in a public arena, with difference as the basis for redressive action. Historically, anthropologists have been supporters of struggles for identity and autonomy of peoples with whom they have worked. To argue that "they" are identical with "us" is certainly progress for the privileged (and by definition unmarked) mainstream white male anthropologists, who still constitute the majority of our profession. Although undermining the grounds of difference may assuage the conscience of the privileged, at the same time it inadvertently undermines identity politics and its claim to the mainstream sympathy on which much of contemporary Third and Fourth World politics rests. Having dissolved the "us" vs. "them" dichotomy, then, we must reconstitute it, without the traditional connotations of the "primitive," to challenge the conditions of power that produced the dichotomy in the first place and continue to sustain it.

Race and Racism: From Biology to Culture

There are several directions from which to rethink the place of the scientific study of race (as opposed to "scientific racism") in the moral grounding of disciplinary practice. The history of anthropology provides some clues as to how the ideas about race and culture that we now take to be self-evident came to be packaged together. I have not suddenly metamorphosed into a physical anthropologist. Rather, I want to argue that the physical anthropology of Franz Boas has had its continuous impact, not so much on the subdiscipline that studies the biological diversity of human populations as on the central place of race and racism in Boas's theory of culture.

In a recent special issue of the *American Anthropologist* devoted to "Race and Racism," Faye Harrison's editorial introduction included key words dissolving the traditional boundaries between cultural and biological anthropology: "race, racism, holistic analysis of race, interdisciplinary dialogue, public awareness" (Harrison 1999:609). Race has long constituted the public face of North American anthropology. In the same issue, Eugenia Shanklin descries the "profession of the color-blind," arguing that the anthropological commitment to tolerance has been appropriated into an extreme right agenda denying the existence of race and therefore of discrimination in order to justify cutting social benefits. The victim is to blame for her or his own plight. Boas provides Shanklin with the model for a more humane intervention into public discourse: "Boas trained his students to renounce the scientific concepts of race that persisted, to ignore the folk concepts of race that existed, and to work toward an egalitarian ideal in society" (Shanklin 1999:670).

Boas's work in physical anthropology represents an anomaly within our collective view of the reorientation of Americanist anthropology in the early years of the twentieth century. Today we remember Boas's biological work, if at all, in terms of establishing the four-subdiscipline structure of North American anthropology: in ethnology the five-foot shelf of Kwakiutl ethnography ambivalently coauthored with George Hunt; in linguistics, the exhortation to produce grammar, dictionary, and texts for each of the continent's endangered languages. Boas may have included archaeology more because he thought it ought to be there than because archaeology before the Pecos classification in the late 1920s had much to offer to his overall interpretation of the history and psychology of the American Indian. His most lasting contribution to archaeology may well be his encouragement of Manuel Gamio in Mexico. Besides, archaeology was neatly sewn up in the crucial years between about 1880 and 1920 by the Bureau of American Ethnology and the Peabody Museum of Archaeology and Ethnology at Harvard. Boas had to forge his alliances elsewhere, and the subdiscipline of archaeology developed largely independently of his program at Columbia (Darnell 1998a).

Physical anthropology as we know it today in North America, had its roots in the same Harvard and Washington variants of Americanist anthropology. After the First World War it became far more specialized and "scientific" than Boas's version, carried out primarily before 1900. Aleš Hrdlička and Ernest Hooton did not do ethnology and linguistics in their spare time. Nor was their version of physical anthropology reliant on Boas's earlier work. Ironically, however, the new "synthetic theory" that emerged around the work of Sherwood Washburn in the 1950s has considerable resonance with Boas's thinking. This parallel, however, consists more of independent invention than of direct influence. Nonetheless, we may wonder what Boas thought he was up to and why he valued his own work as a physical anthropologist. When he collected his own papers into Race, Language and Culture, twenty of them dealt with race, followed by five linguistic, thirty-five ethnological, and five "miscellaneous" papers (Boas 1940:3–195).

In 1940, as in 1911 in the introduction to the Handbook of American Indian Languages, Boas argued that race, language, and culture must be identified as distinct variables and should be expected to produce contradictory classificatory conclusions. It was, therefore, a crucial point of methodology to study them, insofar as possible, independently—and to understand that classification always and necessarily arose from a standpoint rather than existed as an ultimate objective reality.

Race, being biologically grounded, was in some nontrivial sense prior to language and culture, which were by definition cross-culturally variable. But Boas's studies of race were more than a static baseline for ethnology. He began with an anthropometry now so thoroughly discredited that we have virtually forgotten that Boas's work on immigrant head form provided the crucial evidence for that discrediting (Darnell 1982a). The context in which Boas's critique of the racism of American physical anthropology and the more general eugenics movement were met with ridicule, recently explored by Lee Baker (1998), goes far to explain why Boas cared so much about this part of his oeuvre.

In his initial survey fieldwork on the Northwest Coast, Boas carried out traditional anthropometric studies, assuming the accuracy and therefore utility of such traits as head form for the reconstruction of aboriginal American history. This was the methodology expected by his sponsors, the Bureau of American Ethnology and the British Association for the Advancement of Science. When Boas began to worry about the validity of this kind of biological information, he turned in less conventionally ethnological (i.e., cross-cultural) directions for biological data. His first academic job, at Clark University, was in psychology rather than in anthropology; his boss, G. Stanley Hall, provided funding for scientific studies of local populations. Boas studied several human populations—Worcester, Massachusetts, school children; Jewish boys around puberty; and children of immigrants—and amassed an astonishing seventeen thousand cases. He discovered that head form could not be a stable characteristic of racial or ethnic populations because it could change in less than one generation. Differences began early, persisted through life, and were directly correlated with the mother's time in America before birth. Moreover, the American environment affected different ethnic groups differently. This was plasticity with a vengeance! If it could be explained at all, explanation would require a cultural valence.

Biological types, then, could not be reified without becoming meaningless. Variability could be approached only in statistical terms. Head form in this context became, for Boas in 1912, merely an "arbitrary type" that "does not prove the correctness of our subjective classification and the existence of the selected forms as types" (Boas 1940:73). For Boas observations could be organized according to "any fitting theory" but it was rarely possible to *prove* conclusively that any one was correct (i.e., nonarbitrary).

In one sense this conclusion is negative. We can't do what we used to do with racial type traits, and it isn't entirely clear what we ought to do instead. Such a reading, however, is overly facile, if not perverse. Boas's methodological rigor dissolved some of the distance between biology and culture. Because he studied heredity within particular family lines, the specific interaction of biology (i.e., race or ethnicity) and culture or environment could be captured in an interactive process but not clearly distinguished. Plasticity meant that biology, like culture, could change rapidly.

Boas never elaborated the implications of variability in cultural form within a population; he was not interested in the merely statistical regularities that were the fashion in physics as well as in biological anthropology. He did become virtually obsessed with sorting out the diverse effects of culture and biology. In this context it is no accident that he supported Margaret Mead's insistence on going to Samoa, encouraging her to find out if trauma at adolescence was universal, as G. Stanley Hall's classic psychological work on adolescence had assumed in the absence of cross-cultural evidence one way or the other. Boas formulated the question for resolution through anthropological field-work. Margaret Mead was neither a physical anthropologist nor a sociobiologist; *Coming of Age in Samoa: A Psychological Study of Youth for Western Civilization* (1928) emphasized the cultural patterning of female adolescence in Samoa. At the species level, environment was more important than heredity; her work confirmed Boas's conviction that human populations varied substantially in the forms of marking and channeling adolescence. The implicit model of culture is characteristic of both Mead and Kroeber, whose "The Superorganic" (1917) addressed the Boasian problem of nature vs. nurture from another angle. Kroeber wanted to carve out a niche for an autonomous anthropology organized around the concept of culture. The antithesis of culture was race. In contemporary terms Kroeber's "superorganic" reads like a caricature of human social order—reified, static, invariant, abstracted from individual agency. But cultural process is almost incidental to the actual paper. Kroeber was concerned rather with anthropology's relations to the natural sciences—organic and inorganic, biology vs. ethnology—arguing that culture was something different, worthy of study in its own right. By the time the paper became a "classic," Kroeber's point could be taken for granted, leaving exposed the inadequacies of his treatment of culture. Sapir and Goldenweiser spearheaded a relatively rare show of disagreement within Boasian ranks that has usually been read as a polarization, although I have argued in this study that it was more a question of emphasis. Culture and the individual were sides of the same coin, standpoints from which to proceed. Although Sapir's position would seem to lead to the study of individual variability within particular cultures, he did not pursue this line of argument. As the star linguist among the early Boasians, he alone evaded Boas's infamous seminar on statistics. So he lacked the quantitative model most of his cohort had for analyzing the variability of biological traits within human populations. Statistics didn't help with problems that interested Sapir; in any case Boas's statistics were increasingly outdated (Jonathan Marks, personal communication). Ironically, biological plasticity left culture rather than biology as the reified typological category. A similar "revolution" in cultural thinking never came together, although Sapir suggested the parameters it might follow and Wallace (1952, 1961) developed a viable methodology, one that was in good part quantitative.

In the 1920s Boasian anthropology shifted from trait-oriented survey ethnology to a more processual focus on what Mead and Benedict called culture and personality and Sapir called "the impact of culture on personality." Like Kroeber, Mead and Benedict treated culture in practice as applying equally to all of its members because of uniform socialization. Culture and personality could be expected to correlate in a one-to-one fashion.

This line of reasoning had the potential to be a real dead end, but instead the study of race reemerged within cultural anthropology as antiracism. By 1934, when Ruth Benedict's *Patterns of Culture* appeared, cultural relativism—understood as tolerance for alterity—had been established in the popular consciousness of North America. The exotic could be interesting, even titillating, as long as it was at a safe distance; closer to home, of course, judgments were made, for example, against Nazism. Mead's adolescent Samoan girls really were different from their North American counterparts. Culture, not biology, was the key, and North American society could remake itself under anthropological advisement.

Cultural relativism was *the* anthropological message of the interwar years. Other cultures were comprehensible in their own terms, had their own integrity and consistency, and were worthy of respect. The position was not quite as knee-jerk naive as it seems in retrospect. The lessons of the so-called primitive were brought home (although we would now want to raise issues of paternalism and appropriation of cultural knowledge that would have been incomprehensible in the earlier period). Samoan adolescents, or at least their culture, had solved a problem that still plagued then-contemporary North America. Ergo, "we" could learn from "them." The study of alternative cultural forms would amass a database for social engineering. This is a long way from the eugenics Boas applied to studying immigrant head form and policy recommendation to restrict United States immigration. Culture was now the focus, along with the human capacity to create "genuine" culture that fulfilled the needs of its individual members.

How would we know what kind of a culture to build? The Boasians answered that we study as many cultures as possible and adapt their strengths and weaknesses to our own circumstances. Anthropologists and those who take their findings seriously can see from more than one standpoint. They can thereby escape from the fetters of tradition, the blinders created by socialization, using what Whorf called "multilingual awareness."

Creating utopia in North America based on the lessons of Boasian ethnography evolved rapidly during the 1930s in response to political events. The anti-Semitism of Nazi Germany challenged the moral foundations of cultural relativism. It was impossible to be nonjudgmental of Hitler's version of German culture; Boasians, many of German origin, had been neutral or pacifist during World War I but could no longer separate their science from the distorted consequences of nationalism and racism. In the critique of racism, the cross-culturally sophisticated anthropologist was in a unique position to subordinate race to culture, to assess the relative civilizational capacities of diverse cultures, and to exhort fellow citizens toward the creation of a more tolerant world. North American society would lead this brave new world because it incorporated the widest possible variety of solutions to the human condition. Culture, after all, could be changed. Boas devoted the last years of his life to developing this position, as did Benedict (1940). Benedict, Mead, and Rhoda Métraux's "Culture at a Distance" project (typified by Benedict 1946; Mead and Métraux 1953) advised American politicians during and after World War II. Isolationism was breaking down, and anthropologists labored mightily to mitigate the perceived threat of cultural diversity run rampant. For the Boasians race turned out to be about biology, but *racism* became a question of culture.

Identity Politics and Standpoint Epistemology

Americanist anthropology has maintained a consistent and productive tension between antiracism and relativism, identity politics and equality of access to power and quality of life. Such tension, however, carries a responsibility to continuously interrogate the ethics and epistemology of anthropological praxis. I want to explore these issues in contemporary versions of the historicist pole of Boasian theory—how to interpret documents, oral as well as written, in collaboration with the peoples whose stories they tell. Massive evasions of responsibility for coevalness are deeply embedded in the disciplinary practices of history, ethnohistory, and anthropology. Whatever our abstract convictions, in practice anthropologists have not always been altruistic when the legitimacy of their premises is challenged. Withdrawal and denial are defense mechanisms firmly set in human psychodynamics—and academics are far from immune. Two moves, possibly contradictory, operate within our disciplines:

First, many historians are learning to talk to people—and to take seriously that what they are told is evidence of happenings in the past and how they affect the present and the future. That is to the good, although there is a long way to go. I recently served on a thesis committee in history where the candidate was instructed to go back and take out most of "that stuff about the Indians." The second draft lost the quality of immediacy, the juxtaposition of two versions, or histories, of the same events (cf. White 1973); their incommensurability went far to explain the poignancy of the outcome for the First Nations communities in question. I was impressed that the candidate found someone to introduce her to people in the contemporary community so she could talk to them about events well within the memories of living elders. This young historian, representing a new generation, clearly intends to enter into further conversations with real people. But I worry that, without reinforcement, her legitimate love of archival research will overwhelm the love of being-in-the-world, which must be the other face of historical scholarship, at least in anthropology.

The second trend I want to highlight is that many Native American communities have been for some time off-limits to non-Native researchers. Therefore, goes the logic in some circles, we had better all find something else to do, something where *our* standards of doing research can legitimately continue to predominate. Palestinian-born literary critic Edward Said, the most articulate spokesman against the appropriation of indigenous voices by outsider scholars, including anthropologists, led the challenge to comfortable assumptions of the universal validity of cross-cultural work and the right to represent the "other" in terms constructed by the powerful (Said 1978, 1993).

A challenge more personalized to the usefulness of our discipline is leveled by Lakota activist, lawyer, writer, and university professor Vine Deloria Jr., whose focus has shifted from long service as the self-appointed ethical conscience of anthropologists to baiting lawyers, apparently on the assumption that Americanist anthropologists have learned something in the interval since his initial critique in 1969.

Use of expressive forms characteristic of communities studied by outsider-students partially mitigates appropriative distortions. Deloria declined to comment on Ray DeMallie's paper evaluating the impact of *Custer Died for Your Sins* in an American Anthropological Association session in 1989, twenty years after its publication. DeMallie framed his paper with a narrative of his own experience meeting Ella Deloria and went on to explore the double vision implicit in her study of her own Lakota culture and that of the related Assiniboines; her correspondence with her mentor Franz Boas reflected her perplexity about the "thin-ness" of the latter, whether because of its own attenuation of cultural features or because of her own inability to interpret it from within, as she did for the Lakota. If the roles of anthropologist and subject of study are sometimes interchangeable, then conversation across the divide of "us" and "them" must be possible.

Vine Deloria's (1997) afterword to the published version of the session, titled "Anthros, Indians and Planetary Reality," implies that many "anthros" live in a world of science fiction fantasy. Common anthropological reactions to *Custer Died for Your Sins: An Indian Manifesto* were denial, withdrawal, and secrecy: "Each secluded conversation ended with the anthro confiding in me that he or she had always been an ethnohistorian anyway and did not much truck with anthros unless academic protocol demanded it" (Deloria 1997: 209). Presumably many such conversations took place in the corridors of anthropology meetings. (Deloria goes on to say some nice things about some of us.)

Ethnohistory should not be defined as cop-out ethnology or as a substitute for ethnography. Nor should it proceed in splendid isolation from the descendants of the folks whose histories are reflected, albeit through a glass darkly, in the documents we read in archives. Ray Fogelson, in his presidential address to the American Society for Ethnohistory, advocated an "ethno ethnohistory," "a kind of anthropological ethnohistory in which a central role would be given to intensive fieldwork, control of the native language, use of a native time perspective, and work with native documents" (Fogelson 1989:146). These are the proper challenges for contemporary anthropology.

Moreover, the places where a closet archivist can retreat from contact with the subjects of study are shrinking rapidly. It used to be possible to argue that archaeology had nothing to do with living people. Many anthropologists trained in the mid-twentieth century or earlier saw nothing wrong with practices that make us shudder today. Dead Indians, presumably, don't talk back. I particularly recall the meticulous documentation in the otherwise chaotic archive of a major North American museum (unnamed for obvious reasons), gloating over the ease of smuggling artifacts out of Mesoamerica.

When confronted by real people, the archaeologist of this ilk was inclined to say self-righteously: "You'll just have to trust me," that is, to assume that I am ethical and that I will decide what is best for you, weighing in the counterclaims of my vested interest in "science." It should be no surprise that Native American communities were unimpressed. Voluntary regulation didn't work.

So we now have a package of legislative control, which most contemporary archaeologists have come to take for granted. In order to continue working, archaeologists had to change quite dramatically. And there is a wonderful literature in archaeology these days that explores how to establish collaborations and common interests (e.g., Pinsky and Wylie 1989).

Perhaps it was easier to take these hesitant first steps in archaeology than in linguistics, ethnology, or ethnohistory. Stones and bones are visible, and ours is a property-oriented and materialistic culture. *Intellectual* property is a considerably more slippery issue. To be sure, ethnologists have learned that certain rituals are not to be made public. Many have decided to publicize (i.e., analyze) only those that are already in the public domain—as if it somehow didn't count, regardless of how surreptitiously details of these rituals got into the public domain in the first place.

I am told that in the Southwest, where many Native people study anthropology, books are regularly stolen or particularly offensive parts of them excised. Just because we *can* avoid meeting contemporary ritualists does not mean that we can continue with business as usual, at least not ethically. Taking an example from the literary side, in a recent volume on the interaction of Natives and academics over research and writing about American Indians, Paula Gunn Allen discusses her recurrent trauma in teaching Leslie Marmon Silko's novel *Ceremony* (1977). Her violent reaction to its speaking of things that titillate her New Age literature students is rendered further offensive because 1) Silko ought to know better, and 2) the ritual detail is not really necessary to the plot. Such detail presumably functions primarily to establish Silko's own credentials as a cultural insider, her authenticity as a teller of this particular story. So Gunn Allen and other contributors to the volume (Mihesuah 1998), all of them Native Americans, talk a lot about who is and is not an Indian. Mixed blood is an issue, but so is respectful conduct. And "fiction" doesn't fix the problem, anymore than material objects did. For most Native Americans, I suspect, the line between the social sciences and the humanities that is so significant for most anthropologists is blurred, to say the least.

What about linguistics? In the Vine Deloria session quoted above, Dell Hymes argued that linguists are often welcome when ethnologists are not because of their technical expertise. Those willing to let themselves be used for their expertise get along fine. I have no quarrel with this variant of Native American pragmatism, but I also think it's important to train at least some linguists who are also native speakers or at least community members. And, yes, we can work together. Linguists are close seconds to archaeologists in collaborative endeavors.

But there is a significant evasion inherent in this discourse too. We could retreat to analyzing already published texts, the archival strategy again. In Canada at least, copyright protection for intellectual property, as for texts recorded from oral tradition, applies *only* when those texts are written down. And anthropological authorship, until quite recently, resided by convention with the amanuensis. I would like to think that voluntary self-regulation is enough here. Certainly there are wonderful exemplars of rich collaboration, but persistent vigilance remains more appropriate than self-congratulation.

Non-Americanist anthropologists, not to speak of colleagues from other disciplines, too often take the critique of disciplinary praxis at face value. Americanists must be far worse, they assume, than anthropologists working elsewhere (preferably somewhere more safely distant from surveillance of scholarship by its subject-objects) or than sociologists, political scientists, economists, historians, and so on. There is something wrong with this picture. Ethnographers get the brunt of the critique precisely because we are the only ones who are out there talking to people. So they tell *us* what is on their minds. Whether or not it has been forced upon us, and I concede that it has been, at least in part, the contemporary Americanist discourse about fieldwork ethics confirms that the rest of our colleagues in the other social sciences still have their heads in the sand.

I suppose we all proceed in light of those occasional moments of insight when something clicks about the nature of our professional practices. Such moments become Kenneth Burke's "representative anecdotes." As teachers we are continually searching for stories that will convey to our students the nature of our cross-cultural encounters and more or less successful attempts to establish dialogue. Let me share one that isn't Americanist: I recently had occasion to chat with a young colleague who explained that his next project would be a life history of his "favorite informant." "Ummm," I mumbled. The young man then reported cheerily: "He's dead." We were interrupted before I could pursue what he intended to use for data. But another colleague, more linguistically inclined, reported to me that the same man had remarked—on seeing her tape recorder—"Oh, I took one of those to the field. I never turned it on." I have, to put it mildly, some problems with the methodology, if indeed we deem it sufficiently reflexive to qualify as methodology at all. I guess he thought it was safer to work with someone who couldn't talk back. Lamentably, I suspect that the attitudes that allow such cavalier dismissal of "the Native point of view" are more common than I at least would wish, perhaps even among Americanists. I am not trying to attack this hapless colleague personally. What appalled me was how matter-of-factly he failed to see the problem that bothered me. And we, whose teachings enable our successors, have let him get away with it.

In thirty years of teaching, I've managed, for the most part, to maintain my optimism. We are, and should be, in the business of putting ourselves out of business. I succeeded once: I taught Cree language and culture in collaboration with native speakers at the University of Alberta between 1970 and 1985; when Cree language later became the first course offered by the university's brand new School of Native Studies, it was taught by a Cree woman who had been a student of one of the women who first taught me Cree, a full circle in which I take some pride. And I've found other things to do; it still seems to me that there will be a need for anthropologists in my lifetime and beyond.

I usually respond to critiques of anthropology with personal examples from my own situated positions. Most Native people are far too polite to insist upon identifying the solecism: "Well, you're a known person, not an anthropologist, or at least not *only* an anthropologist." Personal relationships outgrow stereotypes. Less often I have been told, usually gently, that not all anthropologists take for granted the ethical and epistemological positions that, for me, define anthropology. I worry about lack of consensus on these matters more than I used to.

So what can anthropologists still do? My answers are necessarily personal and experientially based.

1 / We can enter into conversations that are not different in kind from those we have with our students, colleagues, friends, and families (categories that presumably overlap for all of us). Even if we don't like what we hear, we can try to extend and enrich the conversations.

2 / Insofar as we have useful expertise, we can offer it, without placing conditions on its use. We should neither offer unsolicited advice nor set conditions, either on friendship or on more formal, institutionalized interactions.

For me these interactions have most often been in the private domain: family violence, child custody, alcohol abuse, and avoidance of well-meaning but ethnocentric social workers, with whom confrontations have abounded between many Native communities and individuals and the larger society within which they have been engulfed for many generations. The roles of counselor and intermediary-to-bureaucracy are, in my view, as significant in their own domains as expert testimony on land claims or self-government. Women's and children's lives matter too.

Even such intensely personal experience became reciprocal in my own life. When I left a relationship because of child abuse and alcohol, male colleagues were sympathetic but largely irrelevant, whereas Native women I already knew well gathered around me and my children and supported us until we could again walk alone. I have not forgotten. It's a good enough metonym for the possibilities of subverting relations of power through human interaction.

3 / I do fieldwork among anthropologists as well among Indians. Specialization in history of anthropology has led me into ethical and epistemological dilemmas not different in kind from those of the more conventional "field." I've gotten to know many of the elders of our anthropological tribe, the descendants of our founding mothers and fathers. I've listened to them respectfully, even when I have gone on to frame their words and actions differently than they do. I have not written about many things that I know—in either "fieldwork."

Unfriendly critics sometimes suggest that both history of anthropology and Americanist ethnography are largely matters of "gossip." Margaret Mead is reported to have quipped that the two husbands with whom she did fieldwork (Reo Fortune and Gregory Bateson) might have been smarter than she was, but that *she* always knew whose pig had died. Anthropologists are people who care about people and their pigs. I am a proponent of the "hanging out" style of fieldwork; it has something to do with removing the exotic. We frame our gossip; history of anthropology entails historicism, things seen through the eyes of actors as agents.

4 / Anthropologists can teach members of our own culture, at least some of them, how to enter into cross-cultural conversations. My course about First Nations in Canada has increasingly focused on the problematics of representation and on accessing the cultural structures of First Nations imagination. Students examine Hollywood movies, National Film Board of Canada documentaries, mainstream and First Nations media reporting, life history texts in English, and fiction and poetry by First Nations writers. Public awareness, informed citizenship, and lobbying are all ways to support political initiatives that arise from within communities.

A few years back, while driving across Canada, I had a flat tire on the out-skirts of Brandon, Manitoba. Three young Native men stopped to help. While two of them were changing the tire, I was chatting with the third when a police cruiser pulled in behind us. The officer was highly suspicious, assuming that I must be in need of rescue. "Thank you, officer. Everything is fine. These gen-tlemen have everything under control." I had to be quite blunt before he reluc-tantly went away. And it made those young men's day that a white lady treated them like she would anyone else. It was one of the few occasions in my career when I found it the better part of valor not to mention that I was an anthro-pologist.

The Anthropologist as Public Intellectual: Educating an Audience for Contemporary Anthropology

Anthropological knowledge regularly finds itself on trial in North American public discourse; its defeats are frequently ignominious, their rationales al-most always disquieting. We have not always communicated our perspective effectively. Micaela di Leonardo laments the "deformed legacy" of American anthropology in its public interface, distinguishing between the wider effects of our scholarship and political activism as such (di Leonardo 1998:367).

I want to illustrate the difficulties of conveying what anthropologists know in light of a single case, well known in Canada, perhaps less so in the United States. The "reasons for judgment" of British Columbia Justice Allan McEa-chern in Delgamuukw' vs. the Crown, presented in 1991 after a four-year trial, challenged virtually every premise of the Americanist-derived anthropological stance toward contemporary cross-cultural research and collaboration. Al-though the Supreme Court of Canada overturned some of the most egregious parts of the decision in 1997, systematic distrust of anthropological methods and nonmainstream cultural knowledges remains.

Thirty-five Gitksan and thirteen Wet'suwet'en chiefs laid claim to 133 indi-vidual territories of some twenty-two thousand square miles (Culhane 1998:114–15). These First Nations elders performed their Adaawk, "sacred rem-iniscences," in which genealogies were traced back in some cases to non-human ancestors, and Kungax, "songs of the trails between territories," as ev-idence for their land claims (Culhane 1998:118). The British Columbia court ruled that the hearsay evidence from oral tradition could be heard, but the judge reserved the right to "weigh" its import. He eventually concluded that the oral history of what Dara Culhane (1990:122) called this "Indigenous aristocracy, gerontocracy and intelligentsia" was merely anecdotal, could not be interpreted literally as history, and therefore was not germane to his decision, which had to be made on legal rather than on cultural grounds. McEachern, who also read more conventional history literally rather than critically, was not prepared to recognize alternative or contradictory stories.

The anthropological expert witnesses for the Native case were systematically discredited on the stand and in the decision. Antonia Mills, Richard Daly, and Hugh Brody's firsthand knowledge based on extensive fieldwork resulting in some degree of "custom adoption" was interpreted as having "gone native," thereby relinquishing all claim to objective knowledge. The court restricted cultural relevance to land use and ecological knowledge, explicitly marginalizing Mills's specializations in religion and symbolism. Her "alleged romantic biases" invalidated whatever she might say about history and contemporary social and political life; her academic research project on Wet'suwe'ten concepts of reincarnation was the last straw. Culhane emphasizes the ethnocentric application of standards of bias: "The Crown's 'critique of romanticism,' however, seems to be based on the simplistic idea that any evidence that the Gitksan and Wet'suwet'en peoples were NOT [sic] war-like, naked, slave-owning cannibals at the time Europeans arrived in the late eighteenth century, is romantic, and therefore not believable. End of conversation: facts are a nuisance in this monologue" (Culhane 1998:133).

The Crown anthropologist, in contrast, had made a career as "professional witness" against land claims; her lack of fieldwork was seen as an advantage. The court failed to ask if she "disliked Indians" (Mills 1994:20), while Mills and Daly were charged to like them. The Crown steadfastly privileged positivist scientific research methodology, requiring evidence to be consistent, cumulative, and predictive (Culhane 1998:153). Some anthropologists whose work entered as evidence, however, changed their minds as ethnography and theoretical insight developed; this change of heart was taken to invalidate the current position of any anthropologist and the value of any information from their discipline. Science, to be of use to the court, could not be open-ended.

Moreover, the American Anthropological Association Code of Ethics, with its emphasis on primary responsibility to the people and communities studied, was used to further discredit the possibility of any valid evidence from anthropologists (Daly and Mills 1993:1, 6). McEachern read the ethics code as mandating anthropologists to "avoid telling the truth" (Culhane 1998:272).

McEachern failed to notice that Daly and Mills laid out a complex system of government and inheritance of land title, translating local concepts in terms the court should have been able to understand. Mills (1994) focused on eagle down, the symbol of peace, as the "law" of the people; Daly's report was called "Their Box Was Full," emphasizing the richness of the traditions and the environment in which they emerged (Mills 1994:4). Culture as symbol is a deeply entrenched Americanist representation.

We could, at this point, give up and change our strategies as expert witnesses, turning off our academic brains and speaking in the rigid absolutes of an outmoded social science. Some of our colleagues have used the fuzziness of our contributions to legal and other institutional decision-making settings to argue for a so-called scientific anthropology that avoids any stench of advocacy. In contrast, I suggest that we must educate citizens and public institutions alike to think as social scientists do about ethnocentrism, cultural difference, and cross-cultural miscommunication. Anthropologist Michael Asch and lawyer Norman Zlotkin argue that extinguishment of aboriginal land title "at the pleasure of the Crown" is ethically and politically unacceptable:

> The focus of negotiations between the Canadian government and Aboriginal peoples should be on reconciliation based on an affirmation of Aboriginal title and rights, according to the principle of equitable sharing of ownership and jurisdiction. . . . The present approach does damage to Canada's ethical core, for it founds negotiations on the premise that one party is inherently superior to the other.
>
> We argue that without a legitimate Aboriginal title there cannot be a legitimate Canadian state. (Asch and Zlotkin 1997:208)

Other models exist for a more equitable Canadian polity. Within the legal profession itself, "critical legal studies" are bringing postmodernist revisionisms of the social sciences into the courtroom, often along anthropologically sophisticated lines. Although Culhane (1998:355) is certainly correct that political will is "absent" to implement the extensive recommendations of the Royal Commission on Aboriginal Peoples (Erasmus et al. 1996), the theoretical basis for reordering Native-mainstream relations is laid out for reflection by intellectuals (both Native and non-Native), politicians, and ordinary citizens. Canadian political commentator John Ralston Saul (1997), for example, envisions Canada with the First Nations as a third founding nation, alongside the English and the French.

McEachern concluded that the Gitksan and Wet'suwet'en, lacking writing, horses, and wheeled wagons, lived in a Hobbesian state of nature, transcended only after European contact. The country was empty at contact (the legal doctrine of *terra nullius*) because the land was not utilized in a way familiar to Europeans. "They" had customs rather than laws, did not recognize land boundaries, and were nomadic, in short, peoples without culture, possessing civilization, if at all, at "a much lower, even primitive level" (Culhane 1998: 249). Their spiritual growth had been enhanced by European contact. McEachern felt that his "drive-by ethnography," a brief visit to some of the territory in dispute, gave him as much expertise as the anthropologists after long-term fieldwork (Culhane 1998:297). Mills concludes that McEachern "convinced himself that the Wet'suwe'ten and Gitksan were/are so primitive, so barbaric, so different, foreign, and 'other' that they would not make good stewards of their aboriginal territories" (Mills 1994:183).

McEachern's position is particularly bizarre given the cultural attributes of the Gitksan and Wet'suwe'ten, who lived in settled villages, had clear concepts of property and territory, vested considerable ritual and political authority in their chiefs, and developed a rich art and monumental architecture. No aboriginal group in North America could make a stronger claim for precontact civilization. McEachern apparently felt it necessary to determine a single legal status lumping all First Nations peoples in the same category, ignoring their differences relative to European claims to right of appropriation over their lands.

The Supreme Court of Canada ruled in 1997 that land title could not be extinguished solely on grounds of political intent on the part of the Province of British Columbia; future efforts to extinguish Aboriginal title would have to involve "Aboriginal initiative, participation, and consent" (Culhane 1998:361–66). Further, "evidentiary difficulties" in presenting the case were sufficiently severe to merit a new trial (although the court recommended a negotiation process as better suited to the interests of the plaintiffs). "The factual findings cannot stand" because the failure to consider evidence from oral tradition, when only oral tradition existed to make the case, placed an undue evidentiary burden on any aboriginal group. Nonetheless, the Supreme Court upheld the dismissal of expert testimony from anthropologists as the right of the trial judge to decide, ignoring the inextricability of this testimony from the evidence of oral tradition received directly from First Nations witnesses. Moreover, the ruling did not mandate consideration of oral evidence but merely made it admissible for a judge to use it at his or her discretion. Case law will clarify whether this landmark decision trickles down to lower courts faced with similar cultural dilemmas.

These issues are not restricted to Canada or to this case. James Clifford's postmodernist reading of the complex mix of stories around the courtroom construction of Mashpee identity emphasizes the permeability of community boundaries, the narrative continuity of history and identity, and the slippery distinction between a tribe and an ethnic group (Clifford 1988:277–346). His vignettes are purportedly presented with rhetoric supporting both sides, although he notes with apparent approval the subversive effect of the jury decision that the Mashpees were "inconsistently a tribe" over 350 years of inadequately documented history (Clifford 1988:333). The land claim case came down to an eerily familiar standoff between the relative expertises of history and anthropology. Recurrent issues include positivist interpretation of written documents as objective evidence, the assumption that the absence of documents means there is nothing to document, and the dismissal of ethnographic fieldwork as too fuzzy to serve as a basis for reliable historical inference. The Mashpee/Wampanoags lost their court case but were recognized as a tribe by the Bureau of Indian Affairs in 1987.

. . .

Anthropologists can, indeed must, claim the role of public intellectual, "speaking truth to power" (Said 1994:xvi). One who speaks in the public sphere risks career stability as well as the possible failure to communicate. Like Paul Radin, Edward Said argues that intellectuals arise in every society, holding a crucial public role as "outsider, 'amateur,' and disturber of the status quo." They are bound to ask embarrassing questions and are not easily co-opted; their "raison d'être is to represent the people and issues routinely forgotten or swept under the rug" (Said 1994:11); "the intellectual belongs on the same side with the weak and unprotected" (Said 1994:22). "The life of the mind" is lived in society, although the intellectual should not be seduced by "gregariousness," the desire to be liked (Said 1994:45). Intellectuals grow inured to dissatisfaction, maintaining a "necessarily ironic, skeptical, even playful—but not cynical" stance (Said 1994:53).

Although Said formulates his argument from a cultural position outside the

Western mainstream, his vision of what intellectuals do is consistent with the Americanist anthropological tradition we have been exploring. Having deconstructed much of the baggage of an earlier anthropology, we are now poised for reconstruction. Culture is something that belongs to people, that defines their personal identity and community membership—in our disciplinary culture as well as in the cultures in which we work.

BIBLIOGRAPHY

Ahenakew, Freda, and H. C. Wolfart, eds. 1992. *Kôhkominawak Otâcimowiniwâwa: Our Grandmothers' Lives as Told in Their Own Words*. Saskatoon: Fifth House.

Allen, Paula Gunn. 1998. Special Problems in Teaching Leslie Marmon Silko's *Ceremony*. In D. Mihesuah, ed., 55–64.

Anderson, Benedict. 1983. *Imagined Communities: Reflections on the Origin and Spread of Nationalism*. London: Verso.

Andresen, Julie. 1990. *Linguistics in America, 1769–1924*. New York: Routledge.

Angrosino, Michael V. 1998. *Opportunity House: Ethnographic Stories of Mental Retardation*. New York: AltaMira Press.

Appadurai, Arjun. 1996. *Modernity at Large: Cultural Dimensions of Globalization*. Minneapolis: University of Minnesota Press.

Asad, Talal, ed. 1973. *Anthropology and the Colonial Encounter*. Atlantic Heights NJ: Humanities Press.

Asch, Michael and Norman Zlotkin. 1997. Affirming Aboriginal Title. In Michael Asch, ed., *Aboriginal and Treaty Rights in Canada: Essays on Law, Equality and Responsibility for Difference*. Vancouver: University of British Columbia Press.

Atkinson, Paul. 1990. *The Ethnographic Imagination: Textual Constructions of Reality*. London: Routledge.

Baker, Lee. 1998. *From Savage to Negro: Anthropology and the Construction of Race, 1896–1954*. Berkeley: University of California Press.

Bakhtin, Mikhail. 1981. *The Dialogic Imagination*. Edited by Michael Holquist. Austin: University of Texas Press.

Bandelier, Adolph. [1890] 1971. *The Delight Makers: A Novel of Prehistoric Pueblo Indians*. Reprint, New York: Harcourt Brace Jovanovich.

Basso, Keith. 1996. *Wisdom Sits in Places*. Albuquerque: University of New Mexico Press.

Bateson, Gregory. 1958. *Naven: A Survey of the Problems Suggested by a Composite Picture of the Culture of a New Guinea Tribe Drawn from Three Points of View*. Cambridge: Cambridge University Press, 1936. Reprint, Stanford: Stanford University Press.

Bauman, Richard, and Joel Sherzer, eds. 1974. *Explorations in the Ethnography of Speaking*. Cambridge: Cambridge University Press.

Becker, Jean. 1993. The Implications of Post-Modern Theory for Aboriginal Studies. Unpublished Master's thesis, University of Guelph (Ontario).

Behar, Ruth, and Deborah Gordon, eds. 1995. *Women Writing Culture*. Berkeley: University of California Press.

Benedict, Ruth. 1923. *The Concept of the Guardian Spirit in North America*. American Anthropological Association Memoir 29.

———. 1934a. Anthropology and the Abnormal. *Journal of General Psychology* 10:59–82.

———. 1934b. *Patterns of Culture*. Boston: Houghton Mifflin.

———. 1940. *Race: Science and Politics*. New York: Viking.

———. 1946. *The Chrysanthemum and the Sword*. Boston: Houghton Mifflin.

Benjamin, Walter. 1968. The Task of the Translator. In *Illuminations*, edited by Hannah Arendt. New York: Harcourt, Brace and World.

Berkhofer, Robert. 1978. *The White Man's Indian: Images of the Indian from Columbus to the Present*. New York: Random House.

Bernstein, Richard J. 1991. *Beyond Objectivism and Relativism: Science, Hermeneutics, and Praxis*. Philadelphia: University of Pennsylvania Press.

Berman, Judith. 1996. "The Culture as it Appears to the Indian Himself": Boas, George Hunt, and The Methods of Ethnography. In G. Stocking, ed., 215–56.

Berreman, Gerald. 1966. Anemic and Emetic Analyses in Social Anthropology. *American Anthropologist* 68:346–54.

Bieder, Robert. 1986. *Science Encounters the Indian, 1880–1920: The Early Years of American Ethnology*. Norman: University of Oklahoma Press.

Biolosi, Thomas, and Larry J. Zimmerman, eds. 1997. *Indians and Anthropologists: Vine Deloria Jr. and the Critique of Anthropology*. Tucson: University of Arizona Press.

Bloch, Maurice. 1998. *How We Think They Think: Anthropological Approaches to Cognition, Memory, and Literacy*. Boulder CO: Westview.

Boas, Franz. 1887. The Study of Geography. *Science* 9:137–41.

———. 1889. On Alternating Sounds. *American Anthropologist* 2:47–53.

———. 1891. Dissemination of Folk Tales among the Natives of North America. *Journal of American Folklore* 4:13–20.

———. 1894. The Anthropometry of the Northwest Coast Indians. In C. Stanisland Wake, *Memoirs of the International Congress of Anthropology*. Chicago: Schulte Publishing.

———. 1895. The Growth of Indian Mythologies. *Journal of American Folklore* 9:1–11.

———. 1896. The Limitations of the Comparative Method of Anthropology. *Science* 4: 901–8.

———. 1898. Introduction to James Teit, The Traditions of the Thompson Indians of British Columbia. *Memoirs of the American Folklore Society* 6:1–18.

———. 1904. History of Anthropology. *Science* 20:513–24.

———. 1906. Some Philological Aspects of Anthropological Research. *Science* 23:641–45.

———. 1907. Some Principles of Museum Administration. *Science* 25:921–33.

——. 1909. *The Kwakiutl of Vancouver Island.* Memoirs of the American Museum of Natural History 8.

——. 1911a, 1922. *Handbook of American Indian Languages.* Washington DC: Smithsonian Institution.

——. 1911b. *The Mind of Primitive Man.* New York: Macmillan.

——. 1914. Mythology and Folk Tales of the North American Indians. *Journal of American Folklore* 27:374–410.

——. 1916a. The Development of Folk Tales and Myths. *Scientific Monthly* 3:335–43.

——. 1916b. *Tsimshian Mythology.* Bureau of American Ethnology Annual Report 31.

——. 1917. Introduction. *International Journal of American Linguistics* 1:1–11.

——. 1920. The Classification of American Languages. *American Anthropologist* 22: 367–76.

——. 1929. The Classification of American Indian Languages. *Language* 5.

——. 1934. Introduction to Benedict 1934b, v–viii.

Boas, Franz, ed. 1938. *General Anthropology.* Boston: D. C. Heath.

——. 1940. *Race, Language and Culture.* New York: Free Press.

Bock, Philip. 1980. *Rethinking Psychological Anthropology.* New York: W. H. Freeman.

Boddy, Janice, and Michael Lambek, eds. 1997. *Culture at the End of the Boasian Century.* Social Analysis 41.

Bohman, James. 1991. Holism without Skepticism: Contextualism and the Limits of Interpretation. In D. Hiley, J. Bohman, and R. Shusterman, eds., *The Interpretive Turn: Philosophy, Science, and Culture,* 129–54. Ithaca: Cornell University Press.

Boon, James. 1982. *Other Tribes, Other Scribes.* Cambridge: Cambridge University Press.

Brady, Ivan, ed. 1991. *Anthropological Poetics.* Savage MD: Rowan and Littlefield.

Briggs, Charles. 1986. *Learning How to Ask: A Sociolinguistical Appraisal of the Role of the Interview in Social Science Research.* Cambridge: Cambridge University Press.

Bright, William. 1976. *Variation and Change in Language.* Stanford: Stanford University Press.

Bringhurst, Robert. 1998. *Native American Oral Literatures and the Unity of the Humanities.* Vancouver: University of British Columbia Press.

——. 1999. *A Story as Sharp as a Knife: The Classical Haida Mythtellers and Their World.* Vancouver: Douglas and McIntyre.

Brown, Jennifer. 1992. Preface to *The Ojibwe of Berens River, Manitoba: Ethnography into History* by A. I. Hallowell, xi–xvii. New York: Holt, Rinehart and Winston.

Brown, Jennifer, and Elizabeth Vibert, eds. 1996. *Reading Beyond Words: Contexts for Native History.* Peterborough ON: Broadview Press.

Brumble, David. 1988. *American Indian Autobiography.* Berkeley: University of California Press.

Buckley, Thomas. 1996. "The Little History of Pitiful Events": The Epistemological and Moral Contexts of Kroeber's Californian Ethnology. In G. Stocking, ed., 257–97.

Bunzel, Ruth. 1929. *The Pueblo Potter: A Study of Creative Imagination in Primitive Art.* New York: Columbia University Press.

Bunzl, Matti. 1996. Franz Boas and the Humboldtian Tradition: From *Volksgeist* and *Nationalcharakter* to an Anthropological Concept of Culture. In G. Stocking, ed., 17–78.

Burling, Robbins. 1964. Cognition and Componential Analysis: God's Truth or Hocus Pocus? *American Anthropologist* 66:20–28.

Burrow, John W. 1966. *Evolution and Society: A Study in Victorian Social Theory.* Cambridge: Cambridge University Press.

Caffrey, Margaret. 1989. *Ruth Benedict: Stranger in This Land.* Austin: University of Texas Press.

Campisi, Jack. 1991. *The Mashpee Indians: Tribe on Trial.* Syracuse: Syracuse University Press.

Cannizzo, Jeanne. 1983. George Hunt and the Invention of Kwakiutl Culture. *Canadian Review of Sociology and Anthropology* 20:44–58.

Carroll, John B. 1956. Introduction to Whorf 1956, 1–34.

Casagrande, Joseph B., ed. 1960. *In the Company of Man: Twenty Portraits of Anthropological Informants.* New York: Harper Torchbooks.

Chafe, Wallace. 1962. Estimates Regarding the Present Speakers of North American Indian Languages. *International Journal of American Linguistics* 28:162–71.

Clifford, James. 1986. Introduction: Partial Truths. In J. Clifford and G. Marcus, eds., 1–26.

———. 1988. *The Predicament of Culture: Twentieth Century Ethnography, Literature and Art.* Cambridge: Harvard University Press.

———. 1997. *Routes: Travel and Translation in the Late Twentieth Century.* Cambridge: Harvard University Press.

Clifford, James, and George Marcus, eds. 1986. *Writing Culture: The Poetics and Politics of Ethnography.* Berkeley: University of California Press.

Coe, Michael D. 1992. *Breaking the Maya Code.* New York: Thames and Hudson.

Collingwood, R. G. 1936. *The Idea of History.* Oxford: Clarendon.

Comaroff, Jean. 1985. *Body of Power, Spirit of Resistance.* Chicago: University of Chicago Press.

Comaroff, John, and Jean Comaroff. 1992. *Ethnography and the Historical Imagination.* Boulder CO: Westview.

Cook-Lynn, Elizabeth. 1998. American Indian Intellectualism and the New Indian Story. In D. Mihesuah, ed., 111–38.

Côté, James E. 1994. *Adolescent Storm and Stress: An Evaluation of the Mead-Freeman Controversy.* Hillsdale NJ: Lawrence Earlbaum Associates.

Cowan, William, Michael K. Foster, and Konrad Koerner, eds. 1986. *New Perspectives in Language, Culture and Personality.* Amsterdam: John Benjamins.

Crapanzano, Vincent. 1972. *The Fifth World of Forster Bennett: Portrait of a Navajo.* New York: Viking.

———. 1980. *Tuhami: Portrait of a Moroccan.* Chicago: University of Chicago Press.

———. 1986. Hermes' Dilemma: The Masking of Subversion in Ethnographic Description. In J. Clifford and G. Marcus, ed., 51–76.

Cruikshank, Julie. 1990. *Life Lived Like a Story.* Lincoln: University of Nebraska Press.

———. 1998. *The Social Life of Stories: Narrative and Knowledge in the Yukon Territory.* Lincoln: University of Nebraska Press.

Culhane, Dara. 1998. *The Pleasure of the Crown: Anthropology, Law and First Nations.* Burnaby BC: Talonbooks.

Daly, Richard, and Antonia Mills. 1993. Ethics and Objectivity: American Anthropological Association Principles of Responsibility Discredit Testimony. *Anthropology Newsletter* 34: (8):1, 6.

Daniel, E. Valentine. 1996. *Charred Lullabies: Chapters in an Anthropography of Violence.* Princeton: Princeton University Press.

Darnell, Regna. 1967. Daniel Garrison Brinton: An Intellectual Biography. Unpublished Master's thesis, University of Pennsylvania.

———. 1969. The Development of American Anthropology 1879–1920: From the Bureau of American Ethnology to Franz Boas. Unpublished Ph.D. dissertation, University of Pennsylvania.

———. 1971. The Professionalization of American Anthropology. *Social Science Information*:83–103.

———. 1974a. Daniel Brinton and the Professionalization of American Anthropology. *Proceedings of the American Ethnological Society*:69–98.

———. 1974b. Rationalist Aspects of the Whorf Hypothesis. *Papers in Linguistics* 7:41–50.

———. 1974c. The Social Context of Cree Narrative. In R. Bauman and J. Sherzer, eds., 315–36.

———. 1975. Towards a History of the Professionalization of Canadian Anthropology. *Proceedings of the Canadian Ethnology Society,* 399–416.

———. 1976. The Sapir Years at the National Museum. *Proceedings of the Plenary Session of the Canadian Ethnology Society,* 98–121.

———. 1977a. Hallowell's Bear Ceremonialism and the Emergence of Boasian Anthropology. *Ethos* 5:13–30.

———. 1977b. The History of Anthropology in Anthropological Perspective. *Annual Reviews in Anthropology,* 399–417.

———. 1979. Reflections on Cree Interactional Etiquette: Educational Implications. *Working Papers in Sociolinguistics* 57:1–22.

———. 1981. Taciturnity in Native American Etiquette. *Culture* 1:55–60.

———. 1982a. Franz Boas and the Development of Physical Anthropology in North America. *Canadian Journal of Anthropology* 3:101–12.

———. 1982b. The History of Anthropology in the Undergraduate Curriculum. *Journal of the History of the Behavioral Sciences* 18:265–71.

———. 1982c. High School Math. Unpublished manuscript.

——. 1984. Interaction et langage: Implications théoretiques degagées de la Culture Cris. *Récherches Amerindiennes au Québec* 14:42–50.

——. 1985a. Kohkom Moskwa, with commentary. In I. Prattis, ed., 129–37.

——. 1985b. The Language of Power in Cree Interethnic Communication. In Nessa Wolfson and Joan Manes, eds., *The Language of Power*, 61–72. New York: Newbury House.

——. 1986a. Personality and Culture: The Sapirian Alternative. In G. Stocking, ed., 156–83.

——. 1986b. The Integration of Edward Sapir's Mature Intellect. In W. Cowan, M. Foster, and K. Koerner, eds., 553–88.

——. 1988a. *Daniel Garrison Brinton: The "Fearless Critic" of Philadelphia.* Philadelphia: Department of Anthropology, University of Pennsylvania Monograph 3.

——. 1988b. The Interactional Consequences of Power. In R. Darnell and M. K. Foster, eds., *Native North American Interaction Patterns*, 69–77. Ottawa: Canadian Museum of Civilization.

——. 1989a. Stanley Newman and the Sapir School of Linguistics. In Mary Ritchie Key and Henry Hoenigswald, eds., *In Remembrance of Stanley Newman*, 71–88. Berlin: Mouton de Gruyter.

——. 1989b. Women's Power. *Anthropology and Humanism Quarterly* 14:124.

——. 1990a. *Edward Sapir: Linguist, Anthropologist, Humanist.* Berkeley: University of California Press.

——. 1990b. Edward Sapir's Poetics. In William New, ed., *Dictionary of Literary Biography 92: Canadian Writers 1890-1920*, 322–27. Detroit: Bruccoli Clark Layman.

——. 1990c. Franz Boas, Edward Sapir and the Americanist Text Tradition. *Historiographia Linguistica* 17:129–44.

——. 1991a. Ethnographic Genre and Poetic Voice. In I. Brady, ed., 267–82.

——. 1991b. Thirty-Nine Postulates of Cree Conversation, Power and Interaction: A Culture-Specific Model. *Proceedings of the 22nd Algonquian Conference*, 89–102.

——. 1992. The Boasian Text Tradition and the History of Canadian Anthropology. *Culture* 17:39–48.

——. 1995a. Deux ou Trois Choses que je sais du Postmodernisme: "Le Moment Experimentale" dans l'anthropologie Nord-américaine. *Gradhiva: Revue d'histoire et d'archives de l'anthropologie* 14:3–15.

——. 1995b. The Structuralism of Claude Lévi Strauss. *Historiographia Linguistica* 22:217–34.

——. 1996. "On Poets and Scientists." *American Anthropological Association Newsletter* (March): 35–36.

——. 1997a. The Anthropological Concept of Culture at the End of the Boasian Century. *Social Analysis* 41 (3): 42–54.

——. 1997b. Changing Patterns of Ethnography in Canadian Anthropology. *Canadian Review of Sociology and Anthropology* 34:269–96.

——. 1998a. *And Along Came Boas: Continuity and Revolution in Americanist Anthropology*. Amsterdam: John Benjamins.

——. 1998b. Camelot at Yale: The Construction and Dismantling of the Sapirian Synthesis 1931–39. *American Anthropologist* 200:361–72.

——. 1998c. Toward a History of Canadian Departments of Anthropology: Retrospect, Prospect, and Common Cause. *Anthropologica* 40:153–68.

——. 2000. The Pivotal Role of the Northwest Coast in the History of Americanist Anthropology. *B. C. Studies* 125/126:33–52.

Darnell, Regna, ed. 1971. *Linguistic Diversity in Canadian Society*. Edmonton-Champaign: Linguistic Research, Inc.

——, 1973. *Canadian Languages in Their Social Context*. Edmonton-Champaign: Linguistic Research, Inc.

——, 1974. *Readings in the History of Anthropology*. New York: Harper and Row.

——, 1977. *Language Use in Canada*. Edmonton-Champaign: Linguistic Research, Inc.

Darnell, Regna, and Judith Irvine, eds. 1994. *Ethnology. Collected Works of Edward Sapir* 4. Berlin: Mouton de Gruyter.

Darnell, Regna, Judith Irvine, and Richard Handler, eds. 1999. *Culture. Collected Works of Edward Sapir* 4. Berlin: Mouton de Gruyter.

Darnell, Regna, and Lisa Valentine. 1991. Cultural and Linguistic Correlates of Reserve English of Ojibwe and Mohawk Speakers in Southwestern Ontario. SSHRCC grant proposal.

——. 1994. Performing Native Identity through English Discourse: A Comparison of Algonquian and Iroquoian Language Use in Southwestern Ontario. SSHRCC grant proposal.

Darnell, Regna, Lisa Valentine, and Allan McDougall. 1997. Discourse, Power and Ethnicity in the Construction of First Nations Identity. SSHRCC grant proposal.

Deacon, Desley. 1997. *Elsie Clews Parsons: Inventing Modern Life*. Chicago: University of Chicago Press.

Deloria, Philip. 1998. *Playing Indian*. New Haven: Yale University Press.

Deloria, Vine, Jr. 1969. *Custer Died for Your Sins*. London: Collier-MacMillan.

——. 1995. *Red Earth, White Lies: Native Americans and the Myth of Scientific Fact*. New York: Scribner.

——. 1997. Conclusion: Anthros, Indians and Planetary Reality. In T. Biolosi and L. Zimmerman, eds., 209–21.

Deleuze, Gilles, and Felix Guattari. 1987. *A Thousand Plateaus: Capitalism and Schizophrenia*. Minneapolis: University of Minnesota Press.

DeMallie, Raymond. 1989. Ella Deloria's Anthropology. Paper read at the American Anthropological Association meetings.

Diamond, Stanley. 1981. Paul Radin. In S. Silverman, ed., 67–97.

Diamond, Stanley, ed. 1960. *Culture in History*. New York: Columbia University Press.

di Leonardo, Micaela, ed. 1991. *Gender at the Crossroads of Knowledge: Feminist Anthropology in the Postmodern Era*. Berkeley: University of California Press.

———. 1998. *Exotics at Home: Anthropologists, Others, American Modernity*. Berkeley: University of California Press.

Durkheim, Emile. [1912] 1961. *Elementary Forms of the Religious Life*. [*Les Formes Elémentaires de la Vie Religieuse*]. Reprint, New York: Collier.

Dyk, Walter. 1938. *Left-Handed: Son of Old Man Hat*. New York: Columbia University Press.

Erasmus, George, et al. 1996. *Report of the Royal Commission on Aboriginal Peoples*. Ottawa: Government of Canada.

Evans-Pritchard, E. E. [1937] 1976. *Witchcraft, Oracles and Magic among the Azande*. Reprint, Oxford: Clarendon Press.

Fabian, Johannes. 1983. *Time and the Other: How Anthropology Makes Its Object*. New York: Columbia University Press.

———. 1998. *Moments of Freedom: Anthropology and Popular Culture*. Charlottesville: University Press of Virginia.

Fajans, Jane. 1997. *They Make Themselves: Work and Play among the Bainang of Papua New Guinea*. Chicago: University of Chicago Press.

Fletcher, Alice C., and Francis LaFlesche. 1911. *The Omaha Tribe*. Washington DC: 27th Annual Report of the Bureau of American Ethnology.

Fogelson, Raymond D. 1989. The Ethnohistory of Events and Non-Events. *Ethnohistory* 36:133–47.

———. 1999. Nationalism and the Americanist Tradition. In L. Valentine and R. Darnell, eds., 75–83.

Fox, Richard, ed. 1991. *Recapturing Anthropology: Working in the Present*. Santa Fe: School of American Research.

Fredson, John. 1982. *John Fredson Edward Sapir Haa Googwandak*. Fairbanks: Alaska Native Language Center.

Freeman, Derek. 1983. *Margaret Mead: The Making and Unmaking of an Anthropological Myth*. Cambridge: Harvard University Press.

———. 1999. *The Fateful Hoaxing of Margaret Mead: A Historical Analysis of Her Samoan Research*. Boulder CO: Westview.

Friedlander, N. 1989. Elsie Clews Parsons. In Ute Gacs, Aisha Khan, Jerrie McIntyre, and Ruth Weinberg, eds. *Women Anthropologists: Selected Biographies*, 282–90. Urbana: University of Illinois Press.

Gare, Arran E. 1995. *Postmodernism and the Environmental Crisis*. London: Routledge.

Geertz, Clifford. 1973. *The Interpretation of Cultures*. New York: Basic Books.

———. 1983. *Local Knowledges: Further Essays in Interpretive Anthropology*. New York: Basic Books.

———. 1984. Anti-anti-relativism. *American Anthropologist* 86:263–78.

——. 1988. *Works and Lives: The Anthropologist as Author*. Stanford: Stanford University Press.

——. 1991. Interview with Richard Handler. *Current Anthropology* 32:603–13.

——. 1995 *After the Fact: Two Countries, Four Decades, One Anthropologist*. Cambridge: Harvard University Press.

Gleick, James. 1987. *Chaos: Making a New Science*. New York: Penguin.

Goddard, Ives. 1996. Introduction to *Handbook of North American Indians 17: Language*, 1–16. Washington DC: Smithsonian Institution.

Goldenweiser, Alexander. 1910. Totemism: An Analytical Study. *Journal of American Folklore* 23:179–294.

——. 1917. The Autonomy of the Social. *American Anthropologist* 19:447–49.

——. 1922. *Early Civilization: An Introduction to Anthropology*. New York: Alfred A. Knopf.

——. 1941. Recent Trends in American Anthropology. *American Anthropologist* 43:151–63.

Goldschmidt, Walter, ed. 1958. *The Anthropology of Franz Boas*. American Anthropological Association Memoir 89.

Gordon, W. Terence. 1990. C. K. Ogden, Edward Sapir, Leonard Bloomfield, and the Geometry of Semantics. In Hans-Josef Niederehe and Konrad Koerner, eds., *Papers from the Fourth International Conference on the History of the Language Sciences, Trier, 24-28 Aug. 1987*, 821–32. Amsterdam: John Benjamins.

Gould, Stephen Jay. 1989. *Wonderful Life: The Burgess Shale and the Nature of History*. New York: Norton.

Grinnell, George Bird. 1892. *Blackfoot Lodge Tales*. New York: C. Scribner.

Gumperz, John, and Stephen Levinson, eds. 1996. *Rethinking Linguistic Relativity*. Cambridge: Cambridge University Press.

Gupta, Akhil, and James Ferguson, eds. 1997. *Anthropological Locations: Boundaries and Grounds of a Field Science*. Berkeley: University of California Press.

Gurvitch, George, and W. E. Moore. 1945. *Twentieth Century Sociology*. New York: Philosophical Library.

Haas, Mary. 1978. *Language, Culture, and History*. Stanford: Stanford University Press.

Hale, Kenneth, and Albert Alvarez. 1972. A New Perspective on American Indian Linguistics. In Alfonso Ortiz, ed., *New Perspectives on the Pueblos*, 87–133. Albuquerque: University of New Mexico Press.

Hallowell, A. Irving. 1926. Bear Ceremonialism in the Northern Hemisphere. *American Anthropologist* 28:1–175.

——. 1955. *Culture and Experience*. Philadelphia: University of Pennsylvania Press.

——. 1960. The Beginnings of Anthropology in America. In Frederica de Laguna, ed., *Selected Writings from the American Anthropologist 1888-1920*, 1–90. New York: Harper and Row.

——. 1964. Anthropology at the University of Pennsylvania. *Papers of the Anthropological Society of Philadelphia*: 1–11.

——. 1965. The History of Anthropology as an Anthropological Problem. *Journal of the History of the Behavioral Sciences* 1:24–38.

——. 1967. Anthropology in Philadelphia. In Jacob W. Gruber, ed., *The Philadelphia Anthropological Society*, 1–31. New York: Columbia University Press.

——. 1976. *Contributions to Anthropology: Selected Papers of A. Irving Hallowell*. Chicago: University of Chicago Press.

——. 1992. *The Ojibwa of Berens River, Manitoba: Ethnography into History*. Edited by Jennifer Brown. New York: Holt, Rinehart and Winston.

Handler, Richard. 1986. The Vigorous Male and Aspiring Female: Poetry, Personality, and Culture in Edward Sapir and Ruth Benedict. In G. Stocking, ed., 127–55.

Haraway, Donna. 1988. Situated Knowledges: The Science Question in Feminism and the Privilege of Partial Perspective. *Feminist Studies* 14:575–99.

Harding, Sandra. 1991. *Whose Science? Whose Knowledge? Thinking From Women's Lives*. Ithaca: Cornell University Press.

Hare, Peter. 1985. *A Woman's Quest for Science: Portrait of Anthropologist Elsie Clews Parsons*. New York: Prometheus.

Harries-Jones, Peter. 1995. *A Recursive Vision: Ecological Understanding and Gregory Bateson*. Toronto: University of Toronto Press.

Harris, Marvin. 1968. *The Rise of Anthropological Theory*. New York: Thomas Crowell.

Harris, Zellig. 1943–44. Yokuts Structure and Newman's Grammar. *International Journal of American Linguistics* 10:196–211.

Harrison, Faye V. 1999. Introduction: Expanding the Discourse on Race and Racism. *American Anthropologist* 101:609–31.

Hatch, Elvin. 1973. *Theories of Man and Culture*. New York: Columbia University Press.

Herskovits, Melville. 1953. *Franz Boas: The Science of Man in the Making*. New York: Charles Scribner's Sons.

Herzfeld, Michael. 1987. *Anthropology Through the Looking Glass: Critical Ethnography in the Margins of Europe*. Cambridge: Cambridge University Press.

Highway, Tomson. 1988. *The Rez Sisters*. Saskatoon: Fifth House.

——. 1989. *Dry Lips Oughta Move to Kapuskasing*. Saskatoon: Fifth House.

——. 1998 *Kiss of the Fur Queen*. Toronto: Doubleday Canada.

Hill, Archibald. 1980. How Many Revolutions Can a Linguist Live Through? In Boyd Davis and Raymond O'Cain, eds., *First Person Singular*, 69–76. Amsterdam: John Benjamins.

Hill, Jane, and Bruce Mannheim. 1992. Language and Worldview. *Annual Review of Anthropology*: 381–406.

Hill, Sarah. 1997. *Weaving New Worlds: Southeastern Cherokee Women and Their Basketry*. Chapel Hill: University of North Carolina Press.

Hodgen, Margaret. 1964. *Early Anthropology in the Sixteenth and Seventeenth Centuries*. Philadelphia: University of Pennsylvania Press.

Hoijer, Harry, ed. 1946. *Linguistic Structures of Native North America*. New York: Viking Fund Publications in Anthropology 6.

——, 1954. *Language and Culture*. Chicago: University of Chicago Press.

Hong, Keelung. 1994. Experiences of Being a "Native" Observing Anthropology. *Anthropology Today* 10:6–9.

Hoy, David. 1991. Is Hermeneutics Ethnocentric? In D. Hiley, J. Bohman, and R. Shusterman, eds., *The Interpretive Turn: Philosophy, Science, and Culture*, 155–75. Ithaca: Cornell University Press.

Hymes, Dell. 1962. On Studying the History of Anthropology. *Kroeber Anthropological Society Papers* 26:81–86.

——. 1966. Two Types of Linguistic Relativity. In William Bright, ed., *Sociolinguistics*, 114–67. The Hague: Mouton.

——. 1971. Morris Swadesh: From the First Yale School to World Prehistory. In Joel Sherzer, ed., *The Origin and Diversification of Language*, 228–70. Chicago: Aldine.

——. 1981. *In Vain I Tried to Tell You: Essays in Native American Ethnopoetics*. Philadelphia: University of Pennsylvania Press.

Hymes, Dell, ed. 1964. *Language in Culture and Society*. New York: Harper and Row.

——. 1969. *Reinventing Anthropology*. New York: Random House.

Hymes, Dell, and John Fought. 1975. American Structuralism. In Thomas A. Sebeok, ed., *Current Trends in Linguistics: Historiography of Linguistics* 13, 903–1176. The Hague: Mouton.

Irvine, Judith, ed. 1994. Edward Sapir's *The Psychology of Culture*. Berlin: Mouton de Gruyter.

Joseph, John E. 1996. The Immediate Sources of the "Sapir-Whorf Hypothesis." *Historiographia Linguistica* 23:365–404.

Jung, C. G. 1923. *Psychological Types*. New York: Harcourt Brace.

King, Thomas. 1993. *Green Grass, Running Water*. Toronto: Harper Collins.

Knauft, Bruce M. 1996. *Genealogies for the Present in Cultural Anthropology*. New York: Routledge.

Koerner, Konrad. 1992. The Sapir-Whorf Hypothesis: A Preliminary History and a Bibliographic Essay. *Journal of Linguistic Anthropology* 2:173–98.

Krauss, Michael. 1986. Edward Sapir and Athabaskan Linguistics. In W. Cowan, M. Foster, and K. Koerner, eds., 147–90.

Kroeber, Alfred Louis. 1908. *The Ethnology of the Gros Ventre*. New York: The Trustees.

——. 1917. The Superorganic. *American Anthropologist* 19:163–213.

——. 1919. Order in Changes of Fashion. *American Anthropologist* 21:235–63.

——. 1922. Introduction to E. Parsons, ed., 5–16.

——. 1923. *Anthropology*. New York: Harcourt, Brace.

——. 1931. Historical Reconstruction of Culture Growth and Organic Evolution. *American Anthropologist* 37:539–69.

——. 1936. So-Called Social Science. *Journal of Social Philosophy* 1:317–40.

——. 1938. Historical Context, Reconstruction and Interpretation. Lectures at the University of Chicago. In A. L. Kroeber, *The Nature of Culture*, 79–84.

——. 1939a. *Cultural and Natural Areas of North America*. Berkeley: University of California Publications in American Archaeology and Ethnology 38.

——. 1939b. Basic and Secondary Patterns of Social Structure. *Journal of the Royal Anthropological Institute* 68:299–309.

——. 1943. Structure, Function and Pattern in Biology and Anthropology. *Scientific Monthly* 56:105–13.

——. 1944. *Configurations of Culture Growth*. Berkeley: University of California Press.

——. 1946. The Ancient Oikoumene as a Historic Culture Aggregate. *Journal of the Royal Anthropological Institute* 75:9–20.

——. 1948. Have Civilizations a Life History? Paper read to the American Association for the Advancement of Science. In A. L. Kroeber, *An Anthropologist Looks at History*, 1963:9–13.

——. 1949. The Concept of Culture in Science. *Journal of General Education* 3:182–96.

——. 1950a. A Half-Century of Anthropology. *Scientific American* 183:87–94.

——. 1950b. The History and Present Orientation of Cultural Anthropology. Paper read at the American Anthropological Association. In A. L. Kroeber, *An Anthropologist Looks at History*, 39–59.

——. 1952. *The Nature of Culture*. Chicago: University of Chicago Press.

——. 1953. Demolition of Civilization. *Journal of the History of Ideas* 14:264–75.

——. 1957. *Style and Civilizations*. Berkeley: University of California Press.

——. 1958. Reconstitution within Civilization. Paper read to the Wenner-Gren Foundation for Anthropological Research. In A. L. Kroeber, *An Anthropologist Looks at History*, 39–59.

——. 1959. A History of the Personality of Anthropology. *American Anthropologist* 61:398–404.

——. 1962. *A Roster of Civilizations and Culture*. Chicago: Aldine.

——. 1963. *An Anthropologist Looks at History*. Berkeley: University of California Press.

Kroeber, Alfred Louis, ed. 1925. *Handbook of California Indians*. Bureau of American Ethnology Bulletin 78.

Kroeber, Alfred Louis, and Clyde Kluckhohn. 1952. *Culture: A Critical Review of Concepts and Definitions*. Cambridge MA: Peabody Museum of American Archaeology and Ethnology.

Kroeber, Alfred Louis, with Jane Richardson. 1940. Three Centuries of Women's Dress Fashions: A Quantitative Analysis. *University of California Anthropological Records* 2:111–54.

Kroeber, Karl. 1998. *Artistry in Native American Myths*. Lincoln: University of Nebraska Press.

Kroeber, Theodora. 1961. *Ishi in Two Worlds: A Biography of the Last Wild Indian in North America*. Berkeley: University of California Press.

——. 1970. *Alfred Kroeber: A Personal Configuration*. Berkeley: University of California Press.

Krupat, Arnold. 1989. *The Voice in the Margin: Native American Literature and the Canon.* Berkeley: University of California Press.

——. 1990. Irony in Anthropology: The Work of Franz Boas. In M. Manganaro, ed., 133–45.

——. 1992. *Ethnocriticism: Ethnography, History, Literature.* Berkeley: University of California Press.

——. 1996. *The Turn to the Native: Studies in Criticism and Culture.* Lincoln: University of Nebraska Press.

Kuhn, Thomas S. 1962. *The Structure of Scientific Revolutions.* Chicago: University of Chicago Press.

Kuper, Adam. 1983. *Anthropology and Anthropologists: The Modern British School.* London: Routledge.

——. 1988. *The Invention of Primitive Society.* London: Routledge.

——. 1999. *Culture: The Anthropologists' Account.* Cambridge: Harvard University Press.

Kuznar, Lawrence A. 1997. *Reclaiming a Scientific Anthropology.* Walnut Creek CA: AltaMira Press.

Latour, Bruno. 1987. *Science in Action: How to Follow Scientists and Engineers Through Society.* Cambridge: Harvard University Press.

Leach, Edmund. 1961. *Rethinking Anthropology.* New York: Humanities Press.

Lee, Penny. 1996. *The Whorf Theory Complex: A Critical Reconstruction.* Amsterdam: John Benjamins.

Leeds-Hurwitz, Wendy, and James M. Nyce. 1986. Linguistic Text Collection and the Development of Life History in the Work of Edward Sapir. In W. Cowan, M. Foster, and K. Koerner eds., 495–531.

Le Guin, Ursula K. 1968. *A Wizard of Earthsea.* New York: Parnassus.

——. 1969. *The Left Hand of Darkness.* New York: Ace Books.

——. 1971a. *The Lathe of Heaven.* New York: Scribner.

——. 1971b. *The Tombs of Atuan.* New York: Atheneum.

——. 1972a. *The Farthest Shore.* New York: Atheneum.

——. 1972b. *The Word for World is Forest.* New York: Berkley Publishing Corporation.

——. 1974. *The Dispossessed.* New York: Harper and Row.

——. 1985. *Always Coming Home.* New York: Harper and Row.

——. 1989. *Dancing at the Edge of the World.* New York: Grove.

Lemert, Charles. 1997. *Postmodernism is Not What You Think.* Malden MA: Blackwell.

Levinson, Stephen. 1996. Introduction to Gumperz and Levinson eds., 21–36.

Lévi-Strauss, Claude. [1949] 1969a. *Elementary Structures of Kinship [Les Structures Elémentaires de la Parenté].* Boston: Beacon.

——. [1950] 1987. *Introduction to the Work of Marcel Mauss.* London: Routledge.

——. [1955] 1975. *Tristes Tropiques.* New York: Atheneum.

——. [1962] 1966. *The Savage Mind [La Pensée Sauvage].* Chicago: University of Chicago Press.

——. [1964] 1969b. *Mythologiques I: The Raw and the Cooked [Le Cru et Le Cuit]*. New York: Harper and Row.

——. [1966] 1973. *Mythologiques II: From Honey to Ashes [Du Miel aux Cendres]*. New York: Harper and Row.

——. [1968] 1978. *Mythologiques III: The Origin of Table Manners [L'Origine des Manières de Tables]*. New York: Harper and Row.

——. [1971] 1981. *Mythologiques IV: The Naked Man [L'Homme Nu]*. New York: Harper and Row.

——. [1973] 1976. *Structural Anthropology, Volume II [Anthropologie Structurale]*. New York: Basic Books.

——. [1975] 1982. *The Way of the Masks [La Voie des Masques]*. Vancouver: Douglas and McIntyre.

——. [1983] 1985. *The View from Afar [Le Regard Eloigné]*. New York: Basic Books.

Lévi-Strauss, Claude, and Didier Eribon. 1991. *Conversations with Claude Lévi-Strauss*. Chicago: University of Chicago Press.

Lévy-Bruhl, Lucien. [1923] 1966. *Primitive Mentality*. Reprint, Boston: Beacon.

Lewin, Roger. 1992. *Complexity: Life at the Edge of Chaos*. New York: Collier Books.

Lewis, Herbert S. 1999. The Misrepresentation of Anthropology and Its Consequences. *American Anthropologist* 100:716–31.

Liberty, Margot, ed. 1978. *American Indian Intellectuals*. St. Paul: West Publishing Co.

Lindahl, James. 1999. Anthropological Approaches to the Philosophy of Translation. Unpublished Ph.D. diss., University of Western Ontario.

Linton, Ralph, ed. 1943. *Franz Boas 1858–1942*. American Anthropological Association Memoir 61.

Lips, Julius. 1937. *The Savage Strikes Back*. New Haven: Yale University Press.

Liss, Julia E. 1996. German Culture and German Science in the *Bildung* of Franz Boas. In G. Stocking ed., 155–84.

Lowie, Robert H. 1919. Review of Edward Sapir, Time Perspective in Aboriginal American Culture: A Study in Method. *American Anthropologist* 21:75–77.

——. 1920. *Primitive Society*. New York: Harper.

——. 1937. *History of Ethnological Theory*. New York: Holt, Rinehart and Winston.

——. [1935] 1956. *The Crow Indians*. Reprint, New York: Holt, Rinehart and Winston.

——. 1959. *Robert H. Lowie: A Personal Record*. Berkeley: University of California Press.

——. 1963. *Collected Writings of Robert H. Lowie*. Edited by Cora DuBois. Berkeley: University of California Press.

Lowie, Robert H., ed. 1965. *Letters from Edward Sapir to Robert H. Lowie*. Berkeley CA: privately published.

Lucy, John. 1992. *Language Diversity and Thought: A Reformulation of the Linguistic Relativity Hypothesis*. Cambridge: Cambridge University Press.

——. 1996. The Scope of Linguistic Relativity. In J. Gumperz and S. Levinson eds., 37–69.

Lynd, Robert, and Helen Lynd. 1929. *Middletown: A Study in Contemporary Culture*. New York: Harcourt, Brace.

Lyotard, Jean-François. 1979. *La Condition Postmoderne: Rapport sur le Savoir*. Paris: Editions de Minuit. Published in English as *The Postmodern Condition: A Report on Knowledge*, translated by Geoff Bennington and Brian Massumi. Minneapolis: University of Minnesota Press, 1984.

Mahmood, Cynthia Keppley. 1996. *Fighting for Faith and Nation: Dialogues with Sikh Militants*. Philadelphia: University of Pennsylvania Press.

Malinowski, Bronislaw. 1922. *Argonauts of the Western Pacific*. New York: E. P. Dutton.

——. 1923. The Problem of Meaning in Primitive Languages. In C. K. Ogden and I. A. Richards, eds., 451–510. London: K. Paul, Trench, Trubner.

——. 1935. *Coral Gardens and Their Magic*. London: G. Allen.

Mandelbaum, David. 1949. Introduction to Sapir 1949, v–xii.

Manganaro, Marc, ed. 1990. *Modernist Anthropology: From Fieldwork to Text*. Princeton: Princeton University Press.

Marcus, George E. 1998. *Ethnography through Thick and Thin*. Princeton: Princeton University Press.

Marcus, George E., and Dick Cushman. 1982. Ethnographies as Texts. In B. Siegel, ed., *Reviews in Anthropology* 11:25–69.

Marcus, George E., and Michael Fischer. 1986. *Anthropology as Cultural Critique: An Experimental Moment in the Human Sciences*. Chicago: University of Chicago Press.

Matthews, Maureen, and Roger Roulette. 1996. Fair Wind's Dream: Naamiwan Obawaajigewin. In J. Brown and E. Vibert, eds., 330–59.

McGlade, James. 1995. Archaeology and the Ecodynamics of Human-Modified Landscapes. *Antiquity* 89:113–32.

Mead, Margaret. 1928. *Coming of Age in Samoa: A Psychological Study of Youth for Western Civilization*. New York: New American Library.

——. 1974. *Ruth Benedict*. New York: Columbia University Press.

Mead, Margaret, ed. 1959. *An Anthropologist at Work: Writings of Ruth Benedict*. London: Secker and Warburg.

Mead, Margaret, and Rhoda Métraux, eds. 1953. *The Study of Culture at a Distance*. Chicago: University of Chicago Press.

Mihesuah, Devon, ed. 1998. *Natives and Academics: Researching and Writing about American Indians*. Lincoln: University of Nebraska Press.

Milliken, Barry, ed. 1997. *Annie Rachel Mshkikiikwe: Stories from an Elder of the Kettle and Stony Point First Nation*. London, Ontario: Centre for Research and Teaching of Canadian Native Languages, University of Western Ontario.

Mills, Antonia. 1994. *Eagle Down Is Our Law: Witsuwit'en Law, Feasts, and Land Claims*. Vancouver: University of British Columbia Press.

Mintz, Sydney. 1981. Ruth Benedict. In S. Silverman, ed., 141–66.

Moerman, Michael. 1965. Ethnic Identification in a Complex Civilization: Who are the Lué? *American Anthropologist* 67:1215–30.

Morgan, Lewis Henry. 1877. *Ancient Society.* New York: Holt, Rinehart and Winston.

Müller-Wille, Ludger, ed. 1998. *Franz Boas among the Inuit of Baffin Island 1883-1884: Journals and Letters.* Toronto: University of Toronto Press.

Murray, Stephen O. 1981. The Canadian Winter of Edward Sapir. *Historiographia Linguistica* 8:63–68.

——. 1983. The Creation of Linguistic Structure. *American Anthropologist* 85:356–62.

——. 1986. Edward Sapir in the "Chicago School" of Sociology. In W. Cowan, M. Foster, and K. Koerner, eds., 241–92.

——. 1994. *Theory Groups and the Study of Language in North America.* Amsterdam: John Benjamins.

——. 1998. A 1978 Interview with Mary Haas. *Anthropological Linguistics* 39:695–713.

——. 1999. The Non-Eclipse of Americanist Anthropology during the 1930s and 1940s. In L. Valentine and R. Darnell, eds., 52–74.

Nemesvari, Richard. 1997. Strange Attractors on the Yorkshire Moors: Chaos Theory and *Wuthering Heights. The Victorian Newsletter* 92:15–21.

Obeyesekere, Gananath. 1992. *The Apotheosis of Captain Cook: European Mythmaking in the Pacific.* Princeton: Princeton University Press.

Ogden, C. K., and I. A. Richards. 1923. *The Meaning of Meaning: A Study of the Influence of Language upon Thought and of the Science of Symbolism.* London: Kegan Paul, Trench, Trubner.

Ortner, Sherry B. 1984. Theory in Anthropology Since the Sixties. *Comparative Studies in Society and History* 26:126–66.

Pace, David. 1983. *Claude Lévi-Strauss: The Bearer of Ashes.* London: Routledge.

Parsons, Elsie Clews, ed. 1922. *American Indian Life.* New York: B. W. Huebsch.

Payne, Kenneth W., and Stephen O. Murray. 1983. Historical Inferences from Ethnohistorical Data: Boasian Views. *Journal of the History of the Behavioral Sciences* 19:335–40.

Perry, Helen. 1983. *Psychiatrist of America: The Life of Harry Stack Sullivan.* Cambridge MA: Belknap.

Pinsky, Valerie, and Alison Wylie, eds. 1989. *Critical Trends in Contemporary Archaeology: Essays in the Philosophy, History and Socio-Politics of Archaeology.* Cambridge: Cambridge University Press.

Powell, John Wesley. 1878. *Report on the Arid Region of the United States*: New York: Belknap Press.

——. 1891. *Indian Linguistic Families of America North of Mexico.* Bureau of American Ethnology Annual Report 7 for 1885–86:7–139.

Prattis, Iain, ed. 1985. *Reflections: The Anthropological Muse.* Washington DC: American Anthropological Association.

Prigogine, Ilya, and Isabelle Stengers. 1984. *Order Out of Chaos: Man's New Dialogue with Nature.* London: Fontana.

Rabinow, Paul. 1977. *Reflections on Fieldwork in Morocco*. Berkeley: University of California Press.

———. 1986. Representations Are Social Facts: Modernity and Post-Modernity in Anthropology. In J. Clifford and G. Marcus, eds., 234–61.

Radin, Paul. 1913. Reminiscences of a Winnebago Indian. *Journal of American Folklore* 26:293–318.

———. 1919. The Genetic Relationship of the North American Indian Languages. *University of California Publications in American Archaeology and Ethnology* 14:489–502.

———. 1920. The Autobiography of a Winnebago Indian. *University of California Publications in American Archaeology and Ethnology* 16:381–473.

———. [1927] 1957. *Primitive Man as Philosopher*. Reprint, New York: Dover.

———. 1933. *Method and Theory in Ethnology*. New York: Basic Books.

Redfield, Robert. 1930. *Tepoztlan, a Mexican Village*. Chicago: University of Chicago Publications in Anthropology.

———. 1941. *The Folk Culture of Yucatan*. Chicago: University of Chicago Press.

———. 1950. *The Village that Chose Progress: Chan Kom Revisited*. Chicago: University of Chicago Press.

———. 1953. *The Primitive World and its Transformations*. Ithaca: Cornell University Press.

———. 1963. *Little Community and Peasant Society and Culture*. Chicago: University of Chicago Press.

Redfield, Robert, with Alfonso Rojas. 1934. *Chan Kom, a Maya Village*. Washington DC: Carnegie Institute.

Redfield, Robert, Ralph Linton, and Melville Herskovits. 1936. Memorandum for the Study of Acculturation. *American Anthropologist* 38:149–52.

Ridington, Robin. 1988 *Trail to Heaven: Knowledge and Narrative in a Northern Native Community*. Vancouver: Douglas and McIntyre.

———. 1990. *Little Bit Know Something*. Urbana: University of Illinois Press.

———. 1991. On the Language of Benjamin Lee Whorf. In I. Brady, ed., 241–61.

———. 1999. Theorizing Coyote's Cannon: Sharing Stories with Thomas King. In L. Valentine and R. Darnell, eds., 19–37.

Ridington, Robin, and Dennis Hastings. 1998. *Blessing for a Long Time: The Sacred Pole of the Omaha Tribe*. Lincoln: University of Nebraska Press.

Rohner, Ronald P., and Evelyn Rohner, eds. 1969. *The Ethnography of Franz Boas*. Chicago: University of Chicago Press.

Rollins, Peter. 1980. *Benjamin Lee Whorf: Lost Generation Theories of Mind, Language and Religion*. Ann Arbor MI: University Microfilms International.

Rorty, Richard. 1979. *Philosophy and the Mirror of Nature*. Princeton: Princeton University Press.

———. 1989. *Contingency, Irony, and Solidarity*. Cambridge: Cambridge University Press.

Rosaldo, Michelle, and Louise Lamphere, eds. 1974. *Women, Culture and Society*. Stanford: Stanford University Press.

Rosaldo, Renato. 1989. *Culture and Truth: The Remaking of Social Analysis*. Boston: Beacon.

Rosenau, Pauline. 1992. *Post-modernism and the Social Sciences*. Princeton: Princeton University Press.

Rouse, Joseph. 1987. *Knowledge and Power: Toward a Political Philosophy of Science*. Ithaca: Cornell University Press.

Rowe, John. 1965. The Renaissance Foundations of Anthropology. *American Anthropologist* 67:1–20.

Ryan, Allan J. 1999. *The Trickster Shift: Humour and Irony in Contemporary Native Art*. Vancouver: University of British Columbia Press.

Sahlins, Marshall. 1985. *Islands of History*. Chicago: University of Chicago Press.

——. 1995. *How "Natives" Think: About Captain Cook, for Example*. Chicago: University of Chicago Press.

Said, Edward. 1978. *Orientalism*. New York: Pantheon.

——. 1993. *Culture and Imperialism*. New York: Knopf.

——. 1994. *Representations of the Intellectual*. New York: Pantheon.

Sangren, P. Steven. 1988. Rhetoric and the Authority of Ethnography. *Current Anthropology* 29:405–34.

Sanjek, Roger, ed. 1990. *Fieldnotes: The Makings of Anthropology*. Ithaca: Cornell University Press.

Sapir, Edward. 1916. *Time Perspective in Aboriginal American Culture: A Study in Method*. Canadian Department of Mines, Geological Survey, Memoir 90, Anthropological Series 13.

——. 1917. Do We Need the Superorganic? *American Anthropologist* 19:441–47.

——. 1918. Tom. *Canadian Courier*. December 7:7.

——. 1921a. A Bird's Eye View of American Languages North of Mexico. *Science* 54:408.

——. 1921b. *Language: An Introduction to the Study of Speech*. New York: Harcourt, Brace and Co.

——. 1921c. The Blind Old Indian Tells His Names. *The Canadian Bookman*: 38–40.

——. 1921d. The Life of A Nootka Indian. *Queen's Quarterly* 28:232–43, 351–67.

——. 1922a. Sayach'apis, a Nootka Trader. In E. Parsons, ed., 297–323.

——. 1922b. Review of E. C. Parsons, ed., *American Indian Life*. A Symposium of the Exotic. *The Dial* 73:568–71.

——. 1923. An Approach to Symbolism *The Freeman* 22 August: 572–73.

——. 1924. Culture, Genuine and Spurious. *American Journal of Sociology* 29:401–29.

——. 1925. Sound Patterns in Language. *Language* 1:37–51.

——. 1926. Note on Psychological Orientation in a Given Society. Hanover NH transcript. In E. Sapir, *Collected Works*, 73–98.

——. 1927. Anthropology and Sociology. In W. F. Ogburn and A. Goldenweiser, eds., *The Social Sciences and Their Interrelations*, 97–113. Boston: Houghton Mifflin.

——. 1929. Central and North American Languages. *Encyclopedia Britannica* 5:138–41.

——. 1930. *Proceedings of the Second Colloquium on Personality Investigation.* Baltimore: American Psychiatric Association.

——. 1931a. Custom. In *Encyclopedia of the Social Sciences.* Vol. 4, 658–62. New York: Macmillan.

——. 1931b. Fashion. In *Encyclopedia of the Social Sciences.* Vol. 6, 139–44. New York: Macmillan.

——. 1932a. Cultural Anthropology and Psychiatry. *Journal of Abnormal and Social Psychology* 27:229–42.

——. 1932b. Group. In *Encyclopedia of the Social Sciences.* Vol. 7, 178–82. New York: Macmillan.

——. 1933. La Realité Psychologique des Phonèmes. *Journal de Psychologie Normale et Pathologique* 30:247–65.

——. 1934. The Emergence of a Concept of Personality in a Study of Cultures. *Journal of Social Psychology* 5:408–15.

——. 1938a. Introduction in W. Dyk.

——. 1938b. Why Cultural Anthropology Needs the Psychiatrist. *Psychiatry* 1:7–12.

——. 1949. *Selected Writings of Edward Sapir.* Edited by David Mandelbaum. Berkeley: University of California Press.

——. 1999. *Collected Works of Edward Sapir 3: Culture.* Edited by Regna Darnell, Judith Irvine, and Richard Handler. Berlin: Mouton de Gruyter.

Sapir, Edward, and Morris Swadesh. 1946. American Indian Grammatical Categories. *Word* 2:103–12.

Sarris, Greg. 1993. *Keeping Slug Woman Alive: A Holistic Approach to American Indian Texts.* Berkeley: University of California Press.

Saul, John Ralston. 1997. *Reflections of a Siamese Twin: Canada at the End of the Twentieth Century.* Toronto: Viking.

Schneider, David. 1995. *Schneider on Schneider.* Told to Richard Handler. Durham: Duke University Press.

Scholte, Bob. 1969. Toward A Reflexive and Critical Anthropology. In D. Hymes, ed., 430–57.

Shankin, Eugenia. 1999. The Profession of the Color Blind: Sociocultural Anthropology and Racism in the 21st Century. *American Anthropologist* 100:669–79.

Shaul, David, and N. Louanna Furbee. 1998. *Language and Culture.* Prospect Heights IL: Waveland.

Sherzer, Joel. 1976. *An Areal-Typological Study of American Indian Languages North of Mexico.* Amsterdam: North Holland.

Shostak, Marjorie. 1981. *Nisa: The Life and Words of a !Kung Woman.* Cambridge: Harvard University Press.

Shryock, Andrew. 1997. *Nationality and the Genealogical Imagination: Oral History and Textual Authority in Tribal Jordan.* Berkeley: University of California Press.

Silko, Leslie Marmon. 1977. *Ceremony.* New York: Viking.

Silverman, Sydel, ed. 1981. *Totems and Teachers: Perspectives on the History of Anthropology*. New York: Columbia University Press.

Simmons, Leo. 1942. *Sun Chief*. New Haven: Yale University Press.

Smith, Henry Nash. 1950. *Virgin Land: The American West as Symbol and Myth*. New York: Vintage.

Sontag, Susan. 1961. The Anthropologist as Hero. In *Against Interpretation*. New York: Doubleday Anchor.

Spier, Leslie. 1921. *The Sun Dance of the Plains Indians*. Anthropological Papers, American Museum of Natural History 16.

——. 1943. Franz Boas and Some of His Views. *Sobretiro de Acta Americana* 1:108–27.

Spier, Leslie, A. Irving Hallowell, and Stanley Newman, eds. 1941. *Language, Culture and Personality: Essays in Memory of Edward Sapir*. Menasha WI: Sapir Memorial Fund.

Stegner, Wallace. 1954. *Beyond the Hundredth Meridian: John Wesley Powell and the Second Opening of the West*. Boston: Houghton Mifflin.

Steward, Julian. 1946–59. *Handbook of South American Indians*. Bureau of American Ethnology Bulletin 143.

Stewart, Omer. 1998. *Cannibalism Is an Acquired Taste and Other Notes*. Compiled and edited by Carol L. Howell. Niwot CO: University Press of Colorado.

Stocking, George W., Jr. 1968. *Race, Culture and Evolution*. New York: Free Press.

——. 1974. The Boas Plan for the Study of American Indian Languages. In Dell Hymes, ed., *Studies in the History of Linguistics: Traditions and Paradigms*, 454–84. Bloomington: Indiana University Press.

——. 1985. Philanthropoids and Vanishing Cultures: Rockefeller Funding and the End of the Museum Era. *Objects and Others: Essays on Museums and Material Culture*. History of Anthropology 3:112–45.

——. 1991. *Books Unwritten, Turning Points Unmarked: Notes for an Anti-History of Anthropology*. Bloomington: Indiana University Press.

——. 1992. *The Ethnographer's Magic*. Madison: University of Wisconsin Press.

Stocking, George W., Jr., ed. 1974. *The Shaping of American Anthropology, 1883-1911*. New York: Basic Books.

——. 1976. Ideas and Institutions in American Anthropology: Toward a History of the Interwar Years. In *Selected Papers from the American Anthropologist, 1921-1945*. Washington: American Anthropological Association.

——. 1980. Sapir's Last Testament on Culture and Personality. *History of Anthropology Newsletter* 7:8–11.

——. 1986. *Malinowski, Rivers, Benedict and Others: Essays on Culture and Personality*. History of Anthropology 4. Madison: University of Wisconsin Press.

——. 1989. *Romantic Motives: Essays on Anthropological Sensibility*. History of Anthropology 6. Madison: University of Wisconsin Press.

——. 1996. *Volksgeist as Method and Ethic*. History of Anthropology 8. Madison: University of Wisconsin Press.

Strathern, Marilyn. 1987. Out of Context: The Persuasive Fiction of Anthropology. *Current Anthropology* 28:151–281.

——. 1991. *Partial Connections*. Savage MD: Rowan and Littlefield.

Swadesh, Morris. 1951. Diffusional Cumulation and Archaic Residue as Historical Explanations. *Southwestern Journal of Anthropology* 7:1–21.

Swann, Brian, ed. 1992. *On the Translation of Native American Literatures*. Washington DC: Smithsonian Institution.

Swann, Brian, and Arnold Krupat, eds. 1987. *Recovering the Word: Essays on Native American Literature*. Berkeley: University of California Press.

Tedlock, Barbara. 1991. The Ethnographic Gaze. Unpublished manuscript.

——. 1992. *The Beautiful and the Dangerous: Encounters with the Zuni Indians*. New York: Viking.

Tedlock, Dennis. 1983. *The Spoken Word and the Work of Interpretation*. Philadelphia: University of Pennsylvania Press.

——. 1990. *Days from a Dream Almanac*. Urbana: University of Illinois Press.

——. 1995. Interpretation, Participation and the Role of Narrative in Dialogical Anthropology. In D. Tedlock and B. Mannheim, eds., 252–87.

Tedlock, Dennis, and Bruce Mannheim, eds. 1995. *The Dialogic Emergence of Culture*. Urbana: University of Illinois Press.

Thomas, W. I., and Florian Znaniecki. 1927. *The Polish Peasant in Europe and in America*. New York: Knopf.

Torgovnick, Marianna. 1990. *Gone Primitive: Savage Intellects, Modern Lives*. Chicago: University of Chicago Press.

Toynbee, Arnold. 1972. *A Study of History*. New York: Oxford University Press.

Trager, George. 1946. Changes of Emphasis in Linguistics: A Comment. *Studies in Philology* 43:461–65.

Tsing, Anna Lowenhaupt. 1993. *In the Realm of the Diamond Queen: Marginality in an Out-of-the-Way Place*. Princeton: Princeton University Press.

Turner, Victor. 1990. Are There Universals of Performance in Myth, Ritual, and Drama? In Richard Schechner and Willa Appel, eds., *By Means of Performance: Intercultural Studies of Theatre and Ritual*, 8–18. Cambridge: Cambridge University Press.

Tyler, Stephen. 1987. *The Unspeakable: Discourse, Dialogue, and Rhetoric in the Postmodern World*. Madison: University of Wisconsin Press.

——. 1986. Post-Modern Ethnography: From Document of the Occult to Occult Document. In J. Clifford and G. Marcus, eds., 122–40.

Valentine, Lisa, and Regna Darnell, eds. 1999. *Theorizing the Americanist Tradition*. Toronto: University of Toronto Press.

Van Maanen, John. 1988. *Tales of the Field: On Writing Ethnography*. Chicago: University of Chicago Press.

Vibert, Elizabeth. 1997. *Traders' Tales: Narratives of Cultural Encounters in the Columbia Plateau 1897-1846*. Norman: University of Oklahoma Press.

Vidich, Arthur J. 1966. Introduction. In Paul Radin, *Method and Theory*, vii–cxv. New York: Basic Books. Original edition, New York: Basic Books, 1933.

Wallace, Anthony F. C. 1952. *The Modal Personality Structure of the Tuscarora Indians, as Revealed by Rorschach Tests*. Washington DC: Bureau of American Ethnology Bulletin 150.

———. 1961. *Culture and Personality*. New York: Random House.

———. 1999. *Thomas Jefferson and the Indians: The Tragic Fate of the First Americans*. Cambridge: Harvard University Press.

Wallace, Anthony F. C., and John Atkins. 1960. The Meaning of Kinship Terms. *American Anthropologist* 62:58–80.

Wallerstein, Immanuel et al. 1996. *Open the Social Sciences: Report of the Gulbenkian Commission on the Restructuring of the Social Sciences*. Stanford: Stanford University Press.

White, Hayden. 1973. *Metahistory: The Historical Imagination in Nineteenth Century Europe*. Baltimore: Johns Hopkins University Press.

White, Leslie. 1963. The Ethnology and Ethnography of Franz Boas. *Bulletin of the Texas Memorial Museum* 6.

———. 1966. The Social Organization of Ethnological Theory. *Rice University Studies* 52:1–66.

Whorf, Benjamin Lee. 1956. *Language Culture and Reality: Selected Writings of Benjamin Lee Whorf*. Edited by John Carroll. Cambridge: MIT Press.

Winkin, Yves. 1988. Erving Goffman: Portrait du Sociologue en Jeune Homme. In Yves Winkin, ed., *Les Moments et Leurs Hommes*, 13–92. Paris: Minuit.

Wissler, Clark. 1917. *The American Indian*. New York: Dutton.

———. 1923. *Man and Culture*. New York: Thomas Y. Crowell.

Wolf, Eric. 1982. *Europe and the People Without History*. Berkeley: University of California Press.

———. 1999. *Envisioning Power: Ideologies of Dominance and Crisis*. Berkeley: University of California Press.

Wolf, Margery. 1992. *Thrice-Told Tales: Feminism, Postmodernism and Ethnographic Responsibility*. Stanford: Stanford University Press.

Wolfart, H. C., and Freda Ahenakew, eds. 1993. *Kinêhiyâwiwininaw Nêhiyawêwin. The Cree Language is Our Identity: The La Ronge Lectures of Sarah Whitecalf*. Winnipeg: University of Manitoba Press.

———. 1997. *Their Example Showed Me the Way: A Cree Woman's Life Shaped by Two Cultures*. Told by Emma Minde. Edmonton: University of Alberta Press.

Young, Virginia. Beyond Relativism. Unpublished MS.

Zengotita, Thomas de. 1989. Speakers of Being. In G. Stocking, ed., 74–123.

Zumwalt, Rosemary. 1992. *Wealth and Rebellion: Elsie Clews Parsons, Anthropologist and Folklorist*. Urbana: University of Illinois Press.

INDEX

Mashpees, 339

Mason, J. Alden, 222

master narrative, 30

Matthews, Maureen, 243–44

Mauss, Marcel, 287

May, Mark, 130–32

Mayas, 18, 155–56, 175–76, 182, 201, 264, 268, 314

McEachern, Allan, 335–36, 338

McKay, Mabel, 249–51

Mead, Margaret, 10, 23, 27, 35, 37, 43, 45, 79, 85, 110, 134, 146, 153, 157, 174, 180, 195–96, 199, 325–28, 334

memory culture, 234

Mendel, Gregor, 79

mentalism, 66, 189, 191, 201, 204, 276, 289

Merton, Robert, 26

metalanguage, 184, 197

metanarrative, 285, 309, 319

Métraux, Rhoda, 10, 26, 328

Meyer, Adolf, 133–34

Michelson, Truman, 152, 227

Mide, Midewewin, 221, 234

Middletown, 72, 133, 199

Mills, Antonia, 336

Mind of Primitive Man, 99, 132, 211

Mink, John, 234–35

modernism, 290, 293

Moerman, Michael, 314

Mooney, James, 10

Morley, Sylvanus, 175

Morgan, Lewis Henry, 2, 11

multilingual awareness, 178, 186, 198, 327

Murdock, George Peter, 132, 180, 278

multi-sited ethnography, 314

mythopraxis, 276

mythworld, 273

Na-dene language family, 181

Naquayouma, Ernest, 182

narrative ethnography, 269, 320

national character, 85

National Film Board of Canada, 334

National Research Council, 133

"Native point of view," 17–18, 37, 50, 67, 71, 105, 111–12, 134, 138, 151, 198, 212–13, 218, 228, 277, 284, 333

Navajos, 21–24, 130, 224, 294

Nazism, National Socialism, 99–100, 310, 328

Ndembus, 276

negative ethnography, 219

Nelson, N. C., 224

Nemesvari, Richard, 93

neocolonial, 312

neo-evolutionary synthesis, 78, 92, 276

new criticism, 254, 259, 281

new ethnography, 272

Newman, Stanley, 66, 129, 133, 177, 181, 183

New School for Social Research, 174

Newtonian mechanics, 77, 91, 116

Nietzsche, Friedrich, 185

nilhilism, 185–86, 263, 293

Nootkas, 13, 47, 54, 130, 229

normal science, 3, 107, 154, 301

Northwest Coast, 14, 215, 221, 284, 306

nostalgia, 217, 235

Obeyesekere, Gananath, 277

objectivity, 110, 150, 203, 212, 225–26, 233, 270

observer: bias of, 42, 43, 213; effect of, 35, 41, 44, 94, 178; position of, 17, 111, 150, 186; and scale of observation, 94

Ogburn, William Fielding, 109, 118, 127

Ogden, C. K., and I. A. Richards, 188–91

Oikoumene, 85

Ojibwes, xix, 4, 241–46

Old Tom (Sayach'apis), 229

Omahas, 180, 194, 208–9, 269